100 YE

LEEDS
UNITED

100 YEARS OF
LEEDS
UNITED

1919   2019

DANIEL CHAPMAN

ICON

First published in the UK in 2019
by Icon Books Ltd, Omnibus Business Centre,
39–41 North Road, London N7 9DP
email: info@iconbooks.com
www.iconbooks.com

This edition published in the UK in 2020 by Icon Books Ltd

Sold in the UK, Europe and Asia
by Faber & Faber Ltd, Bloomsbury House,
74–77 Great Russell Street,
London WC1B 3DA or their agents

Distributed in the UK, Europe and Asia
by Grantham Book Services, Trent Road,
Grantham NG31 7XQ

Distributed in Australia and New Zealand
by Allen & Unwin Pty Ltd, PO Box 8500,
83 Alexander Street, Crows Nest, NSW 2065

Distributed in India by Penguin Books India,
7th Floor, Infinity Tower – C, DLF Cyber City,
Gurgaon 122002, Haryana

Distributed in South Africa
by Jonathan Ball, Office B4, The District,
41 Sir Lowry Road, Woodstock 7925

ISBN: 978-178578-635-8

CONTENTS

LIST OF ILLUSTRATIONS

14. Billy Bremner, 1966.

15. Albert Johanneson at Wembley, 1965.

16. Don Revie, 1961.

17. Billy Bremner holds the FA Cup aloft, 1972.

18. The first team in the dressing room following Billy Bremner's testimonial, 1974.

19. Eddie Gray vs Liverpool in the 1974 Charity Shield at Wembley.

20. Brian Clough glances over at Bill Shankly, Wembley, 1974.

21. Allan Clarke takes on Franz Beckenbauer of Bayern Munich, 1975.

22. Tony Currie, Chelsea vs Leeds United, 1978.

23. John Sheridan, Coventry City vs Leeds United, 1987.

24. Mel Sterland, Vinnie Jones and Chris Fairclough celebrate promotion from Division Two, 1990.

25. Howard Wilkinson during the 1989/90 season.

26. Leeds United celebrate with the First Division Trophy, 1992.

27. Gary Speed, Tony Yeboah, Brian Deane and Gary McAllister at Upton Park, 1995.

39. Jack Harrison scores a late winner away at Reading, 26 November 2019.

40. Ezgjan Alioski applauds an empty Elland Road after beating Barnsley 1-0, 16 July 2020.

41. Pablo Hernández scores a vital goal to beat Swansea 0-1, 12 July 2020.

42. Liam Cooper celebrates victory over Barnsley at full-time, 16 July 2020.

43. Fans of all ages gather outside Elland Road to celebrate promotion to the Premier League, 17 July 2020.

44. Leeds United players and staff greet the fans stood outside the East Stand at Elland Road, 22 July 2020.

45. The Leeds United squad celebrates after winning the Championship, 22 July 2020.

46. Leeds United player are presented with the Championship trophy, 22 July 2020.

47. Left to right: Kalvin Phillips, Gaetano Berardi and Gjanni Alioski celebrate winning the Championship, 22 July 2020.

48. Manager Marcelo Bielsa lifts the Championship trophy, 22 July 2020.

1877–1905

THAT'S THE PLACE FOR ASSOCIATION FOOTBALLERS

That Leeds City – United's precursor – survived as long as they did in the early days of the twentieth century, coming within one win of promotion to Division One of the Football League, was a triumph of stubborn faith over equally stubborn indifference, stubbornness a trait readily associated with people from Leeds.

For years soccer was regarded with indifference and hostility in Leeds and the West Riding of Yorkshire. Two days after Christmas 1877, earnest missionaries from the soccer-mad city of Sheffield in south Yorkshire brought teams, officials, balls and even goalposts to Holbeck Recreation Ground in south Leeds, putting on an exhibition match and drawing a large enough crowd that the promoters believed their zealous sermon on the kicking game may have found ears to hear it. That belief lasted until they counted the takings: the congregation had been mostly season ticket holders from the local rugby club, enticed to watch as a freebie. At the end of the match they tugged down their caps, thrust their hands deep into their overcoat pockets, and went home to await the next proper rugby football fixture. Hands, scrums and skill, not this kicking and dribbling rubbish.

Nobody has really accounted for the West Riding's suspicion of association football; even contemporary writers, tracing the development of the game prior to Leeds City, were at a loss. The stubborn local character seems to have played a part, and a respect for institutions that often meant Leeds was a slow city to change. Rugby was played there first, since 1864, and with limited leisure time the working population were content to stick with what they liked. A lot of rugby clubs switched to cricket in the summer, meaning loyal club-men's calendars were fully booked. The 'muscular Christianity' inherent in rugby meant a proliferation of church teams and a tight bond between sport, church and social life that was hard for soccer – a more individualistic, dilettante sport – to break. It was also difficult for soccer to compete with the quality of the local rugby clubs: Leeds St Johns, Hunslet FC, Bramley and Leeds Parish Church all fielded excellent teams, creating fierce local rivalries that captivated the public.

Soccer lagged far behind. In 1878, after the exhibition at Holbeck, Hunslet Cricket Club's Sheffield-born professional Sam Gilbert founded Hunslet AFC and, as captain, took them down the road for a creditable 1-0 defeat at Sheffield Hallam. Despite that bright start, and matches with Kirkstall that were educational as much as competitive – according to reports, on one occasion Kirkstall caused 'much amusement by mixing a little rugby into the game' but won 2-0 anyway – the club closed within five years. Following them were Leeds FC (1885–87), Leeds FC take two (1888–90) and Leeds Albion (1888–92). Despite the constant foundings and founderings, by 1894 there was deemed enough interest to support an amateur West Yorkshire League, six years after the beginning of the national and professional Football League, with Leeds AFC and a new Hunslet AFC the teams to beat.

Leeds AFC were formed at the Cardigan Arms pub in 1894 and had a nomadic existence, trying to escape the shadows of rugby. Finally they moved to Headingley, and that was the end of them; the ground was bought by the ambitious Leeds Cricket, Football and Athletic Company Ltd, a group of businessmen chaired by the 'father' of Yorkshire cricket, Lord Hawke; they were co-opting Leeds St Johns as their football section. A pavilion and main stand were built, costing £30,300, and Leeds AFC were told to pay their way. The club folded in 1889, and Leeds St Johns rugby club moved in.

Hunslet AFC managed better, originally forming as Leeds Steelworks in 1889. The enormous steelworks dominated Hunslet, employing 1,500 workers on a 25-acre site entangled within the Midland Railway; by the 1920s, it had made more than half of all the tram rails embedded in England's streets. Leeds Steelworks' team were renamed Hunslet AFC in readiness for the West Yorkshire League in 1894, but always kept their nickname: The Twinklers. While the Steelworks' tall chimneys sent sulphuric sparks like industrial starlight into the smoky skies above Leeds, its workers sparkled in the streets; tiny graphite particles, called kish dust, were impossible to clean from their twinkling skin.

For a time the Twinklers' team was almost entirely made up of men who came to work at the steelworks from Thornaby-on-Tees, and the local standard meant Hunslet's Teesmen were soon dominating local soccer. In 1896 they shared the West Yorkshire League title with Bradford FC, and from 1897 won both the West Yorkshire Cup and the Leeds Workpeople's Hospital Cup in four consecutive seasons. Their second victory in the West Yorkshire Cup – a 1-0 win over Harrogate on 23 April 1898 – was the first competitive soccer game played at the Old Peacock Ground, on Elland Road.

Hunslet were the first Leeds club to make a mark outside the city, reaching the quarter-finals of the FA Amateur Cup in 1895/96 and 1900/01. The cup run in 1896 included a high-profile match with Old Etonians, twice winners and four times runners-up in the FA Cup itself between 1875 and 1883. The game drew much from the Twinklers' reserves of character; within seven minutes their famous visitors were leading 2-0. Hunslet 'seemed nervous and excited', but showed aptitude for the new style of combination passing play, contrasting with Old Etonians' older-fashioned individualism. Hunslet dominated the second half, winning 3-2 thanks to goals from Collinson, 'Tipper' Heffron and Callaghan.

Soccer was gaining popularity, and if the Twinklers could find a permanent home with the proper facilities, an application to join the professional Football League's Second Division was not out of the question. Instead, they wandered. There were numerous new association clubs in the city, while rugby's split into two codes after 1895 meant new teams competing for pitches. Hunslet started at the Wellington Ground on Low Road, moved to Hunslet Rugby Club's Parkside and Laburnum Grounds, then back to Low Road at the Nelson Cricket Club's ground.

In September 1902, Hunslet were expected to be one of the top sides in a reformed Yorkshire League, but were advertising desperately for somewhere to play. As options for alternative venues dwindled away, so did the club's highly rated players, and on Friday 3 October the *Leeds Mercury* reported the inevitable, that had once seemed impossible: 'The Hunslet Club Defunct.'

The Twinklers were mourned, not only for themselves, but for the blow the demise of the leading club dealt to what was becoming a forlorn dream for Leeds' 'sockerites' and 'sockerists': a proper league team. But all was not lost. A meeting at the club's headquarters, the Royal Exchange Hotel in Hunslet, reaffirmed the desire to keep the club going in some capacity, and even the players who had transferred elsewhere promised to return if Hunslet could find a ground. The club was put on hiatus, with fundraising events and friendly games planned to keep the Twinklers' lights lit, however dimly.

The lead dreamer was Fred W. Waterhouse, rare in the West Riding for being seduced by soccer before rugby could claim him. As a boy of twelve, gazing across the fields below his window in Rothwell on a winter night in 1878, Waterhouse saw a crowd of sporting spectators for the first time, and saw what they were watching: a demonstration of association football, played beneath electric lights.

Two traction engines had been brought to the field, supplying power for lamps on tall poles that lit up the playing area, the sky, and young Fred's imagination. Although the lights soon failed – the sockerists took to playing leapfrog during the blackouts – and with them another attempt to win the public over to association, one twelve year old was convinced. Waterhouse became fanatical about promoting the game, first as player and referee, then committee member and later president of the West Riding Football Association, inaugural president of the Leeds and District FA, and in later years senior life member of the West Riding County FA, all while working in John Barran's clothing factory. An article on the growth of soccer in Leeds described Waterhouse as 'straight through and through', although not everyone thought so; encountering Waterhouse in a pub, fundraising for Hunslet AFC, a rugby fan offered him five bob – cab fare to the nearest lunatic asylum. 'That's the place for association footballers,' he said.

Waterhouse was secretary of Hunslet AFC when they began sweeping the local cups in 1897, and by summer 1904 he was an energetic man of 38, determined the Twinklers should shine again. A revival was confirmed at the Royal Exchange Hotel that May, when Waterhouse announced the club had been made members of the West Yorkshire League and would once again play at the Wellington Ground.

Expenses were not expected to be more than £50 for the season, small when compared to the £1,000 Middlesbrough paid to sign Alf Common from Sunderland in 1905. But ambition was growing. At the end of the following month's meeting of the Hunslet enthusiasts, Waterhouse was elected club president, entry was decided for the English FA Cup, and the title of the club was changed to 'Leeds City Association Club'.

The dream that sustained Waterhouse's enthusiasm, of taking the game in West Yorkshire from local to national, had begun to come true during Hunslet AFC's absence. But it was coming true in Bradford, not Leeds.

The nearby city, as full of self-importance and wealth as Leeds, had been as firmly for rugby as the rest of the West Riding. But rugby's great schism, dividing it between paid professional players and amateurs, was not a clean split. The cracks were revealing opportunities for soccer.

Professional rugby clubs became dominant in the north, but fierce competition meant increasing expenses as clubs vied to form the sport's new elite. In 1896 Bradford was home to the Northern Union's first champions, Manningham FC, but they soon fell behind their cross-city rivals Bradford FC. By 1904 Manningham had been relegated and given up. A fundraising archery contest was organised in summer 1903, but the club's directors and supporters decided it would be better to switch to playing association football, and spend the money on entry to the Second Division of the Football League.

Soccer had captured the national imagination; 110,000 people watched Tottenham Hotspur and Sheffield United draw the FA Cup final in 1901, and the sporting public of West Yorkshire were not immune. In the *Yorkshire Evening Post*, Mr T.H. Fitton of the West Yorkshire Football Association recorded northern rugby supporters demanding something 'more interesting and scientific than the eternal line-out and scrummage ... more skill and less brute force'. Soccer was becoming that skilful, scientific game, particularly in the north, where Scottish imports introduced short-passing and broke the hegemony of the founding public-school clubs. The West Riding's thoughtful sporting spectators, engaged by day in the increasingly technical manufacture of steel, railway locomotives and fine quality clothing, took a second look at soccer, with its sweeping lines and quick movements. The only letdown, in the local leagues, was the standard.

The Football League was keen to help any club that wanted to fill its lack of representation in West Yorkshire; Manningham could be the West Riding's first entrant into the league, moving them at a stroke from the backwaters of rugby to the head of local soccer. Renamed Bradford City AFC, they were welcomed into the Second Division before they even signed a full team of players, let alone played a game. When they did play, thrust straight into league action against Gainsborough Trinity in 1903, 11,000 spectators – 9,000 more than had come to Manningham's last match – saw them lose 3-1. 16,000 came to the next home game, a 1-0 win over Bristol City. Manningham's president, Alfred Ayrton, had predicted soccer was the 'game that would pay', and in 1904 there was no need for a summer archery contest to guarantee Bradford City's progress.

That progress had been closely watched in Leeds, at Holbeck Rugby Club. Holbeck were late but ambitious entrants into the Northern Union, but had failed in their aim of becoming the city's dominant club. Holbeck

had two rivals to contend with, with the leading club
– Hunslet – on their doorstep. The second were Leeds
St John's at the enormous Headingley stadium, now
known simply as Leeds. When Leeds won promotion
to join Hunslet in the First Division in 1903, rugby fans
in the city were guaranteed a top-class game of rugby
every Saturday. Who was left to come to Elland Road to
watch Second Division Holbeck? Their only hope was
promotion, as quickly as possible, before the public forgot them entirely.

Holbeck gave everything to their attempt in 1903/04,
but let a two-point lead over St Helens slip on the final
day of the season, leaving them tied for the second promotion place. A play-off match completed the letdown;
St Helens took a 7-0 lead at half-time and won what the
Yorkshire Post & Leeds Intelligencer called 'an uninteresting game'.

It might have been uninteresting, but it had serious
consequences. Two weeks before the play-off, football
reporter Flaneur in the *Leeds Mercury* had outlined
what was at stake. 'There have been hints of Socker at
Holbeck in case of the Northern Union team's failure to
get into better company next season,' he noted. Some of
the club's wealthier backers were impressed by develop-
ments at Manningham, and during the summer, took
note of Hunslet AFC's revival as Leeds City.

In mid-July the city's sports pages were reporting
that Leeds City had no greater aspirations than a good

showing in the West Yorkshire League. There were hints, however, that private discussions in drawing rooms and offices across the city were opening Fred Waterhouse's club up to new influences. A meeting was announced for Monday 29 August. 'Negotiations have, we understand, been going on for some time,' wrote Flaneur, 'in furtherance of a scheme which includes an application for admission to the English Association in the season of 1905/06.' Most significantly, he added that 'a number of sportsmen from the North side of the river are interesting themselves' in the club.

In Leeds, the river was as much a metaphorical as a geographical divide. The city's industrial factories – its engine – lay south of the River Aire, in Hunslet and Holbeck; its financial centre was just to its north, and north of that the residences of the well-to-do were found on whatever high ground could be built on above the smog, lately in fashionable Headingley. The sportsmen Flaneur referred to had north Leeds money, but strong links to Holbeck.

Charles Hoyle was managing director of Bentley Brewery, whose pub the Old Peacock Inn stood on the edge of the Elland Road ground. Bentley had sold the sporting pitches to Holbeck FC – there was a cricket pitch too – and retained rights to serve refreshments there. Councillor Joseph Henry was president of Holbeck Football & Athletic Company, which owned Elland Road and ran the rugby and cricket clubs; a self-made

man, he owned a large iron foundry in Holbeck, lived
in a house by Holbeck cemetery named Grand Vue,
and served as liberal councillor for Holbeck ward for
so long that he had the nickname 'King of Holbeck'.
Norris Hepworth, who built his own grand house in
Headingley, was another man of influence at Holbeck,
once an eccentric captain of its cricket team, then keenly
interested in its rugby club. He was partner, managing
director and the 'son' in Joseph Hepworth & Son, a
clothing manufacturer growing rapidly thanks to Norris'
innovations: he cut out the retail middleman, establish-
ing more than a hundred Hepworth's stores to sell direct
to the public, transforming the clothing industry. Across
Leeds, Montague Burton's took the model, and with
additional flair for branding became world famous in the
1930s; Hepworth's were more cautious, but prospered
until the 1980s when they rebranded as Next.

Only Joseph Henry was present at the crucial meeting on 29 August 1904, but Hepworth and Hoyle sent
apologies and messages of support, and their influence
on the new club was clear. The venue – and Leeds City's
headquarters – was relocated from the Royal Exchange
Hotel, a pub tucked among crowded industrial yards in
the centre of Hunslet, to the Griffin Hotel, across the
street from the city's prestigious stock exchange. Some
'forty or fifty gentlemen' were present, giving enthusiastic support to a scheme that wasn't quite as simple as
Manningham's switch to association the season before.

Leeds City was a confluence of clubs, interests and timing, not strictly a succession from one club to another, nor a merger. It depended on combining the history and know-how of Fred Waterhouse and the Hunslet AFC committee, who had reorganised the club and found the players, several Twinklers among them; the financial backing of Norris Hepworth; the support of Joseph Henry, meaning Holbeck Rugby Club effectively ceased to exist and Elland Road was available; and the Elland Road ground itself, upon which the new venture depended. Elland Road would be rented for the season and later purchased, a new company would be floated to provide finance, 'the object being the establishment of a first-rate team, which will secure the favourable notice of the Football Association', and so bring top-class league football to Leeds. Some early reports attached Hunslet AFC's earlier successes to the new name of Leeds City, but the club was looking to the future, not anxious about retaining any sense of its past.

Fred Waterhouse, whose passion for excellent soccer conflicted with his stance against professionalism, faded from view, but his arrangements were crucial, as three days after the meeting at the Griffin Leeds City kicked off their first match in the West Yorkshire League, a 2-2 draw away to Morley. It was a whirlwind week; two days later City played their first home game, a 2-1 defeat to Altofts, although Elland Road was not yet ready so the match was played at the Wellington Ground, as

was a high-profile friendly two days after that against
Bradford City, who won 3-0. The club's first win in the
West Yorkshire League came on 24 September, 3-1 at
Huddersfield Town, and after finally confirming arrange-
ments to play at Elland Road, a crowd of 3,300 watched
Leeds City's first friendly game there, a 2-0 defeat to
Hull City. City's first competitive game at Elland Road
was on 12 November, a 3-2 win in the first round of
the Leeds Hospital Cup over holders and heirs to the
Twinklers' dominance, Altofts, inside-forward Gordon
Howard scoring all three City goals before half-time.

Leeds City made it to the third round of the Leeds
Hospital Cup, losing 2-1 to Upper Armley Christ
Church, but competitive fixtures were almost an unwelcome distraction in 1904/05. While promising the West
Yorkshire League its strongest team, City only completed
23 of 26 fixtures, and the club often double-booked itself
with friendlies against big-name clubs: Second Division
West Bromwich Albion, Leicester Fosse, Lincoln City
and Barnsley, and First Division Sheffield United, Derby
County and Preston North End were all welcomed to
Elland Road; all won except Sheffield United, with
whom Leeds drew 2-2. The aim was demonstrating
that Elland Road was a top-class football venue, and
Leeds a favourable city. The charm offensive worked:
on 29 May 1905, Leeds City won the vote for election
to the Football League.

1905–14

YOU ARE THE BIGGEST
LIAR IN BEESTON

Leeds had its Football League club. Leeds City floated as a limited liability company in April 1905, initially offering 5,000 of 10,000 £1 shares. The major shareholders were Ralph Younger, landlord of the Old Peacock on Elland Road; A.W. Pullan, a sports journalist writing as 'Old Ebor' in the *Yorkshire Evening Post*, who became deputy chairman; and Norris Hepworth, who was unanimously elected president in November, and now confirmed as chairman. Hepworth's contributions were already vital. As well as becoming majority shareholder, he was arranging to buy Elland Road for the club's use, at a price revised downwards from an initial £5,000 to a still substantial £4,500.

It was well remembered at Leeds City that the lack of a home ground prevented Hunslet AFC applying to join the Football League and hastened their demise, and the new club's shareholders had seen what success the investments at Headingley had brought to the rugby and cricket clubs there. Elland Road already had a cricket pitch, and improving the Old Peacock Ground alongside it for soccer presented an opportunity to build a Headingley stadium for south Leeds. Announcing the company's prospectus in April, the *Yorkshire Post* claimed: 'Already a gentleman who has been concerned in the erection of such stands at the Bramall Lane ground, Sheffield, at Middlesbrough, Fulham, Woolwich Arsenal, and Stamford Bridge, has paid a visit to the ground in order to give the directors the benefit of his experience and advice.' That CV belonged to Archibald Leitch, then in the early stages of becoming football's foremost architect, responsible for iconic grandstands at Villa Park, Goodison Park and Ibrox. Built during the summer of 1905 for £1,050, Leeds City's new stand stood between the side of the pitch – then oriented east-west – and Elland Road itself, but it was built by Messrs H. Barrett and Sons of Bradford and is not known to have shown any of Leitch's distinctive influence; 75 yards long and 35 yards deep, it had room for up to 5,000 spectators under cover, and a 'commodious press box'. At the same time, Holbeck Rugby Club's old timber stand at the north end was taken down, and bank-and-cinder terraces put in place around the three uncovered sides, with room for 20,000 or 30,000, depending on which version of the club's hype you believed.

Although the team's performance in Leeds City's first league match was talked up by the supportive local press, the 1-0 defeat at Bradford City that announced Leeds to Division Two may have dampened enthusiasm for their home debut. At Elland Road on 9 September 1905, 6,800 paying customers saw West Bromwich Albion win 2-0. Just half that number came to see Tommy Drain score Leeds' first two league goals in a 2-2 draw with Lincoln City two days later, but after news of a 1-0 win away to Leicester Fosse was communicated to the reluctant public back home, they understood City might be getting their act together. For the next match, on 23 September, more than 13,000 turned out at Elland Road and saw Hull City soundly beaten, 3-1. Wearing jerseys of deep blue with gold trim, the team were nick-named the Peacocks, both for their appearance and for their ground's association with both the Old Peacock Inn over the road, and the New Peacock Inn by the cricket ground. The team colours were completed with the city coat of arms on the breast, the Peacocks hoping soccer could become a source of civic pride.

Attendances were roughly estimated, but takings on the gate were counted to the penny. When Chelsea came in late November, around 20,000 were not dismayed by the 0-0 result; the *Leeds Mercury* reckoned the game was, 'perhaps, the finest that has been played in the city'. On 30 December Bradford City won 2-0 at Elland Road, and records were set: some 22,000 were in the ground, and for the first time late arrivers had to be turned away for lack of space. The same day Leeds Rugby League played Oldham at Headingley; just 6,000 turned out there to watch Leeds' 8-2 win. The *Yorkshire Evening Post* noted sombrely that 'it was a delightful day for football, but the big association game at Elland Road was evidently a bigger attraction to the local public', with Flaneur adding in the *Leeds Mercury*: 'Socker has hit the popular taste in Leeds, and the Northern Union game will have to look to its laurels.'

Hunslet and Leeds were engaged in a terrific season in rugby's Northern Union, eventually finishing second and third respectively behind Leigh, but falling attendances at Headingley were causing losses so severe that the club were publicly considering closing the ground altogether. At Parkside annual subscriptions were down from £462 to £242, and Hunslet directly blamed the new soccer club down the hill. Leeds City's directors, totting up their profits for the season of £122, insisted soccer would not bring about the downfall of rugby in the city; Hepworth suggested the problems at Headingley were due to its distance from the working-class districts from which sporting crowds were drawn.

Although Leeds City's directors were satisfied with 6th place at the end of their profitable first season of league football, soccer at Elland Road was not booming as they wished. Summer 1906 brought more building work; £3,000 was spent on a new 4,000-seat Main Stand to the west of the pitch, with dressing rooms, officials' rooms, and an indoor running track for the players underneath; there was even a motor garage, said the *Leeds Mercury*, 'so that the management are quite up to date'. The West Stand's inauguration against Chelsea marked the opening of a magnificent new ground and a new beginning: 'And it is only natural to expect that the same business capacity which has been shown in the provision of the ground will now be directed towards getting together a team worthy of the highest honours.'

The stadium now contrasted sharply with the team playing in it. The game with Chelsea was Leeds' sixth defeat, and a trip to Wolves brought a seventh. The changes at Elland Road included rotating the pitch, so the new West Stand was against its longest touchline; it was hoped the new orientation, relaid turf and improved drainage would solve the flooding and waterlogging that had stuck Leeds' attempts to play short passing soccer in the mud.

City's directors had advertised for a manager before their place in the Football League was confirmed, selecting Gilbert Gillies from over a hundred applicants. Gillies had been secretary-manager at Chesterfield and helped them win election to the Football League in 1899, and he quickly demonstrated his administrative skills in the same role at Leeds; but even with George Swift working with him as trainer, his soccer abilities remained hidden. The first season was promising, with just three defeats at Elland Road; goals were hard to find, but thirteen came in fifteen games from top scorer David 'Soldier' Wilson, a veteran of the Boer War signed from Hull City in December for £150. He was a big, stocky player, with a thick moustache that gave the 22 year old a much older appearance. Not fast or mobile, he looked indifferent to the game going on around him, but he was strong and clever, an intelligent passer to the wings, always in the right place to score.

City were much changed for the start of 1906/07, retaining Wilson as the focal point, but he didn't score in the first two games and missed the next four through injury. His return lifted the team; Leeds beat Burton United, Grimsby Town and Burslem Port Vale, and signs of improving form brought 14,000 fans to Elland Road for a match with Burnley.

Wilson's commitment to the cause of what was still only a provincial Second Division club in its infancy cost him everything that day, and made him Elland Road's first hero. Fifteen minutes into the second half Wilson was still searching for his first goal of the season, getting some rough treatment from Burnley's defenders – he was badly winded in the first half when sandwiched between two of them – and sending two efforts just over the bar. A third, headed at goal, caused some sort of strain and left Wilson feeling such severe pains in his chest that he headed for the dressing rooms.

Police constable John Byrom followed Wilson, and finding the player in agony on the ground, he sent for the Leeds and Burnley club doctors, and a third found in the stands. They moved him to the comfort of the directors' room, where he began to recover a little from what City's Dr Taylor presumed had been a heart attack. A taxicab was called to take him home.

Even before Wilson went off, Jack Lavery had been knocked unconscious in a tackle, and was now a passenger on the fringes of the game; now Harry Singleton was injured, and limped away to the dressing rooms, leaving Leeds down to eight fit players.

'Though his chest was very sore,' reported the *Yorkshire Evening Post*, 'Wilson said he could not remain there [the directors' room] while the Leeds City team were in such straits. So, although many of those in the room endeavoured to dissuade him from his purpose he went out to resume play, his reappearance being greeted by a storm of cheers.'

Wilson managed three minutes, only going near the ball once, before leaving the pitch again in agony. While Burnley took an inevitable lead, in the dressing rooms Constable Byrom was helping Wilson into a hot bath the player thought might restore him. Instead, Wilson suffered violent spasms, lost consciousness, and was quickly moved to a table and attended by Dr Taylor.

Sarah Wilson was at the game and, worried by her husband's behaviour, had set off for their home in Catherine Grove, not far away at the top of Beeston Hill, to wait for him there. When the game ended the players found a shocking situation in their dressing room, and Gilbert Gillies found a car to overtake Mrs Wilson, bringing her back to the ground to attend to her stricken husband. When she made the trip away again, it was in an ambulance, with her husband's body. Despite the efforts of the doctors, David 'Soldier' Wilson had died just as the game was ending.

It was agreed at the inquest that 'over eagerness to be of service to his club was Wilson's undoing'; 'His devotion to the game and to the club proved fatal,' wrote the *Leeds Mercury*. As well as Sarah, Wilson left a ten-month-old daughter. He was just 23 years old. A few days later, after a service at Catherine Grove, his coffin was draped in a Leeds City flag for the journey north, to be buried near his family in Leith.

The shadow over the shocked and grieving club took a long time to lift; they didn't score for three games following Wilson's death. Leeds began 1907 17th in the twenty-team division, but two wins gave them hope; Clapton Orient were beaten 3-2 at Elland Road on 1 December, then promotion hopefuls Stockport County were seen off 6-1. Each game included a goal from a new £350 player, Billy McLeod, a 21 year old signed from Lincoln City to replace Wilson; with the bravery to head any ball that came near him, and shooting power with either boot, he was the season's top scorer with fifteen in 23 matches. Form improved, but there was no consistency; Leeds finished 12th.

The directors were growing impatient. Chelsea, elected at the same time as Leeds, had won promotion; Gilbert Gillies could no longer argue this was a new club that needed time to develop, and a line had to be drawn under the tragedy of Wilson's death. The stadium was first class, and so was Billy McLeod; 21-year-old Fred Croot was signed to serve him from the wing, and Tom Hynds, a 23-year-old centre-half with top-flight experience, to stiffen the defence and take on the captaincy. Leeds reached 2nd in the table in 1908/09, but after that their form fell dramatically; they didn't rise above 11th after November, a far cry from promotion. McLeod scored seventeen goals, but the next best was Croot; he had a brilliant season, but only scored eight.

Gilbert Gillies didn't last the season. As at most clubs, City's side was picked by a selection committee, and despite showing a good eye for players, Gillies was not trusted with player recruitment, left to work instead on the administration of the club and its grounds. But Gillies was being blamed for the team's failure, and fed up with being made the scapegoat, he resigned in February, five days after a surprising 5-1 home win over Derby County. Leeds played their next game, away to Lincoln City, in a storm that tore the roof from the stand at Sincil Bank, injuring five spectators and delaying the game by 40 minutes; they lost 5-0.

Gillies was not replaced until April, ample time for dissatisfaction to transfer from Gillies to the club's directors. City's supporters couldn't understand why, after spending so much on the stadium, the directors seemed unwilling to invest in a team worthy of it. After 22,000 watched Leeds' defeat to Bradford City on 30 December 1905, Elland Road recorded just five league attendances over 20,000 in the next six seasons, the last in September 1908.

The new manager was Frank Scott-Walford, brought north from Brighton & Hove Albion. He was given more freedom, and more funds, but his radical team-building relied on players he knew from the Southern League, who brought no improvements in 1908/09. Leeds City were risking the same fate as Holbeck Rugby Club, of poor performances leading to low attendances, meaning fewer funds for players, all while soccer was becoming more competitive and expensive; in 1909, the Players' Union successfully campaigned to increase the maximum wage to £5.

Scott-Walford's priority was building a good team, and fast, and his response was another busy summer of transfers, but now with a much-reduced budget. McLeod and Croot stayed and were as productive as they could be, but the new players were either youngsters or cheap imports from Ireland, and if one was successful, offers from elsewhere were hard to resist. Billy Halligan signed from the Irish League and rivalled McLeod, with twelve goals in 24 games, but by March he was sold to Derby County for £400. 19th of twenty clubs with six games left, McLeod and Croot stepped up, between them scoring all of City's goals after 7 March, gaining 17th place and safety.

The team was safe, but the directors were not, and a series of stormy meetings with shareholders dominated the summer. After losing £1,200 in 1908/09, City's loss in 1909/10 was £1,904; income was down by £1,600. 'If you want my own candid opinion,' Joseph Henry told a meeting at Salem Hall, 'it is this – that the in and out play of the team was so unsatisfactory that people would not come to the ground to watch it.'

It was the same story that had beset Leeds City from the start: nice ground, shame about the team. But attempts to make more money from Elland Road were chaotic; City's boasts about capacity won the opportunity to host an FA Cup semi-final between Barnsley and Everton in 1910, but with 36,000 inside, around 14,000 fans were locked out; for an FA Cup fourth-round replay between Barnsley and Bradford in 1912 45,000 squeezed in, 11,000 of them without paying. After Manchester United opened their new ground at Old Trafford in February 1910, designed by Archibald Leitch to include tea rooms, a billiard room and space for 80,000 spectators, Leeds City's hopes that Elland

Road might become the major football ground of the north looked forlorn.

Norris Hepworth spelled out the financial situation at Salem Hall in September. Trouble had begun at the club's outset, when difficulty raising funds for the new stands at Elland Road meant a change of bankers. The new bank had allowed an overdraft of £7,000; Hepworth, Henry and two others had personally loaned the club £2,500 to keep it going, while another £840 had come from Frank Scott-Walford to pay players' wages over the summer while Hepworth was abroad, when the rest of the board refused to put in another penny.

Hepworth told the Hall that £12,000 had to be found to save the club. He proposed a scheme of debentures at 5 per cent, and if the shareholders would raise £4,000, he and a few of the other directors would contribute the £8,000. The club's option to buy Elland Road had lapsed, but Hepworth was arranging to buy it personally and convey it to the club in exchange for a mortgage. The alternative, under pressure from the bank, was liquidation. 'It would not show very great sportsmanship,' added Joseph Henry, 'if we could not find this money. I believe we have got over the difficulties, really. Managing an association club is quite a new feature, and it is a huge business concern, but now the club is in a fair way towards prosperity. In my judgement the team for the present season are all men of character, and that is something for a start.'

The shareholders were not convinced. One, Harry Riley, accused the board: 'When we come to consider the fine ground, the great industrial population of Leeds, the splendid railway and tramway facilities, it is remarkable that they should be grovelling in the mire. They are actually asking their servants for money.' There had to be radical changes if shareholders were to hand over more cash: the board would be reduced to five, consisting of Hepworth and four elected shareholders: Joseph Henry, Alf Masser, J.C. Whiteman and James Bromley.

Some wanted the reorganising to extend to Frank Scott-Walford, but Joseph Henry supported him, and dismissed rumours that Scott-Walford had been seeking new players at the Glasgow Labour Exchange. In any case, the option of simply dismissing the manager for the team's poor performance was complicated now the club was in debt to him, and his position became a focus of tension.

Ahead of the election of the new board, angry words were exchanged between Scott-Walford and one of the founding directors, Walter Preston. What caused the argument remained in dispute: whether it was Preston's attempts to remove Scott-Walford; or his accusation that Scott-Walford was trying to become a director himself; or Scott-Walford's allegation that Preston was trying to take money out of the ailing club. But what was agreed when the matter went to court was that Scott-Walford walked with Preston into the middle of the Elland Road pitch, away from the watching players, and told him: 'I have got you across here to tell you what you are. You are the biggest liar in Beeston. You are a pig. You are a damnable liar. You are not an honest man. My players have more honesty in their toes than you have in your body.' Pushing and shoving followed, Mr Preston gesturing with an umbrella and threatening to call his solicitors; with a swing of his fist, Mr Scott-Walford broke Mr Preston's jaw.

The magistrate helped the pair to an amicable settlement; they had shaken hands before leaving Elland Road after the fight. But the club was under strain, and Scott-Walford in particular. He hadn't been to Glasgow Labour Exchange, but to Ireland, signing five new players. In a bizarre stunt to make them feel at home, he sent the team out in green shirts for the first game of the season and added green flags to the centre line markings. There were five other signings, but Scott-Walford struck a defeatist tone in his message to the players at the start of the season: 'Should your efforts deserve success, and it is denied you, we shall extend our sympathy; when you do badly we shall still think you have done your best.'

City didn't move clear of the re-election places until after February. They finished 11th, but another poor season impacted attendances; 50,000 were at Stamford Bridge to watch Chelsea beat Leeds 4-1 in April, but just 6,000 came to Elland Road to see Leeds win their last game of the season, 1-0 against Wolves.

Another eight raw recruits came from Scott-Walford's summer pilgrimage to Ireland, but the best of his finds, twenty-year-old Billy Gillespie, after ten goals in 24 appearances, was sold to Sheffield United for a City record fee of £400. He played there for 21 years, in 575 games, and held the record as Ireland's top international goalscorer for 80 years. 1911/12 was another season of gloom. McLeod was out of form and fitness, and there was no time for the young players to mature. There was a rousing home win over Glossop in the first round of the FA Cup, confirming that attractive fixtures could still draw 21,000, but by March the team were 19th, and attractive fixtures were few and far between.

At a meeting at Salem Hall in September, Alf Masser had given details of yet another scheme to clear debts, buy Elland Road, provide money for new players, and stabilise the finances. If £16,000 could be raised, the debts – most owing to or underwritten by Norris Hepworth – could be cleared. Hepworth got the ball rolling by putting in the first £3,000 himself.

The plan failed, and Frank Scott-Walford was told to come up with another at the end of January. Already fighting against re-election to the league, owed more than £3,500, and now under pressure to find a financial solution and save the club, Scott-Walford cracked, although this time no jaws were. Instead, at the end of February, he delivered an ultimatum to the board, citing his ill health and his duty to his wife and children:

either the club paid what he was owed by 31 March, or he would submit his resignation.

Scott-Walford's impaired state can be read from his toothless ultimatum. He had in fact presented an ideal situation to the board: they accepted his resignation and, rather than repay his debt, presented him with an inscribed silver flower bowl, an inscribed gold medal, and a silver-mounted oak biscuit box for his wife. They thanked him for his work and advertised for a replacement.

The local papers filled with rumours: of a takeover by local businessmen Ed Wood and Samuel Samuel; that only eight players were staying; that Woolwich Arsenal manager George Morrell had been appointed. There was some truth in the last one, but Morrell's friends persuaded him to stay in London. Without a manager, Leeds were sinking, winning only one of the last eleven games and finishing 19th. Leeds City were out of the league, and had to apply to be voted back in.

There was no patience at the bank. In March, the £8,000 overdraft was called in, and Hepworth appointed accountant Tom Coombs as receiver to manage the club's finances. At an extraordinary general meeting at Salem Hall in August 1912, it was explained that the club had liabilities of £16,000 and assets of £7,000, in the form of Elland Road; but if there was no club, Elland Road would be worthless. Leeds City were only surviving through Hepworth's generosity, albeit with renewed determination, and a tighter hand on its purse thanks to Coombs. 'Association football in Leeds ought to be successful, can be successful and will be successful,' he told the *Yorkshire Evening Post*. 'If only the public of Leeds will stand by the club and have a little patience and confidence we shall yet have a club at Elland Road capable of taking its place in the front rank of Association football.'

The club had, for once, reasons to be optimistic. Re-election was secured in July, as was a new manager. Herbert Chapman had taken Northampton Town from two consecutive last-place finishes in the Southern League to first place within two seasons, aiming to take them into the Football League. But election was unlikely given Northampton's small population and rugby union inclinations, and the authorities were unimpressed by Chapman's far-sighted ideas about promotion and relegation beyond the two national divisions. When Leeds City offered Chapman a league management job at an ambitious club in a big city in his native north, Northampton's chairman Pat Darnell allowed him to leave with his blessing.

Although Chapman was not yet an innovator, he prospered at Northampton Town through tactical thought, developing a counter-attacking style based on creating space in front of the opponent's defence for his forwards to drop deep and unsettle their markers. He gave unusual attention to physical conditioning, overseen by trainer Dick Murrell, who followed Chapman to

Leeds. Much of Chapman's best work was done off the pitch. In his office, he had a large tabletop with a football pitch painted on it, bringing a practical element to discussions about the game. He had observed the fervour with which soccer players debated games of billiards and cards, but never football, so before every match he would gather his players at a hotel for lunch and a group conversation about the game.

The talks were a success thanks to Chapman's skill at drawing the players from their reticence, breaking the ice and ensuring fairness. He wore a keen expression, as if listening ready to respond with an intelligent joke, followed by a serious analysis of the problem; his sober suits would be topped off with a flamboyant choice of hat, sometimes a straw boater, sometimes a bowler or a fedora. His emphasis was on creating a family atmosphere and a positive environment. At Leeds he had a flagpole installed on the West Stand roof to give Elland Road a sense of place and pride.

Chapman put his tact and good humour to work on football chairmen as well as players. At Northampton, he persuaded Darnell to put aside his principles and begin paying transfer fees. He insisted on control of team selection, but made sure the directors understood the value he placed on their support. If they left the team to him, he told them, it would make their lives considerably easier; they could enjoy the sport and let Chapman do the worrying.

Intelligent, keen, persuasive and full of ideas, Chapman was 34 when he met Norris Hepworth to talk about Leeds City. They immediately took to each other. City's financial difficulties now worked in their favour, because with Tom Coombs as receiver, the influence of directors and shareholders was reduced. As long as Hepworth underwrote the debts, Coombs managed the money and Chapman worked without interference, Leeds City had a formidable management team.

'I am here to get Leeds City into the First Division,' said Chapman. 'It is, of course, a matter of time, but if it is humanly possible, it shall be attained.' First, he had to make something of the team Scott-Walford had left behind. Chapman's first principle was 'soundness', and the brittle young players were not robust enough. Only ten who played in 1911/12 featured under Chapman, and several of those were sold as the rebuilding continued throughout the season.

Three experienced internationals – centre-half Evelyn Lintott from Bradford City, full-back George Law from Rangers and goalkeeper Billy Scott – were signed for the defence; Scott was an FA Cup winner. But the signings caused trouble with the Football League; their previous contracts ended two months before they joined Leeds, but Chapman paid them for a full year, meaning their weekly wages exceeded the maximum allowed. Chapman reported the situation himself, but there was no lenience, just a £125 fine and a severe telling off, although City were praised for taking the 'honourable course' of handing themselves in.

Chapman used thirteen new players during the season, but was left distraught by one that got away. 'In no instance have I personally suffered so great a disappointment,' he said when attempts to sign tiny outside-right Fanny Walden from his old club Northampton Town were thwarted, by a 'shilling fund' established by fans to keep him there. Chapman wanted Walden to feed Billy McLeod from the right as effectively as Fred Croot from the left; Walden 'would be the making of the Leeds City team, if only I could get him to Elland Road.' For now, Chapman found cheer in a new inside-left from Bradford City.

Jimmy Speirs was a Scottish international, scorer of the winning goal for Bradford City in the 1911 FA Cup final replay, but he was disillusioned by the way they were being run. It was the perfect opportunity for Chapman. He persuaded Speirs that his future lay in dropping down a division to ambitious Leeds City, and convincing Coombs that the club record £1,400 transfer fee was good business. Both Speirs and Coombs agreed to the biggest deal Leeds City had ever made, for the most famous player the club had ever signed. 'The enterprise of the Leeds City management in securing Speirs would have staggered those responsible for the club a few years ago,' said the *Yorkshire Evening Post*.

The team was looking better, thanks to greater 'dash and enthusiasm', and crowds were returning; 15,000 were at Elland Road to watch City play local rivals Huddersfield Town on 21 December. But that crowd saw City's first home defeat, and the next three games, all at home, were also lost. The *Yorkshire Evening Post* said Christmas 1912 would be 'marked in the records with black borders.'

But Speirs had the desired effect. City's attack had a new look; McLeod and Croot stayed at centre-forward and outside-left, with Speirs at inside-left; on the other wing were recent signings Simpson Bainbridge and Arthur Price. At Blackpool on New Year's Day they had 'vim', 'dash', 'speed' and 'understanding', according to the *Leeds Mercury*; they were 'well-nigh irresistible' in a 3-0 win.

The City defence was still suspect, but the forwards gave the team every chance. In nineteen games Speirs scored ten, finishing second top scorer; McLeod was ahead of everybody, scoring in nine consecutive games between 1 March and 5 April, including a hat-trick and a brace, ending the season with 27 goals in 38 appearances. Leeds finished 6th, the best since the club's first season, and there were only four defeats at home, where the division's top four teams were all beaten. Elland Road in the summer was far from the grim enclosure it had seemed during so many seasons of failure. Chapman was busy installing new baths for the players, and a recreation room with a billiard table.

The good mood extended to City's Annual General Meeting at the YMCA Hall in Albion Place, not quite deflated by the balance sheet. A proposed financial reconstruction scheme was still just proposed: 'It was found impossible to induce any one to put down any fresh capital for the company,' reported vice-chairman Joseph Henry. Another £2,100 came from Norris Hepworth's pockets, and the season showed an overall loss of £1,865. In all other respects, though, the club was healthier than it had been for years.

It all hinged on Chapman building a team worth paying for; the transfer fees and wages paid by Coombs and Hepworth, the entry paid on the gate by supporters. Twelve players departed, and two much-needed centre-halves arrived: Jack Hampson, whom Chapman had managed at Northampton, and Harry Peart, who followed Speirs from Bradford City. The summer's big attacking signing was 24-year-old Ivan Sharpe, who won the gold medal with Great Britain's team at the 1912 Olympics, and the Second Division title with Derby County. He played as an amateur while working as a journalist, and when he took a job at the *Yorkshire Evening News* he also took Fred Croot's place on the left wing for City.

McLeod began the season by scoring four in the first three games, the last a 5-1 thrashing of Bradford Park Avenue. But the 'baffling business', as the *Yorkshire Evening Post* put it, of City's inconsistency returned when they lost the next match 4-0 away to Notts County. In pursuit of steadiness, team changes were kept to a minimum, and results improved; City were 2nd in the league on Boxing Day. Speirs and Sharpe were creating goal after goal for McLeod, who hit four in an 8-0 win over Nottingham Forest at Elland Road at the end of November. January 1914 brought an FA Cup fourth round visit from West Bromwich Albion, one of the top five teams in the country; in front of 29,733 spectators, Leeds held them until the last seconds, when West Brom snatched two cruel goals.

Chapman was still searching for 'soundness', and with £1,397 taken on the gate for the West Brom game, Hepworth and Coombs were willing to spend. Huddersfield Town's decision to sell their captain, Fred Blackman, caused such a sensation that the directors and the manager, Arthur Fairclough, refused to discuss the fee, only revealing it was 'upwards of £1,000'. Blackman was a full-back, 30 years old, stylish, polished and reliable, with 'few equals as a tackler.' Huddersfield fans could not believe their club had let him go, but they'd lost out to Chapman's art of persuasion, and Hepworth's readiness to fund success.

Norris Hepworth never saw Blackman play for Leeds. On the eve of the next match, away to Hull City, Hepworth died at home after a brief illness. He was 57 years old and at the height of his career; chairman of one of the largest clothing manufacturers in the country, and on the verge of having his long and expensive commitment to Leeds City rewarded with First Division soccer. It was only after his death that his true commitment could be seen: City's debts had been rearranged so that Hepworth owned them all, and overall he had put almost £16,000 behind the club's hopes, more than a sixth of the total £103,000 estate he left in his will, and roughly equivalent to a whole year's profits at Hepworth & Son.

In the circumstances it was unsurprising that the game at Hull ended in a 1-0 defeat, although Blackman showed his coolness and maturity with an assured debut, but four wins and two draws at Elland Road took Leeds into the last round of matches in 4th. Promotion was still possible if they beat Birmingham City at Elland Road, and with Speirs back from injury, Leeds did their bit. Birmingham equalised twice before McLeod made the final score 3-2 to Leeds, but scores elsewhere broke their hearts, and Bradford Park Avenue were promoted.

Leeds ended the season 4th, with a record number of points and a record number of goals, made bitter by falling two agonising points short of promotion, and the loss of Norris Hepworth. But Leeds City's future without Hepworth did not look as grave as it might had he not found Chapman in time. Coombs reported a profit of £383, the first time the club had made money since its first season. 'The income from gate receipts and season tickets has been a record,' he said, to applause and laughter at the AGM. 'We have paid a record amount for transfer fees, and made a record profit. There was also a record expenditure, but that was counterbalanced by the other records,' on the pitch.

With Herbert Chapman's intelligent management, Spiers, McLeod, Sharpe and Hampson's top-class skills, and fifteen home wins bringing large crowds to Elland Road, Leeds City entered their tenth league season ready for rewards: everything was in place for promotion.

3

1914–19

HE PLACED IN OUR HANDS CERTAIN INFORMATION

By 1914, association football had overtaken all other sports to become the English national pastime, played and watched by hundreds of thousands of people every week. But their soccer seasons were becoming complicated by questions of destiny much larger than the fates of their favourite football teams.

On 26 September 1914, 20,000 people lined the pavements of Boar Lane and filled the platforms of Leeds City station to cheer 1,275 soldiers who had signed up for the Leeds Pals battalion, departing for their training camp en route to fight in the Great War declared that July. There were no such crowds at the station the next morning, to watch the Leeds City team depart for their match with Clapton Orient, or to greet them when they came home defeated. As national debates decided whether soccer ought to carry on being played at all, the uncertainty, and poor form, soon meant City's hopes of promotion would be frustrated; Leeds ended the season 15th; a disappointment, but no longer a tragedy.

Leeds had its share of the sorrows that were to follow. Among the Pals was Evelyn Lintott, one of Herbert Chapman's first signings, and his captain; he didn't miss a game in his first season at Leeds. By January 1915, Lintott was promoted to lieutenant, the first professional footballer to hold a commission. On the first day of the Battle of the Somme, 1 July 1916, he led the Leeds Pals out of the trenches and over the top. He was hit by enemy fire; but with his revolver in hand he continued leading the advance. It took two more shots to bring Lintott down, aged 33, one of more than 500 Leeds Pals killed or wounded within moments of stepping into the battle.

Jimmy Speirs had another fine season for Leeds in 1914/15, captaining the side and scoring ten goals. Married with two children, Speirs could have gained exemption from service, but chose to sign up in Glasgow in May 1915. In May 1917 Speirs was recommended for the Military Medal for bravery; in June he was promoted to sergeant. In August, after writing on a postcard to his wife that he hoped 1917 would be the last year of the war, he was killed in action in the Battle of Passchendaele.

Five other past or current Leeds City players lost their lives: Frederick Hargraves, John Harkins, Gerald Kirk, Thomas Morris and David Murray.

The club itself continued. The Football League was replaced by regional competitions, and Leeds City enjoyed their first successes. In the first season of the war, they finished 10th in the Midland League, but won the post-season 'subsidiary' tournament against five other northern clubs; Leeds then won the Midland League twice running, and a two-legged League Championship play-off against Stoke City in 1918, finishing 3rd in 1919.

Leeds were helped by the closure of teams such as Newcastle United and Sunderland, giving them access to players including Charles Buchan, the best in England. The movement towards work for the war effort also moved players to new clubs. Fanny Walden moved from London to work at a motor engineering works near Leeds, and Herbert Chapman was finally reunited with his former Northampton Town winger; Jack Peart from Notts County and Clem Stephenson from Aston Villa became City's key attackers.

Despite their sporting successes, City's existence remained precarious. Receiver Tom Coombs made it clear that he could not go on running Leeds City on behalf of Norris Hepworth's estate, particularly not in wartime, and was ready to hand it back to the shareholders whose debts had been liquidated by Hepworth as soon as they were ready to pay for it. As ever, when funds were required at Elland Road, there were none forthcoming.

Instead, in summer 1915, came a proposal from Headingley: the Leeds Cricket, Football and Athletics Company would buy Leeds City outright – players, stands, fixtures, fittings and their place in Division Two – and transfer it all to their stadium in north Leeds, replacing Leeds Rugby League club, leaving Elland Road a wasteland. Such upheaval was not popular: City drew its support from working-class districts south of the River Aire, from Beeston, Holbeck, Hunslet and Morley; for many supporters, travelling to Headingley for leisure was out of the question. There was anger north of the river too; many of the spectators at Headingley were rugby diehards, and where was their beloved Leeds RL club to go?

Hours before a meeting of Leeds City shareholders, the proposal was withdrawn, and Joseph Connor, a cloth merchant and president of the West Riding FA, went public with an alternative. By paying an initial £1,000, and a further £250 from any incoming transfer fees, Connor and a syndicate – J.C. Whiteman, Sam Glover, George Sykes and W.H. Platts – would take over Leeds City, meeting all expenses and leasing the ground, still rented with an option to purchase from Bentley's Brewery. The aim was not profit, as there was little prospect of that in wartime, but to ensure soccer survived at

Elland Road. The shareholders, invited to either match Connor's offer or back it, opted overwhelmingly for the cheaper option of backing it. Connor became chairman; 'Johnny' Whiteman, theatre agent and manager of the City Varieties music hall, became vice-chair.

Connor was expected to be the ideal foil for the progressive management of Herbert Chapman, but they only worked closely together for a year, until summer 1916. Chapman, whose years of management experience included mining operations as well as soccer clubs, became one of the senior managers of Barnbow, a munitions factory built on a heroic scale, employing 16,000 people in three shifts filling 24 hours, six days a week. While the war front had accounted for thousands of men, at factories like Barnbow women matched their effort: 93 per cent of the workforce was female.

It was carried out with utmost secrecy; Chapman was described in the *Yorkshire Evening Post* as holding simply 'an important munitions appointment'. The secrecy extended to the night in December 1916 when an explosion killed 35 women; many more were seriously injured. It was the worst disaster the city of Leeds had ever known, but not made public until 1924.

Chapman remained as a consultant at Leeds City, and was included in the club photograph in 1917. Day-to-day management was divided between Connor and Whiteman, in charge of team selection, and Chapman's personal assistant George Cripps, a schoolteacher and referee, who Chapman recommended should take on the administrative work.

Connor and Cripps became bitterly entrenched against one another. The origins and facts of their disputes at Leeds City are not clear, but were spilled in letters written after the fact to the *Yorkshire Evening Post*, conflating unrelated issues and laying blame at each other's feet. What is clear is that Connor had an extremely low opinion of Cripps' work, claiming at the end of 1916/17 that the club's accounts were in such a poor state that either Cripps went or he did; a clerk was employed to take over.

Cripps disputed this, claiming he was paid a bonus of £30 by the other directors for his work, and that the clerk was paid a fraction of his own salary and was effectively his assistant. In any case, Cripps said, if he was 'an incompetent man', why did he continue to be employed?

Connor seems to have been asking that same question, citing Cripps' position as the cause of friction between the directors, the players and Chapman. Chapman had more involvement in 1917/18, the season he appeared on the club photograph, taking over team affairs from Connor and Whiteman, with Cripps assisting him. But Chapman was soon absent again and Cripps was left in charge of the team, effectively usurping Connor's role.

According to Connor, the directors had so much trouble with Cripps they stipulated that only one director should travel with the team, and it should never be

Cripps. In February 1918 Cripps turned up at an away match at Nottingham Forest anyway, and after the match Chapman received a letter from the team captain, Jack Hampson, stating that the players would strike unless Cripps was allowed to start going with them again. It took a personal intervention by Chapman to convince the players to accept the directors' conditions and continue playing. Connor viewed the incident as scurrilous insurrection instigated by Cripps, but Cripps simply pointed to another £30 bonus he received at the end of another season's work.*

The Great War was ending in Europe, but not at Elland Road. Chapman returned for the 1918/19 season, and Cripps was out of a job: some accounts say he was put to work again as Chapman's assistant, but simmered at the demotion; Connor claimed the directors decided to sever all ties with him; Cripps himself claimed Chapman told him the club could not afford them both. However it came about, by Christmas 1918 Cripps was out, and claiming damages for wrongful dismissal.

---

* This tale has been told elsewhere as the players refusing to travel with Cripps, but Connor's letter of 14 October 1919 is clear that they wanted Cripps with them: 'An arrangement was made that one director, and not Mr Cripps, should go away with the team, unless under special instructions. The result was that after a match at Nottingham, which Mr Cripps attended, a letter, written by J. Hampson, was sent to Mr Chapman stating that unless Cripps was allowed to go with the team they would all go out on strike!'

Chapman may have been tiring of all this, or found at Barnbow that there was satisfying work outside soccer; he only ever meant to try football management as an experiment anyway. It might simply have been that the offer to become superintendent of labour at one of Europe's largest mills, the Olympia Oil and Cake Works in Selby, was too good to refuse. But Chapman's letter of resignation was the worst Christmas present Leeds City could have received; he left Elland Road, and football, on 31 December 1918.

Connor and Whiteman took control until the end of the season, then appointed Bob Hewison as manager, a popular player for City during the war who retired after breaking his leg once, then again in his first match after recovering. The *Yorkshire Evening Post* expected he would be successful, adding: 'He will not be without encouragement and service from his predecessor, Mr Herbert Chapman.' Hewison took the job amid circumstances that would have been familiar to Chapman; Connor and Whiteman were making good on their intention to hand the club back to the city and preparing to float it to shareholders. The club was paying its way after years of hardship, and Connor had no doubt the soccer fans of Leeds would provide the backing to make Leeds City a post-war success.

They had the makings of a team. The Football League was reinstated for the 1919/20 season, and although City's new beginning was a 4-2 defeat at Blackpool, they won the next three matches without conceding a goal. Jack Hampson was a powerful captain at the back; Arthur Price, who played more than anyone else for Leeds during the war and was only outscored by Jack Peart, was an experienced and valuable inside-right; Billy McLeod, the talismanic centre-forward, had returned the season before and started scoring straight away. His hat-trick in a win at Wolverhampton Wanderers on 4 October took his goalscoring total for Leeds, including the war, to 184 in 314 games, moving City up to 7th in Division Two.

The problem of Cripps, however, had returned in a new form. Cripps engaged a solicitor, James Bromley, a former Leeds City director, to pursue his claim for wrongful dismissal, now backed up with evidence he said proved Leeds City paid improper expenses to players during the war. The charge was serious, in that it exposed City to accusations of unsporting conduct while being so successful; but also frivolous, as it was an open secret that most clubs had done the same. Cripps was claiming between £300 and £400; in January 1919 he settled for £55, although the terms were later disputed in the press.

Connor said Cripps was persuaded by Bromley to give a written undertaking not to disclose any information about the club, and to hand over all club documents in his possession, including private chequebooks and correspondence, and that these were given to club solicitor Alderman Clarke, in Bromley, Connor and Whiteman's presence. Cripps denied handing anything to Clarke, claiming he had already given the relevant documents to Bromley anyway, and that there were no private chequebooks, only a club chequebook and passbook bearing his name. Bromley said he had done the handing-over, with conditions attached: the documents would be held in trust by Alderman Clarke on behalf of Bromley and Connor, only to be revealed if they both agreed to it; and a £50 donation must be made to the Leeds General Infirmary by August to keep Bromley from reporting the club to the authorities. Connor claimed he never agreed to that condition; and at the start of September he replied to Bromley's request to see a receipt for the £50 by refusing, through Clarke, to discuss any of the club's affairs with Bromley.

By then there was much more at stake than a £50 donation to the local hospital. In the summer, as the club was signing players on for the new season, among them was Charlie Copeland, a full-back Chapman had signed in 1912. He played 44 games in three pre-war seasons, decent enough until replaced by Fred Blackman; he made a further 53 appearances during the war. His pre-war wage was £3 a week, plus £1 for playing in the first team. City now offered him £3 10s a week, with a 'substantial advance' for playing in the first team; if that wasn't acceptable, he would be a granted a free transfer. The Football League was allowing a 50 per cent increase in wages, but Copeland calculated that without summer wages he was now being offered a reduction, and wrote to the club to refuse their offer.

Again, the stories differ about what happened next. Copeland claimed he spoke to Mr Sykes, a City director, who advised him to write agreeing to take £4 10s. Copeland said the club replied, stating they had in fact offered him £6 a week and, as he had refused it, they would do nothing further. Connor claimed Copeland had demanded £6 a week, or he would report the club for making illegal payments, and that the directors chose to ignore such blackmail, giving him a free transfer. Whatever the truth, Copeland engaged James Bromley as his solicitor, and in July 1919 sent his complaint, with documents, to the Football League and Football Association.

What documents Copeland had, or had heard about, was also disputed. Bromley stated that Copeland 'placed in our hands certain information, with instructions to make the necessary report to the Association and the League'; he denied Connor's insinuation that he gave Copeland copies of the documents held by Alderman Clarke. But it was hard to imagine that Bromley didn't use what he knew to bolster his client's case, and his letter about the unpaid donation to the Infirmary removed his obligation to keep silent anyway.

Bromley's motivation is not known. He was president of the Leeds Albion Cycling Club, 'one of the stalwarts of the road' who 'delights in a road race', sponsoring an annual outing to Boston Spa that was particularly popular with the Albion's female members. He was one of the shareholders elected alongside Alf Masser, J.C. Whiteman and Joseph Henry to form, with Norris Hepworth, Leeds City's streamlined board in 1910; he was one of City's official representatives at Hepworth's funeral in February 1914. The next month, with George Cripps, he 'organised one of the best concerts in the history of Leeds City Football Club' as part of benefit fundraising for Fred Croot. It was after this that Connor, Whiteman and their syndicate took control of the club to prevent its move to Headingley; presumably Bromley lost his position on the board, and what was left of the value of his shareholding. We'll probably never know if that lay behind his involvement with taking Cripps and Copeland's complaints to the authorities, but the manner in which all parties dealt with each other – contradicting statements, press allegations, non-disclosure agreements, blackmail attempts – tells of the infighting at Leeds City by the end of the war.

Joseph Connor, for his part, seems guilty of failing to take the situation seriously. He assumed Bromley's silence was secured, and ignored Copeland's threats, thinking that transferring him to Coventry City would end the problem. Even when Leeds City were summoned to Manchester to appear before an investigating commission on 26 September, Connor seems to have underestimated the gravity of what was happening. 'I may say we were very much surprised', he told the *Yorkshire Evening Post*, 'to find present not only the six members of the Commission, but at least a dozen members of the FA and the League, including the members of the selection committee. This did not appear to be exactly a fair proceeding.'

If Connor was surprised by the size of the inquiry, the inquiry was amazed by Leeds City's response. Its members had been informed of the existence of the documents relating to the allegations, and asked for them to be produced. All of Leeds City's directors were present, represented by Alderman Clarke, who told the commission it was not within the club's power to produce the documents. It was widely reported in the press, and obviously known to the commission, that the documents were in Alderman Clarke's strong room; it was also reported, in the *Leeds Mercury*, 'that the package had not to be opened except with the consent of all parties concerned'. But James Bromley had apparently already revealed the contents to the authorities, and it seemed that the Leeds City directors were simply refusing to comply. A deadline was set of 6 October. It came and went.

Perhaps this was another misjudgement of the possible consequences. The game at Wolves on 4 October turned out to have been City's last. They were photographed at the start of the journey, as a railway strike meant they set off from City Square in a charabanc, an open-top motor bus normally used for pleasure trips; an unusual enough sight, made even stranger when it stopped on the way back to give lifts to a number of stranded people, including Charlie Copeland. With no sign of the documents by the 6th, the commission met in Sheffield on the 8th, and declared the club was suspended.

All that prevented the suspension being permanent was the intervention of Joseph Henry, now the Lord Mayor of Leeds, who offered the resignations of the Leeds City directors and asked to be allowed to run the club himself, 'on behalf of its supporters and the public of Leeds,' until a new company could be formed. He had with him W.H. Platts, a chartered accountant, who would pay off the club's obligations and finance its future. A purge of directors, the promise of a clean slate from Alderman Henry, and the importance of league football in West Yorkshire were Leeds' three threads of hope; when the commission agreed to consider the offer and meet again on Monday, that was a fourth.

On Monday, the Football Association's ruling came first: Leeds City were suspended until the requested documents were produced. The four directors – Connor, Whiteman, Glover and Sykes – were all suspended from football indefinitely, 'not allowed to attend any football matches or take any part in football matches', as were George Cripps and Herbert Chapman. Following the

FA decision, the Football League announced Leeds City had been expelled, and Burslem Port Vale were elected to take their place.

The commission were believed to have insisted that the documents be produced as a matter of principle; but Joseph Henry was convinced the punishment would have been merely a fine if not for determined lobbying. 'I am sure that Burslem Port Vale did not act in a sportsmanlike way in pressing their claim before the final decision was arrived at,' Henry told the *Yorkshire Evening Post*. 'I was also very much handicapped by several local people sending letters to members of the League, making suggestions, of which no copy had been sent to me.' Without the documents to prove what happened during the war, Leeds City's silence had been overwhelmed by exaggerated and malicious rumours of what might have happened, and by the eager noise from Burslem Port Vale.

Herbert Chapman, arguing he had been at Barnbow, had his ban overturned within a year. The others appealed, but the ban was reinforced: no documents, no football. Joseph Connor was replaced at the West Riding FA by Fred Waterhouse, and a dinner was held at the Griffin Hotel in honour of his long service to Yorkshire football. Perhaps feeling he would become *persona non grata* in Leeds, Connor accepted a silver cigar case from Waterhouse, and retired to Harrogate to run pubs and race horses. In 1942 he was the last of the syndicate to die, at the Talbot Hotel, a pub he ran in Scarborough.

Around eighteen months before he died, Connor wrote to a friend that once the Second World War was over, he intended to write a series of articles for a Sunday newspaper, giving a full account of the events of Leeds City's suspension that would 'make interesting and sensational reading.' Alderman W.H. Clarke had died, and for all anyone knew, the documents were still locked in his office strong room at 12 South Parade. Connor went on: 'I never saw the contents of the parcel [of documents]; but so far as I knew, it contained mostly letters from players from other clubs, some of whom had assisted us in the war period, and it was to save these players from being involved that we refused to give up the documents.'

For years the documents were thought lost. But in the mid-1980s Tony Arnold, an academic working with the University of Essex, located the papers as part of his research into the growth of soccer in the West Riding. There were indeed letters from players. One, Tom Cawley, who divided his wartime career between Sheffield Wednesday and Leeds, wrote disputing his expenses: 'I don't want more than is due to me and I don't want less,' he said, after a game at Birmingham in September 1918. He added, 'My wife wishes me to ask you if you have any chocolate as she cannot get any for Baby at all.'

But as well as letters, there was more concrete evidence. The documents included a set of expenses for every match City played between 21 October 1916 and 5 May 1917, written on headed notepaper, showing the wages paid to each player. Leeds had paid between £1 7s and £2 2s, around half the pre-war maximum wage, and unlikely to be much different from amounts paid by other clubs. The papers proved Leeds' guilt, though, and bundled with them were statements from the account Leeds used for the payments, in George Cripps' name, at Bradford District Bank.

While the expense and accounts sheets laid out the facts of City's activities, a small blue notebook contained the scandal. Handwritten by George Cripps, this was the trump card in his claim for wrongful dismissal, a diary of events during his time working at Leeds, although it appears to have been written in hindsight after he was dismissed. While it was his name on the bank account and expense sheets, Cripps' notebook records who was involved in the payments and how they were done. Amounts shown in the annual accounts for staff wages and printing costs were falsely inflated so that the difference could be transferred to the expense account, all at the suggestion of the directors, and added to undeclared cash taken from programme sales, as suggested, Cripps wrote, by Herbert Chapman.

How far Cripps' diary can be believed is difficult to determine, as it was intended to support his claim for up to £400 for wrongful dismissal and doesn't do much to disguise his bitterness. The illegal payments are secondary to his record of personal acrimony among the board, much of which appears to have been instigated by Cripps. He repeatedly draws the rest of the board's attention to expenses paid to Joseph Connor, for such items as 'drinks + cigars with which he entertained various people at Newcastle' and 'giving [Fanny] Walden a wedding present and paying for same out of club funds'. As a result of Cripps' information, the account at Bradford and District was replaced by one at the National and Provincial, in the names of directors Sam Glover and George Sykes, with new controls over payments.

On another occasion, when Connor and Chapman were against playing the 1917/18 season due to the financial risk involved, Cripps records that he 'wrote privately to League Sec [Secretary] pointing out how it might be possible to persuade Leeds City to play. Plan successful and City played'. After this overstep of his authority, it seems little wonder that around the same time, Cripps wrote, 'JCo Chairman [Connor] now hostile to GHC [Cripps] for no apparent reason'.

The other theme of the notebook is Cripps' constant disputing of his own pay compared to Herbert Chapman. Although Cripps had been Chapman's personal assistant, and it was Chapman who recommended him to City while he went to Barnbow, Cripps resented that he was 'now doing all [the] work' while Chapman continued to draw a higher wage than him. According to Cripps, the other directors did not know Chapman was still being paid a wage, thinking he was only being repaid for debts – until he made them aware.

It's hard to say whether Cripps was genuine in his attempts to keep Connor and Chapman honest, causing petty conflicts in protest at his own wages, or slanting his account with retrospective bitterness about being under-paid then dismissed, for which he blamed Connor and Chapman. His claims are not helped by their notes of paranoia. After exchanging letters with Robert Hewison about his playing expenses, Cripps writes that he real-ised, 'JC [Connor] friend of Hewison and latter forwards all my letters to JC without letting me know'. In summer 1918, Cripps writes, 'JC and HC [Chapman] had just returned from Bridlington where they had been on holi-day – I think they schemed there to dispense with me'.

Whether or not they schemed, Chapman tried to get rid of Cripps in September, but he refused to hand his keys over, claiming he had a season-long agreement; then again in December, when Chapman, 'not knowing of any further appt [job] and fearing Barnbow would close told me the Directors could not afford wages to us both'. Cripps' implication was that Chapman was guaranteeing his own salary by forcing Cripps out. 'I said I should fight the case,' he writes, and after engaging James Bromley as his solicitor, a letter dated 23 January 1919 'authorising a settlement' is sent, enclosing the notebook and all the other documents, leading to the disputes described earlier.

Without evidence confirming that illegal payments were made, the permanent suspension against Leeds City and its directors was imposed for refusing to hand over these documents when the club was being investigated in October 1919. Chapman, by that time, had found his new appointment away from association football at the Olympia Works, and was able to overturn his ban because he was no longer part of the club and took no part in that decision; his war work at Barnbow also helped place him away from involvement in day-to-day goings on at Elland Road. In 1921 he returned to football with Huddersfield Town, and over the next thirteen years he was responsible for seismic transformations in soccer tactics and the role of managers, winning the FA Cup and two First Division titles with Huddersfield, then again with Arsenal.

But if the documents had been made public in 1919, Chapman would have been in a very different position, faced with evidence claiming he was involved in designing the scheme of illegal payments and signing off accounts, and that he was drawing wages from the club throughout the war. Cripps even claimed that, after September 1918, 'all Leeds City business [was] done by Barnbow clerks'. Hardly proper use of the munitions factory workers with peace not yet declared.

Chapman would, however, have been able to call

Cripps' evidence into doubt. The expense sheets and bank accounts spoke for themselves, but clubs across the country were hiding similar paperwork. But the diary is filled with too much bitterness and contradiction to be accepted without question. While implicating Chapman in the ongoing work of the club, Cripps also complains, '[I was] now doing all work [c.1916, and I] complained of inadequate payment ... I did work of club during summer [1918] and got no pay. Signed on practically all the present team ... had season tickets printed and made all gate arrangements'. Cripps seems adamant that he was the most important figure at City between 1915 and 1918, and it's hard to trust his claims that Connor and Chapman were conspiring against him, while he admits writing to the League to undermine them.

And, ultimately, the price for Cripps' silence was low, just £55, not the £300–400 he first demanded, suggesting the City directors didn't think his testimony would be worth much in public. It was not Cripps but Charlie Copeland, with James Bromley, who went to the authorities and began the chain of events leading to Leeds City's suspension. As Joseph Connor wrote in 1940, City's directors may have calculated then that if they refused to give up the documents and sacrificed their own football careers, then the wartime players, the club and its staff would survive. In Herbert Chapman's case, they were right. But about the future of Leeds City, they miscalculated badly.

1919

UNLESS I HAVE YOU
BEHIND ME, I FINISH

Alf Masser would have been interesting company on
17 October 1919. He would have been interesting
company any day. Born in Leeds, the son of a travelling
cotton salesman, young Masser won a scholarship to the
Yorkshire College – later the University of Leeds – and in
1900, aged 23, began his own long practice as a solicitor,
soon averaging a scarcely believable 2,000 court appearances per year, defending people accused of everything
from traffic offences to murder.

That was not enough to dissipate Masser's reserves
of civic energy. He was elected liberal councillor for
Leeds North-West in 1910, beginning a record-breaking
40 years of continuous membership of the council.

Masser was on the Tramways Committee, judged gymnastics competitions, helped found Headingley (Rugby) Football Club, and was active in Leeds Lifeboat Fund, Yorkshire Flying Club and Yorkshire Automobile Club, at whose speed trials he was often near the front. In 1912 he won the motoring 'musical chairs' at the Automobile Club gymkhana, by successfully transporting Mrs F. Catton around the rugby pitch at Headingley, 'a highly diverting pastime' according to the *Yorkshire Post*.

In October 1919 Masser, now 42, was giving his attention to the 'tragedy', as the newspapers called it, of Leeds City. Joseph Connor may have wanted to protect players at other clubs who had committed no wrong, but that noble stance did nothing to help the equally innocent players of Leeds City. They now belonged to the Football League, who promised to meet their wages and provide assistance, but whose idea of assistance was to auction the players off to the highest bidders. On 17 October a committee, led by the Football League's president John McKenna, came to one of Leeds' grandest hotels, the Metropole, as did representatives from more than 30 league clubs. Such a meeting of sockerists in West Yorkshire would have been highly desirable twenty years earlier, but now they were arriving like vultures, in town to feast on Peacocks. McKenna advised them to come and, 'have a look at the Leeds "stock" and bid for it.'

The players were summoned to the Metropole; the clubs looked, and looked at the league's guide prices, and complained they were too high. Sealed bids were placed in envelopes, and the players' futures were decided. Notts County secured legendary goalscorer Billy McLeod by bidding £250 above his guide price, to £1,250; Harold Millership, John Hampson and Simpson Bainbridge fetched £1,000 each. Aston Villa, Lincoln City, Sheffield Wednesday and South Shields each took three players. Willis Walker, a goalkeeper taken for £800 to South Shields, began a new matchday routine of rising early to catch the 7.25am train via Newcastle, and not getting home until after midnight.

It was a 'melancholy spectacle', wrote the *Yorkshire Post*. Masser must have watched in sorrow, but perhaps vindication. As one of the first shareholders of Leeds City, he had been among the most active trying to reform its management. In 1910, he led efforts to raise money from shareholders to relieve Hepworth of his increasing burden. He appealed again when Connor and his syndicate thwarted the plan to move City to Headingley; if £5,000 could be raised from shareholders, he argued, the club could be run more democratically than if it was sold to a group of businessmen. At the crucial meeting, while A.W. Pullan was remarking that 'to attempt to raise £5,000 for football [in wartime] was wholly impracticable', Masser was busy raising £200 from the people sitting around him, proving it was possible. He was not believed; the vote for the syndicate was unanimous.

The results of the syndicate's ownership could now be seen. They were banned from football for life; the players were being sold off like upmarket cattle; and not only did Leeds not have its First Division football club, it had no football club at all. Masser was even more convinced that 'the cause of the failure has been the autocratic governance of the club. There has been no democratic government from the start, owing to the bulk of the capital having been found by one gentleman.' But now that failure was total, more than vindication, Masser sensed opportunity.

'I have always been of the opinion', he told the *Yorkshire Evening Post*, 'that the Leeds City Association Club, to be really successful, should be not run by a small syndicate but by a Committee of Management representative of the football interests of the city as a whole. It would be infinitely better for 2,000 supporters of the club to put down £5 apiece, and appoint a proper board of directors, than for four or five gentlemen to find the money to run the club.'

The shock of losing its club altogether, in such public and scandalous circumstances, was the impetus Masser needed. There was no time for sorrow at the City players' auction; along with Mark Barker, Charles Snape and former City player Charles Morgan, Masser went to the Metropole to canvass support for a new club, to be named Leeds United. They spoke to the League committee before the auction, then again in the afternoon.

That evening they were joined by Joseph Henry Jr, son of the Lord Mayor, and spoke to the people of Leeds at Salem Hall.

Around a thousand soccer enthusiasts packed the building. The *Leeds Mercury* reported that, judging by their appearance and unwashed hands, 'many of those present had obviously come straight from artisan work.' Masser told the meeting that the League committee said Leeds ought to have an association club, so long as no attempt was made to build up a team out of the ashes of the old one. 'Isn't t'spectators part o' t'ashes?' asked someone amid much laughter, but his joke accorded with Masser's views. Leeds City's players had just been sold off at a fancy hotel in the centre of the city's legal and banking district; now, south of a river hemmed by mills and warehouses, in a church hall between a brewery, a soap works and a leather market, Leeds soccer's only remaining asset – the industry of its supporters – was being put to use making a new club.

They would have to start at the bottom, registering a new club, and hoping the two-year probationary period for applying to join the Football League might be shortened. A ground was needed; W.H. Platts had let Elland Road to Yorkshire Amateurs for the rest of the season, resisting offers to buy it outright to mine its clay for a brickworks. Money was needed too; Masser proposed that '2,000 sportsmen could be found in the city who would put down £5.' They would get a team together, find a place to play and a league to play in, and work towards applying to join the Second Division. 'My view is that Leeds is such an important centre that it deserves full recognition,' said Masser, to loud applause. 'If the "powers that be" refuse to entertain our application, they will be cutting off their noses to spite their faces.'

'I hope the vote will not be taken lightly,' Masser added, as the proposal to form the new club was moved and seconded. 'Unless I have you behind me, I finish.'

The motion was carried unanimously, as was a proposal to form both a limited company and a separate supporters' club, and a fortnight of work commenced. Another well-attended meeting was held at Salem Hall on 29 October, two nights ahead of schedule, and heard that the new club had been registered with the West Riding Association 'under the title of the "Leeds United Club"'; the item in the *Yorkshire Post* was headed: 'The Leeds United A.F.C.'. The Leeds United Supporters' Club was established, and all 'well wishers of the Association code of football in Leeds and district' were invited to send two shillings and sixpence to be enrolled, and notified by post of all meetings 'in support of the movement to reestablish Association football in Leeds'. Yorkshire Amateurs agreed to share Elland Road for the rest of the season. Charles Morgan and another ex-player, Dick Ray, were putting together a new team, and more than a hundred applications had been received; a trial was being held the following Monday, and a game was scheduled against Sheffield United Reserves at Elland Road for Saturday. The new club had been invited to take the place of Leeds City Reserves in the Midland League, and 'seized that opportunity', said Joseph Henry Jr, joining 'in the name of the Leeds United Association Club'.

Joseph Henry Sr made a popular speech, condemning the Football League for expelling Leeds City, declaring: 'It was nothing less than a scandal that the feelings of a city should have been so entirely ignored by a body of men who acted as autocrats, scarcely hearkening to reason, and swayed by passion, as some of them were, because they were probably interested in some other club which aspired to get into Leeds City's place.' He had been ready to have no more to do with soccer; but the resentment vanished beneath his desire to see association football prosper in Leeds. In his words: 'What has already been done to resurrect the game since Leeds City was executed as a club will show the football authorities in London and Sheffield that there is no lack of Association vitality left in Leeds.'

Leeds would show 'em. All that was needed now was the money. A company with nominal capital of £25,000 would be floated, of which £10,000 should be paid up. 'What is needed,' said Masser, 'is that all supporters should subscribe in order to establish the club on a thoroughly democratic basis.' One gentleman offered to put in £1,000, and others £100 or £200, but they would rather have sums as small as a pound from a much wider circle of subscribers. Promises amounting to £400 came from the hall that night, and subscription forms were distributed to raise the rest.

After such slow beginnings to the local game, the city was to have a new professional club in place of the old within a month, brought about through energetic leadership, civic pride and fervent local support. Crowds of 1,000 had gone straight from work to attend packed meetings to get the thing done, while down the road in Huddersfield, barely 2,500 went to see Huddersfield Town, a team yet to lose a home game that season, beat Fulham 3-0. The gate receipts that day were just £90, less than a quarter of what the Leeds public had drummed up in a church hall the night before.

J. Hilton Crowther, one of four brothers whose family owned a successful local mill, had been underwriting Huddersfield Town's attempts to establish association football in the area, building a stadium that could hold 50,000; he gave the club credit worth £27,000, while he and his brother D. Stoner held a further £18,000 of debentures. Jack Cock, a forward with six goals in nine games, was sold to Chelsea for £2,500, but that didn't make up for the lack of support coming from the town.

The problem was rugby. While Town took £90 on the gate, Huddersfield's rugby club took in £1,600. Arrangements for the two clubs to alternate home matches failed: if the rugby team was not at home, its supporters stayed in theirs.

The solution was Leeds. Without consulting his fellow directors, Hilton Crowther met the committee in charge of Leeds United. They were expecting a quiet day looking at new players, but instead received a shocking proposal. Soccer in Huddersfield was, Crowther said, finished. So the Town club would merge with the new Leeds club and move to Elland Road, bringing its players and staff – including respected manager Arthur Fairclough, and former Leeds City trainer Dick Murrell – and carrying on its Second Division season under the name Leeds United.

A meeting of the Leeds United Supporters' Club was called for the YMCA Hall in Albion Place that Friday night. It was only a week since the last, but Crowther's idea meant there was much to discuss. He had quickly won the support of the committee, of some of Huddersfield's players, and of Platts, who remained in control of Elland Road; he said Crowther's scheme was so impressive that, whether or not Leeds United were involved, Huddersfield Town's directors could have Elland Road if they wanted it.

Crowther, knowing he needed public goodwill, was intent on an amicable merger; there was talk of calling the club Leeds Trinity to reflect the three clubs combined: Huddersfield Town, Leeds City and Leeds United. The new board of directors would consist of an independent chair, along with Crowther plus three from Huddersfield, and Platts plus three from Leeds. The Football League's approval would be required, but few problems were anticipated there; as away clubs took 20 per cent of gate receipts, the rest of the Second Division regarded playing against Huddersfield Town as a form of tax.

Among the speakers in favour was Joseph Henry Sr, acknowledging that it might be preferable for a Leeds club to be built by Leeds people, but that he would 'sacrifice my "patriotic" feelings to bring about League football in the city'. One path offered expense and time wasted; the other would have Leeds United playing Coventry City at Elland Road in Division Two a week tomorrow. There were few, if any, arguments against the scheme that night; the merger was enthusiastically approved by the supporters.

Crowther was cheered when called upon to make a speech; a chorus of 'For He's A Jolly Good Fellow' rang around the room. 'I have never spoken in public before,' he told the crowd. 'I want to come amongst you. I want to help you, and I want you to help me. I want to do everything fair and square.' A vote of thanks followed, 'to Crowther and his Huddersfield friends.'

Alf Masser's feelings about putting aside his demo-cratic scheme in favour of the merger are not known. The committee was not unanimous before putting Crowther's proposal to the supporters; Masser may have needed persuading to place the city's soccer fortunes once more into the hands of one rich man. In any case, he was reconciled, speaking of Crowther's 'magnificent offer', adding that his willingness to write off a large portion of the money owed him by Huddersfield Town 'showed his sportsmanship'. Although the merger involved no funds being raised by Leeds fans at the present time, there was provision to pay off the £25,000 debt to Crowther that the new club would carry with it from Huddersfield – written down from £40,000 – if ever the supporters wanted the board to be elected freely with no need for Huddersfield representation. Crowther was, said Masser, 'a real sport, prepared to give to Leeds something which Huddersfield had never appreciated'.

In Huddersfield, the few who did appreciate soccer were not willing to let their club leave quietly. When the news broke, a campaign started that was very much in keeping with Masser's democratic ideas, threatening Crowther's plans. 3,000 people – more than often came to watch the football – gathered for a meeting at Leeds Road stadium, demanding a chance to prove soccer was wanted in the town. It was proposed that the club converted to public ownership with 20,000 £1 shares, so ordinary supporters could invest; already 1,150 workmen, none pledging more than £5 each, had promised between £3,000 and £4,000; another £2,000 had been pledged by loyal supporters. They would find a way to pay off the Crowthers and make the club pay its way in its own town. The club chairman, William Hardcastle, was compelled to take a deputation – with Amos Hirst, one of the club's founders, and Captain Moore, a former player – to the Football League to persuade them to refuse the transfer to Leeds.

Interviewed by the *Yorkshire Evening Post* the night before the meeting, League chair John McKenna sounded doubtful about the merger, his main concern being Joseph Henry Sr's involvement; Henry had 'made charges and statements which the Management Committee could not be expected to forget.' Henry replied that he would have nothing to do with the management of the new club. McKenna's second concern was for the good of soccer in Huddersfield. 'We have heard a lot about the Leeds public wanting football,' he said. 'But what about the Huddersfield public whom it is proposed to deprive of it? Their interests cannot be ignored.' That could have drawn another pointed statement, about how the Leeds public were ignored when McKenna executed Leeds City, but Henry kept quiet.

McKenna agreed that Town's finances were a problem, but listened readily to the deputation's speeches about the growth of football in the town, and the speed with which funds were forthcoming to keep the club in Huddersfield. The League decided to give Huddersfield one month to raise the money owed to Crowther. If they could not find a way to pay him, the club would move to Leeds.

Leeds were forced into stasis; Huddersfield into action. Fairclough and his players beat Coventry right enough, 5-0, but they did it at Leeds Road in the name of Huddersfield, rather than Elland Road in the name of Leeds. Leeds United hastily arranged a friendly with Elland Road's outgoing tenants, Yorkshire Amateurs; they won their debut 5-2, but with only five players signed on it was neither the performance, the standard or the occasion Leeds had wanted. A week later, while Huddersfield were beating Bristol City at home in the Second Division in front of almost 8,000, Leeds United were submitting themselves to the Midland League, drawing their first match 0-0 at Elland Road against Barnsley Reserves.

Leeds had its professional soccer team again, but enthusiasm was now all to be found in the town Crowther wanted to leave behind. The fundraising challenge was steep but the Huddersfield people relished the fight; enthusiasm didn't equal money, however, and only around £8,000 was raised. In preparation for the deadline, Leeds United put their Midland League season on hold, again expecting confirmation that Huddersfield's players could come and play Division Two football in Leeds.

Again, Leeds were disappointed. The Football League, impressed by Huddersfield's efforts, extended their deadline to the end of the year. That was only three weeks to raise another £17,000, but now they introduced a legal angle, pointing out that Hilton Crowther was no longer a director of Huddersfield Town, and the actual directors had not applied to transfer it. Indeed,

they were all against it, and the question was what right
Crowther had, as merely a debenture holder, to move
their club to Leeds. The Crowthers tried forcing the
issue, using £10,000 owed to Stoner Crowther as leverage to put the club into receivership, but Town's answer
to the writ delayed the case into January, and at the
start of 1920 the Football League removed themselves
from the affair until the legal situation was resolved.
Permission to transfer the club was effectively revoked.

Amid the delays Leeds United's directors were stuck,
unsure whether to start building a new club when a
functioning Second Division outfit might be imported
any day. Eventually Hilton Crowther advised them to
make peace with the Midland League and build a team
for the rest of the season. He joined United's finance
committee, and signs of growth became visible all that
spring: trials were held, players signed on, a reserve team
started, friendly matches arranged.

Huddersfield Town, meanwhile, were settling matters on the pitch. Ambrose Langley replaced Fairclough
as manager in December, and the team was performing
miracles. From 13 December Huddersfield only lost one
of 25 League matches, winning promotion; they reached
the FA Cup final against Aston Villa, only losing 1-0
after extra time. Success filled their bank account, so
the Crowthers could be paid off; Huddersfield Town
were staying in Huddersfield. They appointed Herbert
Chapman as their new secretary-manager.

Leeds United were playing catch-up. Crowther now devoted himself to the club, bringing Arthur Fairclough with him as manager, but while Leeds had been waiting for Crowther, Cardiff City had been gathering support for election to the Second Division. The vote would take place on 31 May, but Leeds United's efforts did not begin until late April. Crowther was personally canvassing every club in the League, and it was suggested he was mentioning to some that they owed the city something, given City's sacrifice over certain documents. Everything else was in place; Dick Ray had a respectable side in the Midland League, Fairclough was finding players for the following season, and the club was £200 in profit; steps were being taken to purchase Elland Road, but two gentlemen offered another ground if that fell through, 'which would be second to none in this part of the country'. Alf Masser was to present the club's case to the League, and first there was a meeting of supporters at Salem Hall, at which he emphasised the need for the public's backing. The Supporters' Club were engaged to solicit subscriptions district by district; Crowther said every club he spoke to asked the same thing: 'Are the public behind you? We want no more one-man clubs.'

This time the public showed their support. At the League meeting Masser reported that more than £12,000 had been raised from 1,500 supporters, earning a round of applause. £520 had come from Beeston, £300 from Armley, £500 from 'Jewish subscriptions'. It was said that no other club applying to join the Football League had been so well supported; Leeds won the election with 31 votes, securing one of two places with Cardiff City, who had 23.

Crowther was elected president, Joseph Henry Jr chairman, H. Meek secretary, and Mark Barker as treasurer; the board would be Crowther, Masser, Barker, W.H. Platts and Kaye Aspinall. Crowther and Platts negotiated the purchase not just of Elland Road but of an adjoining strip of land, allowing the terraced embankment to the north to be enlarged to hold 20,000; the Main Stand would have a new roof, while the stand on Elland Road had fallen into disrepair, and would be replaced by a new covered stand for 6,000 spectators. Overall capacity would be around 40,000, with 60,000 the ultimate aim, and there were plans for a road through the low fields to the east to connect Elland Road to Gelderd Road, and a station on the Great Northern Railway passing next to the ground. The Football League formally discharged what remained of Leeds City, granting Platts £1,500 from the players' auction to cover his losses while he'd been responsible for Elland Road, clearing the way for the ground to belong to Leeds United.

The next Saturday night Salem Hall was filled again, 'a fraternal gathering of kindred spirits', to cheer the return of league football to Leeds. Masser told the crowd it was a proud moment, 'a striking testimony to the zeal and enthusiasm of the sportsmen of Leeds that they were never downhearted, that they stuck to the old ship, flew a tattered flag in October last, and decided to sail the ship into fair weather'. He wouldn't rest, he told them, until supporter subscriptions totalled £15,000. Hilton Crowther, still unused to public speaking, said: 'The whole thing to me is very wonderful indeed.' He added that he was not a native of Leeds, and an audience voice replied: 'But we like you!' Amid laughter and applause, Crowther concluded: 'I am just trembling all over, and I just thank you.'

1920–27

NO SET OF PLAYERS CAN HAVE TRIED HARDER

Leeds United's first Football League season began on 28 August 1920. Huddersfield may have left them behind, but the association still lingered; United wore identical colours to Town, blue and white striped shirts with white shorts. Fate immediately involved itself in the club's affairs, sending them for their first match to Burslem Port Vale, the team that seized Leeds City's place in the Second Division. Fortune did not help Leeds; they lost 2-0.

City's manager Arthur Fairclough – strong, tall and genial, a Barnsley man never seen without a bowler hat, winner of the FA Cup as Barnsley's manager in 1912 – preached patience to supporters. 'They must remember that though individually men might be good players, they do not always blend in the first year.' It would take three years or so to be challenging the Second Division's leaders, he said, four years to be at the very top. For now, they had inexperience to contend with: the team at Port Vale included four teenagers and a twenty year old, goalkeeper Billy Down; the youngest was left-half Jimmy Walton, aged just sixteen.

The first home match, against South Shields on 1 September, was also lost, 2-1. Len Armitage had the honour of scoring Leeds United's first league goal, an equalising drive from outside the penalty area, across the goalkeeper and into the far corner; the 18,000 crowd were inspired to 'shouting themselves hoarse' by United's second-half fightback. The team was not out of its depth, and proved it in the next game, again at home; dominant 3-1 revenge over Port Vale, watched by 15,000. Down was ever present and Walton missed only one game; nineteen-year-old George Mason played 35 times; and with such young players, experience alongside them proved vital. Fairclough brought 28-year-old centre-half Jim Baker from Huddersfield and made him captain; a strong, hard tackler, he was the heart of the team in every game. With Bert Duffield and Jimmy Frew constants behind Baker as full-backs, Leeds conceded just 45 goals, and only fourteen at home. At the other end centre-forward Ernie Goldthorpe, a promising goal-scorer signed from Bradford City, was injured after six games and two goals, and Leeds struggled until £1,750 was spent on Bristol City's centre-forward Tommy Haworth, who scored six of United's last seven goals of the campaign, spread across eleven matches. Despite humdrum results, crowds were respectable, 20,000 coming to United's last home game of their first season, on their way to finishing 14th.

As Fairclough warned, it was not a fast start, but it gave United a sound basis for improvement. A new goalkeeper, Fred Whalley, and the emergence of young centre-half Ernie Hart meant an even firmer defence in 1921/22, but scoring remained a problem. The second half of the season was enlivened by Bill Poyntz's inclusion on the wing; he scored his first goal in a 2-0 win over Bury at Elland Road, but when Leeds lost the return match 2-1 a week later, Poyntz became the first Leeds United player to be sent off, accused of trying to kick Jimmy McCrae in the last minute. United's next fixture was a postponed match against Leicester City at Elland Road; the rearrangement clashed with Poyntz's wedding, which he dutifully attended in the morning, before scoring a hat-trick in United's 3-0 win in the afternoon. More Poyntz goals in home wins over Barnsley and Fulham raised hopes of a late attempt at promotion, but Leeds could only manage one goal and one win in their last five games, finishing 8th.

Fairclough kept the defenders together and kept them fit and playing: goalkeeper Whalley, full-backs Duffield and Frew, and half-backs Baker, Hart and Harry Sherwin just got stronger: they set another record for meanness in 1922/23, conceding 36. Top scorer Percy Whipp, a new signing at inside-forward, inspired seven wins and three draws after a debut hat-trick, but only managed fifteen goals for the season. Leeds improved to 7th, four points from promotion.

It was frustrating, but Fairclough was not flustered, even after assistant manager Dick Ray resigned; his replacement, Will Norman, had worked with Fairclough at Barnsley and was said to 'appreciate the value of good team spirit' and physical fitness. With trainer Dick Murrell they set about tweaking a team that was stubbornly refusing success. Billy Down had matured and took over in goal; Frew was replaced by Scottish youngster Bill Menzies. The defence set another new record of 35 conceded, but the real improvement was, at last, in attack. Jack Swan was leading scorer with eighteen, Whipp did well again with eleven, while three more of the previous season's signings clicked: wingers Alan Noble and Joe Harris provided; centre-forward Joe Richmond scored fifteen.

Leeds went top, but struggled to seal promotion, buckling under the pressure in April. Bury were just a point behind Leeds, Blackpool three points and Derby five, with a game in hand. After four consecutive draws and now a defeat, with three games left, if Leeds didn't start winning they would throw promotion away.

Instead they threw all they had at Stockport County at Elland Road. Leeds won 4-0 in front of 22,145 people, while Bury and Blackpool both lost; promotion was won in emphatic style. The crowd was 'more demonstrative than perhaps any that has assembled on the ground since the war', said the *Yorkshire Post & Intelligencer*, who credited United's confidence, tenacity and effective tackling for the win. The next game was harder going, against relegation-threatened Nelson at Elland Road, in front of an expectant crowd that put the Leeds players' nerves on edge; but a goal in the last few minutes by Walter Coates secured the league title, before an hour of celebrations and speeches on the pitch. There were more celebrations a week later, when a 3-1 defeat away to Nelson was ignored by the crowd of 20,000 people waving blue and white umbrellas to greet Leeds United on their return to the city that Saturday night. The players were put in a charabanc and paraded with a brass band along Boar Lane, Duncan Street, Vicar Lane and Lower Headrow, ending with an enthusiastic reception at the Empire Theatre.

Arthur Fairclough had made good on his prediction that Leeds United would top the table in four seasons, and credit was given to the work Fairclough had done, with assistants Dick Ray and Will Norman and trainer Dick Murrell. Four of the side that won promotion were with United from the very first season – Down, Duffield, Hart and Baker – and Leeds had spent less than £6,000 in transfer fees since 1919, a sum the *Yorkshire Evening Post* contrasted with £25,000 spent by Middlesbrough in one season while being relegated from Division One. 'Though cleverer teams may have won promotion', added the *Yorkshire Post*, 'no set of players can have tried harder or trained more conscientiously.'

'We may not have had what you would call a "star" in our side', said Hilton Crowther, 'but we have had a fine spirit and a dogged determination to win through. We have a team of triers.' He said that he 'found satisfaction and pride in the fact that I have redeemed the promise I made to Joe Henry when I came from Huddersfield to Leeds'; Joseph Henry Sr., regrettably, had died in December, when the club he helped found were top of the table, but not yet champions.

Not all of Hilton Crowther's time at Leeds had been so satisfying. The team was timid in the title decider because they rarely played in front of big crowds at Elland Road. Despite publicity about the new Lowfields Road making travel to the ground much easier, and the excitement of charging to the title, the championship was won against a strange and listless backdrop; there was only one crowd over 20,000 until the very end of the season. If it wasn't a big game, the public didn't seem interested. The Supporters' Club only had around 700 members.

Shareholders were another problem. Only around £9,000 of the club's share capital was taken up, leaving

Hilton Crowther to pay the rest, which soon became an issue between him and his adopted city. At the club's first Annual General Meeting in October 1921, it was announced that W.H. Platts had resigned and wouldn't be replaced 'until we find some local gentleman who is prepared to come to Mr Hilton Crowther's financial assistance'. Alf Masser, chairing the meeting, set out what would become a constant theme over the next three seasons: 'It is hardly fair that, in a city like Leeds, with half a million population, and with many men with money in their pockets, so few should come forward and show sufficient local interest in the football club to relieve the burden on Mr Hilton Crowther's pockets.' By the time Leeds were promoted, Crowther had put £54,000 into Leeds United, including £20,000 on ground improvements, and £10,000 to buy the freehold of Elland Road; he did not charge United any rent for using it, nor any interest on his loans.

Although the shareholders were small in number and light in financial assistance, they were noisy, agitating for greater influence, at one point campaigning for Masser's resignation after he refused to post copies of the club's balance sheet to all shareholders. Masser was sanguine: 'I remember being carried onto the platform as the heaven-sent deliverer of association football in Leeds,' he said, 'and I told them that within three years they would be demanding my resignation. And so it came to pass.' They argued more people would attend matches if tickets were cheaper; Masser replied that, as only £9,000 had been put into the club by the Leeds public, low attendances were more likely due to apathy. Even Crowther's investment drew criticism: so much money for football seemed 'very dear'; the money spent on the ground was 'squandered'. In 1923 the shareholders formed a new association and started fundraising, but not to invest alongside Crowther; they reckoned they could do better, and wanted to buy him out.

That was, in fact, just what Hilton Crowther wanted. With promotion to the First Division Crowther had, he said, 'completed my mission.' It had cost him £54,000, and perhaps some regrets. The sporting public of Leeds had proved much less enthusiastic for football than he had thought, while in Huddersfield – where Crowther still lived and owned mills – soccer enjoyed a boom after Crowther tried to move Town to Leeds; Huddersfield won the FA Cup in 1922 and the league title in 1923/24. Now Leeds were at least in the First Division, it was the right time to part. Crowther resigned as chairman in June, declaring it was time for the Leeds public to own their own club, and asked for his money to be paid back at the earliest opportunity. His sporting nature prevailed; he would take £35,000, writing off £19,000, and although he asked for most of it to be paid by August, his generosity suggested he would not be pressing for the money.

His successor was Major Albert Braithwaite, a popular young man who was sent to South Carolina

as an army instructor during the First World War, so
charming his hosts that he married Anne Anderson, the
youngest of four daughters of an Augusta family, who
soon acclimatised to Leeds weather and Leeds United
football. Braithwaite used First Division football as an
occasion for raising Crowther's money, suggesting as
slogans 'Support Your Sport!' and 'Lend Us A Fiver!'
for a scheme offering 7,000 £5 bonds, paying interest
at 7.5 per cent. The opening match of the new season,
at home to Sunderland, was a big event, with a new
uniform in club colours for the Elland Road band,
performing a new 'war song' specially written by a well-
known London composer; every member of the crowd
was given a souvenir programme containing an application form for the bonds. In the evening a mass meeting
took place at the Town Hall, where Crowther presented
medals to the players who won promotion, and the
Supporters' Club gave them gold watches. The aim was
to generate publicity and enthusiasm, and bring home
to the public that the club was their responsibility from
now on. 'Until it is properly stirred up,' said Braithwaite,
'Leeds is the most lackadaisical place in the world, and
will let anybody else do its job. But with sound backing and enthusiastic workers I have no doubt about the
success of our effort.'

He had the first part right. 50,000 were expected for
Leeds United's First Division debut; the attendance for
the 1-1 draw with formidable Sunderland was a record,

but only 33,722. 41,800 filled the ground for a 1-1 draw with league champions Huddersfield, but the sterner test of the First Division was not gripping the fans: from November to the end of the year only a 6-0 hammering of Aston Villa at Elland Road on Christmas Day relieved four draws and six defeats.

The poor form came at the worst possible time. In mid-November 1924, Hilton Crowther revealed an urgent need for his need for his money. He had been divorced in February, offering no defence to Maud Evelyn Crowther's allegations that her husband had been seen at London hotels with other women. Mr and Mrs Crowther had lived apart for some time; Maud became suspicious of her husband in 1917, after two years of marriage, and moved out to a house he owned in London in 1920. Whether the divorce caused his financial difficulties is not clear, but at some point Crowther used the debt Leeds United owed him to raise a mortgage. Repayment was due by 31 December, and Crowther had to have his £35,000 before then, otherwise the lenders would seize the club. It was a serious situation; £35,000 would be equivalent to around £2 million in 2019.

'I know,' said Crowther, 'that the people who will take over the club have been in communication with two or three London clubs to ascertain what the players are worth. They have discovered that they can realise £25,000 in transfer fees. It is as certain as night follows day that if they do not get their money they will do this. In that case the club could have no hope of remaining in the First Division, and you can take it from me that English League football would know it no more. I should be very sorry indeed if things were to come to that pass, but I am quite powerless to save the club.'

The Football League, dismayed by more financial trouble in Leeds, pressed for answers; and several clubs tried to take advantage of the crisis, at least three managers travelling to Leeds to make immediate offers for players, recalling bitter memories of Leeds City's final auction. One local businessman, confessing he was not much interested in football but sensing a profit, offered to buy the club outright. Braithwaite refused them all, convinced that the definite deadline for catastrophe would focus minds in the city and make the 'Lend Us A Fiver' campaign a success. Within a week he reported that half the money had been found, and more was coming in regularly to the campaign office in the Corn Exchange, where the public could sign up to buy bonds in instalments if they could not find a whole fiver at once. One woman paid in £10, much of it in gold she had been saving; a miner came from Normanton and 'thumped 100 £1 treasury notes on the counter', according to the *Yorkshire Evening Post*, saying: 'I doan't get ter t'game ivery time they're at heam, but I dew want 'em to keep going.' One man from Roundhay, who had 'long ceased to be interested in football', added £100 to £10 from his gardener, who was an ardent fan. On one Saturday more than £7,000 was taken at the Corn Exchange.

Finding money from local businesspeople was more difficult. Braithwaite got together a 'flying squad' to make personal visits to the city's wealthiest inhabitants, sent prospectuses to every shop and business, and had some success touring breweries; but only two shopkeepers and two restaurateurs offered any support, despite lengthy lectures on the economic benefits of First Division football. 'To the shop-keepers, theatres, music-halls, cinemas and business folk generally,' Braithwaite wrote to the *Yorkshire Evening Post*, 'it must be an asset to have large crowds of people coming from the outlying districts to spend the afternoon in Leeds, and I contend that the Leeds United Football Club is fulfilling a function quite as important as the municipal parks of the city, inasmuch as it is getting our workers out into the fresh air to watch clean, healthy, vigorous sport.'

£20,000 was raised by the start of December, but there the campaign stuck while time was running out. 9,000 prospectuses had been sent out, but only 632 had responded, and Braithwaite promised a 'Roll of Honour' on the Main Stand at Elland Road listing all who contributed; 'A permanent memorial to those who practically saved the club.' If they saved the club. Braithwaite was asked what would happen if the campaign failed; he said the money would be returned, he would resign, and matters would have to take their course.

The campaign office began opening at night and Braithwaite announced a new tactic: a sale of 10,000 ordinary shares at £1 each. A three-month-old baby from Horsforth took out a bond, causing an appeal in the press when the club realised they did not know whether to address correspondence 'to Dear Sir or Dear Madam'; it was then claimed that a three-day-old baby boy from Harehills had taken out a bond at the start of December. On 29 December, Braithwaite told the press he had refused a £30,000 offer to buy the club outright, and was going to London with Crowther to beg a week's extension from the lenders. 'Only 500 Leeds people have done anything at all for [the fund],' said Braithwaite. 'I cannot say what will happen at the meeting, but there is a distinct possibility that the club may be lost to the city.'

Braithwaite and Crowther returned with four extra days, and met with their fellow directors at the Queens Hotel next to the railway station, discussing the situation until late into the night. If £35,000 was not ready to hand over at 3.30pm on Monday 5 January 1925, the club and all it owned would belong to the lenders. On New Year's Day, £2,803 was still required. On Sunday night Braithwaite prepared to make a speech at the Leeds Sportsmen's Concert at the Majestic Theatre, expected to be one final appeal for support.

Instead, he declared Leeds United was saved. More than £1,500 in small sums had come into the campaign office on Saturday, and with more cash expected on

Monday morning, the directors had secured promises that any shortfall would be made good by wealthy subscribers when the 3.30pm deadline came. 'There is no danger of the city losing a First Division football team,' Braithwaite told the theatre, paying tribute to the working people of Leeds who paid what little they could to save the club from ruin. 'Whether those present are enthusiastic or not with regard to this particular game, you can not but realise that it forms a very great asset to the city, and to thousands of the city's workers it represents a very great pleasure to which they look forward week by week. It would be disastrous if it came to an end, and, on the other hand, I hope we will live to see in Leeds one of the greatest football teams in the country.'

With that, an exhausted Braithwaite finally followed his doctor's advice and left for a month's rest in Switzerland, leaving his fellow directors to deal with Crowther's creditors. Braithwaite's unexpected declaration that United were saved might have been a calculated display of confidence to buy more time; there was not quite the full £35,000 to hand, but enough to keep the lenders at bay, and with the deadline lifted the directors found another few thousand pounds over the following weeks, returning to wealthy bondholders and asking for more.

Paying the debt became a celebration. Crowther was retaining a small shareholding and his place on the board, and in the team selection committee with

Fairclough and Norman; at a meeting at Salem Hall, he was presented with an album containing photographs and signatures of Leeds United's players and officials, inscribed to 'J.H. Crowther Esq., on the occasion of his handing over to the Leeds public a First Division football club'. The club was taking what positives it could from its flirtation with extinction, praising the civic spirit of the few who had contributed rather than dwelling on the vast majority in the city who ignored the club's plight. But the optimism of another new start still had to deal with the situation of the team: 19th in the First Division.

Leeds won their first game after financial safety was announced, 4-1 away to Preston North End, but the Second Division champions were finding the top level difficult. The famous backs, Duffield, Hart and Baker, were letting in almost twice as many goals; the attack was blunt against First Division defences. The new board had to act, and in a few days in March, they plunged into the club's overdraft to bring in three new players: Willis Edwards, a 21-year-old wing-half who cost £1,500 from Chesterfield; Russell Wainscoat, £2,000 from Middlesbrough, an inside-left; and 23-year-old Tom Jennings, a prodigious goalscorer in the Scottish leagues, bought from Raith Rovers. The fee was 'not disclosed, but it is understood to be substantial'.

After a troubling start – Edwards, Jennings and Wainscoat's first game together was a 4-1 defeat at Newcastle United – Leeds found safety. Form was still erratic, but Wainscoat scored four and Jennings three, including one each in a 2-1 home win over Bolton Wanderers that kept Leeds in the First Division.

A First Division future was assured, and with it came a touch of glamour; United director Mark Barker, an actor whose frame resembled Oliver Hardy's, appeared as a 'noble-hearted football director' with screen stars Mabel Poulton and Dorothy Boyd, and Manchester City's Billy Meredith playing himself, in football mystery film *The Ball of Fortune*. Several scenes were filmed at Elland Road, continuing a relationship with the world of showbiz stretching back to J.C. Whiteman, the Leeds City director and famous theatrical agent.

The club was now financially stable, although it would soon have to face the problem of paying annual interest on £35,000 to the new bondholders. For now, after promising that no more would be spent improving the stadium until the team was top quality, the board gave their backing to Arthur Fairclough for the new season: fourteen players departed and five were brought in, joined at Christmas by centre-half Tom Townsley, bought for £5,000 from Falkirk.

The new football season brought a major change to the offside law, intended to rival cinemas and music halls for entertainment. Full-back pairings were so expert at stifling attackers that a change was needed. Now only two players including the goalkeeper, rather than three, must be between the forward and the goal, and Tom Jennings proved the ideal player to take advantage of the new space and uncertainty in opposition defences. In one spell he scored in five consecutive matches, including twice against West Ham United and a hat-trick against Arsenal, and with 26 goals he was United's top scorer.

Despite Jennings' goals, however, Leeds couldn't win. Their defence was struggling with the new rule as much as anybody's, and Leeds were regularly outscored during three months when they only won twice. Willis Edwards was playing well enough at the back to win his first England caps, and things improved when Townsley replaced Hart and new goalkeeper Jimmy Potts replaced Bill Johnson, but there was no consistency around them.

Four defeats and a 0-0 draw in April left Leeds with a simple task for the final match: beat Tottenham at Elland Road, or be relegated. The club's plight finally caught the attention of the city, where the prospect of relegation was much discussed among non-soccer fans, but only 16,158 came to see the team's fate decided. Bobby Turnbull gave Leeds the lead, but a Spurs equaliser and a difficult, muddy pitch sapped United's hopes in the second half until, with fifteen minutes left, Turnbull lobbed the ball into the middle where, despite colliding with the keeper, Jennings put the ball in the net. Within five minutes Percy Whipp and Jennings again made it 4-1, and the *Leeds Mercury* praised the team's pluck and perseverance; 'The last memory of the season, indeed, is of a gallant set of fellows pulling out the last ounce for the honour of the club.'

Leeds hoped to capitalise on that gallantry the following season. Despite the almost disastrous end to the previous season, the directors felt £19,000 in transfer fees had been well spent, and the departure of Jim Baker, the club's first captain, was the only significant change.

Tom Jennings was superb again, missing only one game, scoring 35 in the league, and two more in the FA Cup. He was unstoppable in the autumn: he got nineteen goals in nine matches, scoring in seven consecutive games, including a three-game sequence when he got three against Arsenal, four against Liverpool and four again against Blackburn Rovers. But unless Jennings scored at least twice, Leeds still could not win. Tom Townsley and Willis Edwards were able replacements for Baker's experience, and Jimmy Potts was strong in goal, but all around them continued to be chaos in the wake of the new offside law. Friction was developing; in September Russell Wainscoat was dropped and placed on the transfer list – 'some difference has arisen between the United club management and the player' – but he returned after three games out.

Fairclough entered the transfer market in February and spent a big fee, £5,600, on John White from Hearts of Midlothian. White was an excellent player, skilful and quick, but he was an inside forward, not a defender.

A 3-1 home win over struggling West Bromwich Albion raised hopes of another late season revival, and the players were allowed to follow their custom for big cup games by training at the seaside ahead of a vital match away to Bury, another team fighting relegation.

Leeds lost 3-1, and although relegation was not yet certain, Arthur Fairclough sent in his resignation. Rumours of disagreements between Fairclough and the directors had circulated for some time; Fairclough said he did not want 'to refer to things which have been unpleasant'. After a week, and a three-hour board meeting at the Griffin Hotel, Leeds announced that while Fairclough's resignation was accepted, he would carry on until a successor was named. Two days later a 4-1 defeat at Spurs finally sent United down.

Fairclough, who came with Hilton Crowther from Huddersfield and made good on his promise of delivering First Division football, was finally released from his duties with Leeds back in the Second Division again. Their old club, in the meantime, won the First Division three times in a row, and finished 2nd in Leeds' relegation season; Herbert Chapman moved on to Arsenal after the first two titles, but Huddersfield were staying strong. After a change to Leeds United's articles of association removed his and Crowther's life directorships, Alf Masser quietly retired from the board in October 1926; an angry letter to the *Leeds Mercury* complained that, apart from 'a touching and welcome reference' at the annual meeting, no tribute was paid to Masser for his work in founding Leeds United.

Hilton Crowther, meanwhile, was anything but quiet. In May 1927 he caused a sensation by suddenly marrying revue and pantomime star Miss Mona Vivian at the Strand registry office in London, 'an alluring coquette' according to publicity, and one of the biggest theatrical stars of the day. The gossip papers made much of the fact that Hilton was 47 and Mona 29. The happy couple had arrived with only the bride's mother for company, meaning an urgent search in nearby offices for a second witness. 'Really and truly,' Vivian told the press, 'we wanted no one to know about it until later. I have not even let Mr Cowan, in whose show I am now appearing, into our secret.' She wore a hat and dress of lavender blue beneath a pale grey squirrel coat, and gave her address as the Waldorf Hotel; Crowther gave his as the Eccentric Club, St James's, London, a celebrated gentleman's club with a night-owl for its emblem. Vivian said she met Crowther 'some years ago' when she was appearing in Huddersfield; she had been billed twice nightly at the Huddersfield Palace Theatre in May 1917. 'I cannot tell you about our romance,' she said, with an enigmatic air. 'It would take a whole week to do so.'

A condition of their marriage was said to be that Miss Vivian would retire from the stage, and in Leeds she found new distractions, racing her champion greyhound Champagne Jim at the new Greyhound Stadium on Elland Road, and flying aeroplanes from Sherburn Aerodrome. But even on her wedding day there was only time for lunch before that evening's performance in Mr Cowan's revue, 'Hello Charleston', and there was no time for a honeymoon before the show moved from Camden to Leeds Hippodrome. Mona, performing constantly since she was four years old, when she was known as 'Wee Mona', was as busy and enthusiastic for bookings and tours as ever in the years that followed, not content to stay at home with her mill-owning husband. In the 1930s the marriage faltered, ending in another expensive divorce. This time, at least, Leeds United was not affected.

1927–39

FOR GOODNESS' SAKE, LET'S HAVE A NEW BAND

Back in Division Two after three top-flight seasons, Leeds United's directors must have been tempted to start again with a fresh approach. But they took more than a month to decide on a replacement for Arthur Fairclough, and gave the job to as near a stalwart as the young club had.

Richard 'Dick' Ray was the first player Gilbert Gillies signed for Leeds City in 1905, signing him from his old club Chesterfield at dawn on the day he became available. Ray was then a 27-year-old full-back, formerly captain of Manchester City when they won promotion to the First Division, fêted for scoring a last-minute winner against Newton Heath, the team that became

Manchester United. He was captain of Leeds City during its first league season – the 'Chief Peacock' – dependable, cool, courteous and encouraging, with soccer so ingrained that he had reportedly never so much as seen a game of rugby. He played 44 distinguished games for Leeds before leaving in 1908.

With another of the class of 1905, Charles Morgan, Ray came back to help resurrect a soccer club in Leeds after City's closure, becoming Leeds United's first manager in the Midland League. When Arthur Fairclough arrived, Ray worked as his assistant for three seasons, looking after the reserves, before becoming manager of Doncaster Rovers in 1923. In his last season at Doncaster he got them up to a best-ever 8th place in the Third Division (North).

As a manager, Ray was confident and blunt. One Christmas, after Leeds played three games in four days, a reporter telephoned Elland Road to ask if the players were training. 'No, I'm the only man here,' replied a less-than-festive Ray. And how were the players spending their day off? 'How should I know?' he replied. 'Playing golf chiefly, or perhaps at the pictures.' Were they very tired after the recent games? 'No,' said Ray. 'You don't feel tired when you've worked three days at your job, do you?'

As soon as he could Ray signed Charlie Keetley, a 21-year-old centre-forward who scored 80 in one season for Alvaston and Boulton. More signings followed: Joe

Firth, Tom Cochrane, George Milburn, Alex Stacey; but they were all players for the future. Doing things Dick Ray's way, at Leeds, meant carrying on where Fairclough left off.

Ray was content to trust the squad he found. Joshua Atkinson, Willis Edwards, Ernie Hart, Tom Jennings, Bill Menzies and Russell Wainscoat had profited by three years' experience together in the top league, and Jimmy Allan, Jimmy Potts, Tom Townsley and Bobby Turnbull by their two; George Reed, Tommy Mitchell and John 'Jock' White had been signed on the way down, but all had the quality to take Leeds back up again. Leeds refused a bid of £6,000 from Sheffield United for White; they knew he could supply even more goals for Jennings. Willis Edwards continued as a first-choice international defender for England.

It was Arthur Fairclough's team; on the eve of the season, a dinner was held at the Griffin Hotel to recognise his part in Leeds United's beginnings. 'Long before I became connected with United, I had thought that Leeds was a wonderful city which deserved a good football club,' said Fairclough, 'and I did my best to bring that about. Fortune was very cruel to them last season, but when I look at the players Leeds have got – most of them quite young – I feel sure it will not be long before the club is back again in its rightful place.'

The team began in exactly that spirit; South Shields were thumped 5-1 on the opening day. Leeds won half their opening sixteen games, climbing to 4th, then really hit their stride. Ernie Hart was restored to centre-half while Tom Townsley, the captain, moved to right-back, and after a defeat at Clapton Orient, Leeds won their next seven.

Another run of eleven games without defeat took Leeds to the top; nobody put a goal past them for nine games in a row. The twelfth match was tough; Chelsea were 3rd, trying to keep their promotion chances alive, while a win for Leeds would guarantee their return to the First Division, and contribute to a big day for West Yorkshire. While Leeds were at Stamford Bridge, Huddersfield Town were at Wembley, facing Blackburn Rovers in the FA Cup final, and all through the night trains were bringing Yorkshire folk down to London.

At half-time Leeds led 2-0, and early in the second half Keetley added a third. That roused Chelsea, and as White and Edwards succumbed to injury and left Leeds short of players, only the agility and determination of Jimmy Potts in United's goal kept Chelsea down to two goals. Huddersfield were beaten 3-1 at Wembley, but Leeds United won 3-2, and promotion was theirs.

A slightly haphazard homecoming greeted them that night; 2,000 supporters packed the approaches to Wellington Station, and although the police formed a passage, it led the players straight into 'two motor drivers, a man and a woman' whose cars were blocking each other's way at the station entrance. While they 'sat in their seats exchanging candid comments on the other's lack of manners', the team were seized by the crowd. Keetley was lifted shoulder high and carried around, until he made his escape to the nearby Midland Hotel.

The following Wednesday a record crowd for a league match at Elland Road, 48,470, plus hundreds more listening outside, came to see if Leeds could beat Manchester City and claim the title; but City's need for points to secure their own promotion was greater, and they won 1-0. Leeds had to make do with winning a silver cup at the Fullerton Park dog track, one of two new greyhound racing stadiums next to the football ground; after the match United and City nominated dogs for a special race, and Leeds' Kind Lady beat Manchester's Wee Murray.

There was one more chance for the championship, but a 5-1 defeat at Stoke City meant Leeds finished in 2nd place. That didn't dim the civic reception organised by the Lord and Lady Mayor upon the team's return by train that night, the Leeds City Prize Band leading a procession in front of thousands of people. The crowd cheered for captain Tom Townsley to salute them; he was popular for the way he 'took the fortunes of his team almost too keenly to heart.' Those who could crammed into the stylish King Edward restaurant to hear speeches, calling first for Townsley, then Jimmy Potts, although he was too shy to say anything. Tom Jennings, missing through illness since early March, paid tribute to stand-in centre-forward Charlie Keetley's eighteen goals in sixteen games: 'Keetley has done more for the team than any international player could have done.'

The vice-chairman, Kaye Aspinall, paid tribute to the team spirit and togetherness that had taken the same group of players, plus Keetley, from relegation to glory. 'I am so pleased we have got promotion without securing any fresh players,' he said, perhaps also thinking of the club's bank account. 'The players have trained for this, and they have pulled together both on and off the field as one man. They are a fine lot of men, and there has never been the slightest unpleasantness throughout the season. That spirit helps a side enormously. The way the men are playing at present makes me think that we have nothing to worry about in meeting First Division sides. We shall do well.'

That confidence was well judged. Had Jennings been fit, the side that faced Aston Villa on the new season's opening day at Elland Road would have entirely comprised players from the relegation season; Keetley was the only addition, but he signalled his First Division intentions by scoring a hat-trick in United's 4-1 win. Promotion added confidence and a winning habit to their previously misused quality, while Dick Ray's training methods were given credit for the players' improved deftness of passing and control. Eight of the first twelve games were won and United started November in 3rd place, the press calling them 'quite one of the wonder teams of the present soccer campaign.'

They could not maintain that form. Willis Edwards was still an England regular, and Ernie Hart joined him after keeping Everton's prolific striker Dixie Dean quiet early in the season – forward Russell Wainscoat was the team's third England international – but the defence had a hard time. After conceding just 49 on the way to promotion, Leeds now let in 84, finishing 13th, losing five of the last six games.

Despite the disappointing end, mid-table had been the target and 13th was the club's best ever finish. Ray looked for improvements from within. Injury to Menzies gave a chance to Jack Milburn, signed from Ashington in Northumberland with his brother George; the family extended to Jimmy Potts, their brother-in-law. Jack was just 21 but didn't miss another game that season, playing alongside Harry Roberts, who took over from Townsley.

In autumn Leeds were unstoppable. Seven wins were followed by a draw, then a 6-0 win over Grimsby Town; only six goals were conceded, and 23 scored. Their form was even more remarkable given the problems in attack. Keetley had surgery for appendicitis but required another operation for a chest problem; he didn't appear until April. Jennings was struggling again with blood poisoning. Jock White was tried for one game at centre-forward, but was needed at inside-left. For a match against Burnley Ray threw in Dave Mangnall, who had just celebrated turning 24 with a hat-trick in a win over Manchester City for the reserves, then scored an unbelievable ten goals in the reserves' 13-0 demolition of Stockport. He was rejected as a youngster by Huddersfield and Doncaster, finding his way to Elland Road through non-league football; there was no fairytale goal on his debut, but what followed was the stuff of dreams. In nine matches Mangnall scored six times, making a solid claim as a long-term replacement for Jennings, not just for his goalscoring, but for 'inspired' distribution to the wings that the *Leeds Mercury* said showed 'a touch of genius'.

Leeds United were top of the First Division throughout October, and the city was buzzing with excitement about a real challenge for the championship by a side that seemed to fear no one; they beat the champions, Sheffield Wednesday, and FA Cup holders Bolton Wanderers. Through steady progress and trust in their abilities, United had built the first genuinely great team in the club's history. They were relegated together, promoted together, amassed hundreds of appearances together. They were well known in the city, committed to each other and to the blue and white striped shirts of Leeds United. The club reported its best ever profit of £1,893, and membership of the Supporters' Club increased by more than 300; these dedicated fans were now fundraising to put a roof over the Lowfields Road side of the stadium. Ernest Pullan, of nearby building firm J.P. Pullan's, joined the board and his company were using building waste to build up the terraces, and capacity was said to be nearing 60,000. The area was becoming a campus for sport; the cricket ground was in use, and large sports pitches were formed for Whitehall Printeries across Lowfields Road. The greyhound stadium to the south of Elland Road was a success, while the track on Fullerton Park was converted to speedway. All this, and the team had a two-point lead over Manchester City at the top of the First Division. Glory was there to be grasped.

It was missed. The team lost five matches in a row, dropping to 6th, a frustrating spell summed up in the fifth game when Longden kicked Blackburn's Willie Imrie to the ground and needed police to protect him from the Blackburn crowd. Then, amid rumours linking Jennings to Bradford City, the directors, despite vowing not to sell, accepted £3,000 from Huddersfield for Dave Mangnall. He had lost his place to Jennings, but kept going in the reserves, scoring three in five minutes away to Manchester United. Leeds had Keetley on his way back, and the offer was larger than for any player before, but two seasons later Mangnall set a Huddersfield record, scoring 42 goals in one season.

Home form kept Leeds in contention for the title, but twelve away defeats condemned them to 5th. It was by far United's best ever season, but could have been so much better had Jennings or Keetley been at their best. Leeds lost eight games by one goal, and were the lowest scorers of the top eight teams.

The longevity of so many quality players was United's strength, but in summer 1930 Ray and the selection committee began looking for the next generation. Some changes were enforced; George Reed was injured, so 21-year-old Wilf Copping stepped in at wing-half. Jock White, now 33 years old, returned to Hearts, and five players were used in the attempt to replace him. Other changes were due to form. After two poor opening games, drastic measures were taken for a match at Arsenal, the entire forward line replaced by reserves. They lost 3-1.

When the line-up settled down it was considerably changed. Copping kept his place, while George Milburn partnered brother Jack at full-back. Billy Furness replaced White, and Harry Duggan was preferred to Bobby Turnbull. Tom Mitchell, a crowd favourite, was replaced by Tom Cochrane, and Charles Keetley played rather than Tom Jennings. Russell Wainscoat, now 32, was more important than ever, while Willis Edwards and Ernie Hart – aged 27 and 28 – were at their peak.

At first the youthful impetus seemed to invigorate Leeds, but 1931 brought six defeats, and they dropped into the relegation places, with little hope of escaping. Milburn, Copping, Furness and Cochrane had quality, but lacked knowhow; a 7-0 win over Middlesbrough was brilliant, but at Ayresome Park Middlesbrough took revenge, 5-0.

Manchester United were bottom by a large margin, but on the final day Leeds were in the other relegation place, two points behind Blackpool. Everything rested on beating Derby at Elland Road, and hoping Manchester City would beat Blackpool.

A depleted Leeds team dug deep and did their part, winning 3-1. A 2-0 lead after ten minutes switched the attention of the crowd to the scoreboard, showing the latest from Manchester, and for a long time displaying a 2-1 score in favour of City – and Leeds. The crowd of 11,190 – and the players, directors and staff – thought Leeds had done it, until a late update: Albert Watson scored an equaliser for Blackpool at the very end. Leeds, the potential champions, were going down.

There was dissent and condescension in the city, where the public had little interest in watching a losing team, and little belief that Ray's players could again go straight back up; the youngsters had endured severe barracking from the unimpressed home crowds. Ray, however, was as confident as always. He signed no new players, and allowed Reed, Mitchell, Underwood, Johnson, Wainscoat, Townsley and Jennings to leave, players with 948 appearances between them. Tom Jennings, who went to Third Division Chester, was the saddest loss; he was only 29, but illness meant his days of scoring 35 in a season were behind him; he played only eight times in his final season, although he scored four goals. If he had stayed fit he might have set extraordinary records, but his record of 112 league goals in 167 games stood the test of time.

There was another important change. While Leeds were relegated, Arsenal won their first league title under Herbert Chapman. As at Leeds City fifteen years earlier, Chapman had insisted on being solely responsible for team selection, and that was becoming the norm. United's selection committee was disbanded, and the team was now entirely Dick Ray's responsibility.

He followed the same principle as the last promotion season, trusting the relegated players had learned from the experience. Ray reckoned he had the youngest set of players in the league, and some important alterations helped consistency; Menzies was full-back alongside Jack Milburn; Furness took over from Wainscoat at inside-left; and 22-year-old Joe Firth filled the gap Leeds had struggled with since Jock White left. Cochrane and Copping, promising but uncertain in the top flight, asserted themselves in the Second Division. Copping in particular stood out, forming a formidable half-back line with Hart and Edwards, and maintaining the team's defensive strength after Edwards was injured. By then Leeds were top of the table, and they went straight back to the First Division, but were again frustrated runners-up, this time to Wolves; and there was a disappointing lack of appreciation from the public.

The team battled for promotion in three home matches in April, none of them watched by more than 13,500. Gate receipts were down £7,500, while barracking of players was up: 'An absolute scandal', said Major

Braithwaite. Elland Road was developing a reputation for sarcasm, unlike the more supportive crowds for Hunslet Rugby League up the road at Parkside. Hugh Whitfield observed in the *Leeds Mercury* that comments about home players at Elland Road could be so barbed you would think you were among fans of the other team.

Despite a fine season, there was a feeling that United were drifting. The team of 1932 had done what was necessary, but without the finesse of 1928; one fan described the play as 'very poor, and often ridiculously so' and 'an agony'. Supporters were agitating for expensive signings, pointing to Bradford, who were paying big fees despite a large overdraft. It wasn't only the team; the price of car parking was faulted, amid calls for more 'showmanship' and 'personality' at Elland Road: 'For goodness' sake,' one fan wrote to the press, 'let's have a new band.'

There was also strong debate about new colours. United had stuck with the blue and white stripes Hilton Crowther brought from Huddersfield, and for years he promoted a plan to consolidate colours across football: home teams would wear blue and white stripes, away teams red and white. But a new Leeds chairman, E.J. Clarke, thought that using the colours of the city might bring crowds back through civic pride. A new kit design was considered, of dark blue shirts with cuffs and a deep collar of primrose; primrose was soon updated to gold, and the plan met with enthusiasm. 'To thousands of people all over the country,' wrote the *Yorkshire Evening Post*, '"Leeds" means chiefly the Association football team that plays at Elland Road ... anything, therefore, that is distinctive about the team and gives it a sense of character is surely all to the good.' After a meeting to consider the matter, the directors did make a change: black socks with a small blue and white top were replaced by blue socks with a large white top, starting rumours that the club could not even afford to buy new shirts, let alone new players.

Dick Ray was typically defiant. 'I am the most pleased man in Leeds,' he said. 'I had never any doubt that the team was good enough to secure promotion, but at one time I believe I was the only man in Leeds who did think so. I am now going to prophesy further, and say that this team will do well in the First Division. Never mind about getting any new men. Our players are nearly all young, they have football ability, and they will improve. I am not going to say that they will top the league. But they are going to play good football, and the conditions will suit them a little better than in the Second Division.'

True to his word, the only significant change was the departure of Turnbull, but Ray could still surprise with players from the juniors; Firth was injured, and at inside-forward was Arthur Hydes, a small but aggressive young recruit from a toffee factory. The first match, a 2-0 home defeat to Derby County, led the *Leeds Mercury*'s

Hugh Whitfield to remark: 'No club's supporters, I suppose, are divided so sharply into two bands as Leeds United's. We may call them the Pessimists and the Optimists. Doubtless the Pessimists will soon be saying, "I told you so."'

Any signs of optimism were overwhelmed by a serious cruciate injury to Edwards that kept him out until the end of December. Alex Stacey took his place, and Leeds found some resolve, only losing once in eighteen games ahead of a Boxing Day trip to runaway league leaders Arsenal, who had just beaten Sheffield United 9-2.

'The Xmas Cracker' read the *Leeds Mercury*'s headline. 'United Have The Pull – Arsenal Go Bang.' In front of 55,876 people shrouded by fog at Highbury, Arsenal were outplayed; Keetley opened the scoring early in the second half, and although Arsenal quickly equalised, it was the only time United's aggressive defenders were beaten. Leeds had spirit, and six minutes from the end Keetley headed the winner; Leeds moved up to joint 2nd place.

The return match was at Elland Road the next day; tickets had been selling for weeks, mainly to people who wanted to see Herbert Chapman's innovative W-M formation in action. Few had thought either match would be won by Leeds, but the United directors seized the occasion anyway, organising a presentation of the players to Lord Harewood and hoping for a performance that would make the city think Leeds were worth watching, as well as Arsenal.

Victory at Highbury gave the day even more impetus. 56,796 was the largest ever crowd for a sporting event in Leeds and the largest in the country that day, and hundreds more watched from the new roof on the Lowfields Stand, or the old roof of the Old Peacock Inn; crowds climbed Beeston Hill for a view. The game was almost everything Leeds hoped for; played at a frenetic pace, dictated by Leeds' relentless attacking. Edwards was back, and the defence became more important as Leeds tired, but the Milburns were tackling with the same efficiency that controlled Arsenal at Highbury, Hart was turning defence into attack, and Copping was described in one report as playing for 'death or glory'. The crowd roared throughout and although the game ended 0-0, nobody could complain about quality or excitement. 'By taking three points out of four from The Arsenal,' wrote the *Yorkshire Evening Post*, 'Leeds United have achieved perhaps the greatest performance in Association football in Leeds.' What more could the public want?

The United directors were asking the same question eleven days later, when just 14,043 came to Elland Road to see Leeds beat Blackburn Rovers 3-1. As ever it was impossible to understand how a stadium that sold out one week could be only one quarter filled the next. Leeds managed another outstanding result in the FA Cup, winning 3-0 away at cup holders Newcastle United; 47,554 turned out at St James' Park for that one, but it was no use back in Leeds. There was not another attendance above 20,000 all season. It didn't help that there were only four more wins as Leeds finished 8th, ending the season at Bolton, where they lost George Milburn to injury after ten minutes and lost 5-0 to a team that ended the day relegated.

Leeds found it difficult to recover from the lethargic end to 1932/33. Next season there was a consistent core of six players who only missed twelve games between them, but there were crucial long-term absences, and Leeds were 17th on Boxing Day. That was after another Christmas double-header with Arsenal, this time without any glory – Leeds lost 1-0 at home and 2-0 away.

Early in 1934, Leeds reached a nadir in front of one of the few large crowds of the season; 29,158 watched them lose 1-0 in the FA Cup third round to Second Division Preston North End. Alf Masser had returned to the board and been elected chairman, and was forced to publicly acknowledge 'the seriousness of the situation … It is not as if one or two players were off form,' he said, 'but the team never worked as a team.' Captain Ernie Hart was summoned to a board meeting, and improvement after February lifted Leeds to 9th. But on the last day Leeds beat Chelsea 3-1 in front of just 6,092 at Elland Road.

Ernie Hart passed 400 appearances, but while his consistency and loyalty justified his status as one of the club's great players, that he signed in 1920, before Leeds United even had a league to play in, suggested Leeds were not moving forward as quickly as they might. In autumn 1933 seven players were eligible through long service for benefit matches, and given cheques instead. The roof over the Lowfields side was extending as and when supporters raised money for it, reflecting the slow progress of Dick Ray's team; while the papers filled with letters demanding thousands be spent on new players, Ray continued his policy of introducing promising youngsters once another player became too old, as if he was replacing worn-out parts in an old motor engine. It meant the machine glided on the same as ever; but it was being overtaken by newer models, making it look distinctly slow and old-fashioned.

Masser claimed that money was not the issue, but Leeds did not want players with only a few years of their career left, and could not convince other clubs to part with their best players at any price. But money could buy, and did buy, Wilf Copping. Herbert Chapman admired the way United's young half-back was developing into a nerveless bruiser, taking to the field deliberately unshaven to add to his intimidating physique, then sternly battering opponents into fearful submission. To his hard-tackling game he added vision, understanding and forward passing. Tragically, in January, just before his 56th birthday, Chapman died from a sudden bout of pneumonia, brought on by ignoring his doctor's advice and braving winter weather to watch Arsenal's third team. In Leeds Chapman was the manager who might have been, in Huddersfield he was the manager who had; at Arsenal he won two league titles and an FA Cup, and revolutionised every aspect of the club. He was taken in his prime, but Arsenal still worked to Chapman's plans, and in June they bid £8,000 for Copping.

It was more than Leeds could turn down, because although Masser denied it, the question of money was always vexing. Dwindling interest in the club's league matches meant dwindling income, and the club was still paying the debenture holders who bailed them out of debt to Crowther. Ray maintained that signing cheap players from junior football was the way he liked to do things, and no doubt he was proud that so many of his discoveries were gems. But the finances didn't allow any other option.

Leeds were characteristically thrifty with the Copping cash. A new half-back arrived – Stan Wilcockson, a 29 year old from York City – along with the usual handful of juniors. Leeds were confident that even without Copping, and despite the effects of age on Hart and Edwards, much of the team – the Milburns in defence, Hydes and Furness in attack – were reaching their peak. Some concessions were made to popular opinion: admission prices were cut and the team colours were changed, to blue and old-gold halved shirts, with white shorts and blue socks with old-gold tops; it was tested as a change kit, but was immediately popular enough to become the official colours.

The new colours did nothing to lift the general gloom. Life without Copping began with a 4-2 defeat to Middlesbrough at Elland Road, then a stunning 8-1 collapse away to Stoke City; things got worse when Hart broke his ankle. It was no longer a matter of poor entertainment, but that Leeds were heading to the bottom of the table, and in November 1934 United spent significant money on a player for the first time since 1927. The board didn't just deviate from its policy but completely reversed, paying Sunderland £2,000 for 33-year-old centre-half Jock McDougall. He only played eleven games. Centre-forward Jack Kelly was younger, just 22, and cheaper at £1,150, but ten games and one goal were not much reward. There was a chance of earning the money back from a big crowd by being drawn at home to Sheffield Wednesday in the FA Cup, but the chance went to Second Division Norwich City, who came to Leeds and won 2-1 in a fourth round replay.

The club's inertia was leading it towards disaster. Rumours about big changes proved true; at the end of a long board meeting at the Griffin Hotel, Dick Ray's resignation was accepted. No official reason was given, but reports hinted at irreconcilable differences between Masser and Ray, who was not only paid £1,000 a year but was a shareholder, as well as having sole control of team selection: by some distance he was the most powerful man at the club. Ray had some right to be; his resignation ended an association that began when he was named Leeds City's captain for the first league season in 1905. The Football League had recognised his skill by asking him to manage an English League XI against a Scottish League team in 1934, and his achievements as Leeds manager were obvious: two promotions, a 5th place and two other top-half finishes established Leeds for the first time as a First Division club, and a place for developing fine young footballers: Copping, Hydes, Keetley, Furness, Cochrane, the Milburns. But his long service also attracted volumes of criticism, and there was widespread disagreement about how one of the most significant statistics of his tenure should define him: transfer fees received, £25,000; transfer fees spent, £3,000.

There was little sign of a plan for replacing the manager; only Masser's appeal to the club's supporters to 'rally round', 'make the turnstiles click' and 'let others learn to respect and envy the Elland Road roar'. A 7-1 defeat away to Chelsea left Leeds just a point clear of the relegation places, and while Ray took over as general manager of Bradford City, the only sign of an appointment at Elland Road was a single line in the *Leeds Mercury*: 'Leeds United F.C. have decided to advertise for a secretary-manager.'

One of the directors, Ernest Pullan, took charge of the team, but it was Billy Furness who saved Leeds

United. He scored seven of United's last eleven goals of the season, and was the only scorer in a 2-1 win at Derby and 1-1 draws with Birmingham City and Aston Villa that secured vital points. He was not on target in the 2-0 win at Preston that guaranteed safety, but signed off with two in the final day's 4-3 win over Spurs at Elland Road.

Change was obviously needed, and it looked like the directors were going to deliver it, retaining just 25 of 44 players, decimating the third team Ray used to trial and develop juniors. But their choice of manager, after 100 applicants were reduced to eight interviewees, was a familiar name if not a familiar figure: William 'Billy' Hampson, a 52 year old who played 91 games for Leeds City during the war, although he had never lived in Leeds, never seen any of the current team play, and never managed a First Division club. His previous experience was with Carlisle United and Ashington; he was working as an FA coach in Northumberland schools when he applied for the Leeds job. Hampson made more of a mark as a player, winning the FA Cup with Newcastle in 1924 and playing for South Shields until he was 47, and was well respected as a polished footballer and a gentleman.

The United directors decided to continue their new habit of meeting weekly rather than monthly, and while Hampson would have 'complete control' of selecting the team and its style of play, his lineups would be submitted to the board before each match, so they could discuss it, 'but without seeking to interfere with his selection.' After a meeting to discuss their policy for the new season, the board announced they were seeking to sign players for centre-forward, inside- and outside-right, and half-back.

When the team lined up for its opening match of 1935/36, there was only one new player: Albert McInroy, a 34-year-old goalkeeper signed on a free transfer. The Supporters' Club heralded a new era by presenting the club with a new blue and old-gold flag, but perhaps sensing disquiet, Hampson placed an item in the papers headlined 'An Appeal For Support', saying he understood the previous disagreements with the board's policies, but that 'no effort will be spared to build up a "United" team worthy of the City of Leeds.'

It would have to happen quickly. Leeds lost four and drew two of their opening six games, scoring just twice. Two big home wins in November restored some faith, and much-needed new players were arriving to ease concerns that Leeds were only capable of more of the same as under Ray. One aspect remained the same: despite Hampson's promise at the AGM that he would take the team to Wembley, Leeds were knocked out of the FA Cup by a Second Division club yet again, this time Sheffield United in the fifth round. One of Ray's last discoveries, Bert Sproston, was the new star of the team, taking over from George Milburn at right-back, while McDougall and Kelly began making steady contributions. Of the new signings, 32-year-old centre-forward George Brown was top scorer with eighteen, and tiny wing-half Bobby Browne, bought for £1,500 from Derry City, became a regular at the back.

The team finished a respectable 11th, and crowds averaged over 20,000 for the first time in six years. But Hampson had not got to grips with the rebuilding job. In the summer Ernie Hart left, to Third Division Mansfield Town. Although he only played four games in his final season, and despite Leeds spending £3,750 on a replacement, Tom Holley from Barnsley, Hart's absence hit them hard. That was probably inevitable. Hart was the fifth player to sign for United, as an eighteen-year-old miner from Burton upon Trent, so that for as long as there had been Leeds United, there had been Ernie Hart. He played in 472 league and cup games, was a captain, an international, and a formidable attacking centre-half; irreplaceable.

Hart was not the only experienced player to leave. Duggan, Brown and Cochrane left early in the season; and while Edwards and McDougall were elder statesmen, their age proved more hindrance than help at the back; Leeds conceded 80 in 1936/37. Winger Arthur Buckley was bought for £2,500 to replace Cochrane, but the stability of the Ray era was gone; Hampson used 29 players, the last of them 34-year-old striker Gordon Hodgson, signed in desperation from Second Division Aston Villa for £1,500.

Hodgson signed at the start of March, when Leeds were 18th, just two points above the relegation places.

He was South African, signed by Liverpool in 1925 after scoring fifteen goals on his national team's tour of Britain, and left them in 1935 after 241 goals in 378 matches. He scored on his debut for Leeds, but it was no consolation as Leeds were taken apart, 7-1 away to Everton; the third match in a spell that brought two draws and six defeats, putting Leeds bottom of the league.

But in Hodgson's time Liverpool were often fighting relegation, and his goals helped Leeds to three wins that raised them to 20th with one game left. A point at home against Portsmouth would mean safety; defeat could put them bottom. For once, everything went United's way, Furness, Kelly and Milburn scoring in a 3-1 win that sent Sheffield Wednesday down with Manchester United. Leeds finished 19th.

In the summer Ernest Pullan won the annual vote for chairman, but there was no change in policy. Leeds fans felt like they were stuck in the Ray years, being promised a brilliant team next season when the club's youngsters had developed, while being criticised for not giving enough support to a team many fans felt was a disgrace to such a proud city. One letter writer pointed out that the Supporters' Club had paid for the roof over their heads on the Lowfields; was it 'crying for the moon' to ask the club to pay for some quality players to watch?

The directors weren't interested in the moon. As far as they were concerned, they had a reserve team full of stars. They had won the Central League, and several players – including McInroy, George Milburn and Furness – were allowed to leave so youngsters could take their place. Full-back Bert Sproston and inside-forward Eric Stephenson had already made significant contributions, and the new-look first team had just three players over 25, one of them Hodgson; his vast experience was almost as important as his goals, and he gave freely of both, scoring 45 in 68 games over the next two seasons.

With sad inevitability, the best of the young players, right-back Bert Sproston, an England international reputed to be the league's fastest full-back, was sold to big-spending Second Division club Tottenham Hotspur in summer 1938, but Leeds had little choice: Spurs offered £9,500, and the British record had been £10,890 for a decade. Despite the fee, chairman Pullan voted to refuse: 'I said I would look after the supporters' interests,' he said. 'This, I think, is going against it.'

There was some talk of fans boycotting games to protest, but Sproston's departure did not destabilise the team the way Copping's had in 1934. The young players brought stability and team spirit in 1937/38, most of them playing at least 30 games as Leeds rose to 2nd amid optimistic talk of the title, until winter stopped their momentum. The team was solid enough for more young players to be introduced, including David Cochrane, a tiny winger worth all the £2,000 Leeds paid to sign him from Portadown.

Crowds were lifted by the exciting youngsters, even after Sproston was sold; Leeds simply promoted another in his place, Ken Gadsby, and made more use of Willis Edwards, now player-coach. 1938/39 was another trip to the top, reaching 3rd in November, but another tale of inconsistency after early promise, this time with a significant step taken to prevent any serious decline. In March 1939 United shocked their fans by paying £5,000 to bring Wilf Copping back, and he made his second debut at Elland Road against Arsenal, the team he had just left, helping Leeds to a 4-2 win that ended a streak of five defeats. Leeds only lost three games with Copping in the side; 29 years old, winner of two league titles and one FA Cup at Arsenal, a player who knew the Leeds club and city, he was the perfect inspiration for Hampson's crop of precocious youths who, if they kept up their performances, had the potential to take Leeds United to glory at last.

There was, however, a subplot, as Copping had not returned purely for football reasons. The prospect of a second war in Europe, this time in an age of technology threatening air raids and flying bombs, led Copping north before London became a target. Leeds were glad to welcome him back, but weren't to enjoy him on the pitch for long. Three games into the 1939/40 season, war was declared on Germany, and the Football League was suspended.

1939–49

CHANGES FOR THE BETTER
– AND SOON

The First World War cost Leeds its football club. Leeds United Football Club survived the Second World War, but the cost was Billy Hampson's impressive young team.

Football continued as it had in the first war, but this time air raids brought the fighting closer to home and made organised football even more chaotic. Some clubs closed down, but Leeds carried on. Stanley 'Tiny' Blenkinsop, a board member with 'a claim to be the largest, widest and heaviest football director in the Old World' according to the *Yorkshire Evening Post*, said that matches should be used for relaxation: 'Enjoy a couple of hours of the finest tonic for tired, troubled, taxed and income-taxed people. And bring your lady friends.'

Although Elland Road was in the hands of the army, United were allowed to use it on match days, fielding whatever players they could find in a series of complicated regional leagues, with final positions settled on goal average. They borrowed talented local amateurs like Albert Saxton, an outside-left from Yorkshire Amateurs, and thought they struck lucky when Chelsea's star winger Alf Hanson was rumoured to be stationed nearby; a taxi was sent to bring him to the ground for a game with York, but ten minutes after kick-off, amid much confusion, a portly Irishman named Sidney Anson took his place on the field.

Alf Hanson must have been somewhere, but mobilisation dispersed most teams to far-flung quarters; the availability of United's Tom Holley to London clubs was headline news. The end of the war brought some normality, as clubs reorganised for the resumption of league football, and a last regional season was played in 1945/46; but Leeds were not promising, finishing bottom of the northern section.

Billy Hampson stayed as manager throughout, and now counted his players back in. The toll was considerable. Leslie Thompson, Robert Montgomery, Vernon Allen and Maurice Lawn were killed in action, as were former player Alan Fowler and wartime guests Tom Farrage and Harry Goslin. Jim Milburn, the third and youngest Milburn brother to play for Leeds, was badly wounded; twins Bill and Alf Stephens were prisoners of war. The biggest loss was Eric Stephenson, who came through the junior ranks at Leeds to become an England international, the heir to Jock White that United sought for so long. He turned 25 as war was declared, a brilliant footballer reaching his peak. Instead he became a major in the Gurkha Rifles in Burma, where he was killed in 1944, four days after his 30th birthday.

The players who made it back were no longer the fledglings who showed so much promise before the war, but they were all Leeds had. Wilf Copping and Gordon Hodgson retired, but the team of 1946/47 was built around pre-war lads: Twomey, Gadsby, Holley, Browne, Ainsley, Heaton, Goldberg, Johnson, Powell, Cochrane and Jim Milburn all turned out in front of enthusiastic crowds, boosted by the optimistic spirit of peacetime. They were coming to the wrong place. Hampson was loyal to his players, but they were not young any more, and stood little chance of becoming the formidable team that had seemed their destiny. They lost fifteen of the first 25 games, but Hampson had little choice but to stick with them.

The Leeds United board had been severely impacted by old age, illness and absence; running the club in war-time fell on the shoulders of chairman Ernest Pullan. He, with Hampson, Alf Masser and James Bromley, was an effective manager, minimising losses and even turning a small profit in one season. But the war years had the worst possible financial start. The large fees paid in 1939 for Wilf Copping and a centre-forward, Len Dunderdale, caused a £5,243 loss for which Leeds got a couple of months of league football from each before war intervened.

More significantly, the club was still carrying the burden of the bond holders who paid off Hilton Crowther in 1925. Their rate of interest was reduced to 5 per cent in 1934, and they agreed to forgo that for the duration of the war plus one season, as well as delaying the scheduled buyback of all bonds by ten years, from 1944 to 1954; they even helped by meeting some tax and rates bills. But the end of the war meant a revival of their payment terms. Although some large bond holders agreed to convert them to shares, the club needed £1,400 a year to pay interest, and had to find £28,000 to redeem the remaining bonds by 1954, all before any money could be spent on the team.

It was hard to see a way out. The team was heading for the Second Division, and even smaller income. A meeting was held at the YMCA to gather fundraising ideas, but the suggestions hardly scratched the surface, and one – moving to a ground nearer the city centre than 'distant' Beeston – was dismissed straight away. New appeals to bond holders reduced the overall debt, allowing the club to accept other loans and freeing up cash for players in the spring: defender Con Martin was bought for £8,000, and centre-forward Harry Clarke for £4,000. They were no help. United's final points total of eighteen was the worst the First Division had seen, or would see for many years. Bizarrely, the public was so starved for entertainment that more spectators than ever came to watch the disaster unfold.

The association with Billy Hampson stretched back to Leeds City and the First World War; and he had now managed Leeds for twelve years, longer than anybody else, building up a good First Division side after a difficult start and guiding the club through the Second World War. It was hard to think of a bad word to say about him, so it was not until April, after relegation was confirmed, that a change was made. Even then, Hampson was dealt with respectfully; a new post of chief scout was created for him, until he decided to work freelance.

The new manager was another with a long history at Leeds: Willis Edwards, whose 444 games rivalled Ernie Hart's record; for eleven seasons theirs was the partnership upon which United's defence was built, and Edwards kept playing during the war until he was three months from his 40th birthday. Although he was born near Alfreton, he was as Leeds as they came; while he was a player, his mother ran the notorious Robin Hood Inn near the city markets – famous years later as a music venue, the Duchess of York – and Willis lived upstairs.

Edwards was coaching the reserve team, and the directors hoped he could find ways of improving the

first team, repeating previous tricks of turning relegated teams into promotion material. There was no
other option. The only new player was Jimmy Dunn,
bought for £200 from Scottish junior football. Five wins
from the opening seven matches were a hopeful sign
that Edwards could make something of the team, with
a 5-0 win over Plymouth Argyle the highlight; thanks to
Aubrey Powell, Albert Wakefield and John Short, Leeds
had scored eighteen goals already. But then they came up
against the division's better teams, plunging them back
into losing habits.

In late October, there were already moves to replace
Edwards. Hull City manager Major Frank Buckley was
photographed talking to Ernest Pullan, and although
Buckley insisted he was enquiring about a goalkeeper,
that ruse soon fell apart. It was not Buckley's first
pleasant conversation with the Leeds board, while his
relationship with the directors at Third Division Hull
was anything but. An unnamed Leeds director declared
the odds were 'a million to one on' that Buckley would
take over, and a journalist visited him at home, reporting discussions about where to live in Leeds, how much
Mrs Buckley was looking forward to shopping in the
city, and Buckley's views on Elland Road: 'I think I could
do a good job there.'

He didn't come. Buckley sent a letter to the Hull
directors that he described as 'more or less an ultimatum', then left to watch the horse racing at Newmarket.

He returned early, making an unexpected entrance at Hull's board meeting, and after an hour's discussion agreed to stay.

Buckley was a big name and the offer from United was front-page news, but while many fans were pleased to see the board taking action, they were disappointed it had failed, and demanding to know what would happen now. New players were arriving, including Jim Bullions, an £8,000 half-back, Kenneth Chisholm, a £6,000 forward, and James McCabe, a £10,000 half-back; Leeds made an audacious £15,000 offer to sign England international Wilf Mannion from Middlesbrough, who had already refused bids of £20,000 from First Division clubs. The search for players even led to Heinrich Mosch, a German ex-prisoner of war at the Butcher Hill camp in Leeds, who signed on as Henry Meek and turned out in the reserves.

But Willis Edwards was doing no better. A 2-0 defeat at home to Luton Town was seen by a large Boxing Day crowd and condemned as United's worst performance in years; then Leeds went to Luton and lost 6-1. As a player Edwards reached the top, playing regularly for England, but he was always the entertaining member of the Leeds back line, concentrating on ball skills and control. That was now reflected in Edwards the manager; he lacked the ruthless edge to inspire his players, and the authority to make tough decisions; the directors and trainers seemed as involved in team policy as

Edwards. In a match at Bury, Hilton Crowther, now living in Blackpool, was spotted reorganising the team on the hour mark, with Edwards nowhere to be seen. His changes did, at least, secure a draw.

The board denied interfering in Edwards' work, and instead put the blame on the players. The latest loss was enormous, £12,783, half of it spent on benefits to long-serving players. 'I am upset that they have not responded better,' declared Pullan at the club's AGM at Christmas 1947. 'No club treats its men better than we do. We have found them houses. We take great care of them in every way.'

The players demanded a meeting with Pullan. He claimed he only meant he was disappointed that extra training had not improved them; that was not good enough for the captain, Tom Holley, who asked for a transfer. 'I may be unpolished as a player,' he told the *Yorkshire Evening Post*, for whom he also worked as a part-time journalist, 'but I have always played for United with every ounce I have. I resent the chairman's criticism.' Holley was replaced as centre-half and captain by Con Martin, and Leeds announced they would listen to offers. But at the end of the week Edwards had to coax him back; a long injury list left Leeds without a centre-forward in the FA Cup third round at Blackpool, and they turned to Holley in desperation. With fifteen minutes of the game left he was moved back to centre-half to keep the score down. Blackpool won 4-0.

Three important wins improved United's league position, but that these were being attributed to a lucky blue and gold tie worn by Robert Wilkinson, one of the directors, said a lot about Edwards' position. Even the tie failed eventually, and Wilkinson was advised that United needed something bigger, like a lucky suit. Rumours were fuelled by an advert in the *Yorkshire Post* in February, by an anonymous Second Division team, inviting applications for the post of manager to be made to a solicitor in London. United denied all knowledge, stating: 'There will be no change in management at Elland Road this season,' but were nonetheless reported to be in talks with Derby County player Horatio 'Raich' Carter about becoming manager. Carter claimed he was only in Leeds to do some shopping, but was linked again at the start of April, just before he joined Hull City as player-assistant to Major Buckley, in place of Frank Taylor.

Buckley and Carter never had the chance to work together. Buckley was said to be unhappy that Taylor had been dismissed, although he did speak to Carter by telephone once the deal was agreed. Carter departed for international duty as an England reserve, while Buckley composed his letter of resignation. His disagreements with the Hull board had continued, and 'it would simplify things' if he was released from his job at the end of the season.

His decision may have already been known in Leeds. Two days after a 3-1 defeat at home to Tottenham, players and directors joined fans at a social organised by the Supporters' Club at the People's Hall on Albion Street. News of a defeat for relegation rivals Doncaster Rovers put the gathering in a more cheerful mood, and two directors made rousing speeches; Robert Wilkinson, who was also president of the Supporters' Club, congratulated the supporters on their loyalty; and Sam Bolton told them that the players were touched by the affection being shown by the fans despite their poor performances. He promised 'changes for the better – and soon.'

The next morning Hull received Buckley's letter of resignation, and in the afternoon the Leeds directors met for a board meeting. Bolton, a director of Holbeck haulage firm Thomas Spence & Son, formed with Wilkinson, Percy Woodward and Harold Marjason a 'progressive' group of directors who had pressed for Buckley all season, but Pullan was adamant Major Buckley would not be a success at Leeds. After 80 minutes of arguing Pullan resigned his chairmanship and walked out, although in the confusion the board did not realise he resigned his directorship as well. Bolton was elected chairman, and an hour later he and secretary Arthur Crowther were seen 'dashing' away from Elland Road by car, presumably bound for Hull.

It was a sad end for Ernest Pullan, who was literally part of building up Elland Road – for years his building firm tipped waste behind the goal to form an ever-increasing Kop – and more involved than most in keeping Leeds United going, running team affairs after Dick Ray's departure, ensuring it survived the Second World War. Nobody held back with their praise, but in the post-war era people were no longer interested in what people had done, but what they were doing now. The 'progressive group' represented the younger generation of Leeds businessmen, working to establish themselves rather than retain their pre-war status. Pullan, after dragging Leeds United from pre-war to post-war, seemed reluctant for it to change, hence the loyalty to Billy Hampson and Willis Edwards, and belief in the old method of waiting patiently for young players. That policy was misguided after the war, when the generation who might have become the footballers Leeds needed was decimated by the fighting; that was felt across football, and it was estimated it would be three years before new juniors would come through. Until then, clubs had to compete for the best players available, and Marjason believed United would get greater support, and greater gate receipts, if they worked with more enterprise.

In that sense, Frank Buckley was an odd choice. Now aged 65, he had joined the army while still only seventeen. Excelling in fitness, his ability as a footballer caught the eye of a scout, and after three years he bought himself out to join Aston Villa. In the First World War Buckley was first to sign up for the 'Footballers' Battalion', climbing the ranks to major, although army snobbery qualified that Buckley was only a 'temporary' major. His war experiences, though, were permanent. During the second phase of the Battle of the Somme, Buckley was felled by a German hand grenade, its metal piercing his chest and puncturing his lungs. A passing stretcher party took the apparently dying man to the casualty clearing station, but Buckley's excellent physical condition sustained him until the shrapnel could be removed and recovery started at a military hospital in Kent.

The story of the brave footballer who survived such dreadful wounds made Major Buckley a wartime celebrity, mixing with literary figures like Thomas Hardy, J.M. Barrie and Rudyard Kipling as part of fundraising efforts for the Red Cross; but with all help needed at the front, Buckley was pressed into action again in 1917 and was 'mentioned in dispatches' for his bravery at Argenvillers.

The war affected Buckley profoundly. At its outset he had just joined Bradford City; nine of their players were killed. The bond of the Footballers' Battalion meant losses were keenly felt by survivors. William Brewer, a QPR player, was killed by a sniper while standing guard on Buckley's orders; Buckley, out of guilt and sorrow, offered to pay for the education of Brewer's three children. The offer was refused, but the support networks were important.

Buckley was 36, his excellent physical health ruined, his football career over, and his perspective changed by all he had lived through; he suffered the dislocating loss of identity felt by many young soldiers returning to Britain. But he was allowed to retain the title of major, and bolstered by his brush with celebrity, he began to embody the role of military gentleman, standing out from the crowd in the flat cap, baggy 'plus four' trousers and brogue shoes of the landed gentry, often accompanied by one or two terriers. It looked odd in 1919, and when he arrived in Leeds in 1948 it was eccentric; but it gave Major Buckley the gravitas of a military man whose experiences demanded respect.

There was a great deal to respect about the Major by 1948. In 1919 an old Footballers' Battalion contact, Frederick Wall, pointed Buckley towards the newly reformed Norwich City: financially broke, with a football ground, The Nest, at the bottom of a quarry, and less than a full team of players, it was the challenge Buckley needed to lift him from post-war despondency. The Footballers' Battalion became his scouting network; comrades would tip Buckley on to a good new player, some of whom were sold on for large fees. The team was playing well and gate receipts were flowing in, until the end of his first season when a dispute over City's refusal to report an illegal approach for one of its players caused a split, with Buckley, five directors and several players walking out.

Buckley spent three profitable years as a travelling sweet salesman – who wouldn't buy sweets from such a distinguished and well-spoken gentleman? – but a chance meeting on a train directed him to the manager's job at Blackpool FC. The same methods used at Norwich gave Blackpool success for the first time; Buckley also gave them an identity, replacing the team's white shirts with bright tangerine that one of the club's directors had seen worn by the Netherlands' national side. No other club in England wore brilliant orange; Buckley was advertising Blackpool as a vibrant, modern club, in keeping with its Pleasure Beach and Illuminations.

At Wolverhampton Wanderers Major Buckley made himself a household name. With a large stadium in the centre of a dense industrial population and trophies in the cabinet, Wolves believed success was theirs by right, but had plunged into Division Three (North). On their return in 1924 they emblazoned their old-gold shirts with a black V for victory and continued as they had since 1906: spending money on stands and players but coming no nearer to promotion.

Wolves were held back by boardroom infighting, and Buckley, with his military bearing and bark, promised to stamp out the nonsense. The club had an overdraft of almost £15,000 and was losing money every year, but Buckley said they could reach the top in five years. And if the directors did not like his first year's work, he told them, they could kick him out.

He was quick to sell players but slow to transform the team. Promotion didn't come until his fifth season, winning the Second Division two points ahead of Leeds; then gradually the 'Buckley Boys' matured into rivals to Arsenal's dominance. When Herbert Chapman died, Arsenal were a rich, stylish club, paying enormous fees to bring players to a beautiful art deco stadium, where the team played with tactical flair. Wolves were dragged up by Buckley on the cheap, his transfer policies all about recouping – he took in £110,000 by selling players, generating £68,000 of profit. The stadium at Molineux had size rather than style, and so did Buckley's team; fit, well-drilled, they played long diagonal balls to their forwards rather than meandering through midfield like Arsenal.

In 1937/38 the championship was heading to Wolves, until defeat at Sunderland on the final day gave Arsenal their fifth of the decade; then Buckley sold them Bryn Jones for £14,000, a world record fee. As if to underline the relish he took in profiting despite the fans' anger, Buckley named his new Welsh terrier Bryn Jones; and as well as another 2nd place in the league, he took Wolves to Wembley. Despite a shock 4-1 defeat to Portsmouth, the FA Cup final ought to have been the start of Wolves' glory years with the Buckley Boys. Instead, it was an ending; the Second World War intervened and in 1944 Buckley resigned, accepting a large contract to begin again from the bottom, at Third Division Notts County.

Buckley did not last long there, or at Hull, who promoted Raich Carter to manager after Buckley left. Buckley's interest was still in long-term building jobs;

there had been a nice ring to the 'Buckley Boys', and it was said that he and Wolves made each other famous. Playing for him at Molineux was 'like being in the laboratory of some mad professor' according to one player, and although war had prevented him from reaping the rewards, few could doubt the singularity of his science. His success as a manager had depended on the identity he created after the First World War, and the success of his teams depended on it too. Major Buckley wanted to build a football club, and he wanted to build it his way.

That suited Leeds United. The progressives in the boardroom recognised what the rest of football learned from Herbert Chapman: running a football team was a job best handled by an expert. Although Buckley's methods were no longer cutting edge, they were proven, and there was no one better to bring Leeds up to date. With no money and few good players, Major Buckley would have to produce both. His salary was high, and so were expectations.

'This is a great day for Leeds United,' announced Sam Bolton as Buckley signed his contract. 'The directors have every confidence in the ability of Major Buckley to make Leeds United the Arsenal of the north.' Buckley was succinct: 'I have come here to do a job and I mean to do it. There is plenty of scope in Leeds. Leeds is potentially a very big soccer centre, and I am sure I shall enjoy the task of making it into the stronghold of the game the club and its public would like it to be.'

Before Buckley could begin, it remained Willis Edwards' responsibility to keep Leeds in the Second Division. With Major and Mrs Buckley among 28,794 watching at Elland Road, a 3-0 win over Chesterfield made Leeds safe with two games to go, and brought Edwards' time as manager to an end. He returned to the coaching staff, and Buckley set about making his presence felt.

Prices were raised for the popular stands, and Buckley spoke in support of a council scheme to build a £1 million sport complex with a 150,000 capacity stadium near the city centre at Torre Road, a sign of where the club and city wanted to be in ten years. The team jerseys were changed, from blue and old-gold halves, to old-gold with blue sleeves and collar; the old shirts had been 'unlucky', wrote one supporter in the *Yorkshire Evening Post*, but 'now we shall see them coming out looking like a football team.'

They came out without their two best players. Buckley agreed to Aubrey Powell's transfer request and let him go to Everton for £10,000; he was replaced at inside-forward by Tommy Burden from Chesterfield, a former Buckley Boy at Wolves, less skilful but harder working. Another £10,000 was received for Con Martin, sold to Aston Villa, and the fees were put towards clearing United's overdraft. New players were predominantly juniors. 'I want as many young players as possible for the rebuilding at Elland Road,' said Buckley. 'I want to organise plenty of trials, and while I can find, see or hear of many young players, I cannot know of them all. I would be glad to hear of any young fellow who fancies a trial with Leeds United. I don't want to hear of Leeds and district boys going off to Lancashire or London, or indeed anywhere else except Leeds United. I know they have been going in the past, but I would like that to stop.'

Buckley would, 'develop players, train them and teach them, inculcate loyalty and service.' The squad were issued with small yellow books Buckley began using at Wolves; they contained eighteen rules covering times of training and meeting for matches, banning smoking on match days and going out dancing after Wednesdays, backed up by hefty fines. Buckley was abrasive, ruling with barrack-room fear, his half-time diatribes strong enough to make grown men cry; but he took genuine interest in the players' welfare, securing their loyalty. Learning the worn-out shoes worn by a junior player named Jack Charlton were the only pair the youngster had, Buckley presented him with a pair of Irish brogues, 'the strongest, most beautiful shoes I had ever seen', said Charlton, who kept them for years.

Changes were slow, Buckley allowing a chosen team to play at least four or five games together. The difference was the style of play, and the greater effort brought from Buckley's training methods, that mixed science and absurdity. There were new machines that fired footballs at the players like balls from a cannon; and simpler technology, like piles of bricks with a ball on top, that would either teach the players to kick properly or leave them with severely bruised toes. To improve dribbling skills Buckley tied balls to the players' feet; to improve balance he paired the players up for sessions of ballroom dancing on the pitch. The Supporters' Club had paid for a public address system for music and announcements, and Buckley made full use of it during training, berating his players from a seat in the stands, until local residents complained about his amplified bad language echoing through their quiet streets.

Then there were the gland treatments. Buckley's teams played a physical form of football, neglecting wing play in favour of sending the ball forward as quickly as possible, and he sometimes veered into unsporting territory – at best by heavily watering pitches to leave away teams fatigued in the mud, or at worst by injuring opponents to reduce teams to ten or nine. The players had to be extremely fit, and at Wolves in 1937 he began using the services of a chemist named Menzies Sharp, who claimed to have a 'secret remedy' to improve mental and physical fitness and stamina, popularly believed to be 'monkey gland serum'. When word began to spread the controversy reached the House of Commons, but the Football League could find no reason to ban it, so the argument centred on whether it had any effect. Leicester City complained when Wolves' 'supermen' beat them

10-1; Everton's Tommy Lawton claimed the Wolves players had 'glazed eyes', as if hypnotised, while beating his team 7-0. But Wolves' own Stan Cullis claimed he felt nothing, and when Buckley introduced the injections at Elland Road, Harold Williams dismissed the idea: 'I don't require needles up my backside to play football.'

Whether with needles or a hefty kick, Buckley had the team playing better, if not getting better results. United ended his first season 15th; only one point better than the season before, but no worse for selling Powell and Martin and clearing the overdraft, and supporters had detected a new 'fighting spirit'. Buckley had steadily overhauled the side, and was determined to keep developing his squad, searching for juniors he could mould.

Then there was the case of the player he found. Three games before the end of 1948/49 Buckley introduced the last new face of the season, a new centre-half. He was just seventeen years old, a giant from Swansea named John Charles.

1949–53

CONFRONTED BY AN
ADONIS OF A YOUTH

The accusation, and fear, of opponents criticising Major Frank Buckley's use of potions like monkey serum was that he was trying to build a team of supermen.

Even without chemicals, Buckley's concentration on strength was unusual in a game that still thought training was a few laps and a kickabout. He collected gym equipment, believing fit players would recover better from injuries. Weight training developed upper bodies, neglected in a game about kicking. Leg muscles were strengthened, so that Buckley's teams could play on watered pitches, while weaker opponents would flounder in the mud. He demanded versatility, seeking players with two strong feet and making them practise different positions. A lifetime's obsession with physical fitness, honed in the trenches of the First World War and the dugouts of the Football League, refined Buckley's view of the ideal team: he sought eleven strong men of skill and character, and if he couldn't find them, he would create them.

And in September 1948 a sixteen year old walked into his office. Tall, straight-backed, arms by his sides, silent until spoken to, John Charles had come from Swansea for a trial. 'I was confronted,' remembered Buckley, 'by an Adonis of a youth.'

A scout hired by Billy Hampson, Jack Pickard, spotted Charles playing in a Swansea park. He found out that the big lad with the ball glued to his feet was on the ground staff at Swansea Town – later Swansea City – and assumed he was signed as a player. But he couldn't resist going back to watch him and getting to know his father, Ned. Ned played in his youth but now worked in the local steelworks, and was considering pulling young John away from football to join him and earn some real money. Swansea Town, he told Pickard, weren't giving John a chance. He was paid a pittance to sweep the stands, and was only registered as an amateur anyway. 'He hasn't signed anything?' asked Pickard. He had not. That was Pickard's opportunity. He telephoned Major Buckley and told him he'd found the greatest footballer in Britain.

The teenager arriving at Leeds had everything. 'Somehow,' Buckley said later, 'he looked like a footballer. He looked like a fine, upstanding young man, but he was far too shy and modest to say much about himself.' Buckley bought Charles a new suit, found him a place to live and signed him on, causing a storm in Swansea when they realised the town's most talented schoolboy had been stolen while they weren't looking. Charles' modesty was a product of his humble upbringing and the distance he travelled for the opportunity; his mother thought there was no hope of her Swansea boy attending a trial in Leeds, because he didn't have a passport. But he had a sense of humour to rival any juvenile, and confidence in the things he could do on a football field.

Although he was now getting the attention denied him at Swansea, he didn't take kindly to Buckley's training. John Charles might become the greatest footballer in Britain, but he would have to work at it. He was a right-footed left-half, so Buckley put him at right-back in the United 'A' team and gave him extra training in the afternoons with his left foot and his head. As Charles' seventeenth birthday passed, and his height passed six feet, Buckley moved him up to the reserves, and to centre-half.

Buckley said at least some credit should go to coaching and good advice, but anyone seeing Charles at centre-half immediately said the boy was a natural.

An injury to Tom Holley, the former captain who only missed a handful of games in twelve seasons, gave Charles a chance in a late-season friendly against Queen of The South. His opponent was Scottish international Billy Houliston, a star centre-forward who had created three goals against England at Wembley ten days earlier, but Charles didn't let Houliston have a kick. It was the first time Holley had seen Charles play. 'Within twenty minutes I knew that my football days weren't simply numbered,' he said, 'I knew they were finished.' Holley retired at the end of the following season.

Holley couldn't get a game because Charles was ever-present that season, and only missing for eight matches the next. Buckley denied he was building his team around the teenager; he was a confident seller of star players, and always believed he could go and find another. But he recognised there was something different about Charles. With Charles at the centre, Buckley's old boy from Wolves, Tommy Burden, as captain and right-half, and first Jim McCabe then Eric Kerfoot at left-half, Leeds conceded just 45 goals in Charles' first full season, better than all except Cardiff City and runaway champions Tottenham Hotspur, better than their own previous season by eighteen.

When Charles was playing, his height and physique dominated the scene, but he also had exceptional acceleration and top speed so that wherever the ball was, he could arrive like thunder to win it. Then he had the skill to either pass it to where it ought to be, or run there with the ball himself. Anyone hoping to take the ball off him might as well tackle one of Sam Bolton's lorries. Charles was a sensation, but he was still young; Holley's advice from the sidelines helped him adapt to the centre-half's art, while Burden, McCabe and Kerfoot were consistent and enthusiastic leaders.

United's first reward was progress in the FA Cup. Leeds had never had a good cup team, and in Buckley's first season were knocked out by Third Division Newport County at Elland Road. The Major brushed off the criticism.

'In twelve months the people of Leeds will be acclaiming Leeds United and me,' he said. 'Leeds United are suffering an inferiority complex, especially in cupties. That will not be remedied until there is a complete change. Shall I give up the job? Not on your life. I am enjoying it. I am revelling in it. I like a fight. I shall see it through.'

Twelve months later supporters were nervous about playing another Third Division side, away to Carlisle United, but now Buckley's team were in good form and immune to nerves; they led 5-0 at half-time and won 5-2. Next was a league match with Spurs, who had won twenty of their 25 games and only lost one; they were beaten 3-0 in front of 50,476 at Elland Road, the biggest crowd since the First Division clash with Arsenal in 1932.

That was bettered within a fortnight, 51,488 watching Leeds draw 1-1 in the fourth round against First Division Bolton Wanderers. Few thought Leeds had much hope in the replay, but Frank Dudley scored after two minutes, giving United something to defend on a pitch that was a mixture of mud, sand and ice, and Len Browning added another just after half-time. Bolton quickly scored and with twenty minutes left Nat Lofthouse, one of the most dangerous forwards in the game, equalised and forced extra time. Lofthouse would have scored many more were it not for John Charles; instead Dudley scored a winner to crown 210 minutes of heroic defending. Stepping from the train in Leeds, clutching his fox terrier Bryn Jones, Major Buckley hailed the greatest cup display he had ever seen. 'Their spirit was wonderful,' he said. 'The way they fought back after losing a two-goal lead amazed even me.'

Leeds were drawn at home in the fifth round against Second Division rivals Cardiff City, and soccer fever gripped Leeds like never before; angry letters in the newspapers denounced the city for going 'plain barmy' when an important general election was just weeks away. The hysteria extended to naming a doll mascot, brought to matches from the Fleece Hotel by the Stanningley branch of the Supporters' Club, that keeper Harold Searson had been taking into the goal with him. There were more than 2,000 entries in a *Yorkshire Evening Post* competition to name it, suggesting Atomic Annie,

Lena The Loiner, Luwyn – 'Leeds United Win'; Laura – 'Luck Aids United's Rise Again'; and Lucy – 'Leeds United's Cup Year'. The winner, suggested by more than 300 people and chosen by Searson and Burden, was another play on Leeds United's initials: Lulu.

Lulu was lucky again, watching over Searson's astute positioning throughout United's 3-1 win. Leeds were just two games from Wembley, and within minutes of being drawn away to Arsenal fans were contacting coach hire firms about transport to Highbury, and Yeadon (later Leeds Bradford) Airport about organising flights. The Lord Mayor and a member of Parliament tried to intervene with British Railways over a fifteen-shilling hike to train fares, one fan suspecting the authorities were afraid of letting 'the Yelland Road Roar' be heard away from Leeds. 150 coaches took 4,000 fans to London, while two sea cadets and a *Yorkshire Post* journalist tried to hitchhike; they walked as far as Doncaster, but at 4am judged they were likely to miss the match and took the only offer they had, a lift home.

In front of 62,273 at Highbury, Leeds were good enough to deserve a replay against one of the best sides in the country, but Arsenal scored early in the second half and Leeds couldn't find a way through to equalise. 'It was just not our day,' said Tommy Burden, talking to a journalist while preparing a Sunday roast the next day. 'Next year. Leeds United are in the "coming" stage. We have not reached the peak by a long way yet.'

The cup run brought the players and fans together, and at a Supporters' Club concert Tom Holley took the microphone and told the players in the front rows that now was their chance to get their own back on the Elland Road crowd: the players stood, turned to the audience full of supporters, 'and booed long and heartily, with Tom as boo-leader', until the crowd and players together were laughing too hard to boo anymore. But the peak United were aiming for was the First Division.

The FA Cup run was in tandem with superb form in the league. After a slow start Leeds only lost one of fifteen matches, including six consecutive wins in which they conceded just one goal, taking them to 5th. Seats for the home match with Hull City were sold out a month in advance, and 49,465 watched John Charles celebrate his first call-up to the Welsh national team by controlling Hull's player-manager Raich Carter and recent signing Don Revie, in a 3-0 win that moved Leeds up to 4th. Spurs were eleven points clear at the top, but Leeds were four points behind 2nd placed Sheffield United, with two games in hand.

The defence was consistently solid, but a lack of goals left no margin for error; near the end of a game against 3rd placed Sheffield Wednesday at Hillsborough, the defence suffered a rare collapse, turning a 2-2 draw into a 5-2 defeat in eleven chaotic minutes. Harold Williams, a short, speedy and two-footed outside-right, had come to United's attention in Newport's team in 1949, and signed in the summer for £12,000; Frank Dudley was signed to partner gangly local lad Len Browning up front, and David Cochrane continued on the left. But United's 54 goals were only three more than bottom team Bradford Park Avenue; Leeds only won four of their last eleven games, finishing 5th.

United's problem was a lack of creativity, but quality inside-forwards were hard to find, driving prices up; Hull paid £20,000 for Don Revie, and Derby £25,000 for Johnny Morris; that was almost ten times United's profit for the season. Buckley had a new contract until 1953, and was resolute against spending money the club didn't have. Sam Bolton said that when results had gone against Leeds the board went to Buckley, 'almost in panic, prepared to ask him to buy players, but he won't do it, not until he finds the right man'.

That meant the next season was a paler imitation of the one that captured the city's imagination. There was no cup run, and although Browning scored nineteen goals, the next best was Frank Dudley with eleven, and Buckley swapped him at the start of February to sign one of his old Wolves juniors, Ernie Stevenson. Late in the season Buckley tried moving Charles and Burden up front, first as a partnership, then just Charles alone, then just Burden; together they didn't work, but separately Charles scored two against Hull City and one against Grimsby Town, and Burden scored against Leicester

City, during a late-season burst that moved Leeds from 13th to again finish 5th, one point nearer to 2nd.

Leeds had to disguise their disappointment and call it progress, but it was a difficult argument to win with impatient supporters. 1951/52 opened with six dull, winless matches, reducing attendances and profits, diminishing Buckley's chances of signing the player who would provide the liveliness that was missing. When Hull tried to sign one of Leeds' defenders they were told it would cost them Don Revie in exchange, and retreated, but Sunderland's interest in John Charles had Buckley thinking the unthinkable. Publicly he dismissed any thought of selling, but privately he must have given serious thought to cashing in, as he had on Bryn Jones at Wolves, and naming a new fox terrier 'John Charles'.

Charles could fetch over £30,000, at a time when the soccer authorities were considering a maximum transfer fee of £15,000; as Charles was doing his National Service, Leeds were not getting the best of him, seeing him at Elland Road only for matches, some of those missed for army duties. He was sidelined by surgery to remove cartilage to solve a problem in his left knee, and it remained to be seen what sort of player would return. In the army Charles discovered a talent for boxing, and was giving serious thought to switching career. During one period of intense press speculation, Tommy Burden asked his manager if he would really sell Charles. 'You watch me,' said the Major. 'I like money in the bank to cover my salary. He'll go if I get the right money.' Sheffield Wednesday's manager Eric Taylor found out what the right money would be; 'We were met by a price from Major Buckley which seemed to us to be the price of Leeds Town Hall.'

Buckley had built a career, and his brilliant Wolves team, on such audacious sales and long-term planning; he had sold Jones knowing he could develop another player who, in a few seasons, would be his equal. But Buckley was older now, with two stated aims in his final job – get Leeds to the First Division and the FA Cup final – and both he and the supporters were already frustrated waiting for his youth policy to produce players. It was too much to expect a second John Charles to appear, but Buckley felt he might yet find an inside-forward somewhere.

Leeds couldn't wait. Don Mills was bought from Cardiff City for £12,000 and put straight into the side, an immediate improvement. But to pay for him United sold local boy and top scorer Len Browning to Sheffield United for £14,000, replacing him with Frank Fidler from Wrexham, who only scored eight. Charles returned at the back but the team's form dipped and lurched as Buckley searched for a solution up front; his experiments continued, using full-back Jim Milburn, centre-half Roy Kirk, inside-forwards Don Mills, Frank Dudley and Ken Hastie, and juniors Ron Barritt and Brian Smith. Leeds stayed in promotion contention, but the last two matches of

1951/52 were typical. If other results went their way, two wins might have meant promotion; Leeds beat Coventry 3-1 then lost to Cardiff 3-1, and ended up 6th, a place and a point worse than before. They lost John Charles again, too, to surgery to remove cartilage from his right knee, injured while playing for the army at Easter.

Charles was fit for the new season, but United's start may have had more superstitious supporters thinking back to the club's Annual General Meeting, when a small black cat jumped onto the top table at the Griffin Hotel, making straight for Buckley. It had been taken as a good omen, but by October Leeds were 18th. Buckley reestablished some stability; the back six were the same throughout, with John Scott in goal, Grenville Hair replacing Jim Milburn as Jimmy Dunn's full-back partner, and Kerfoot, Charles and Burden the solid half-back line, but only inside-forward Ray Iggleden was providing any meaningful threat. It was time for radical changes.

George Meek, an eighteen year old signed from Hamilton Academicals in late August, provided stamina and accurate crosses from the wing. Inside-forward Albert Nightingale came from Blackburn Rovers for £10,000, a physical and crafty battler with a dapper moustache, and a reputation for winning penalties whenever he was tackled outside the penalty area by making sure he fell within it. Veteran Jim McCabe returned at centre-half, while John Charles, for a third time, was moved to centre-forward.

Nightingale scored on his debut, a sixth defeat, 2-1 at Sheffield United. But he scored two more in his next game, with one each from Charles and Mills beating Barnsley 4-1. Another Charles goal secured a 1-1 draw at Lincoln City, then Hull were beaten 3-1 at Elland Road. His third might have been an undeserved penalty, and his all-round play in attack was not as good as at centre-half, but John Charles had a hat-trick, and Leeds had a centre-forward.

Buckley kept switching his players from wing to wing, from inside to outside. But the new constant was Charles at number nine. He truly announced himself with another hat-trick in a 3-2 home win over Brentford. His winning goal, on a pitch covered with snow, involved dribbling the ball 50 yards, avoiding three tackles, taking the ball around the goalkeeper, and recovering his balance to find a one-yard gap between a hurtling defender and the post. 'I hesitate to use the phrase a "one-man win", but this was the nearest I have seen to it for a long time,' wrote Richard Ulyatt in the *Yorkshire Post*; Phil Brown in the *Yorkshire Evening Post* suggested: 'November 29 should henceforward be known at Elland Road as John Charles Day, and (discreetly) celebrated as such.' Major Buckley put the situation simply. 'Charles is the best in the world,' he said. 'I'm very proud of him.'

For five consecutive matches, Charles was the only Leeds player to score, and the team was unbeaten. Gradually his teammates joined in again, but Charles kept going, scoring 26 goals from 28 games in the attack. Charles was still only 21, but now the best young centre-half in the country, about whom more was being said and written than any other young defender, was a sensation.

The move to centre-forward was carefully managed by Buckley and diligently undertaken by Charles. Fame had not changed him. English football's maximum wage meant there was no temptation in transfer speculation; he loved living a short walk from the stadium because it meant long lie-ins, and in April 1953 he married Peggy White, a local girl he'd met at the Astoria dance hall. All he wanted was to start a family and do his best for Leeds United, and for Major Buckley, whose voice had become a stern, constructive and critical influence on the player he always called Jack. 'Jack, you just go out there and play, and that's it,' Buckley told him before his first game at centre-forward, and as Charles learned his new position the Major kept his advice simple, ignoring Charles' doubts and his request, even after eighteen goals in fifteen games, to move back to defence. 'You know all the tricks the centre-forwards use against you,' Buckley told him. 'Now you can use them yourself.' Charles modelled himself on centre-forwards he'd least enjoyed facing, moving across the attack, dragging defenders out of position, then going for goal. The Major had helped Charles to great aerial power, and hours of headaches, by training him to leap into the air and head the crossbar like a football; now Charles took himself behind the Main Stand to practise for hours after training, shooting against the wall to develop power and accuracy.

Charles helped Leeds to 71 goals, their best total since 1935. But without Charles, the defence wasn't strong enough to build a promotion challenge. Buckley had finally found the attacking counterpart to John Charles, but it was John Charles, and now he was 70 years old, he had to consider whether he or the Leeds public had the patience to wait while he found a new centre-half. Jack Marsden, a local apprentice French polisher, was given a run towards the end of the season, to gain some experience; seventeen-year-old Jack Charlton, only just breaking into the reserve side, had his debut in the final match. There was more help for Charles, too: Wales wanted to try him at inside-right, so Buckley helped him practice by moving him there for Leeds against Everton, and again for a match at Swansea, so Charles would not be playing directly against Swansea's centre-half, his brother Mel. There was a simple explanation for these almost paternal late-season experiments; Leeds were safe from relegation and not up for promotion, and at the start of April, Major Buckley had announced he would be leaving after the last match.

Buckley's contract was ending, and he was offered another year, but that was not much use to him. In five seasons he had built the first team, the reserves and the juniors, and knew what each was capable of, and when players like Marsden or Charlton would be ready. His policies were slow but successful; a year wouldn't do it, unless they bought a centre-half to make an impact like Albert Nightingale up front. Buckley's hard work had cleared the debenture holding the club back since 1925 and returned a profit every season, but the government's increased entertainment tax, high running costs and the recent transfer fees contributed to debts over £30,000. The chances of signing a centre-half to win promotion seemed small. As if to make a point about the lack of backing from the board at Elland Road, Major Buckley announced he was returning to the Midlands to take over at Walsall, who were in the process of finishing last in the Third Division (South) for the second successive season. He was going to build them into a footballing force instead.

'I have enjoyed my stay,' Buckley told the *Yorkshire Post*. 'I leave Leeds United with good wishes for the future. We have had a mixed bag of luck, but it has been good fun.'

9

1953–56

WHERE ARE
THE SOCCER FANS?

When Leeds United first spoke to Horatio 'Raich' Carter about becoming their manager, in 1948, there were two significant problems. First was that Carter wanted to continue playing, and was tempted by learning from Major Frank Buckley as player-assistant at Hull City. Second was that Carter wanted a five-year contract, but Leeds only offered three. So Carter went to Hull, not knowing Buckley would immediately take over at Leeds, leaving Carter in charge. Now, five years later, Buckley said his goodbyes at Elland Road, and the next day Raich Carter said his hellos.

Buckley had made his name as an irascible, eccentric but successful manager; Raich Carter was famous simply for being a brilliant footballer. He played his last match days before signing at Leeds, aged 39, giving his career a long post-war coda as if he wanted to settle a question: if not for the Second World War, how good might Raich Carter have become?

His hometown club, Sunderland, gave Carter his debut aged eighteen, and made him captain at 23. Sunderland's manager Johnny Cochrane built an attacking team, and the precocious inside-forward dictated from the front. Legend has it that Cochrane was so confident in his players that, for a team talk, he would pop into the dressing room and ask who they were playing. Someone would reply, 'Arsenal,' and Cochrane would leave the room satisfied, declaring: 'That's okay, we'll beat them.'

Sunderland won the First Division in 1935/36 by scoring 109 goals, the first team to score more than 100. Carter was joint top scorer, with 31 goals from midfield; and top scorer the next season, with 26. He captained the team to victory in the FA Cup, scoring one of the goals that beat Preston North End 3-1 at Wembley. He had won his first England cap three years earlier, and by lifting the cup, aged 23, he had every honour in the game. It was now a matter of how many more times he would win, and by how much.

That's how it should have been, but the Second World War denied Carter the best years of his career. His enormous fame made the war even more painful; he had been living among the severe poverty the economic depression brought to Sunderland's shipyards, and while turning out as a guest player for Huddersfield Town and Derby County, he was accused of shirking the war effort by seeking his living in the fire brigade, the RAF, and as an instructor in a rehabilitation centre for wounded pilots, instead of fighting on the front line. He regretted it all; his decisions, the tarnish to his reputation and the loss of his career. When the war ended he was 32, and had something to prove.

Carter looked even more distinguished when he resumed league football with Derby, not least because his hair had turned a flattering silver. Carter's playing style looked relaxed, almost arrogant; he couldn't look less interested when he didn't have the ball. His arrogance was real, but so was his talent, and few realised his influence on a match until he made it obvious, by drifting into space and cracking in a shot from 30 yards. He was instrumental as Derby won the first post-war FA Cup final, beating Charlton Athletic 4-1.

Carter was 34 when Buckley's resignation thrust him into management at Hull City. Dropping to the Third Division (North) was unusual for such a famous name, and the city was enthralled by its new celebrity, buying up jars of Nufix hair cream to get a free photograph of City's silver-haired player-manager. Carter was determined to give them the full Raich Carter product, as seen in the First Division; his method was to ignore the club's status and play like a top-flight team. Quality would be its own proof.

He was hailed a hero when he delivered the title in his first season, and secured his status by taking Hull to the edge of promotion to the First Division. He bought quality – centre-half Neil Franklin from Stoke City and inside-forward Don Revie from Leicester City – but Carter's methods began to lose their lustre. Twenty-two-year-old Revie was to be his successor, and arrived eager to learn from one of the greats; but Carter was not a teacher, and was disappointed by his £19,000 signing. He felt that weak character, something Carter had never suffered from, was holding Revie back.

Carter's own character inevitably caused rifts with the same board of directors that exasperated Major Buckley. He resigned soon after the start of his third season, referring vaguely to 'a disagreement on matters of a general nature in the conduct of the club's affairs'. Still fit, he was asked not to train with the players he had been managing; he opened a shop and stood selling sweets and tobacco while the city and the directors argued about his future, and the team dropped towards relegation. He returned as a player in December, and his play inspired Hull to avoid relegation; a hero again, the Lord Mayor granted him a civic testimonial match and a reception at the City Hall.

Carter was still not done. Offers regularly came across the counter at his sweet shop, and £50 a match to commute to Ireland and play for Cork Athletic, more than three times the maximum wage in the English leagues, was irresistible. As was the adulation. Gate receipts soared wherever Cork played, and they won the FAI Cup and the Munster Cup; Carter led the team out for the Munster Cup final, his last match, and was photographed surrounded by the players, directors and ballboys, the silver-haired centre of attention.

Two days later he was the centre of attention again when he breezed into Elland Road, declaring his playing days over, ready to devote himself to management and repeat the promotion performed in his first season following Major Buckley at Hull. The two seemed tightly linked, but there were contrasts of character and style. Under the benevolent military dictatorship of Buckley, United craved the First Division and top-class football, and that was what Carter was all about; a thoroughly modern figure, he would drag Elland Road into the 1950s, his Hollywood looks matched by a Hollywood wardrobe and confident assurance that Leeds would rise to a higher level simply by playing better football.

With just one addition to Buckley's team – 40-year-old winger Eddie Burbanks, to cover injuries and call-ups to National Service – United had the perfect start. John Charles scored four as Notts County were beaten 6-0 at Elland Road, then three more in a 4-2 home win over Rotherham United. Charles scored 23 by December, but Leeds only won seven of twenty games. The style had improved; Leeds were getting the ball down and passing to players in space. But First Division football looked as far off as when Buckley was sending his teams up and at the opposition.

Nobody in Leeds craved First Division football more than the player most worthy of it. The summer's press reported record bids for Charles from Cardiff City and Arsenal, and games in London in October brought offers to the team hotel, most persistently from Chelsea. Charles had just performed brilliantly for Wales at centre-forward against England, and Chairman Sam Bolton hid his star inside the hotel and refused to listen. 'Chelsea may be willing to pay £40,000,' he told Tom Holley, now working for the *Yorkshire Evening Post*, 'but we have never yet had a concrete bid from them as I have never given them the chance to make one.'

The maximum wage meant no financial imperative for Charles to move, and he was happy with the extra pound per goal that Bolton slipped under the counter, but at the height of the speculation, Phil Brown managed to squeeze a concession from Charles for the *Yorkshire Evening Post*: 'He was not asking for a transfer in as many words, but he could not get away from the feeling that it would be very nice to play in First Division football. He only hoped United could take him into it.'

Charles was relying on Raich Carter for that, but found him a very different manager to the fatherly Major Buckley. Buckley believed in developing players to get the best from them; Carter held that, in soccer, you either had it or not. 'John is a natural footballer,' said Carter. 'His instincts take him into openings average players don't see. I don't think he could help going for the chances he does, because his instincts are taking him.' Carter had enjoyed the same early fame as Charles had now, and saw a lot of himself in the young player; but when Carter was Charles' age, he was winning the First Division, and FA Cup, and he couldn't resist pulling on the gold-and-blue jersey and showing off alongside Charles in a series of friendlies that autumn. Elland Road's new floodlights attracted 31,000 to a game against Hibernian, who saw Charles score two goals, but when he left the field for stitches in a head wound all eyes were on Horatio Carter, his silver hair flashing beneath the brightest floodlights in the country. He all but scored one of Charles' goals, scored two himself, and Richard Ulyatt wrote: 'Were Carter able to stay in the side for league matches, I should tip them for promotion.'

Carter also enjoyed showing how soccer should be played in training, while lavishing the young pretender Charles with the sort of star treatment that developed the arrogant streak behind Carter's own career. It might have motivated Carter, but it was not the right approach with the shy, polite and unfailingly gentle John Charles. Charles, who thought First Division football would be 'very nice' but wouldn't disrupt anybody to get it, wanted to do his best for the team and win matches; being Carter's golden boy was embarrassing, and he was acutely aware of the disquiet it was causing among his teammates, who despite all his talent and fame had never been jealous of John before.

Charles could not have done more for the team. Despite starting 1954 with an incredible 7-1 home win over Leicester City, the division's clear leaders, Leeds couldn't lift themselves above mid-table and finished 10th, the same as under Buckley the year before. Carter's new emphasis on attacking meant a record-breaking season for Charles, who in 39 games scored 42 of United's 89 goals; but goals against increased from 63 to 81, and Carter could offer nothing to help his beleaguered defence.

'I am no "creeper",' Carter told the Annual General Meeting. 'We have not got a good side, but we have a useful one. One that will not be relegated and one that will do quite well, but it needs improvement. I don't want to spend your money, I want to make some for you. But I do hope the day will come when I can afford to spend, say, £20,000.'

Carter had to stick with Buckley's players, but some of them could only stand his criticism for so long. The new season opened with a 2-0 away win at Hull, but the next five games were lost with sixteen goals conceded, and after a 5-3 defeat at Bury the long-serving captain, Tommy Burden, revolted. Carter was placing the usual vociferous blame on goalkeeper John Scott, and Burden, who felt the manager was happy enough taking all the credit when things went right, told him it was time he started taking responsibility when things went wrong: 'You're the one who's bloody well to blame.'

It was a home truth, and not welcome in Carter's dressing room. Burden was immediately transfer-listed and soon sold to Bristol City; for family reasons, he had spent his six years at Leeds commuting from the south-west, and the press were told he now wanted to be closer to home. But in all that time he had missed just eight league games, served as captain, and guided the development of John Charles and Eric Kerfoot; his dedication to Leeds United was irreplaceable. But even if these were Buckley's players, this was now Carter's team; Scott followed Burden out of the side, replaced by youngster Roy Wood.

Carter now had to make changes, and made arguably an even bigger call than selling Burden, by moving Charles back to centre-half, alongside Kerfoot and Keith Ripley. He surprised many by giving Charles his pal Burden's role as captain; Charles accepted with his usual mixture of pride and embarrassment. He had the desired effect at the back and form improved, but despite the honour of being captain, despite moving to his preferred position, and despite spending Saturday watching a reserve game with United's vice-chairman and Sunday being treated at Elland Road for a groin injury, on a Monday morning at the end of September Charles handed in a written transfer request. 'I want to play in the First Division,' he said. 'I have no quarrel with United, but it is my ambition to get into the highest level of soccer.'

'I am dumbfounded,' said Carter. 'I am staggered,' said Sam Bolton. Leeds were due to play another friendly match with Hibernian on the Wednesday night, and announced they would consider Charles' request before the game. Burnley, Sheffield Wednesday and Glasgow Rangers were interested, Arsenal asked to be notified immediately if the request was accepted, and Cardiff City manager Trevor Morris arrived by train and sat outside the boardroom, ready to do business.

He faced a long wait, for there was much to discuss. United's reflexive stance of refusing to listen to offers was under pressure now the player, whose loyalty had been exemplary, had put his wish to leave in writing. An unhappy captain being kept at Elland Road against his will was a new thought, and if he refused to sign again at the end of the season, Leeds might be forced to put Charles on the transfer list anyway.

Then came the question of his value, and the long-term future of the club. For five years Charles had been their jewel; not only the greatest player in Leeds United's history, but now one of the best in the world. That was hard for a Second Division club to give up; the previous season, when Charles was missing from Elland Road to play for Wales, the attendance dropped by almost 10,000. But Charles alone was not enough; even with the greatest player of his generation in the team, Leeds rarely got the gates they needed to break even. He seemed unappreciated in the city, where casual supporters wanted United to spend large fees on star players, not realising that no star could be brighter than one they'd signed for nothing. There were even some who thought he was unwittingly keeping crowds away; Charles was so good he made the other players look worse than they were, giving spectators the impression that Leeds were a bad side.

'Where are the soccer fans?' Carter had been asking. 'I understand that over a million people live within twenty miles of Leeds. What's happening to all the men folk? Do they all go to bed on Saturday afternoons? Our critics want us to buy star players but they cost a lot of money. If only we could get some more support.'

Charles couldn't bring in the crowds, and he couldn't make the players around him good enough for promotion; and while Carter dreamed of spending £20,000 on players, he had to replace Charles up front with Harold Brook, a 32 year old signed from Sheffield United for £600. Carter did not share Buckley's passion for trawling the country for junior gems. If he was given the money to buy one very good striker and one very good centre-half, instead of owning only one brilliant Charles, Carter felt he could give Leeds promotion.

For now, a man from Cardiff was sitting in the corridor waiting to give Leeds £50,000. He waited for almost three hours, and then was told, no. The crowd, albeit only 12,500 of them, were also told, to loud cheering. And John Charles, preparing to play against Hibs, was called into the boardroom and told his request was being refused. 'What can I say in the circumstances?' he said to Richard Ulyatt before the match. Leeds lost 3-1, and the game was not one of Charles' best; he had been waiting even longer than Cardiff's manager for a decision, time filled with interviews and film crews at his home. They even filmed him in the changing rooms, shaking hands with Carter as his teammates looked on; Charles was all smiles, but not disguising his disappointment. 'I am still anxious to play First Division football,' he told Ulyatt after the match. 'But what can I do? I was called into the meeting and told the club would not let me go. I was not really surprised.'

He did not withdraw his request, but he did not let the decision, or the upheaval of the month since Burden's outburst, upset him or the team. Charles always heeded the advice given him by Jack Pickard, the scout who sent him from Swansea: 'When you report to Leeds, listen to all the coaches and say nowt.' He had a job to do, and if he couldn't get a transfer to the First Division, he could still try his utmost to take Leeds there. With captain Charles at centre-half, Leeds only lost one of seventeen games from September to Christmas, taking them to the top of the table. Performances were not in the class of champions, but results were. Brook was excellent alongside Albert Nightingale in the attack, while Wood in goal, Grenville Hair at full-back and Kerfoot and Charles in the half-back line were giving Leeds stout foundations.

They struggled to maintain consistency through winter, but the whole Second Division seemed to be suffering the same, and just six points separated the top ten at the start of April. Reporters tried writing off United's chances for lacking quality, but began admiring their determination. Promotion would be a battle, and Carter found reinforcements, signing 31-year-old inside-forward Jock Henderson from Rotherham, and promoting two of Buckley's boys, Archie Gibson at right-half, George Meek at left-wing. With Charles in brilliant form in defence, Leeds were top of the table with a game to go. They won 3-1 at Fulham, but it wasn't enough; too many teams had too many games in hand, and with their fixtures complete, United could only watch Birmingham City and Luton Town taking 1st and 2nd places. Leeds finished 4th, a point behind the promoted teams.

There was regret at the early season's poor form, and disappointment at the eventual failure, but hope that United could maintain their late season surge into the new campaign; Carter was given a three-year contract to repel enquiries from Derby County. Cardiff made their regular November offer for John Charles, and were told their regular 'no', but in January they got some joy from Elland Road, winning 2-1 in the FA Cup.

Charles was again the totem around which Carter was building his team, but now Carter didn't seem sure what to do with him for the best. It was simple enough to carry on with the same side, and five wins in the first two months were a decent return. An injury to Archie Gibson caused the first change, Charles moving to right-half and young Jack Charlton taking over at centre-half, but a lack of goals soon had Charles wearing number nine again. United conceded fifteen in the next five games, prompting calls for Charles to go straight back to the defence.

Carter ignored them. When Gibson returned from injury he continued his improvement into a quality right-half, while Wood was another young player becoming established in goal. The remarkably consistent defenders of Buckley's days were still going; between them Jimmy Dunn, Grenville Hair and Eric Kerfoot had missed just 26 of 572 games. And Jackie Charlton, given his debut in Major Buckley's final match, had returned from National Service gangly, opinionated and ready to assert himself in place of John Charles.

Charlton solved one problem for Carter, making his mind up that Charles should play in the attack. Charlton was no longer the awkward seventeen year old who had started his first game without any advice from his

1. Leeds City, 1914/15 season. Back (left to right): George Law, Mr. J.C. Whiteman (Director), Tony Hogg, Frederick Blackman, John Hampson, Mick Foley, Mr Herbert Chapman (Secretary-Manager), Jack McQuillan. Front: R. Murrell (Trainer), Ivan Sharpe, John Jackson, Billy McLeod, James Speirs, Ernest Goodwin, Valentine Lawrence.

2. Leeds United, 1920/21 season. Back (left to right): Jim Baker, R. Murrell (Trainer), Ernie Hart, Billy Downs, Mr Baker (Director), Ralph Rogerson, Mr Hilton Crowther (President), Jimmy Walton. Front: George Mason, Bert Duffield, Tommy Howarth, Merton Ellson, Basil Wood, Jimmy Frew.

3. Ernie Hart,
Leeds United
centre-half
(1921–36).
Colorsport/Shutterstock

4. Tom Jennings,
Leeds United
centre-forward
(1925–31).
Colorsport/Shutterstock

5. Willis Edwards, Leeds United wing-half (1925–43) and manager (1947/48).
Colorsport/Shutterstock

6. Tom Holley, Leeds United centre-half (1936–49).
Colorsport/Shutterstock

7. Major Frank Buckley, Leeds United manager from 1948 to 1953.
Colorsport/Shutterstock

8. John Charles is mobbed by young supporters as he runs into Elland Road following a training run, August 1962.
Gordon Priestley/Associated Newspapers/Shutterstock

9. Horatio 'Raich' Carter, Leeds United manager from 1953 to 1958.

Associated Newspapers/ Shutterstock

10. Left to right: Alan Shackleton, Wilbur Cush, Don Revie and Jack Charlton (August 1959).

Colorsport/Shutterstock

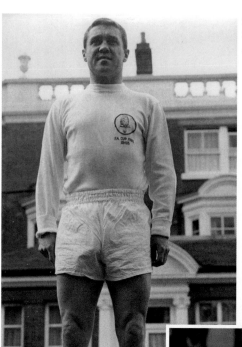

11. Bobby Collins models the 1965 FA Cup final kit.
Associated Newspapers/Shutterstock

12. Norman Hunter ahead of the 1960/61 season.
Colorsport/Shutterstock

13. Paul Reaney,
aged seventeen in 1962.
*David Thorpe/
Associated Newspapers/Shutterstock*

14. Billy Bremner at Manchester
Airport, October 1966.
*Barry Greenwood/Associated
Newspapers/Shutterstock*

15. Albert Johanneson at Wembley, a couple of
days before the 1965 FA Cup final.
Associated Newspapers/Shutterstock

16. Don Revie, August 1961.
Colorsport/Shutterstock

manager; Eric Kerfoot had spotted his confusion and told him: 'Son, they've picked you because they think you're good enough. Now go and prove them right.' He was now two years older and thought himself at least two years more worldly; it would be a brave man who called Charlton 'son' now. He was always head-strong; when he was fifteen, he walked out of the local coal pit that employed almost everybody in Ashington, Northumberland, telling them: 'Nah – I'm not going to do it.' Serving in the armed guards had introduced him to beer, cigarettes, women, and the idea that rather than proving anybody else right, he would go further by proving himself right. Reputations didn't matter; he had taken the number five shirt from the great John Charles, and wasn't giving it back. Near the end of one match, Charles began organising the defence of a cor-ner. Charlton told him abruptly to clear off back up the field. 'We've been handling this all game, we don't need you here!' After the match Charles told Charlton, in no uncertain terms, and with the upstart's back pinned high against the dressing room wall, never to speak to him like that again.

Another young player, Jack Overfield, became a reg-ular on the left wing, aiming cross after cross at Charles' head; but Carter couldn't find a steady combination in attack and moved Harold Williams, Albert Nightingale, Keith Ripley, Bobby Forrest, Peter Vickers and George Hutchinson in, out and around the forward positions.

Again inconsistency didn't hold Leeds back; a 2-1 win over runaway leaders Sheffield Wednesday, watched by 43,268 at Elland Road, put Leeds up to 5th, and just six points separated 2nd place from 12th. But three defeats and a draw put Leeds down to 9th, including a 2-1 loss to Blackburn Rovers at Elland Road. That was United's first home defeat since September 1954, a proud record of 34 matches that was sustaining their ambitions; always solid and sometimes brilliant at home, they only won away twice all season. 'Yelland' Road's fortress-like invincibility had been pierced at the worst moment.

It was the moment for Carter, finally, to find a combination that clicked. Brook took over at centre-forward, and Nightingale returned at inside-left. Meek came in on the right wing to balance Overfield on the left, and the forward line suddenly became productive around a change Carter had made a month earlier: moving Charles to inside-right.

At centre-half and left-half, it was hoped Charles could still influence the attack from the defence. Moving to inside-right, the midfield position where Carter had played, Charles was able to influence the defence from the attack, shaping matches not with the hidden subversion Carter had, but with the dominance his physique and skill allowed him. Charles could break up opposition attacks with his strength and pace, build up a counter-attack with his intelligent reading of play, and score, with a thunderous shot from anywhere near the goal. Against Sheffield Wednesday he was man-marked, but Richard Ulyatt called it 'the best game Charles has ever played for Leeds United ... Charles was the complete footballer in defence and attack.'

Leeds returned to form in a 4-2 win over Plymouth, Charles scoring twice, and he scored ten more as Leeds rose up the table. Crowds also rose from just 12,348 to see the match against Plymouth, to 49,274 for the final home game of the season, a 2-1 win over Bristol Rovers that took Leeds above them into 2nd place on goal average. Two days later they travelled to Rotherham United, along with thousands of fans, who crowded the pitch and climbed a nearby crane to get a view of two Nightingale goals that opened the gap above Bristol Rovers to two points. One more point would make sure.

For the fourth match in a row Carter named an unchanged lineup, and took them to Hull City's Boothferry Park. Without Carter, his old club had lost their grip on Second Division football and were already relegated, but if they were not much competition, Leeds still had to face their own nerves, and the expectations of their fans. More than half of the 31,000 in the ground had come from Leeds, pouring from the railway station behind the East Side terrace long after kick-off. Charles gave Leeds an early lead but Hull equalised, and after an hour's play the score was 1-1, when George Meek was fouled in the penalty area. For seven years John Charles had seemed immune to the drama around him, a full participant in every match and every situation, but somehow on a different plane, out of the reach of ordinary circumstances. He could score from anywhere, and he could certainly score from twelve yards; fans said later that if Hull keeper Bernard Fisher hadn't ducked, Charles' penalty would have taken his head off.

Meek set Brook up for two goals in the last fifteen minutes, giving Leeds a 4-1 win, and the fans an excuse to charge onto the pitch and embrace their heroes. The players toasted their achievement in the dressing room, Raich Carter filling teacups with champagne, and were toasted on their return to Leeds by a crowd of 2,000 outside the Civic Hall. Sam Bolton, Raich Carter and the Lord Mayor made speeches, but it was John Charles they wanted, and what they got was his usual modesty. 'With the support you have given us, we have done very well. Promotion is a great thing.'

That was underselling its significance. Leeds might not have been brilliant, but their home form had been, winning all but four at Elland Road, and they finished the season with style; eight wins and one defeat. Their points total was low, but the division was tough, and all that mattered was that Leeds finished with four more points than 3rd placed Liverpool. After nine frustrating seasons, Leeds United were back in the First Division, and John Charles had the stage he deserved.

10

1956–57

WHAT MORE COULD A FOOTBALLER WANT?

Leeds United's first match back in the First Division had all that was good and all that was bad about the season to come. It was billed as a gala day, the long-awaited reward for a city anxious for First Division football. 49,274 had come to the last match at Elland Road, the win over Bristol Rovers in April that sent Leeds on their way to promotion. But in August 1956 only 31,379 came to see United against visiting giants Everton. It seemed the city was taking the same stance towards Leeds United's return to the top flight as the rest of the football world: watching from afar to find out if Raich Carter's team could cope.

Carter's team started like they meant to cope and more. Jack Overfield opened the scoring after two minutes, John Charles planted his flag in the First Division with a goal, and veteran Harold Brook added three more before half-time; Leeds won 5-1, the performance of the day. There was no money to buy players, so Brook's experience was vital, but Albert Nightingale, the only other with top flight experience, was lost as Leeds won. For four seasons Nightingale's inventive spirit was an answer to anyone who accused 'Charles United' of being a one-man team, but a knee injury ended his career, aged 32.

A brilliant team performance illuminated by Charles but marred by bad luck, played in front of an enthusiastic but small crowd, that would hardly pay the bills at the Peacocks' enormous but decrepit stadium; that first match with Everton was the bare outline of the story of Leeds United in 1956/57. Events soon filled in the rest.

There was an early lesson from Tottenham Hotspur, who won 5-1 at White Hart Lane, but Leeds were 2nd by mid-September. The defence was redoubtable as ever, and through the season only conceded three more goals than in the Second Division; Jack Charlton, despite injuries, began to interest the England selectors, while Roy Wood, Jimmy Dunn, Grenville Hair, Archie Gibson and Eric Kerfoot, with Jack Marsden as Charlton's cover, were tough, and hard to ruffle. Bobby Forrest took over from Nightingale in the attack, but of course everyone was watching Charles, and of course nobody could stop him. With Overfield and George Meek crossing from the wings and Brook distracting defenders at centre-forward, Charles hit goal after goal from inside-right.

Elland Road was becoming an optimistic place; 40,010 watched Leeds beating Bolton Wanderers. United returned from Wolverhampton with a third consecutive win, two goals from Charles beating Wanderers and putting Leeds a point behind Manchester United at the top.

On the night of Monday 17 September Arnold Price couldn't sleep. He owned the fish and chip shop opposite the stadium, and his daughter Audrey had married long-serving full-back Jimmy Dunn; perhaps he was thinking over Jimmy's tale of Charles' two weekend goals at Molineux. As Monday became Tuesday, around 2am, Price was disturbed by the sky lighting up outside his bedroom window; perhaps someone at the ground had turned on the floodlights. When Price opened his curtains, what he saw sent him running into the street in his pyjamas, dashing barefoot to a telephone box. Elland Road was on fire.

There was not much to burn; there had been little money for team building, so none for building the stadium. The Scratching Shed along Elland Road itself was the same as in the 1920s; 30 or 40 shallow steps with a brick wall behind and a barrel roof above. The Kop to the north, and the Popular side to the east, known as the Lowfields, were nothing more than huge mounds of building waste and rubble topped with concrete steps, and a roof perched at the back of the Lowfields, paid for in three stages by the Supporters' Club. The same source had just funded 2,600 seats under this roof, the only seats outside the main West Stand.

The only alteration to the West Stand since it was built for Leeds City in 1906 was a forward extension of the roof in the 1920s, but under that roof was everything. The dressing rooms, the boardroom, the club offices, the physiotherapy rooms, the press rooms, the gym and the indoor running track were all there; as were the shirts, shorts, socks and boots; the balls, the goalposts, the nets, the flags, the trophies, the pennants, the mementoes, the written records; everything that recalled 50 years of Leeds City and Leeds United since the stand was built, everything that was needed for the game against Aston Villa on Saturday. And it was this stand that was burning.

Five fire engines rushed to the ground, with 40 fire-fighters, but within ten minutes of their arrival the flames had spread from end to end and high into the sky, visible for miles. Raich Carter and the club directors were called, but there was nothing anyone could do; the blaze was under control in an hour, but the damage was done. There was no formal investigation but arson was ruled out, and the probable cause was an electrical fault. In the morning, the metal frame stood stripped and charred. Everything else had gone.

'It could have been worse,' said the chairman, Sam

Bolton, that morning. 'We have got our ground and one stand left. Of course, it is a blow at this stage when we were doing so well, but the board are having a meeting tonight and we shall see what we can do. The match with Aston Villa on Saturday will definitely be played at Elland Road.'

It was, and *The Times* reported it was 'rather fun', adding that burning the old Main Stand down 'had been long overdue'. Forty pairs of new boots were bought and given to the players with strict instructions to wear them as much as possible before the game; injured players were treated in the private surgery of former trainer Arthur Campey. Jerseys, shorts, socks and balls were bought, the burnt-out stand was boarded up, and arrangements were made for the players to change at Whitehall Printeries Sports Ground behind the Lowfields Stand, and travel by bus to the back of the West Stand, where they walked through the blackened frame of the old grandstand onto the pitch.

A few fans made their way onto the concrete terraces at the front of the ruin to watch the game, and watch the players trooping back to the bus for their half-time team talk. The Leeds public had often shown its fascination for morbid events at Elland Road, turning out in large numbers during the disastrous relegation of 1947, and more came to view this game and its dramatic backdrop than had watched a win over Manchester City ten days earlier. Comforted by a local company's donation of 400 cushions, the well-to-do of the West Stand sought out the new seats at the top of the Lowfields, and even Blackie, the Leeds United cat, adopted by the ground staff and normally resident in the West Stand, turned up safe and well once the drama was over. Leeds beat Aston Villa 1-0 thanks to Charles, the constant scorer, restoring some normality.

The club had coped well in the aftermath of the catastrophe, and tried to concentrate on the positives. *The Times* was right, although burning it down was going a little far; rebuilding the Main Stand was long overdue, and the directors knew it. They admired the comparatively lavish main stand at Sheffield Wednesday, one of Archibald Leitch's best, and this was their opportunity to surpass all the grandstands erected in the previous 50 years with a lavish and modern construction that could change the tone at Elland Road, and distract from the barn-like Scratching Shed.

But the board also had to face up to reality. Leeds had lost £3,620 in the promotion season, and debts were almost £50,000. First Division football was not pulling in the gate receipts they had hoped, and now the highest-priced seats were cinders. Worse, the lack of attention to infrastructure was exposed when they checked their insurance policy. The stand was critically underinsured, and the club received around £55,000, far short of the amount needed to build a new stand, estimated first at £100,000, then £130,000, then £180,000.

It was like 1925 had come again for Leeds United; they had secured First Division football after years of trying, but having won the prize, they had to appeal to the city for urgent funds. Bolton dismissed the idea of a loan, as heavy interest payments would tie a new millstone around the neck of a club only just freed from 1925's debentures. Supported by the Lord Mayor and the city council, he appealed to business people to provide seven-year interest-free loans, and to the public to buy 1,000 twenty-year season tickets for £100 each.

There were no more illusions on the field, either. There were some big victories: 3-2 over Newcastle United, 3-1 over Sheffield Wednesday, 4-1 over Portsmouth and 5-0 over Blackpool, John Charles accounting for eight of those fifteen goals, but they were the only victories in nineteen games. Worse was a repeat of the previous season's FA Cup third round tie at home to Cardiff City. 34,237 came to the big match at the start of January, and Bolton stressed to the players that a good performance would keep the crowds they needed coming back, while a cup run would provide much-needed revenue for the new stand. He got neither. Cardiff won 2-1, and Bolton was bitterly disappointed, wondering how he was going to find the huge financial support he needed with such a lacklustre side.

Leeds were further up the table than many had expected, playing better than results showed in an unforgiving division. Away to Matt Busby's formidable young

Manchester United team in November, Leeds lost 3-2, but few could remember them playing better since the war. A week later, at home to Arsenal, Leeds were three goals down inside half an hour, but fought back in the second half. Forrest scored one and Charles got two, heading in Meek's cross to equalise with four minutes left.

But glorious defeats and hard-fought draws weren't enough to impress the public, and didn't dispel the jibes that Leeds were just 'John Charles United'. He loathed that old refrain, but as Charlton and Forrest succumbed to injuries and Brook's fitness failed, United's results didn't hide their reliance on him. In March Charles moved from inside-forward to wear number nine again; he already had 27 goals, and now added eleven of United's last fifteen, finishing as the division's top scorer, while Leeds finished 8th.

There were stories in the press about his summer plans, including a tour of Uganda, prompting an invitation from the government of Mauritius; and stories in the press asking for an end to stories in the press gossiping about John Charles and transfers. 'Charles is perfectly happy at Elland Road,' read one typical column. 'He has a nice house, a contented family, a weekday job and has scored more goals than any player in the First Division. What more could a footballer want?'

What John Charles wanted was one thing. What Leeds United wanted, desperately now, was cash to build

the new stand. On 10 April Charles captained Wales for
the first time in a 0-0 draw against Northern Ireland,
watched for the first time by Umberto Agnelli, one of
the millionaire owners of the enormous Fiat automo-
tive company in Turin, and of Turin's principal football
team, Juventus.

Former Juventus coach Jesse Carver and scout Luigi
Peronace had been singing Charles' praises for years.
Peronace first saw him in 1955 while working for Lazio,
and became a regular visitor to Elland Road and to the
Charles family at home. He would tell John and Peggy:
'You will love Italy and they will love you.' After Charles
scored in a 1-1 draw at West Ham in January 1956,
Peronace went back to Turin and told Agnelli about
'the greatest centre-forward in the world'. But Agnelli
was dubious. Italian clubs bought from South America,
not from England, and not from the Second Division;
besides, a player of the size Peronace was talking about
couldn't be very quick. He sent another scout, got
another report of Charles' excellence, and monitored his
exploits in the First Division, while watching Juventus
struggling disgracefully at the bottom of Italy's Serie A.
Eventually Agnelli went to Belfast to see Charles for
himself. 'He did not play well,' said Agnelli, 'but the
greatness was there.'

He made an offer within a week, and Sam Bolton
admitted publicly that United were listening. 'Leeds will
sell Charles to a continental club providing the offer is

substantial enough,' he said. 'And also providing Charles receives a substantial sum.'

United's refusal to sell had always relied on the Football League's maximum wage of £17 per week, and maximum signing-on fee of £10, that meant Charles would be no better off at another English club; the most a player could earn through bonuses and international match fees in an English season was around £1,700. A foreign transfer was a different matter. Agnelli was talking about a £10,000 signing-on fee for Charles, while wages, bonuses and benefits would lift Charles above the ordinary footballer's lifestyle and into the realms of the rich. That was the reason United gave for their willingness to sell. 'This is a chance of a lifetime for Charles,' said Bolton. 'Quite frankly I could not stand in his way and keep him here, as it were, a "slave."' Bolton insisted the fee would be used to buy new players, and would have nothing to do with financing the new stand.

Bolton asked Agnelli to come to Leeds to negotiate, while the wires ran hot with offers. Real Madrid denied offering £70,000 to Leeds and £30,000 to Charles. Lazio and Internazionale wanted to take Charles to Rome or Milan rather than Turin; the first, managed by Jesse Carver, were said to have offered £50,000, and representatives of the second were ready to travel from their match at Birmingham City in the Inter-Cities Fairs Cup.

The press bombarded Agnelli with questions at the airport in London; there was a more sedate conversation

on BBC Television's *Sportsview* programme, presenter
Kenneth Wolstenholme enquiring about footballers'
salaries in Italy. Agnelli retired to Claridge's Hotel, and
Wolstenholme spoke to his agent, Teddy Sommerfield,
who also looked after business affairs for Charles.
Sommerfield was an incisive negotiator, but that was
talking to film companies or the BBC; Wolstenholme
would provide the soccer knowledge. Sommerfield sent
a telegram to Charles telling him to decide nothing until
he and Wolstenholme arrived.

The Charles family home was the other centre of
attention, although the press had to be on their best
behaviour as Peggy was expecting her third child at
any moment, and John Charles, though gentle, was a
giant not to be crossed. He slipped away to room 222
in the Queens Hotel, an imposing art deco building close
enough to Leeds station for its white walls to be blackened by smoke from the trains, where he was joined by
Wolstenholme and Sommerfield, who set up telephone
lines to a lawyer and accountant in London and proceeded through seven hours of preparation for the deal
of Charles' life. The maximum wage meant agents had
not been involved in football negotiations before, but
this was different, and they examined Italian employment contracts, players' salaries, bonus structures and
local regulations. The only interruptions were hotel staff
who took Sommerfield for one of the people come to
buy Charles, and wanted either to tell him to keep his

hands off, or, if they were one of the Italians working in the hotel restaurant, to encourage his efforts.

The actual Juventus delegation had travelled by car – presumably a Fiat – to negotiate a price with Sam Bolton, director Percy Woodward and Raich Carter. The meeting took place in Hunslet, across the road from Tetley's brewery and the Salem Chapel, in the offices of the great Waddington's factory, manufacturer of playing cards, games like Cluedo and that other tense contest of economic negotiations, Monopoly. With Agnelli were Peronace and Gaetano Bolla, Fiat's general manager in the UK. Agnelli was a young man, just 22, entrusted with millions by his family, and deft; he made firm contact with Internazionale's representatives, preventing a bidding war. But abrupt and idiosyncratic Yorkshire businessmen like Bolton and Woodward were not what Agnelli was used to, and they didn't move to the hotel until 8.30pm. There, along the corridor in room 233, negotiations continued until 10.10pm, when Agnelli was finally allowed to speak to Charles.

Agnelli received Charles' entourage too, who didn't let on that Sommerfield spoke excellent Italian. Two more hours of detailed negotiations followed, and Agnelli – who was, in fact, presenting a perfectly reasonable contract – began showing the strain of a long day of travel and talk, sustaining himself with a room service order of boiled eggs, red wine and coffee. At ten minutes past midnight he was finally allowed to update the press waiting in the lobby. The deal was agreed. John Charles would play football for Juventus for the next two years.

In return, Charles would receive that £10,000 signing-on fee, paid over the length of his contract, and a salary that, at £16 a week, was smaller than his current wage, but dwarfed by bonuses: £40 for an away win, and hundreds for winning an important match. There would be an apartment and a supply of brand new Fiats, first-class travel with the team and five-star hotels. His time had come. Diligent use of his talents had brought John Charles wealth and fame, and just as important to such a sportsman, the prospect of trophies.

Leeds United got £65,000, the highest price ever paid for a British player, and just £7,000 below the world record Milan paid for Juan Schiaffino in 1954; Juventus would also visit Elland Road for a money-making friendly match in front of the new main stand, named the West Stand. Once the cheque was written, said Wolstenholme, the Leeds directors didn't hang about to toast the deal; they were straight off to the bank. Charles returned home to give Peggy the news at 1.15am, while Sommerfield and Wolstenholme stayed in room 222, triple-checking contracts until four in the morning.

It was almost unthinkable that John Charles should be leaving Leeds United, but there was a surreal interlude when it was possible to imagine he wasn't. Negotiations had run into Good Friday with a busy weekend of football to end the season, and an exhausted Charles travelled with Leeds to play in a 2-0 defeat at Sunderland. From there they travelled again, for a game at Birmingham City the next day; Leeds lost 6-2, but Charles scored both for United. Sunday was a day of rest, but on Bank Holiday Monday Elland Road said goodbye to John Charles, Sunderland captain Don Revie shaking hands with him before kick-off, then attempting to make the day about Sunderland's rescue from relegation rather than Charles' farewell.

Of course the day was all about John Charles, although there was a sad inevitability about the crowd; there were just 29,328 there, compared to 47,216 who had come to see the marvels of Manchester United play three weeks earlier. Not for the first time during Charles' time at Elland Road, it was remarked how prophets struggle for acceptance in their home town. The fair-weather fans may not have appreciated him, but the truest Leeds United fans didn't disguise their affections, cheering Charles from the moment his car arrived at the stadium, when he ran onto the field, while he played with his usual enthusiasm and grace in a 3-1 victory, and when he scored twice in front of the rising steel-work of the new West Stand; they only stopped cheering when, straining everything to reach a cross and score, he crashed into the back of the net and landed writhing in agony. Amid the anxious hush you might have heard sworn statements of concern in Italian and Yorkshire accents coming from the directors' seats, but of course Charles was okay, and the cheers continued at the end of the game when he was mobbed by the crowd on his slow journey to the dressing room; a crowd that stayed, chanting 'We want John!' for an hour, until he came to walk among them one last time.

Still he wasn't truly gone. He flew to Juventus for his medical the next day, the deal still depending on his new club avoiding relegation; a foreign signing would not be allowed in Serie B, and the Italian season didn't finish until mid-June. From Turin he flew to Holland, where Leeds United had a post-season tour, and played four more times. Of course he added six more goals, his last coming fifteen minutes from the end of a 1-1 draw with PSV Eindhoven.

Eventually, his obligations settled, his third child born and Turin ready for him, John Charles left Leeds. He had played 316 first-class matches, 162 in defence and 154 in attack, and scored 154 goals. He arrived at Juventus still wearing his Leeds United club blazer, but his new fans soon found him a black-and-white striped shirt.

11

1957–61

MY WIFE AND I DECIDED NEITHER OF US LIKED THE PLACE

Elland Road had its new main stand ready for the new season in August 1957, and Raich Carter had his new players. But he only had two, they had not cost £65,000, and neither of them was John Charles.

The stand was the most impressive addition. Built of fire-resistant steel, concrete and brick, there were 4,000 seats behind a terraced paddock where 6,000 could stand, all beneath a propped cantilever roof, one of the most advanced designs of the time. The players had new dressing rooms and an up-to-date gym. The staff had new offices, and the directors had a new boardroom and a lounge for the 100 Club, a members-only association of the club's wealthiest supporters. The grandest feature was the main entrance, three double doors beneath a clean blue facade, with three balconies and three flagpoles, and the words 'Leeds United AFC' above a relief of the city's coat of arms. It was like the executive entrance to some sleek modern factory, befitting a club that only had Sheffield Wednesday as a local rival in the First Division.

The West Stand made an impression: no expense had been spared. But it made quite a different impression on Carter, not allowed to be so lavish with rebuilding the team. Carter had spent £8,000 on inside-forward George O'Brien from Dunfermline Athletic, but that was before Charles left for £65,000. He got just £12,000 of that, to spend on centre-forward Hughie Baird from Airdrie, and the season had a predictable start. Leeds blessed the new stand's first two games with two wins, but they came among five defeats in which Leeds scored just one goal, and conceded fourteen. 'I shall be satisfied if we hold on to a place in the First Division this time,' said Carter.

Carter had several problems. First was the lack of funds, mismatched with his own expensive tastes. He had been one of the game's greatest inside-forwards, and that was the position he needed to fill; no player within United's reach could live up to Carter's standard. Then there was the problem of convincing players to come to Leeds. Carter would lead tours of the new stand, but the balconies opened onto a grim city whose centre was frequently evacuated due to poisonous smog, so that an afternoon stroll through Leeds could be like walking in a dark, deserted town. It took a fortnight, and a 60-mile drive through the Yorkshire countryside, to convince Hughie Baird and his wife that Leeds was for them. England international Ernie Taylor was desperate to leave Blackpool, but told the press in December: 'After looking round Leeds, my wife and I decided neither of us liked the place, so I am not signing for the United.'

Wilbur Cush, a small but wily player, did come from Glenavon in November for £7,000; John Kemp, an outside-left, came from Clyde; Noel Peyton, another inside-forward, took more than a month to decide to sign from Shamrock Rovers for £5,000. South African Gerry Francis, the club's first black player, was signed as an amateur for the reserves, and was not ready for the first team.

Major Buckley's painstaking and fruitful scouting system had been allowed to deteriorate, and the reserves were dry of junior talent. Carter at least had Chris Crowe, a young protégé he was using on the wing. But without Charles either prompting attacks or finishing them, the forward line looked lost and short of ideas.

It didn't help that Carter wasn't sure of his own ideas. He used seventeen players in the first nineteen games, making 34 positional changes, and although Wilbur Cush was a quality addition and soon made captain, he was switched from attack, to add bite and experience in defence. There seemed to be no structure to Carter's signings; each inside-forward he tried offered something different but not complementary to the last. There was one thing in common: they were all short. It felt as if Leeds United's forward line standing atop each other's shoulders still wouldn't reach the height of the giant John Charles. But how could they?

Looking for solutions, Carter and the directors tried to improve training methods, an area the manager had preferred to ignore. They advertised for the new post of trainer-coach and selected Bill Lambton, a former goal-keeper, an army man and fanatical about fitness, who believed in trampolining sessions to keep players supple. The papers reported the team looking 'livelier', but added a barb: 'There has not yet been any evidence of planning.'

The defence, at least, was standing up to its task: Roy Wood in goal, Jimmy Dunn and Grenville Hair the full-backs, Archie Gibson, Jack Charlton and Eric Kerfoot the halves. Charles had always relieved pressure with a well-timed goal, but now that goal wasn't coming, opposing sides were encouraged, and were attacking Leeds with more vigour than before. It was a testament of the quality at the back that they conceded 63, the same number of goals as before, only the top two teams conceding fewer. But the other column showed a severe deficit. With John Charles: 72 scored. Without: 51. Baird scored twenty of them, hard-earned; no other player scored more than eight.

Carter continued blithely on. He had lowered expectations at the start, so didn't see any reason for United's
17th place finish to reflect badly upon him. He con-
tinually deflected blame onto the directors, complaining
they had given him less than half of the fee obtained
for Charles. Jack Overfield recalled Carter moaning
that he wouldn't trust the Leeds directors to go out and
buy a packet of Woodbines, while Carter described his
own season's work as 'a very tough job satisfactorily
accomplished, in helping Leeds to recover from danger
of relegation to a very successful finish to the season'.

It was true that Leeds had won three and drawn three
of their last six matches, but the directors took a very
different view of Carter's work. His three-year contract
was ending, and they asked themselves if they wanted
to continue working with a manager who besmirched
them in the press. The Charles money had paid for debts
and, after the council refused a loan, the new stand; but
the £12,000 fee for Baird was one of the highest anywhere that year. Carter complained about money, but a
group of directors and local businessmen, led by Harry
Reynolds, had just put in a ten-year loan of £58,000 to
pay for further ground improvements and new players.
A fortnight after the end of the season, Sam Bolton told
Carter he wouldn't be asked back.

'This decision has come to me as a great shock,' said
Carter; continuing by repeating his complaints about
the loss of Charles, noting the board's decision was not

unanimous, and staking a claim for the job of managing Newcastle United. 'It has always been my ambition to reach eventually one of the plum managerial jobs,' he said. 'At Newcastle I would feel I had an opportunity second to none to exercise my ideas and my energies to full effect. Such a job, for one of the best supported teams in the country, would offer me greater scope than I have had at Hull or Leeds.'

The problem for Leeds was that, just as there had been disagreement about letting Carter go, there was no agreement about how he should be replaced. Long-serving club secretary Arthur Crowther had retired, replaced by Cyril Williamson, and four new directors were co-opted, expanding the board to ten. That meant an influx of fresh ideas, and plenty of thorny comments about the older generation outstaying its usefulness; Hilton Crowther had been re-elected at Christmas despite being ill at home in Blackpool, and died shortly after; he had been too sick to visit Elland Road for several seasons, but took great satisfaction from their promotion. But for all the new energy, there was no clarity.

Bill Lambton became acting manager, although Sam Bolton gave his actual job title vaguely as 'chief-coach-and-trainer'. He had all the duties of team manager but not the salary, and six directors were involved in team affairs with him; with no money for new players, they were backing his unorthodox training methods to bring about Buckleyesque improvements. The players, though, were far from happy. Raich Carter had always ensured their wages increased in line with the Football League's maximum, but there was now no sign of their pay rise. Without that, the players said, Lambton could forget his petty rule of training at 9.45am instead of 10am, and the directors could expect some transfer requests.

An outright revolt was averted, but the team only won three of its first seventeen matches; a reporter visiting Elland Road for a 0-0 draw with Aston Villa noted an air of depression and gloom even before the game kicked off. Buying Alan Shackleton to play centre-forward improved things after Hughie Baird was sold to Aberdeen for £11,000, but Shackleton's capture was an example of the ad hoc way Leeds were operating. Sam Bolton saw in the morning paper that Reading would be watching Shackleton play for Burnley that night, and telephoned Burnley chairman Bob Lord to find out more. He liked what he heard, so ordered Lambton to go across and watch him, with long-serving coach Willis Edwards and Maurice Lindley, the new chief scout. They were impressed enough to telephone a recommendation to Bolton during that night's board meeting, and an £8,000 deal was soon done – once Shackleton's girlfriend had been convinced of the shopping merits of Leeds.

Positive decisions were far from the norm. Some in the boardroom wanted to bring a top-class manager to Elland Road, and some, like Harry Reynolds, thought

Bill Lambton's esoteric methods would work. Eventually, in November, they decided to advertise for a manager, warning they didn't want any 'minnows' to apply; they were seeking a new Stan Cullis or Matt Busby. Arthur Turner, formerly of Birmingham City, or Bill Shankly, manager of Huddersfield Town, were said to be the men they wanted.

Instead, a week later, they got a new inside-forward, spending £12,000 to bring Don Revie back to the First Division from Sunderland, making him the costliest player in British football; the fees for his moves, from Leicester City to Hull City, to Manchester City, to Sunderland and now Leeds, totalled more than £76,000. He was no longer the tall but introverted youngster trying to learn what he could from Raich Carter at Hull. Playing for Manchester City had brought him recognition, fame, England caps and the Football Writers' Association Footballer of the Year award in 1955.

That year City, inspired by Hungary's shocking 6-3 and 7-1 demolitions of England, adopted the Hungarian style with Don Revie at the centre, or rather just behind; the 'Deep Lying Revie Plan' relied on Revie using his tactical acumen to play as a centre-forward withdrawn behind his two inside-forwards, confusing opposition defenders as he pushed and prompted with the ball from deep to create chances for his team. It caused a sensation, took Manchester City to an FA Cup final, and made Revie a household name among amateur tacticians; but a rift with his manager over a family holiday restricted the Revie plan to just one season of success. He was dropped for most of the following season, but injuries gave him another chance in the next FA Cup final; this time he was man of the match, setting up the first goal and reorganising the team to ensure the cup was won, 3-1 against Birmingham City.

After relegation, Sunderland were rebuilding with young players, giving Sam Bolton the chance to secure a player he'd wanted before he went to Hull. Revie was now 31, but his additional pedigree was more valuable to Leeds now than youth.

Revie stepped into the new-look forward line of a team that might just be on the up. Billy Humphries, a £5,000 signing from Ards, was playing well on the right wing; Shackleton scored on his debut in a 2-1 defeat at Old Trafford, then contributed a hat-trick to a 4-2 win at Blackburn Rovers; a 3-2 home win over Newcastle United followed, inspired by Revie on his debut. Leeds won four in a row, and three weeks after the board's long-awaited decision to advertise for a permanent manager, they changed their minds and unanimously gave the job to Bill Lambton.

Lambton at least knew the club and its situation, and was taking steps to put things right. He set about restoring Buckley's scouting system and returning Leeds to the find-and-develop policy that had served it during all the straitened years since 1925. Lambton and Harry

Reynolds had been watching when the BBC showed the second half of a schoolboy international match at Wembley in April, and despite England's 3-1 win, they noticed the quality of two Scottish boys, Tommy Henderson and Billy Bremner. Arsenal and Chelsea had taken them to London, and Celtic, Rangers, Aston Villa and Sheffield Wednesday were interested, but Lambton and Reynolds won their signatures with a mixture of all-expenses-paid travel from Scotland and Reynolds' down-to-earth attitude that struck a chord with Bremner in particular. They went into the junior teams, and by the end of the season Bremner was in the reserves. Nearer home, the club began paying attention to school-boys being praised by the local press: Paul Madeley of Parkside, Paul Reaney at Leeds City Colts.

But Lambton's work with the first team was not successful. Raich Carter had commanded respect; Bill Lambton inspired derision. His methods were unor-thodox because they had been developed without any knowledge of football. Apart from trampolining, there were five-a-side matches played wearing running spikes, for no logical reason, and a mysterious piece of paper Lambton was always holding; the players presumed it was meant to make him look busy. He said that with proper technique the players ought to be able to cross a heavy leather football in bare feet and not feel a thing; told to show them how it was done, Lambton hobbled away, trying to disguise his pain and blot out the laughter.

Not every situation was comic. Long-serving players Grenville Hair and Jack Overfield, and youngster Chris Crowe, asked for transfers, saying that Lambton was harming their form. His clashes with Jack Charlton were severe; Charlton was always likely to rebel against the rules, but became furious if he saw double standards. He was told only players and directors were allowed on the team coach, so had to leave two relatives behind after a game in London; two weeks later Lambton was giving a lift to four waiters from the team hotel, and Charlton told him it was either a rule for everybody or for nobody, and it was either the waiters on the coach, or Jack Charlton. 'I make the rules around here,' said Lambton, but he had long since lost that authority. 'Get them off the coach,' ordered a director, as Charlton stood fuming on the kerb. 'And get him on.'

The four wins that got Lambton the job became a distant memory. There had been only three more, compared to eight defeats, when Sam Bolton called a meeting and asked the players straight: did they want Lambton to leave? They did, even more so after he begged for another chance. Lambton resigned, after 89 days in charge, claiming 'interference by the board in my training methods'.

The team, with Revie elected captain, found three wins and a draw at the end of the season to finish in 15th place, but the board could not find a manager. Their vision of a new Cullis or Busby working harmoniously in the new West Stand offices was diminished by one look at the Scratching Shed, the ill-disciplined team, or the letters of refusal that answered their approaches to Charlie Mitten at Newcastle United and Willie Thornton of Dundee. Arthur Turner, former Birmingham City manager and the board's best hope, opted to stay at non-league Headington United rather than come into the First Division with a club such as Leeds. 'It has not been easy,' said Turner. 'Leeds are a First Division club. But I consider the Headington board can take its place with any in this country when it comes to allowing a manager to manage.'

Eventually the Leeds board found Jack Taylor, a native of Barnsley, who had done a steady job in nine years at Third Division Queens Park Rangers, often using young players taken from the Leeds area. He brought his brother Frank, who was at least a capable coach, but couldn't bring order to a squad that had lost interest in training. Nor could he fix a defence without two dependable veterans; Eric Kerfoot, now 34, left after 349 appearances; Jimmy Dunn, aged 36, left after 443. Hair, Charlton and Cush held things together, but twenty games finished with three or more goals against Leeds; at Old Trafford, Manchester United beat them 6-0.

In the attack George O'Brien was sold for £10,000, and top scorer Alan Shackleton for £8,250; he was replaced by John McCole from Bradford City for £10,000, a burly character who prowled the penalty area and scored 22 goals. Nineteen-year-old Chris Crowe was fulfilling his promise with eleven goals, but National Service took precedence and his army call-up meant a debut for seventeen-year-old Billy Bremner on the right wing. With Don Revie alongside him Bremner soon looked at home, getting his first goal in a 3-3 draw at home to Birmingham City, and Leeds took a chance by cashing in on Crowe; Blackburn Rovers paid £25,000 for him, and Taylor immediately spent £10,000 of it on defender Freddie Goodwin from Manchester United.

Leeds were in such a bad state that Goodwin could hardly believe they were in the same division as the club he'd left. They weren't for long. With barely a fight Leeds were relegated in 21st place. Taylor was distraught, taking drastic action: Cush, Gibson, Meek and Overfield were all cleared out. They hardly brought in enough money to improve the team, but Taylor couldn't afford to sell Charlton, McCole or Bremner; he needed them on the pitch. £15,000 was paid for winger and part-time nightclub singer Colin Grainger from Sunderland; Willie Bell, John McGugan, Tommy Murray and Eric Smith were all found in Scotland, and £7,000 bought Irish centre-forward Peter Fitzgerald from Sparta Rotterdam.

New players were fine, but they soon fell in with the prevailing atmosphere. Goodwin was dictating defensive systems to Taylor, senior players were slacking off from training runs to buy ice lollies, practice matches were treated as a joke, and league matches soon went the same way. Taylor couldn't even decide on a team, using four different right-backs in the first eleven games. McCole kept banging goals in, scoring twenty, but so did opposition forwards, who put 83 past Leeds. Bremner was homesick, in and out of the team; Revie was considering hanging up his boots to become a manager and, believing he brought the team bad luck, gave up the captaincy to Goodwin. Charlton was raging, as ill-disciplined as anyone, but furious at the lack of professionalism around him. Revie told Charlton he ought to get the chip off his shoulder and knuckle down. 'If I was manager, I wouldn't play you – you're always messing about,' he said. 'Well, you're not the manager,' replied Charlton. 'So what the hell?'

Results, in spite of it all, kept Leeds in mid-table, but that only made things worse. Without a crisis, there was no reason for anybody to care, and attendances at Elland Road were now dropping below 10,000. If all anyone looked at was the league position, Leeds United might have been said to be at their level: 9th in the Second Division. But for the new directors, making do would not do. In March 1961 Jack Taylor had a year left on his contract, but Harry Reynolds was ready to tell the board it was time for him to go, and took Taylor aside to tell him first. Perhaps it was a relief; Taylor took the hint and resigned.

12

1961–66

THAT ONE MAN IN A THOUSAND

That Don Revie had potential as a manager was obvious to anyone who knew his First Division and international experience, his intelligent playing style, his tactical revolution as a deep-lying centre-forward and his thoughtful character. Tranmere Rovers, Chester City, Bournemouth and Adamanstown in Australia were tempting Revie to take over their clubs, and he was keen on Bournemouth; he asked local journalist Eric Stanger and Leeds United director Harry Reynolds to send references.

Reynolds knew Revie's qualities went further than those of most players. He'd taken Revie on a scouting trip with Jack Taylor, a long car journey that must have depressed the struggling manager as he listened to Reynolds and Revie's eager conversation about the future of soccer. Bournemouth were quoted £6,000 for the player portion of the player-manager, and that made them think twice, but they would be getting a sensible and forward-thinking young manager if they hired Revie, and Reynolds was happy to say so. The Leeds board had more use for the £6,000 than for the fading reserve inside-forward.

The exact moment of Harry Reynolds' epiphany is lost to legend. Either he sent the letter, thought it over, and urgently sent another to cancel the first; or he paused in closing, read the letter through, and sent Revie's reference to the bin rather than Bournemouth. Perhaps he kept it to help persuade the rest of the board; it had persuaded him. If Don Revie could be such a good manager for Bournemouth, why couldn't he be manager of managerless Leeds? Taylor had not been replaced, as the directors were preoccupied with growing debts, but even without a £6,000 windfall, the finances worked in United's favour; they could keep Revie on his playing contract and have him take on the management duties for free, saving the time and expense of hiring somebody from outside the club. Revie would know what he was getting into, although when he was called to meet the board in March 1961, he thought it was to confirm he was getting out to Bournemouth. Instead he was offered the job at Leeds.

Who else would have taken it? As the board learned before hiring Taylor, nobody outside Beeston would come near Elland Road. Leeds United were in a desperate state. Too many people had cared too little for too long, allowing debts to pile up, the stadium to deteriorate, results to fail, players to slacken. The Peacocks had been in worse predicaments before, either closed down entirely or threatened with it, but 1961 was different; there was no imminent disaster. The club was just going through the motions, and the direction was slowly, inevitably, down.

Revie's first task, more important than results, was to get the club interested in itself again. 'If everybody pulls together,' he said, 'from the directors right down to the women who do the cleaning and the washing, and is Leeds United-minded, then we shall get somewhere.' To do that, he had to define what being 'Leeds United-minded' meant. There were parts of Leeds United's history that were instructive: the sacrifice of David 'Soldier' Wilson, the dedicated service of Willis Edwards and Ernie Hart, building from youth as advocated by Dick Ray and Major Buckley, gritty promotions achieved by hard-working teams without superstars – even counting John Charles, who put the team before himself by playing in so many positions in the Second Division for so long. But Elland Road, despite its modern West Stand, contained too many reminders of a dour and difficult past of relegations, financial struggles and misplaced loyalties.

Revie knew that, for the sake of its future, Leeds United couldn't look back. Being Leeds United-minded would mean a rejection of the past, and an embrace of the future the rest of football was enjoying.

Revie was not alone in his determination that Leeds had to do better. He inherited a small, disparate collection of frustrated individuals, inspired by soccer's progress and capable of influencing it, but yet to recognise kindred spirits in the smog. Taylor had hidden his incompetence by recruiting staff with ideas far in advance of his own. Les Cocker was the trainer, a fitness fanatic in the Major Buckley mould; but rather than esoteric experiments with gland potions, Cocker was deeply interested in physiological science, and among the first to enrol on the FA's new coaching courses. Like Buckley, he had seen action in the armed forces, but rather than officer-class detachment and an amplification system, Cocker trained his players with the blunt force intensity of a fellow soldier. There were no brogue shoes or tweeds; he was a dervish in a tracksuit and football boots, joining in training matches and mercilessly tackling frail teenagers like midfielder Norman Hunter, until Hunter got the message and was tackling him back just as hard.

Taylor paired him with Syd Owen, a former centre-half and briefly player-manager of Luton Town, who like Revie had been the Football Writers' Association Footballer of the Year; a technician who could tailor

Cocker's physical work to focus on tactical and individual improvement, at least with the club's eager youngsters, if not its cynical first team. Owen had been in charge of the staff under Taylor and oversaw the departure of Willis Edwards, after 35 years as player, manager and coach, and Maurice Lindley, the chief scout; Revie brought Lindley back as his assistant and scout, trusting him to seek and find new players for the junior ranks. These were the beginnings of a system implemented by the three coaches; players were found, strengths and weaknesses were analysed, coaching plans were detailed and sweat was prolific, as raw talents like Billy Bremner were taught how to use their abilities.

Bremner was a willing participant. Although he was the first team's youngest player at eighteen, he already felt Leeds United was not all it could be. He moved from Scotland to join a First Division football club and was, frankly, disappointed. Bremner was too young to have seen much of the football world, but he knew when something wasn't right, and Taylor's pre-match preparation for a vital relegation clash at Blackburn Rovers – stopping at a roadside cafe for beans on toast – did not feel like the right way to approach such an important match. United lost, all but confirming relegation, and Bremner's disillusion grew. He was falling far down the leagues, and feeling further away from home.

Cocker and Owen's lessons were a reason to stay, but the strongest glue was Revie. Revie had given Bremner the news of his debut at Chelsea and taken him under his wing; they roomed together, Revie showing how an international footballer gets ready for a match, with an early night and a long morning walk through London. Bremner was playing on the right wing with Revie inside, and whenever the young player was in trouble, he had Revie to take the ball, tell him what to do, and give it back.

A fatherly interest in the club's young players was important to Revie, because it had been important to his own career. His mother died when he was twelve, and he took her absence hard while growing up in working-class Middlesbrough, filling the gap with the awe he felt watching professional soccer players walking past the end of his street on their daily way to training at Ayresome Park. Following them, and his dreams, was not easy, and Revie was always grateful for a hand on his shoulder to guide him. Arriving at Leicester City aged seventeen, he loitered awkwardly around the players' entrance with his boots under his arm until club captain Sep Smith took a grip of him, a grip he didn't lessen, through coaching sessions that would often leave Revie going home in tears for all the things he did wrong, until he was doing them right.

The manager, Johnny Duncan, treated Revie like a son. When Revie was nineteen, a crunching tackle in a match against Tottenham Hotspur left him in a hospital bed. He was in the dark about his injury, thinking it might be a severe sprain, until Duncan arrived with the truth. 'They say you'll never kick a ball again, son,' he began. 'Your ankle is broken in three places. The doctors say it's a thousand to one against you ever playing again, Don.' Revie always remembered the straight gaze of his paternal manager. 'What say we make you that one man in a thousand, son?'

'I'll be that one man in a thousand if you say so, boss,' replied Revie, and he was as good as his word, playing again in nineteen weeks and becoming so much a part of the Duncan family that he married Johnny's niece, Elsie.

The need for reassurance didn't always lead Revie well; he regretted refusing a transfer to Arsenal, worried he would not be good enough, in favour of staying in the Second Division with Hull City, where silver-haired Raich Carter offered a fatherly example of how to play inside-forward. But he grew in stature, and in the eyes of those around him, until he was valued as much for his leadership as his ability, an ideal captain who would listen to and understand his players.

Revie's mission at Leeds was to make the players care about the club, and he knew that first the club would have to care about them. Getting Bremner to understand that was not easy, because all Bremner cared about was Scotland, his girlfriend Vicky, and going home to her and his family. A bid of £25,000 from Hibernian demonstrated Bremner's growing profile and offered him a route home, the Leeds board some much-needed cash, and Revie a huge headache. It was his grim duty to tell a delighted Bremner that the bid had been made and the board were considering it, and his determined task to fight the problem on three fronts. First, after finding out that £25,000 was all Hibernian could afford, he told the Leeds board they shouldn't accept a penny less than £30,000; they agreed, told Hibs the same, and Hibs promptly withdrew their offer. Second, he gave that news to Bremner, and now it was the manager who was pleased and the player who was bitterly upset, until he listened and started taking in Revie's reasons for wanting him. Revie wanted success more than anything, and he meant to succeed in everything: the league, cups, Europe. To do it, he would build a team around Bremner; he just needed Bremner to stay. Third, Revie attacked the homesickness at its source. Without telling Bremner, he began making trips to Stirling, meeting Vicky and telling her about his plans for her boyfriend, and how she could help. Revie had an advantage here; Elsie was Scottish, and he loved the country and people that Billy was missing so much. He knew how to assure Vicky that life in Leeds would not be so different, and make her understand that the rewards would be worthwhile. She was persuaded, and began talking to Billy on Revie's behalf, slowly convincing him that Leeds was the best place for him, until she and Billy were married; Revie found a house and made all the arrangements for them to be together in Leeds.

That personal touch with young players and their families was vital to filling the junior teams, where the idea of being Leeds United-minded could be planted at source. If Lindley or Owen recommended a talented schoolboy, Revie and Reynolds would travel hundreds of miles to wherever the boy called home, and having come so far, stay as long as they could. They were easy company. In villages in Scotland or Wales, they were politely entering working-class homes where Leeds had never been heard of, but their own upbringings and homeliness put a boy's parents at ease. Here were two men like themselves, so Leeds could not be all that different to home. The officials from First Division clubs could arrive with slick promises of fame and riches; but the fellows from Leeds wore their wealth lightly. Rather than giving their boy a lavish lifestyle just for kicking a ball about, Mr Revie and Mr Reynolds were extending the Leeds United family business to include the boy, his parents, his brothers and sisters. He would be well looked after and made to work hard, which was just what mum and dad wanted to hear.

The boy would find First Division standards, as far as Leeds could provide them. Revie confirmed Bremner's intuition that Leeds had not been doing things as they should. If they were to become a top club, they had to act like one, and that meant good hotels for away games instead of dingy bed and breakfasts, first-class train travel instead of cramped motor coaches, proper pre-match meals instead of the nearest greasy spoon. Making the players Leeds United-minded meant manipulating what was in their minds when they thought about Leeds United, associating the football club with the best until the two were indistinguishable.

Leeds United had never been associated with the best of anything, and Revie was prepared to force the connection. The team's jerseys were blue with gold trim, a regal combination reflecting the city's coat of arms, that adorned the breast. Revie changed all that, introducing gleaming and unadorned all-white shirts, shorts and socks, an unashamed imitation of Real Madrid. Real Madrid were the best team in the world, and fascination with them extended beyond Revie. Bremner attended their 7-3 demolition of Eintracht Frankfurt in the European Cup final at Hampden Park in 1960, one of the best performances in history by any football team, and only the fourth time the brilliant side containing Ferenc Puskás, Alfredo Di Stéfano and Francisco Gento had played on a British pitch. It was the first European Cup final broadcast live on television in Britain; Revie, Cocker, Lindley and Owen will not have missed the chance to study the great team's methods, and Revie was said to have acquired and regularly studied a film of the match.

The Football Association had feared the European Cup in the 1950s, as it had the World Cup in the 1930s, as if it might be a form of contamination; England invented the game of association football and ought not to have to prove its superiority over any nation, nor risk inferior methods damaging the purity of the English game. This stubborn attitude was punctured by Hungary and the USA's impertinent victories over England's national team. Syd Owen played centre-half for England in their 7-1 drubbing in Hungary in 1954, made to look incompetent by the deep positioning of Puskás and Nándor Hidegkuti, but seeing at the closest quarter a fascinating future for the game; Revie didn't play against them, but adapted Hidegkuti's role, amid much disdain, for Manchester City. While the FA objected to European competition, players like Bremner and young coaches like Revie, Owen and Cocker were fascinated, studying the new methods in depth, seeing in Real Madrid a message and a challenge. Their all-white kit was the easiest thing to adopt, but it was a starting point, declaring which side of history Revie wanted Leeds United to be on.

It was visible and immediate, the first thing anyone saw, but it took time for the rest of the club to catch up. Revie brought energy and ideas; above all, he cared. But in the first team he only had two really good players, and one of them, Bremner, was a homesick kid. The other was an overgrown youth who wasn't homesick, but was sick to death of everything.

After so many arguments between them as players, when Don Revie called the team together and asked them to call him 'boss' it was the worst thing that could have happened to Jack Charlton. He was 25, still obviously the best player in the team, but just as obviously no better than he had been at nineteen. If anything he had regressed, and if anybody knew it, it was him. Charlton hoped a move to Liverpool would be his salvation until the fee put them off, and still playing for Leeds now was like a prison sentence. Raich Carter taught him nothing; Bill Lambton was a joke. Jack Taylor's brother Frank, the coach, was at least a football man – 'The first guy who ever took me out on a pitch and taught me how to kick a ball properly' – but Leeds ended up at the bottom of the Second Division anyway.

Charlton was desperate for better, enrolling on the FA's technical courses at Lilleshall, the FA's football school, becoming a fully qualified coach before he was 23; but expanding his horizons only emphasised how gloomy the skies were over Leeds' training pitches on Fullerton Park. Les Cocker and Syd Owen should have been kindred spirits, but Charlton stubbornly refused to conform; how could they be good coaches, if they were stuck here with him in Division Two? Jack thought he could coach better himself, and made that clear; he treated Cocker with contempt, and threatened to 'take his coat off' to Owen, telling Revie that if Owen didn't stop telling him what to do, he wouldn't be responsible for his actions.

Revie, the goody-two-shoes captain who had told Charlton that if he was manager he wouldn't pick him, was now in a position to do just that. Instead, he offered Charlton the captaincy; Charlton turned it down. He also moved Charlton to centre-forward, hoping to recreate the John Charles effect; Charlton scored a few goals but fought the decision, never comfortable in attack. Being shoved out of position was, to him, just another example of how his chance of ever being somebody in football was being taken away by the fools around him.

Charlton knew too much already about wasted talent. His younger brother Robert was playing in the First Division for Manchester United and internationally for England, fêted as one of the best midfield players in Europe; he was part of a brilliant young team, assembled by Matt Busby, that looked destined to win the European Cup. That dream ended on a frozen runway in Munich in 1958 when, travelling back from a match in Belgrade, Manchester United's aeroplane crashed on take-off, killing eight players, three staff, eight journalists and two others. Jack was almost back in Ashington, rushing to his parents' home, when he heard his kid brother had somehow survived; when Jack and his mother collected him from London several long weeks later, Bobby told them everything he could remember about the crash as they drove north, then asked never to speak about it again. Through Bobby, Jack was friends with all the players who died; you didn't have to tell him about wasted talent. This was the atomic age and the Cold War era, when optimism was clashing with fatalism, when if the H-bomb didn't get you, a tragedy like this might. Who had time to waste their best years playing football for a fool like Don Revie, at a club like Leeds United?

Revie's attempts to introduce equal pay, with bonuses based on attendances, were the last straw for Charlton. There had been no improvement in results in the first two months with the new manager, and too many miserable games at centre-forward. Revie was sticking with the same bunch of players, relying on Charlton's enemies Cocker and Owen to improve things; and now, Charlton calculated, his wages were being cut. He'd had enough; his brother had let Matt Busby know, and now Manchester United were making enquiries with the Leeds board. Charlton was delighted to be getting away at last, to a club that was recovering from disaster to retake its place as one of the biggest in the country; he refused to sign a new contract at Leeds, convinced he would be moving.

But the £26,000 Leeds wanted made Busby think twice about Frank Haydock, a 21-year-old in his own youth team. When Charlton heard, he was furious. He had been expecting to travel to Old Trafford any day to sign a contract; now, when he marched into Busby's office to find out what was going on, Busby tried to placate him, saying he might still be interested, later, but he wanted to have another look at Haydock first.

Five years of frustration exploded in Jack Charlton. His anger was fuelled by injustice; he valued fairness above everything, but never felt he was getting a fair chance to fulfil his potential. In this office, hearing those words, he realised in a moment the chances he had been given at Leeds – they took him from the pits at Ashington, paid his wages, gave him his debut, made him a First Division footballer, and suffered his petulance; now they were offering him the training, the professionalism and the ambition he yearned for, even thinking him worthy of the captaincy – and realised that he was the one not being fair. Here he was in Manchester, ready to throw it all back in their faces. And for what? For someone who didn't even want him.

'I have caused ructions at Elland Road,' Charlton told Busby. 'I have refused to sign a contract, nobody there is speaking to me. I have caused bloody havoc in the club. I have been offered a deal and turned it down. And now you're telling me I have got to wait until the beginning of the new season, until you have had a look at someone else? No. I'm not going to do that. I am going back to Elland Road, and I am going to apologise for what I have done. I'm going to sign a new contract with the club, and I'm not bloody coming here.'

Putting things right at Elland Road wasn't as easy as that. The contract was easy enough to sign, and the apology to make, but the anger remained. For blaming Charlton for conceding a goal, Revie was the missed target of a thrown half-time teacup; for playing him upfront again, Revie got all the protests Charlton could muster, until Revie put him in the reserves and told him he could go if he wanted. But Charlton was slowly coming round. When pre-season training changed to introduce competitions, Charlton made sure his group won them all. When Cocker and Owen told him something he'd already learned at Lilleshall, instead of getting angry, he recognised it was right. When Revie brought him back into the side at centre-half he was a revelation, and by the end of the season, it was Revie who was apologising. 'I'm sorry about what I said last year,' he said. 'When I told you that you were not my type of player. You've made yourself one of the best centre-halves in England. If you keep going like that, you'll play for England.' Revie, as Charlton always thought, talked nonsense. But this was the kind of nonsense he would listen to.

Putting the rest of the team right wasn't easy, either, and Don Revie had also been to Matt Busby's office. Within a week of taking his new job, Revie crossed the Pennines for an audience with the man he regarded as the best manager in England; the only one with a team close to Real Madrid. As he was with Raich Carter, Revie was the willing pupil, but it was Busby who was impressed; as much as advice, what he gave was a seal of approval to Revie's instinctive idea that building from youth was the only way for his debt-laden club to grow.

Get all the teams playing the same way; the first, the reserves, right through the juniors. Fill from the bottom with talented, quick-learning kids. Create a culture that makes even the youngest player Leeds United-minded. Tend it every day like a garden, and wait for it to grow.

Waiting was the hardest part. Revie was making a disciple out of Charlton and just about stopping Bremner from running away to Scotland – or worse, to Arsenal, who were making tempting offers to the board – but apart from Grenville Hair, an institution for ten seasons at full-back, only Albert Johanneson offered any hope on the pitch. Johanneson was the club's second black player, a South African like Gerry Francis, recommended to Leeds United in a schoolteacher's letter from Johannesburg; and good enough, after arriving in Britain and taking part in training, for Revie to sign him and put him straight in the team. Johanneson made the wing lively; he was fast, direct, had tricks defenders hadn't seen and scored more goals than many centre-forwards. But the rest of the team was as stale as Johanneson was fresh. In the second half of Revie's first full season United were bottom of the table, and Revie didn't know what would come first: relegation to Division Three, or the sack.

Harry Reynolds also had doubts, but not about Revie. The question for the board was whether to wait for the work being done with schoolboys to develop – a process that could take years of losses they couldn't afford – or to hang the expense, find what money they could, rescue the team from relegation and throw everything at promotion.

With relegation looming, they bought players. Revie wanted six but got three: Ian Lawson, Cliff Mason and Bobby Collins, a forward, a defender and a midfielder. They added enough to keep Leeds in the Second Division, just; five consecutive draws and a final-day win salvaged the cause. Then, while not disregarding Revie's efforts with the youths – Reynolds still had the confidence to let Revie do things his way – the board did something its way, spending £53,000 to buy John Charles.

It took three months of very public, high-profile negotiations to bring King John back from exile. His years in Italy had been extraordinary: in his first season Juventus were transformed from also-rans to champions, Charles' 28 goals making him Serie A's top goalscorer. He helped Juventus win two more league titles, the Coppa Italia twice, and reach the quarter-finals of the European Cup. He scored 108 goals in 155 games and earned the adoration of the fans; they called him *Il Gigante Buono*, the Gentle Giant, for his habit of stopping games to tend to an injured opponent, despite being kicked into hospital several times himself. He had become a pop star with a recording of 'Sixteen Tons', part-owned a restaurant, and mixed with film stars like Sophia Loren.

It was all very different to Leeds, and that thought never left him; he had been talking about coming home since the end of his first season. Partly it was professional pride; Charles had learned to enjoy the limelight, and while he was great friends with forward Omar Sívori, he didn't always like how Juventus were playing to Sívori's strengths rather than his. Juventus had also made it difficult for Charles to play internationally for Wales. But there were personal reasons too; he missed home, and he and Peggy wanted to raise their children in Britain.

Juventus chairman Umberto Agnelli offered Charles another fortune to stay, and only agreed with great reluctance and out of respect for Charles to meet Leeds at the airport in Turin to discuss their offer. But he made a crucial mistake by taking Charles with him, above the protests of Leeds, who weren't used to a player being involved in negotiations. Revie seized his chance, charming Charles into his team, describing how they would play to King John's strengths, how many goals Johanneson and Bremner would lay on with tempting crosses, how celebrated the prodigal son would be when promotion was achieved. Charles was persuaded: he was going back to Leeds. Agnelli was aghast: he resigned, but that didn't make it any easier. The weeks that followed were tense and confusing; United were making a statement, paying a huge fee for one of the world's greatest players, its own son and king, but it was all at risk from Anglo-Italian communication, a scrum of interested clubs, Agnelli's desperation to keep his star player, and Charles' insistence on Juventus properly paying out his contract.

The Leeds directors were relieved when Charles was finally at Elland Road in front of the press photographers, but Harry Reynolds was about to make owning Charles even harder than signing him. The directors personally paid the £53,000 fee in cash, and with the club owing large debts already, they wanted their money back as soon as possible. Calculating the excitement Charles' return would generate, Reynolds increased season ticket prices from £7 7s, to £10. Leeds had just finished nineteenth in Division Two and were now charging almost £2 more than first-division Manchester United; they would be the most expensive team to watch outside London.

The reaction in Leeds was easy to predict for everyone but Reynolds. It had been a struggle to get people to watch Charles in his youth, when prices were fair; the enthusiasm for his return as a 31 year old was killed at a stroke by Reynolds' prices, replaced by a storm of protests and petitions. Reynolds doubled down, accusing the public of wanting something for nothing, and not being interested enough in football in the first place, then increasing the standing prices too, by 150 per cent. Charles' return was supposed to herald a wonderful new age for Leeds United as he led them back to the First Division; instead, Reynolds was told, all he was arranging was a funeral, to which nobody could afford to come.

By the time low gates and bad publicity forced Reynolds to see sense, reduce prices and grovel to the city, reports were circulating about the returning star player's first few games that were unlikely to encourage fans to watch him at any price. Charles was overweight and unfit, and although Les Cocker might do something about that, it was harder to fix his game. In Italy Charles had become used to more brutal centre-halves but slower rhythms; against hectic Second Division defences, spear-heading a team Revie wanted to be quick and aggressive, Charles looked ponderous and easy to read. He scored three goals, but opponents soon got the hang of him. Clearly struggling, he tried a game in defence, where he always felt most at home, and was superb, but nobody could support that solution; if £53,000 was largesse for a goalscorer to attract the crowds, it was an absurd price for someone to stop Second Division forwards.

'I have reached the stage now where I can't sleep at nights,' Charles said, after his seventh consecutive game without a goal. 'This is the first time my football has left me for so long. It was a mistake to come back.' He was missing Italy, and Peggy was too; they were realising British education might not outweigh sun-drenched holi-day homes after all. The whole enterprise was a failure, but the Leeds board showed unusual enterprise in solv-ing it; within a fortnight of his first match, they discreetly fed stories of Charles' unhappiness to the press in Italy, where his fame was still larger than any worries about form or fitness. United's £53,000 buy became a £65,000 sale to Roma, Leeds ending in profit on a deal that had threatened to bankrupt them.

The board's bank of ideas was now well and truly empty, and they turned back to Revie to find a new way forward. Revie, in fact, hadn't stopped searching. The interlude with Charles was a distraction; a goalscoring talisman would have been useful, but Revie had signed his king the previous March. Ten inches shorter and less than half the price, inside-forward Bobby Collins arrived from first-division Everton with international pedigree and a bad mood; aged 31, he could not believe manager Harry Catterick was letting him leave. He dropped a division to join Leeds almost out of spite, determined to prove Catterick wrong.

Doing that required winning, and winning all the time, and all Don Revie's plans for changing the culture at Elland Road now took human form; small, Scottish, furious, violent and exceptionally skilful form. Rules limited the amount of tactical instruction managers could give during a match; in Collins, Revie found a player to take that responsibility, with a motivational force few of United's lackadaisical or inexperienced players had encountered before. The youngsters were in awe of him; the older ones were terrified. And with Collins running things on the pitch, Revie no longer had to wait to promote his most promising young players from the reserves.

One had already made an unscheduled appearance. Gary Sprake, a confident and athletic goalkeeper from Wales, was roused from his bed and rushed to

Manchester Airport when Tommy Younger was taken ill before a game at Southampton. Sprake was also ill on the two-seater aeroplane the club found to rush him to the south coast, where the game was delayed by fifteen minutes so he could make kick-off. Air sickness left him so weak Revie had to carry him from the plane to the police escort that took him to the stadium, and his day didn't improve until the evening, when he finally put away a mixed grill before boarding the train back to Leeds. In the meantime, a Southampton player knocked him out cold for two minutes, Freddie Goodwin scored an own goal past him, and Southampton scored three others he could do nothing about in their 4-1 win. He was sixteen years old, and if there was any danger of such a first-team debut going to his head, it ended when he was back at work scrubbing the team bath on Monday morning.

Sprake was now seventeen, and in September 1962 he joined the first team again for a less hectic journey to a match at Swansea Town, along with Norman Hunter, aged eighteen; Paul Reaney, seventeen; and Rod Johnson, also seventeen. They thought they were going to watch and learn, until Revie gathered them together under the main stand and told them they were all joining nineteen-year-old Billy Bremner in the team that day. 'Get out there and just do what you're good at,' he said.

Revie's meticulous planning, Cocker and Owen's exhaustive training, and Charlton, Hair and above all

Collins taking responsibility on the pitch meant that once their nerves had settled, the transition from the reserves to the Second Division was seamless, even for such young players. Sprake kept a clean sheet and only missed three more games that season. Reaney, a quick full-back who didn't know how to be flustered, only missed one. Hunter, whose relentless tackling in midfield became such a topic of conversation in training that he was moved to defence and bulked up on a diet of sherry, eggs and bone-crunching tackles from Cocker, didn't miss a game until March 1965. Johnson, a nimble striker, scored but was taken off injured, so couldn't secure himself as Charles' replacement. Bremner scored the other goal in a 2-0 win; he had played with the younger four in the juniors and reserves, and lived in digs with Hunter, but was practically an old pro by now.

Bremner's youth occasionally showed through, and another of his sorrowful escapes to Scotland gave another youngster his debut; Peter Lorimer, one of the most sought-after schoolboys in football, played on the wing in a 1-1 draw with Southampton, aged fifteen years and 289 days. More and more often, young players were popping into and not always out of the first team; nineteen year old Mike Addy and sixteen year olds Barrie Wright and Jimmy Greenhoff were each given short spells, and after making good progress at St Mirren, Bremner's nineteen-year-old mate Tommy Henderson was brought back from Scotland to play on the right wing.

After the fiasco with Charles, Collins led the young players up the table to 10th, when an unusually harsh winter became a short-term curse but a long-term blessing. The north was frozen, and so was football; United couldn't play from 22 December to 2 March, stopping any momentum towards promotion, and freezing the already slow cashflow. But there was plenty to learn during two intensive months of fitness work with Cocker, and focused practice with Owen, Revie and Collins to the fore, drilling the three Cs – confidence, concentration and courage – setting the standards that the young players with a taste of first team action, or waiting for a chance like Paul Madeley and Terry Cooper, were expected to put into practice when the season restarted.

Nineteen games had to be played in eleven weeks, making promotion too great a challenge, but their surge up the table to finish 5th, followed by another new-style pre-season of competitive fitness training and practice, put Leeds in good shape for 1963/64. Confidence in the manager again overruled common sense with the bank, as Revie was allowed to spend £33,000 to sign John Giles. Giles was another First Division recruit, this time from Manchester United, another who felt aggrieved to learn, weeks after winning in the FA Cup final, that he wasn't wanted. Giles felt a certain amount of relief getting away from Old Trafford; he hadn't enjoyed the atmosphere playing for Matt Busby, and felt Leeds United, despite their Second Division status, now had the more professional setup. But like Bobby Collins, although without so much hot whisky and language, he was desperate to get back to the top; he privately swore he would 'haunt' Busby. He was not quite 23, young enough to fall under Collins' dynamic spell – playing with him was another reason to join – but experienced and capable enough to add immediate quality and leadership on the right wing.

That meant Revie could move Bremner to where he now felt he belonged, to Jack Charlton's right in the half-back line, where the thunder that Collins' influence had unleashed in the youngster would be more dominant than on the wing. Hunter was to Charlton's left, with Reaney behind them partnering Willie Bell, another player Revie had moved around, finding his best position after three inconsistent seasons. Revie had a talent for this; young players were now signed for their attributes, and coaching would uncover their proper place on the pitch. The midfield was solid, with Don Weston and Ian Lawson helping Collins supply Johanneson and Giles on the wings. Once the season was under way, it was clear Revie had built the best United team in years; they reached the top of the table in October, in the middle of twenty unbeaten games.

If there was concern, it was in attack. Leeds started with Jim Storrie at centre-forward, signed from Airdrie for £15,000 while everyone – including Storrie – was excited about the return of John Charles. After Charles left Storrie became United's number nine, scoring 25 goals; and while in the new season he only scored two in his first nine games, his aggressive running into the penalty area always created opportunities for others. After Storrie was injured Revie couldn't find a replacement that worked, swapping between Weston and Lawson, while the team turned to left-winger Johanneson for goals. Johanneson was brilliant, withstanding the kicks that came for his skin colour as much as his skill, but the workmanlike team around him meant there were few routes to goal other than his and Weston's outright speed. The defence was the best in the division, but for scoring Leeds were mid-table. A second defeat of the season, along with an increasing number of draws, allowed Sunderland to overtake them at the top, with Preston North End just a point behind.

Leeds still needed the centre-forward they'd thought John Charles would be, but all the options looked as expensive or risky as he had been. But attendances were now regularly over 30,000 – though still dropping to 21,000 if the opposition weren't up to much – and with fourteen games between Leeds and a promotion that could transform the club, Reynolds was willing to gamble. For £53,000, the same price as John Charles, plus £5,000 on promotion, Leeds bought Alan Peacock from Middlesbrough; a tall 26 year old who played for England in the 1962 World Cup and was once prolific, now trying to prove himself after a serious knee injury.

Middlesbrough didn't believe in him, and preferred to take the money; Revie offered belief by the bagful, and once Johanneson and Giles discovered Peacock's heading ability and how to aim their crosses, goals followed. In those fourteen crucial games, Peacock scored eight.

He arrived just in time. Going for promotion wasn't quite uncharted territory for the young team, as they had tried the season before; but then they had failed. Suspension denied them Bremner for three matches, unsettling a defence suffering through injuries to Jack Charlton and his experienced deputy Freddie Goodwin; nineteen-year-old Paul Madeley and seventeen-year-old Jimmy Greenhoff were used, as was 32-year-old Grenville Hair; injuries to Johanneson meant the introduction of nineteen-year-old Terry Cooper. Collins, relentless, was holding the team together; but Charlton's return after fourteen games out was vital.

A 2-0 defeat at Preston brought Leeds close to failure; it put the two teams level for second place, two points behind Sunderland. But Leeds had the better goal average, and were prepared to defend their promotion place. Four consecutive wins lifted them to first as they fought back into form; a draw at mid-table Derby County let Sunderland close in, but against Newcastle at Elland Road Johanneson's match-winning skill won another vital point. With fifteen minutes left he controlled a long ball as three defenders closed in. He swept past them one by one, and as the keeper rushed out Johanneson stayed calm, slotting a shot past him for 2-1.

Preston couldn't match Johanneson or Leeds for nerve. They fell away to third, and with three games left Leeds only needed one point for promotion. Now the team had recovered its poise, that was simple. The First Division was reached inside the first half-hour at Swansea Town, Peacock scoring twice and Giles once to send Harry Reynolds to a nearby pub, bringing back champagne for the dressing room, and a promise of fish and chips on the journey home.

At Elland Road a week later Leeds were hailed as champions by a crowd of 34,275, although Reynolds and Revie may have shared bitter glances at the empty spaces where an extra 15,000 had been when Newcastle visited. The players carried a large banner to thank the fans for their support, taking a pre-match lap of honour, but they were not champions yet. They only drew against Plymouth Argyle, so in their last match, a trip to Charlton, they had to either match or beat Sunderland's result at Grimsby.

Harry Reynolds wanted to win because Leeds hadn't won a trophy since 1924, 40 long years. Don Revie wanted to win because his players deserved the title of champions. Bobby Collins wanted to win because it was a football match. And when it came to the Leeds United team, what Bobby Collins wanted, Bobby Collins got. He was the centre of everything as Peacock scored twice and Leeds won 2-0, finishing the season two points clear of Sunderland. Leeds United were Second Division champions.

13

1966–67

I'LL KILL YOU FOR THIS

Leeds United's first major football honour was a World Cup winner's medal that Queen Elizabeth II handed to Jack Charlton at Wembley in July 1966, following England's 4-2 victory over West Germany after extra time in the final. That nonsense Don Revie filled his head with at the bottom of Division Two had ended in 1965 when Charlton made his international debut aged 29, although even with a World Cup winner's medal in his pocket, Jack couldn't quite credit it. At the end of the match, with no energy left to celebrate Geoff Hurst's last-minute goal, Charlton sank to his knees, then rose to embrace the team's star midfielder, his younger brother Robert.

England's victory was a reminder that although Association Football was now the world's game, its inventors were still its masters; vindication of English methods after the embarrassing defeats by Hungary. The glory reflected well upon the Home Nations; Great Britain had the best players, the best teams, the best league, and now the best international football side in the world.

Norman Hunter and Les Cocker were at Wembley too, Hunter in the squad and Cocker the team's trainer, although neither got medals until years later. Alan Peacock had been recalled to England, and Bobby Collins to Scotland; Billy Bremner was established in the Scotland team and Willie Bell had won two caps. Gary Sprake was first-choice goalkeeper for Wales, and Johnny Giles was a mainstay for the Republic of Ireland.

Leeds United players were at the heart of British football's pomp, but while the nation's eyes filled with tearful pride as Bobby Moore lifted the Jules Rimet trophy, the nation preferred to avert its gaze when it came to Leeds, if they weren't regarding the club and its achievements with outright disgust.

Don Revie's side made an immediate and lasting impact after being released from the purgatory of Division Two. United's team was better than most of the First Division, and Revie resisted adding any new players, promoting from within as Jimmy Greenhoff, Paul Madeley, Terry Cooper, Rod Belfitt and Rod Johnson came of age. By January 1965 Leeds were top of the First Division, two points ahead of Chelsea and Manchester United. All three teams were chasing a league and FA Cup double; in the FA Cup semi-finals Chelsea drew Liverpool, and Leeds drew Manchester United. Leeds were brilliant, but they were not popular.

Only Tottenham Hotspur had ever won the Second Division with more points than Leeds in 1963/64, but the reports from visitors to West Yorkshire were that no team had ever won it with more violence. Without a prolific scorer, Leeds bore the imprint of the ultra-aggressive Bobby Collins; Jack Charlton would never turn down a fight, and Billy Bremner and Norman Hunter had grown up fast under their mentors. There had been no television coverage to show off Albert Johanneson's tricks on one wing or Giles' calm quality on the other, only indignant newspaper reports of Revie's players taking one-goal leads then fighting to defend them, a win-at-all-costs mentality nobody looked forward to seeing in the First Division.

The scaremongering was amplified by the authorities. Revie was outraged when the Football Association's official journal published an article about the threat ill discipline posed to the game, citing Leeds United as the main offenders, printing a table showing Leeds had the poorest disciplinary record in the country and supporting the newspapers' view that Leeds were a 'dirty team'. Revie pointed out that the majority of United's disciplinary points were collected by junior and school-boy teams; the first team were rare in their division for not having a player sent off, and only Bremner had been suspended. More important was what such an article by the governing body said to other teams and officials.

'We would point out that we have only had two players sent off at Leeds in the last 44 years,' said Revie. 'We maintain that the "dirty team" tag which was blown up by the press could prejudice not only the general public but the officials controlling the game, and, to put it mildly, could have an effect on the subconscious approach of both referee and linesmen, to say nothing of the minds of spectators, especially some types who are watching football today. It could lead to some very unsavoury incidents.'

It was true that Leeds were harder than most, but when they took to the pitch in Division One, they found opposing teams were not waiting to find out; they were ready to fight Leeds United's reputation, and get their retaliation in first. At Chelsea in September, Giles was stretchered off in the first ten minutes after Eddie McCreadie scythed him down; with no substitutes allowed, Leeds had to fight to stay in the game, Collins and Bremner encountering Chelsea's young hard man Ron Harris for the first time, making sure he didn't forget them.

At Goodison Park in November Giles was involved again, after a 50-50 challenge with Everton's Sandy

Brown left Brown claiming studmarks on his chest, dealing his retribution with a left hook and getting sent off after just four minutes. The Battle of Goodison continued without him, the violence on the pitch and from the stands so severe – Willie Bell, knocked unconscious at one point, called it frightening – that the referee stopped the game before half-time, sending the players to the dressing rooms to calm down. It didn't work; caging the teams only fired them up. Leeds won 1-0, but the match was a national scandal.

To make things worse, Leeds kept winning. They started with three wins, over Aston Villa, Liverpool and Wolverhampton Wanderers, that set their standard. Liverpool were the league champions, but lost 4-2 at Elland Road. Inspired by Syd Owen's detailed scouting reports on potential players, Revie had set Owen, Maurice Lindley and himself the task of preparing equally detailed reports on entire teams, analysing their collective and individual strengths and weaknesses, preparing a plan to contain and exploit them, and teaching it to the players through written dossiers and focused training sessions, using the reserves as replicas of the next opponents. Leeds were prepared to an extent that many found almost chilling. It was revolutionary in an era when coaching was still regarded as unwelcome embellishment of a simple game; computerising football in this way was removing the individual tests of skill the English had always regarded as integral to the sport.

That tension between the old guard's ideals of Englishness and soccer and Don Revie's willing adoption of new and foreign ideas, stretching back to 1955 when he played like a Hungarian, was at the heart of England's loathing of Leeds United's success. While English football was asserting itself as the best in the world, picking up the Jules Rimet trophy to prove it, Leeds had come rampaging into the First Division from the still-mysterious north with a black South African on the wing, dressing like Real Madrid and playing football like Italians. That was where the 'Dirty Leeds' style had come from; John Charles' transfers had given United a close affinity with Italian football. They played against Juventus in Leeds, and Roma, Cremonese and Preto in Italy, games that were friendly in intent but fierce in practice, introducing Leeds first-hand to the fouls, off-the-ball violence and intimidating tactics Charles had experienced in Serie A for five seasons, tales he told the young players in the dressing room during his short time back at Elland Road.

Leeds were not Spurs or Manchester United, teams regularly reaching the later stages of European competitions; they were a young team full of heart but not yet sure of their talent, seeking any advantage. Always studying their opponents, Leeds' players learned from Italy that the limits to what referees would punish lay beyond where other English teams would go, and while never sanctioning violence, Revie approved his players' efforts to exploit those outer limits of acceptability. The English football authorities and the London-based sports press more than disapproved, they were outraged; but in many cases the outrage came before they'd seen Leeds United kick a ball, let alone an opponent. Leeds and Revie stuck to their defence, producing their own lists showing which teams and players committed most fouls in a match; usually not Leeds, although that evidence was taken as proof of how much they got away with; and usually not Bremner, although he would usually be booked anyway.

Two years of fast, aggressive, winning football caught up with Leeds by the end of the season. The battle for honours became a battle with Manchester United, and Leeds won the FA Cup semi-final; a hard-fought 0-0 at Hillsborough was followed by an exciting game at the City Ground in Nottingham, settled in the last minute when Bremner impudently headed a long free-kick backwards into the goal. But as tiredness overcame Leeds, Manchester United took the league title, decided by Leeds' last match away to Birmingham City. Needing to win to force Manchester to get something from their two games in hand, Leeds went 3-0 down after an hour and began easing up, the FA Cup final on their minds; but almost inadvertently they got back into the game, Charlton equalising with four minutes left, and scrambled to find a winner to keep them in the title race. They couldn't, and Manchester United won the title on goal average.

Five days later, at Wembley, Leeds showed why they had needed to conserve their strength. They spent the time between games secluded in a hotel in Croydon, where what little energy they had left was transposed to nervous tension. Leeds froze against Liverpool; even Bobby Collins said he felt awful before the game, and Billy Bremner remembered the match being like a waking nightmare, praying for a replay so they could start again at Maine Road. Liverpool were not an attack-minded team, and the press were infuriated when these two dour northern clubs reached 90 minutes at o-o. Gary Sprake had one of his best days in goal, but couldn't stop Roger Hunt's header at the start of extra time; then Bremner scored one of his best goals, volleying Charlton's header into the corner of the net.

But at 1-1 Leeds were indecisive and tired. The struggle was symbolised by Albert Johanneson. The star of the promotion season, he had lifted his game to the First Division, playing 30 times and scoring nine goals. The racist abuse and attention had gone up another level too, but he was always defended by United's all-for-one approach. It was team policy that if a player was in trouble, either with an opponent or a referee, he would walk away and the combined might of his mates would sort it out; Johanneson was initially reticent around such a tight group, until they stripped him and threw him in the team bath to show there was no barrier between teammates. But at Wembley the focus on Johanneson

was so much sharper, as the first black player in an
FA Cup final, and everything was so much bigger –
with 100,000 in the stadium, millions more watching
on television, and Queen Elizabeth II waiting to present
the trophy – that everything around him became a blur.
All he could hear were the racist 'Zulu' chants from
Liverpool fans; all he could feel were kicks and punches
from Liverpool's defenders; and all his teammates could
do was leave him to it, suffering individual nightmares
of their own. Whatever Johanneson or Leeds tried, they
were trapped. After the equaliser, Leeds couldn't decide
between putting Charlton and Bremner into defence to
play for the replay, or up front to score; Liverpool took
advantage of the uncertainty, Ian St John heading the
winning goal.

Liverpool were not popular winners, but Leeds were
very popular losers. Their critics believed that would
now be enough from Revie's obnoxious upstarts, and
were reassured by early exits from the FA and League
Cups the following season, and poor away form keeping Leeds down in a tolerable 5th place in the league.
But Leeds were finding vindication in the Inter-Cities
Fairs Cup.

If ever a confirmation and condemnation of United's
methods could be rolled into one act, it would be the
vicious foul by Fabrizio Poletti that left Bobby Collins
lying in a heap on a pitch in Turin, his thigh bone
snapped in half, Jack Charlton punching every Torino

player he saw trying to move his seriously injured team-mate until Les Cocker could reach him.

Poletti was not, apparently, one of the more villain-ous in Torino's ranks, and claimed it was a shocking accident; Collins ran much faster than he'd expected, he'd timed the tackle all wrong. Bremner's on-field assessment was different; he told Poletti: 'I'll kill you for this.' But that a supposedly benign player had broken his opponent's femur at a stroke, in Leeds United's first ever competitive European away match, demonstrated why Leeds had felt forced to adopt such a brutal game themselves, lest they become victims of it; and it dem-onstrated the risk of terrible injuries from such a style of play. Collins was fortunate that a nearby hospital specialised in the broken bones of skiers in the surround-ing mountains; their surgeons repaired his broken thigh with a fifteen-inch steel pin.

Leeds, meanwhile, had to play on with ten players, shocked by the fate of their skipper. They were defending a 2-1 lead from the first leg, and for 40 minutes that's all they did: defend. The game finished 0-0, and the Italian press were full of praise for Leeds: 'This team has said a word about British soccer which for years has not been heard and which convinced the crowd. The whole team seemed to be spurred by fire.'

European football held no fear for Leeds United; they were ready for this. Lindley and Owen would fly out to watch their opponents, composing scrupulous dossiers and plans. Despite being thrown straight into European competition, United's second wave of youngsters – Peter Lorimer, Terry Cooper, Paul Madeley, Eddie Gray – slotted easily into the tirelessly practised gameplans. The defence of Sprake, Reaney, Bell, Hunter, Charlton and Bremner gave Leeds security against goals, with the last three giving security against opponents who tried to step out of line.

Leeds beat Leipzig 2-1 on a snow-packed pitch, holding them 0-0 in the return at Elland Road. At home to Valencia, who had won the Inter-Cities Fairs Cup in 1962 and 1963, Leeds came from behind to draw 1-1, playing the last thirteen minutes without Charlton, after Valencia's goalkeeper raised objecting fists to Charlton's challenge and the police became involved in front of the South Stand. The referee took the teams to the dressing rooms for ten minutes to cool off, and to send off Charlton and Vidagany; then he sent off Sánchez Lage for a foul on Storrie. The Spanish FA took no action against the Valencia players, but the English FA were, as usual, appalled, and a special inquiry fined Charlton £20, despite the referee appearing as a witness in his defence.

Leeds defended for all they were worth in the away leg, and fifteen minutes from the end they were worth a counter-attacking goal from Mike O'Grady that took them through. In the quarter-final Újpest Dózsa, who had beaten Everton, were beaten 4-1 at Elland Road; that meant a 1-1 draw in Budapest was enough, and enough for the Újpest players to take Leeds on again in a brawl at the post-match banquet, where they only suffered another defeat.

The semi-final was against 1964's winners Real Zaragoza, famous for five attacking forwards that meant a defensive plan for the away leg. Sprake and Charlton were to the fore in a 1-0 defeat, Zaragoza only scoring a penalty for handball by Bremner. There was another late incident, Giles and Violeta sent off before Violeta's remonstrative push after Giles' hard tackle could become something worse. Leeds had to score twice in the second leg, but on Elland Road's hard pitch the early play went with Zaragoza, until Johanneson forced Charlton's downward header over the line. Zaragoza kept control, a brilliant half-volley from Canario beating Sprake, but they couldn't stop Charlton, who never stopped trying; he headed Hunter's cross to make the final aggregate score 2-2.

A toss of a disc gave Leeds the right to host a play-off match, but now Revie's intuition let him down. Zaragoza had enjoyed passing the ball on Elland Road's firm ground, so the fire brigade were engaged to hose the firmness away, Major Buckley's old trick. But Zaragoza were just as capable in mud, and scored three inside a quarter of an hour. Charlton led the attack but only got a consolation goal with ten minutes left.

Defeat so close to a major European final was tough to take, a year after defeat at Wembley, but Revie's team were growing up in the Fairs Cup. The next season they came even closer, although the process was prolonged. Another meeting with Valencia showed United's development; Valencia had improved too, and collected a vital goal in a 1-1 draw at Elland Road, under the new rule that away goals counted double if a tie ended as a draw. Despite missing key players through injury, and amid the undercurrent of dislike between the teams, Giles gave United's young side an early lead in Valencia; Lorimer added a second with three minutes left, strong defending in between contributing to one of Leeds' best displays yet. More strength and stamina were needed in the quarter-final against Bologna; extra time and the away goals rule didn't solve a 1-0 defeat in Italy and a 1-0 win at Elland Road, so a disc was flipped. Bologna's captain Bulgarelli called 'red', and United's captain Bremner leapt for joy when the disc came up white. Leeds drew Kilmarnock for the semi-final, but European scheduling postponed it until their domestic seasons were over.

Leeds were finding league football tougher than the concentrated bursts of effort in Europe. Bobby Collins, showing strength of leg and character that would be impossible in anybody else, returned from his broken thigh in the last game of that season, and a handful of matches in the next, but Revie had to plan without him. Collins was 35 and couldn't play forever, although he plainly intended to try, but Johnny Giles moved in from the wing to inherit Collins' dictatorship. It took Giles time to find his own style in the number ten shirt; he was not the aggressive bawler Collins had been, and would assert his authority with the rhythm and length of his passing; but he added a new edge to his game borrowed from Collins and Bremner.

That change, and an injury to Alan Peacock's troublesome knee, took some poise out of United's forward line. Revie made a rare purchase, buying Mike O'Grady for £30,000, a tall winger to fill the gap left by Giles and fill the penalty area with crosses. The problem was finding someone to finish them. Teenagers Peter Lorimer and Eddie Gray were maturing into formidable players at inside-forward; Terry Cooper was shifting between left-wing and left-back while Albert Johanneson, profoundly affected by his day at Wembley, was now only occasionally brilliant, struggling with injuries. At centre-forward Rod Johnson, Rod Belfitt and Jimmy Greenhoff weren't growing up to be prolific finishers, and even Paul Madeley was tried there, as he was in every position. Goals were shared throughout the team, Lorimer and Storrie finishing as joint top scorers after a strong second half to the season helped Leeds finish 2nd in 1965/66; but they were eleven points behind champions Liverpool, and fell even further down the table in 1966/67 to 4th, even if the gap to winners Manchester United was only five points in a much closer race. But Manchester United had scored 22 more goals, and United's top scorer was Giles with twelve, three of them penalties.

Leeds had a team that could beat anybody, but the deficiencies were too great to sustain a league-winning season. The Fairs Cup was their best chance, and a parallel effort in the FA Cup. A 1-1 draw at Sunderland in the fifth round was best described as 'bitter'. The replay four days later was chaotic. The Leeds public, still ambivalent about watching United, decided this was the game for them, and 57,892 – a new record – were counted inside, while nobody could count the thousands outside or on the stadium roofs. Elland Road was still the same old ground, its large terraces boasting spaces its infrastructure couldn't cope with being filled. Crush barriers failed on the Lowfields, and an avalanche of people fell onto the pitch. The game was stopped for seventeen minutes while 32 injured people were hauled from the crush and taken away in ambulances, missing another 1-1 draw.

A second replay at Boothferry Park in Hull was also heading for 1-1, and a scheduling nightmare that could have forced Leeds to play Sunderland again on the same day they played Bologna. A late Giles penalty won it, as two protesting Sunderland players were sent off and the referee, Ken Burns, called for police protection from the crowd. A home win over Manchester City followed, Charlton heading the winner above goalkeeper Harry Dowd's claim of a foul, and against City's dominance of the match. Leeds were fortunate to go through, but fortune was always a friend to cup winners.

But fortune was tending to desert Leeds at vital moments, especially when referees were involved. The semi-final was at Villa Park against Chelsea, who had knocked Leeds out of the cup in the fourth round the season before. Chelsea took the lead when Tony Hateley headed in Charlie Cooke's powerful cross just before half-time, and Leeds added Bremner and substitute Lorimer to their attack, trying to evade Chelsea's kicks in midfield. With seven minutes left Bremner headed a long ball into the path of Terry Cooper, who was dashing between defenders from the left and hit a powerful volley into the net to equalise – or so he thought. The referee – Ken Burns again – ruled offside.

Chelsea's defending was desperate, and with seconds left Hunter was fouled 25 yards from goal. Chelsea lined up their wall, and Giles lined up his plan; Leeds had Lorimer, the twenty year old reputed to have the hardest shot in football, but he stayed away until Giles flicked the ball sideways and Lorimer unleashed all his power upon it. Peter Bonetti had no chance; the ball flew into his top corner, an incredible equaliser – ruled out. As disbelieving Leeds players crowded and jostled him, Burns told them Chelsea's wall had not been the required ten yards back, and the kick would have to be retaken. Eventually it was, and this time the ball went nowhere near the net; seconds later the final whistle blew, and the Leeds players went to the floor, unable to take in what had just happened to their FA Cup dreams.

When losing in 1965 they'd had nobody to blame but themselves. This time everybody, whether their sympathies were with Leeds or Chelsea, agreed they were denied by the referee. 'If it had happened to me I would have been very sick,' said Chelsea manager Tommy Docherty; it had happened to Don Revie, who said: 'For about half an hour after the final whistle, I felt completely numb. But the remorse really began to hit me when I met my son, Duncan, outside the ground. He was sobbing – and I felt like sitting down and crying with him.'

There was still the hope of the late-running Fairs Cup, and in mid-May 21-year-old Rod Belfitt scored a hat-trick inside half an hour as Leeds took a 4-2 lead over Kilmarnock, defending it meanly in the second leg. The two-legged final against Dynamo Zagreb wasn't held until the end of August, and United's defending let them down in the away leg, a 2-0 defeat. At Elland Road Charlton spent most of his time in the attack as Leeds aimed every ball into Dynamo's penalty area, but they were guilty of both over-simplification and over-elaboration, unable to crack Dynamo's defensive wall, or draw their opponents upfield to let them round it. The match finished 0-0, and what was left of the 35,604 Elland Road crowd, paying Harry Reynolds' special high prices for the privilege, applauded Dynamo's players as they took the Fairs Cup from FIFA president Sir Stanley Rous, and away from Leeds United.

It was the end of six full seasons under Don Revie's management, without doubt the greatest days Leeds United had known; a Second Division championship, an FA Cup final and semi-final, a European final and semi-final, denied the Football League championship on goal average, finishing 2nd again and now 4th. But the only person with a medal to show for it was Jack Charlton. Leeds had been one of the best teams in Europe for three seasons, but won nothing, and nothing couldn't last forever. Soon the team had to either fade from brilliance or be broken up in the transfer market. Of course, it might win something instead, but West Yorkshire could be a pessimistic place. In 1967 people suspected they'd seen the best of Leeds United already.

14

1967–69

LEEDS UNITED ARE WORTHY CHAMPIONS

Leeds United's players no longer lived in club houses next to Elland Road. The abolition of the maximum wage meant a greater share of the rewards on offer at the top of the national and now televised game, along with the celebrity and scrutiny that came when ordinary lads like them bought big houses and drove fast cars.

While schoolkids chased their favourite players to sign photographs in fan magazines, the wider public identified managers as the key representatives of the teams on *Match of the Day*. Herbert Chapman had started the long change, ending the days when secretary-managers answered applications for season tickets while a committee of directors chose the team. Growing acceptance of the foreign and maligned concept of 'tactics', and post-match interviews discussing them, were encouraging the idea of football teams as expressions of individual managers.

There had been Matt Busby's Babes at Old Trafford, and the public's sympathetic fascination with his attempts to rebuild them after the tragedy in Munich; Liverpool's fans had elevated Bill Shankly to the status of a deity. Younger coaches like Malcolm Allison and Brian Clough were comfortable being quotable for cameras seeking Beatles-style celebrity in soccer. But most scrutinised of all was Don Revie, manager of the country's most consistently successful failures; for his personality as well as his football, and the way one influenced the other.

Leeds United's inscrutable lack of personality made it easy for reporters to project whatever ideas they wanted onto Revie's lads. The all-white strip associated Leeds with the world's greatest team, but where Real Madrid created their success by paying huge transfer fees, Revie's policies took Leeds in another direction; if Johnny Giles and Mike O'Grady were missing, Revie would name a team that had not cost a penny in transfers, and they would win. Taken with their defensive tactics and fierce togetherness, United's plain white shirts emphasised their refusal to allow individual stars to rise above the team, but denied the press the personality stories they craved. The ideal Leeds United player, as far as the team were concerned, was Paul Madeley; fit and versatile, Leeds relied on him to perform better than most specialists in any position on the pitch, so they were rarely weakened by an individual injury: Madeley would fill in. But the media could make little out of a player who looked to them like a competent reserve. It was better to train their cameras on a wayward genius like Manchester United's George Best, at home on the wing or in a nightclub; or on Don Revie.

Revie's playing career had been guided by his sensitivities, but he had won Footballer of the Year when soccer fame did not attract deep analysis. Now in the spotlight of a new, celebrity-obsessed era, all Revie's methods and quirks were scrutinised and discussed as if they held the key to explaining Leeds United's success. In many ways, they did. The loyalty to the boss and to each other that created United's side without stars was due to Revie's insistence on nurturing young players in the sort of family environment that was the making of him as a tearful youth stranded at Leicester City, and his insistence that the whole club should become 'Leeds United-minded' had touched everybody, from the laundry staff to the players' wives and families. Revie would massage the players, ensuring the respect he commanded by the title of 'boss' was tempered by a literally hands-on approach; there couldn't be a closer relationship than when the boss's hands were smoothing the tension from the players' muscles.

The family atmosphere was a source of strength, but Revie's insecurities didn't leave him. He inherited a club used to superstition, from Robert Wilkinson's lucky blue-and-gold tie, to the black cat interrupting Major Buckley, to Lulu, the doll that inspired a cup run. Revie matched, embraced and entrenched that streak. Learning Elland Road might have been cursed by Romany travellers who were once evicted from the land, he brought in Gypsy Rose Lee, a famous fortune teller from Blackpool sea-front, to lift the curse. His matchday routines included placing a rabbit's foot in the pocket of a worn-out blue suit, kept for luck throughout the season if the team started well, and walking to traffic lights near Elland Road, turning around, and walking back. Regular substitutes like Terry Yorath were subjected to Revie's dugout rituals with cigars, mints and chewing gum, and told to count to ten before going back into the changing rooms for spare boots. Believing images of birds were unlucky, he had the civic owl emblem removed from the team's shirts.

Revie's superstitions spread to the players. After spotting Norman Hunter throwing a ball to Bobby Collins before a win, Revie insisted that the otherwise cynical Hunter made it a ritual. The players had a particular order for running onto the pitch. Billy Bremner preferred a short-sleeved shirt. Jack Charlton developed such a convoluted pre-match routine it was taking him an hour to get ready and he had to stop. Dressing rooms everywhere had players going through odd, personal rituals to prepare for matches, and to most these superstitions were no more than habits. But the attention paid to Revie's idiosyncrasies made them seem more significant, combining with United's failure to win a trophy to create an air of vague paranoia, enforced by murmuring about the occult.

Leeds were sometimes trapped between their superstitious rituals and their meticulous practical preparation for matches. The players were the best drilled and best prepared in Europe, and the coaches were not about to abandon methods that brought such rapid success and were still ahead of their time. But some of the players, reading another dossier on a team they had perhaps faced just a few weeks earlier, felt they were thinking too much about the opposition and not enough about themselves. Leeds had players ready to express themselves, but dealing with the opposition came first and foremost. And Leeds would win, so in the end it didn't matter that with a different approach they might have won by more, or with more style.

The players bought into it because they bought into everything Revie told them, because Revie had taken many of them as fifteen-year-old boys from working-class homes and made them into the international footballers they grew up dreaming of becoming. Few of them may have imagined that life as a top-class sportsperson would mean time away from their family before games, playing dominoes and carpet bowls in secluded hotels, but it worked, so they did it. Besides, being with the team was like being with family, with all the love, honesty and arguments that entailed. No squad of players were closer or knew each other better, on and off the pitch, and amid the differences and the explosions of temper, bonds of loyalty grew. There could not be two more different characters than the nervous patriarch Revie and the player who was now his captain, rebellious and self-confident Bremner, and they were frequently at odds; but none would stand up taller for each other than these two, inside and outside Elland Road.

As the years went by without trophies, vilification continued in the press and punishments were handed down by the FA, the familial bond became a siege mentality. The club had come quickly from nothing, with players, coaches and a manager who had grown up knowing what nothing really meant, and that if you wanted something, nobody would just give it to you. Now they were successful, hewn so closely from their manager's brilliance and his neuroses that they were barely distinguishable, as individuals, from Revie, they risked falling victim to Revie's great paranoia: that it would all be taken away.

Revie had felt that as an individual. After promotion he left his new contract unsigned for months, Harry Reynolds arguing to the board that Revie deserved a five-year contract rather than the three they offered, almost leading him to Roker Park as manager of Sunderland. They offered less money than Leeds, but greater security, the one thing Revie craved. Reynolds understood that, and after a serious car accident left him in hospital, he finally got the board to relent by pleading with them from his hospital bed.

By the time illness forced Reynolds to stand down as chairman in 1967, replaced briefly by Albert Morris, then by Percy Woodward, the board had become almost numb in its deference to Revie. He lost a valuable ally and mentor in Reynolds, but gained near-total control. Revie's management had erased a six-figure overdraft, the directors' loans had been paid back, and the club made over £60,000 profit in two successive seasons, boosted by European football. When the club did register losses, it was by paying for ground improvements needed since long before the old Main Stand burned down; the old Kop was levelled and a modern concrete stand built in its place, further north than the old one to create space at the other end to replace the Scratching Shed.

Attendances were still unpredictable but Elland Road was now often full, amplifying the long-standing but less appealing character traits that had always given it a different atmosphere to the city's rugby grounds. Winning often wasn't enough; the crowds would jeer and give slow handclaps against negative football. But when the siege mentality extended from the pitch to the terraces, it made Elland Road an intimidating place for away teams. Sections of the fans could be as prone to paranoid outbursts as the players and manager, as when referee Jack Taylor was attacked during a game, leading to arguments between the club and its supporters; Harry Reynolds 'could not be blunter than he was without swearing' when using the public address system to demand the fans start behaving. Jack Charlton once ran the length of the pitch to stand at the front of the Scratching Shed and yell at everyone within it until they gave West Bromwich Albion the ball back.

Revie was loath to introduce outsiders into this carefully calibrated atmosphere; distrust extended to the transfer market. Leeds pursued midfielder Alan Ball before he left Blackpool, but the price eventually paid by Everton was too high; in any case, Johnny Giles had since filled that position, and now there was nobody better in the league and the money was still in the bank. Mike O'Grady had been a necessity for the wing and was a key player, although Revie fretted about his lack of a steady girlfriend. Striker Tony Hateley was another given long consideration before the fee put Leeds off, but the board were ready to be confident in the transfer market, if Revie was.

He wasn't. Without Alan Peacock a goalscoring centre-forward was the team's conspicuous lack, and it was the one position the junior teams could not fill. Historically Leeds had failed to produce centre-forwards; Elland Road's half-back lines were legendary, thanks to home-grown players like Ernie Hart, Wilf Copping, Bert Sproston and Grenville Hair, but Leeds were always short of goals unless they spent money to sign Billy McLeod or Tom Jennings. The one player Leeds could claim to be a home-grown centre-forward, John Charles, was really a centre-half anyway. None of Jimmy Greenhoff, Rod Johnson or Rod Belfitt were regular scorers, but Revie stood by them, as they were creating goals for the midfield players. But when Leeds only scored one goal in the first three games of 1967/68, Revie had to act.

With typical caution, he signed a striker who would not cause a significant change to the team's style of play. Mick Jones was bought from Sheffield United for £100,000 after a year of consideration and occasional bids; Jones was the scorer of 63 goals in 149 games and an England international, but young enough at 22 for Owen and Cocker to get to work on him. Jones was to add a goal threat of his own, while carrying on the job of occupying centre-halves with his strength and cavalier bravery, fighting for every ball in attack as hard as Bremner in midfield and Hunter in defence, so that Giles, Bremner, Lorimer and Gray could profit. All he lacked was close control to keep possession, and that's where Owen and Cocker's one-on-one training came in. Jones' other target was to fit in, but his easy-going nature meant he was well suited as the new-boy butt of the Elland Road old-hands' joking, a role he never truly stopped playing.

It took a while for Leeds to adjust to Jones, not helped by an ankle injury that kept him out for six weeks in autumn; he was in the side for a brilliant 7-0 home win over Chelsea, but that match was all Bremner, who helped make five of Leeds' goals before scoring himself, a stunning overhead kick, his last act before a month's suspension. The return of Bremner and Jones prompted six consecutive wins in a fourteen-match unbeaten league run, including back-to-back 5-0 defeats of Fulham and Southampton, lifting Leeds to 1st place; but their slow start, difficult away form and the demands of three other cup competitions were taking a heavy toll.

Progress in the cups was almost automatic. Four home matches brought four home wins in the FA Cup, before a first-half penalty for handball against Charlton, after Gary Sprake had given Everton the ball, settled a bad-tempered semi-final at Old Trafford. After beating Spora Luxembourg by an aggregate score of 16-0 in the first round of the Fairs Cup, Leeds overcame Partizan Belgrade and the competition became an Anglo-Scottish affair; Hibernian, Rangers and Dundee were beaten opponents as Leeds again reached the final, again to be held after the start of the next season.

Leeds played their League Cup games without Jones, who was cup-tied, but reached the final at Wembley after overcoming Second Division Derby County in a

two-legged semi-final, either side of beating Derby in the
FA Cup. 'They can teach my lads a lot,' noted Derby manager Brian Clough. 'How hard they have to work, how
much effort and dedication is required – in short, a complete picture of what we have to aim for in the future.'

Leeds United's aim was a trophy. The League Cup
final was played at Wembley at the beginning of March,
and Revie promised his players would offer better entertainment and a better result than against Liverpool in
1965. He was half right. Leeds took the lead over Arsenal
in the eighteenth minute, Charlton's controversial tactic
of standing next to the goalkeeper at corners causing its
usual havoc, and the defenders appealing for a foul as
Terry Cooper volleyed the ball through them all and into
the net. Arsenal had little attacking threat of their own,
and with Charlton, Sprake, Giles and Greenhoff all unfit
but playing, and Madeley in place of Jones in attack,
Leeds forgot about style and concentrated on the one
thing they hadn't been able to do, until now: winning.

The final whistle freed them; now Leeds could
entertain, and Bremner did a forward roll for joy while
Revie ran to congratulate the players. 'Before the final,
I was seriously thinking of goading the lads by opening
an empty trophy case and telling them, "This is what
you have to show for all your sweat and toil in recent
seasons,"' said Revie. 'I hate to think what might have
happened had Leeds lost this one, too. You can only take
so many disappointments.'

And their bodies could only take so much punishment. Leeds played 66 matches that season, but losing the FA Cup semi-final and letting the league title slip away to Manchester City – Leeds finished 4th again – didn't disappoint them the same way as in the past. The League Cup was firmly in the trophy case, and the next season would start with a two-legged Fairs Cup final against Ferencváros. With a trophy, any trophy, now won, the summer of 1968 was focused and relaxed. Rather than follow every route to silverware in another 60-game season, Revie decided to keep things simple: they would start by winning the Fairs Cup, then they would win the First Division. And they would do it, he told the players, without losing a single game.

Ferencváros were one of the best attacking teams in Europe, but the first objective was achieved thanks to Mick Jones, scrambling a goal from a corner to pierce Ferencváros's defensive gameplan in the first half at Elland Road; and Gary Sprake, who made several brilliant saves behind his severely tested defence in Budapest, including the save of his life when a powerfully struck free-kick by Dezső Novák appeared from behind a wall of players, and he hit the ball away one-handed. Sprake's wrist was still smarting when the referee blew for full-time and Leeds became the Inter-Cities Fairs Cup champions.

A second trophy by the middle of September was the perfect accompaniment to the start Leeds made in the league, winning seven and drawing two, although the plan to stay unbeaten only lasted until 28 September and a 3-1 defeat away to Manchester City. Three more wins followed before a shocking 5-1 defeat away to Burnley, then three consecutive 0-0 draws. The away defeats and goalless draws were particularly disappointing as Revie had promised his side would have a new attacking look, 'a policy of free expression by the players' to bring more goals and more wins away from Elland Road; Leeds had only won five and drawn six away the previous season. Leeds were lining up with Madeley behind the midfield four of Gray, Giles, Bremner and Lorimer, themselves behind and profiting from the hard work of Jones. They were sound defensively, but relying on the midfield to get goals, and many observers felt Leeds lacked a winger to replace Johanneson, and a true goalscorer. Revie possibly felt the same. Lorimer was unhappy at how often he was losing his place to O'Grady, having his best season out wide for Leeds, and asked for a transfer; the papers linked Leeds with swap deals for a variety of wingers, but Lorimer stayed.

And Leeds, helped by going out of the League Cup and FA Cup early, didn't lose another match. Revenge over Burnley came in a 6-1 win at Christmas, a hint that Leeds were hitting their stride, and from 24 January, when they were three points behind Liverpool at the top, to 8 March, Leeds won seven consecutive matches, scoring seventeen and conceding three, building an eight-point lead. Liverpool were still a threat with two games in hand, and United's form temporarily left them; they were knocked out of the Fairs Cup in the fourth round by Újpest Dózsa, 3-0 on aggregate, and drew 0-0 away to Wolves and Sheffield Wednesday. Drawing became easier than winning, and nervous tension overcame free, expressive football; at Highbury, Sprake settled a long-running feud by flooring Arsenal's Bobby Gould with a left hook, and was lucky to only be booked. Leeds travelled to Anfield for their penultimate match after another 0-0 away draw at Everton. If Liverpool could take advantage of United's difficulties away from Elland Road and end their unbeaten league run – 30 matches – they would close the gap to three points, with a game in hand.

Leeds would win the title with a win or a draw, possibly a simple task anywhere but Anfield. 'We have a chance,' said Revie. 'And I hope we can take it.' The players were nervous, sleepless, feeling as bad as before the FA Cup final against Liverpool in 1965. But that was four years ago, and those boys had grown up. However they were feeling and whatever was at stake, United's European experiences had taught them how to hold what they had, and they played as if leading on aggregate; Jones defending from the front, Reaney and Cooper marking Liverpool's wingers, forcing play into the middle where Liverpool had to get through Bremner and Giles before they could reach Madeley, Hunter and

Charlton, let alone Sprake. If any team could break through that defence, it was Liverpool; if any team could stop them, it was Leeds. Leeds United's first league title was won with a 0-0 draw.

Such efforts hadn't made Leeds popular, not even in Leeds, where Revie was still perplexed and sometimes fuming with the city's inconsistent support. The home match against Southampton at the start of March only attracted 33,205 people to Elland Road, a top-six clash Revie felt sure would get 40,000 from the 2 million living near the ground. 'What on earth do they want?' demanded Revie.

But at Anfield Leeds found the acclaim Revie wanted. At the end of the game Bremner, after some persuading from the boss, led his players towards the 27,000 standing on Liverpool's famously loyal and intimidating Kop. They responded, chanting 'Champions!', encouraging Leeds to enjoy twenty minutes of celebrations on the pitch, before getting stuck into a crate of champagne in the dressing room, courtesy of Liverpool boss Bill Shankly. 'Leeds United are worthy champions,' said Shankly. 'They are a great side.' Leeds, so starved in their years of glory for compliments and trophies, took these compliments and the Football League trophy to heart. Then they took them back to Elland Road for a final victory over Nottingham Forest, in front of 46,508 who came, at last, to hail Leeds United as champions.

1969–70

WE'VE WORKED TOO
HARD TO FAIL NOW

Five seasons in the First Division had established Leeds United as its best team, but the garlands and trophies they deserved were hard won. Leeds were the only team to finish in the top four in each of those seasons, winning more games and losing fewer than any other in that time, but had to watch as Manchester United twice, Liverpool and Manchester City took their turns at winning it. Leeds reached the FA Cup semi-finals three times, and only Chelsea and Everton could say the same in that period, but Leeds hadn't won it. Since qualifying for the Fairs Cup, Leeds had reached the semi-finals three times; no other team got that far more than once, but Leeds only won it once.

The complex that was developing at Elland Road, about building Europe's most consistent team but becoming Europe's most consistent failures, was dispelled by winning the League Cup, the Fairs Cup, and most importantly the First Division. They were the best ever champions, with more points, more wins and fewer defeats than any previous winners, and the most home wins and home points, unbeatable at Elland Road. Don Revie was voted Manager of the Year. And he was determined to do better.

Winning removed some of the characteristic insecurity from United's manager, allowing his determination, self-confidence and confidence in his players to come forward. The previous season he had set the target of winning the league unbeaten; they missed by two games, but glory was theirs anyway. This time they would aim even higher. Leeds were entering the European Cup, the competition Real Madrid were dominating when they captured Revie and Bremner's imagination. After meeting every type of opponent in four years of long Fairs Cups campaigns, Revie felt Leeds were well prepared to live up to their all-white strip and emulate Real Madrid. He saw no reason not to retain the league title, and while the League Cup would be used to try reserve players, he was aiming to win the FA Cup. Revie wanted a treble, and told the players so.

They could add the Charity Shield at the start of the season, and did, beating FA Cup holders Manchester

2-1 at Elland Road; and during the season it was
reported that FIFA would start regulating the annual
Intercontinental Cup match between the champions of
Europe and South America. It would become a recognised tournament for the champions of six continents,
and the winners would be official world club champions.
Revie made that a target, too. Win the Charity Shield,
the league title and FA Cup at home; become European
champions, then be the first champions of the world.

Achieving any part of that objective was a huge task,
and to do it, Revie took an unusual risk. Leicester City
were relegated and Revie moved quickly, buying striker
Allan Clarke for a British record fee of £165,000. The
previous record was the £150,000 Leicester had paid to
sign Clarke from Fulham a year earlier. He wasn't only
expensive, he was a star, about to turn 23, with 98 goals
to his name; and of all the outsiders Revie could have
chosen to join the Leeds United family, Clarke was the
furthest distant.

'Egotistical, gifted, obsessively in love with success and, some say, with himself,' was one description
of Clarke in the *Sunday Express*. In the *News of
The World* Jimmy Hill, the former chairman of the
Professional Footballers' Association who successfully
fought to abolish the maximum wage, was furious that
Clarke was collecting his second successive 'relegation
bonus', a 5 per cent cut of his transfer fees, after leaving first Fulham and now Leicester after they dropped

into Division Two. He accused Clarke of disrupting Leicester's dressing room, causing disputes about money from their cup final appearance, and putting his selfish interests ahead of the club. 'Football is a team game,' wrote Hill, addressing Clarke directly in his last line. 'You won't half be worth some money if you ever get that into your noddle box.'

Revie had, as ever, given careful thought to the contents of Clarke's noddle box, and whether by accident or design, Clarke was immediately taken in hand by Billy Bremner; they became close friends. The ego and arrogance were obvious, but Leeds United had a title-winning squad of internationals, a collective weight that would crush any needy individualism. 'The longer I am at Elland Road,' Clarke said, 'the more I realise that to be a star at this particular club, with more importance than any other player, is an impossibility.' Far from feeling restricted, after all the turbulence at Leicester and the weeks of arguments Jimmy Hill caused in the press, Clarke was relieved to let the pressure be absorbed and neutralised by the group around him.

Leeds and Clarke also needed to adapt on the pitch. He was to join Mick Jones up front, and switching to a front two was the biggest tactical change Leeds had attempted in years. Jones' job was still to hurl himself towards every ball and every defender, bringing all the attention to him and sending a chance to a teammate; but now the teammate would be Clarke. Louche by comparison, he would lurk deep like Revie in the fifties, until he sensed a chance to score and went to it, putting the ball in the net before anyone else saw the opportunity. If teams tried to mark them both, Peter Lorimer would appear from the right wing, with a shot so powerful he could score from anywhere. After spending much of the title season on the transfer list while Mike O'Grady shone, there were rumours about Lorimer departing when Clarke was signed; instead it was O'Grady who left for Wolves, the large £80,000 fee reflecting his quality and leaving fans wondering if Revie had taken leave of his senses, forgetting someone would have to supply crosses to Clarke. But Lorimer could do that, and Leeds now had the flexibility to play with four across midfield, Lorimer and Eddie Gray as the wide men; or to push Lorimer forward into an attacking three; or Clarke could drop deep to stiffen midfield and leave Jones alone. And all this in one match, dictated by Bremner and Giles, who were now side by side in the middle of the pitch, two telepathic generals organising the game.

It took time to work, and defending was the biggest problem. As well as starting attacks Bremner and Giles had to play with more defensive discipline, as with swift full-backs Paul Reaney and Terry Cooper overlapping to attack, Leeds could be left exposed. Goals against them almost doubled in the league. But Clarke was proving his worth, and Leeds scored twelve more than any other

First Division team, adding eighteen to their previous season's total – seventeen coming from Clarke.

By March, Revie's miracle was no longer a fantastic dream, but a goal within reach. In the league, Leeds led Everton by a point, and were in much better form. Kind draws in the FA Cup were negotiated with only one goal conceded, and Leeds were facing Manchester United in the semi-final at Hillsborough. In the first round of the European Cup Leeds unforgettably dazzled Norwegian football fans by beating Lyn Oslo 10-0 at Elland Road and 6-0 away; they saw off Ferencváros with two 3-0 wins, then two hard-fought 1-0 wins defeated Standard Liege to put Leeds in the semi-finals, against Celtic.

Leeds had seven league games left to hold off Everton. If they won two more games in the FA Cup, beat Celtic over two legs and won the final, an impossible treble would be theirs. But it was the worst possible moment to begin a twelve-match mini-season with so much at stake. The World Cup was taking place in Mexico that summer, and to help Alf Ramsey's squad prepare to defend their title in such a challenging climate, the English football season was shortened by a month. The FA Cup final was scheduled for 11 April, and Leeds were scheduled to play ten games in 28 days.

The result of the FA Cup semi-final meant something had to give. A dour 0-0 draw added a replay at Villa Park to the calendar. That was much more exciting, dominated by Manchester United, before a final fifteen minutes when Leeds struck back, desperate to avoid extra time and possibly another replay. They failed, and a second 0-0 draw meant a third match, at Burnden Park in Bolton, where Bremner gave Leeds an eighth-minute lead, then orchestrated a shutdown of the entire Manchester United team.

Their opponents in the FA Cup final would be Chelsea, and Leeds celebrated getting back to Wembley to put 1965 right, but then they counted the cost. A vital league match against Southampton came two days later, and injuries meant Leeds were without Bremner, Giles, Reaney, Jones and Cooper. With twenty minutes left a 1-0 lead became a 3-1 home defeat, while Everton took a five-point lead of the league by hammering 3rd placed Chelsea 5-2. The extra games against Manchester won Leeds a cup final, but lost them the league; two days later, away to Derby County, armed with a doctor's report that his players were nearing exhaustion, Revie sent out eleven reserves, and Derby won 4-1.

The Football League were not impressed, and fined United £5,000 for fielding a weakened team. The league secretary, Alan Hardaker, had a strong dislike of Leeds and Revie in particular; after agreeing to fixture changes the previous season when flu ruled several Leeds players out, he had taken the brunt of Liverpool's complaints, and felt Revie was trying to take advantage with endless requests to move games. Hardaker was not going to let Revie run him the way referees were run by Revie's team.

Revie argued there was no point seeking medical advice if it wasn't followed, then despaired, when in the now meaningless league matches Reaney suffered a broken leg, ruling him out of United's season and the World Cup, and new centre-half John Faulkner fractured his kneecap in only his second match.

By giving up the league Revie effectively distilled the season to three games; the first at home to Celtic, the FA Cup final against Chelsea, then the second Celtic match to bring about a fourth game: the European Cup final. He rested as many players as he could, with as much coddling as he could lever from his good relationship with their wives, although Jack Charlton spent one of his days off searching the streets of Halton until he was reunited with Corrie, his family's missing puppy. Paul Madeley, chosen by England to replace Reaney in Mexico, indicated the state many Leeds players were in when he declined the call; he had played 57 games already, and would have no energy left for more.

Even getting to the end of the season, shortened as it was, was becoming arduous. The first leg of the European Cup semi-final took place the same night Everton clinched the league title. 'Whoever it was in the Leeds United jerseys that Celtic beat 1-0 at Elland Road,' wrote the *Yorkshire Evening Post*'s reporter, 'it was not Leeds United.' Leeds had hoped to save Celtic for the final, and play one of Legia Warsaw or Feyenoord first; several of the Leeds team were Celtic fans and

Scottish internationals, Celtic's manager Jock Stein was a close friend of Revie, and all involved had relished the thought of a Battle of Britain in the final. Then there was Maurice Lindley's scouting report, declaring Celtic the best team Leeds had faced in Europe. At Elland Road Celtic took the lead inside a minute after United's back line confused itself, then spent the night letting winger Jimmy 'Jinky' Johnstone take on – and usually beat – first Terry Cooper, then the rest of the defence. The referee, Michel Kitabdjian, disallowed a second Celtic goal after half-time and Leeds did better until the hour, when Bremner struck his head on the hard ground. It took ten minutes to get the concussed captain to leave the game, and at full-time, looking for his taxi home, he was found wandering into Celtic's dressing room, as dazed as his beaten team.

Leeds were given a rare and much needed six-day break before Wembley, but only after a 2-1 win over Burnley at Elland Road, enlivened by two extraordinary goals by Eddie Gray; the first an intelligent and accurate lob over the goalkeeper from 30 yards, the second a feat of dribbling skill that took the ball from near Burnley's corner flag, around six tackles from four bewildered defenders, and into the net. Gray had been the last of Revie's youngsters to make his debut and his mark, but had been a regular since he was nineteen and now, still only 22, he was a rival to Manchester United's erratic George Best as the best winger in the league. Perhaps

Gray had the advantage of training every day with Paul Reaney, the one full-back renowned for containing Best. Against Burnley Gray played in midfield, but at Wembley he was restored to the wing.

It was one of the few parts of the pitch where it was possible to play. Months of wet weather and hundreds of hooves at the Horse of the Year show had reduced the pitch to mud, and 100 tons of sand was the groundskeepers' solution. Grass was rare and a bouncing ball even rarer; it just stopped in the sand. Leeds and Chelsea's talented players had to lift their efforts to make anything of the match at all, and the efforts of all 22 meant a fast, skilful and memorable final. But none could touch the performance of Gray, least of all David Webb, the player meant to mark him. Once it was clear Gray had an advantage, and the form to take it, Leeds gave him pass after pass, sending him up the wing to beat Webb with Cooper busily overlapping. Webb was lost, but Gray was controlled, choosing when to pass and when to dribble; and when to shoot, cracking the crossbar with one brilliant effort, having another saved by Peter Bonetti.

Gray took the corner that gave Leeds the lead; a classic to Charlton, whose header landed between two Chelsea players on the line and, without a bounce, evaded them as it went in. The pitch cost Leeds just before half-time, or it was Sprake; he dived on Houseman's low shot, but the ball appeared from under his body and rolled into the net. The second half was all Leeds, and all Gray, until with six minutes left Bremner passed forward to Giles down the right and he lifted a first-time cross to Clarke. Clarke dived and headed from the penalty spot, but hit the base of the post; Lorimer missed the rebound, and Jones ran to the loose ball, striking firm and low inside the far post. The ghost of 1965 was ready to rest, but as against Liverpool, Leeds failed to protect what they had; two minutes later Charlton was penalised for a push, then Hutchinson got ahead of him to head the free-kick past Sprake. Extra time couldn't separate the teams.

That meant Leeds, expecting to face Celtic four days later with the FA Cup settled, had yet another big game in their diary and on their minds, and not much left in their legs. In front of 136,505 at Hampden Park, just 4,500 of them from Leeds, United started nervously, facing five corners in the first eight minutes, and Sprake made some crucial saves to stop Celtic running away with the tie. Instead Billy Bremner scored, a superb long-range strike that held Hampden transfixed and silent as they watched the ball float into the top corner. That was the best moment for Leeds; Cooper and Hunter between them couldn't do anything about Jimmy Johnstone, eventually deciding to kick him, but then unable to catch him; a terrible kick wounded Jones, who had to leave the field for ten minutes; defensive confusion at a short corner gave Celtic an equaliser; a collision with Celtic's

John Hughes severely injured Sprake's knee, and he was replaced by David Harvey; Johnstone beat Cooper again and passed to Bobby Murdoch, who drove a shot past Harvey to give Celtic a 3-1 aggregate lead. They hadn't even played 55 minutes yet. For the rest of the match Leeds were frenetic and, at the end, inconsolable.

The players just wanted it to be over. Reserves ticked off the two remaining league fixtures, both defeats, and the *Yorkshire Evening Post* aimed a dig at the performance against Manchester City at Elland Road, dragging up Revie's old excuse for defending away, that it was up to home teams to entertain: 'United should have pulled themselves together and put on a show ... I suggest they practise what they preach.' It seemed that no matter how much Leeds United gave, someone was always demanding more. In his newspaper column, Charlton declared he was so sick of the game he didn't even want to play 'blow football' with his children; but both he and Bremner were determined to beat Chelsea. 'If we fail to beat them this time we will feel cheated,' said Charlton. 'We simply can't miss out on some silver this season,' said Bremner. 'We've worked too hard to fail now.'

Chelsea were determined not to be outplayed as they had been at Wembley. Old Trafford's pitch promised even better from Eddie Gray, but Chelsea switched his marker, and Ron 'Chopper' Harris gave him a hard match. Although Harris boasted long afterwards about neutralising Gray in the opening minutes, it was almost half-time before he was able to scythe Gray down once and for all, hitting him high behind the knee, a foul calculated to injure. Even then Gray was able to influence the second half; limping but intelligent, he moved inside from the wing, drawing Harris and creating room for left-back Cooper, once a winger himself, to press down that side. But it wasn't a game suited to Gray, or to tactical niceties.

Harris's assault on Gray was only part of the viciousness from both sides. Referee Eric Jennings' policy was to let players sort disputes out between themselves, and with Chelsea determined to assert their strength and Leeds always quick for revenge, disputes were soon being sorted with fists and reckless fouls. Leeds provided the first moment of grace, Mick Jones bursting from midfield with the ball, swerving between defenders and shooting past Bonetti into the top corner; a forceful solo effort from a player usually associated with teamwork and brawn.

Leeds held the lead until the last ten minutes, then again felt the FA Cup slipping away from them. Charlie Cooke crossed from deep and Peter Osgood, unmarked, dived to head past Harvey. Leeds pushed for a winner and should have had a penalty when Jennings refused to punish McCreadie for a flying kick to Bremner's head; Bremner could have had another penalty when he was brought down when running through on goal, and Jones headed a chance just wide. Extra time was inevitable, and when a long throw-in was headed into United's net by David Webb, the player Gray embarrassed at Wembley, that felt inevitable too. Leeds fought back but it was no good. 'I thought we were going to win right up to when Chelsea equalised,' said Bremner later. 'As soon as they scored, I knew we weren't.'

Charlton stormed to the dressing room, never more upset by a defeat, blaming himself. Outside, dejected Leeds players swapped shirts with some of their counterparts, giving the Chelsea players trouble when they tried to collect their medals; nobody believed the men in white shirts could be the winners.

By aiming to win the treble of league, FA Cup and European Cup, Leeds were attempting something no team had ever tried before, and after 63 games, they had come closer than anyone expected: second in the league, second in the FA Cup, semi-finalists in the European Cup. They entertained and endured like no other team, pushing themselves beyond their own world-class limits of skill and athleticism; nobody could ask the players, manager or staff to give more. Had the season not been shortened by a month to help the England team and the FA, Leeds were sure they would have achieved Revie's impossible target. 'But not one piece of silver to show for it,' said Bremner. 'And that's what counts.'

Revie's players had suffered defeats before, but just a year after they were hailed as champions in Liverpool, this harrowing month was a hard setback. Leeds United couldn't find a friend. A civic reception was arranged by the Lord Mayor in Leeds, but after winning nothing, and with four players and Les Cocker already away with England, two more on holiday, and the rest feeling a mixture of exhaustion and despair, Revie sent polite apologies and withdrew. The Lord Mayor, John Rafferty, exploded.

'Their decision is not only rude, but chickenhearted,' he said. 'They promised to come, win or lose, and they have let everybody down … they have failed themselves and their proud record by behaving in a way that savours of a petulant boy taking his bat home.' The cancelled reception was front-page news for the *Yorkshire Evening Post*, who added in an editorial that United had 'let down their fans, their city and their Lord Mayor'. The paper noted that all the civic plate and cutlery had been brought up from the cellars of the Civic Hall, and the council was now cancelling hundreds of pork pies and sandwiches that were being prepared. Revie apologised again, but there was no letup; letters flowed to the paper, calling his decision 'an insult' and 'a shocking display of bad sportsmanship'.

If almost a decade of hard work, culminating in one of the greatest seasons ever known in the game of football, was to be dismissed in Leeds over a cancelled order of pork pies, Don Revie had to be interested when, within a fortnight, a rogue Birmingham City director rejected his board's preference for hiring Brian Clough and offered £100,000 over seven years to Revie. Revie turned it down, as he had turned down Sunderland, Coventry City, Aston Villa, Juventus, Torino and more, saying as he always did that he wanted to finish the job he had started at Leeds. But in the summer of 1970 Revie was wondering, with his players, how much more effort this job would demand, and whether Leeds would ever get their rewards.

16

1970–73

I WILL ALWAYS REGARD
ELLAND ROAD AS
MY REAL HOME

Leeds United started the 1970/71 season determined
that nobody should see how much 1969/70 had hurt
them. Manchester United were beaten at Old Trafford
on the opening day, then Tottenham Hotspur, Everton,
West Ham United and Burnley. Leeds scored twelve
and conceded two, both to Everton. A hard-fought and
badly refereed 0-0 at Highbury cost a point, but Chelsea
were added to the list of beaten teams before Leeds were
finally beaten themselves, away to Stoke City, where
Johnny Giles and Jack Charlton were missed.

It was a temporary setback. Leeds only lost four
more league matches all season, and were their usual

efficient selves in the Fairs Cup, beating Sarpsborg 5-0 and Sparta Prague 6-0, before a 3-2 aggregate win over Vitória Setúbal set up a semi-final with Liverpool. Injuries restricted Paul Reaney, Eddie Gray, Johnny Giles and most worryingly Billy Bremner, but with the rest of the side remarkably consistent despite the previous season's wear, Paul Madeley and Mick Bates covered most absences between them. Arsenal were closest, but nobody could overtake Leeds at the top.

Failure would not destroy them, nor disappointment define them. A large contingent went to Mexico to see the World Cup first-hand – Charlton, Allan Clarke, Les Cocker, Terry Cooper and Norman Hunter on England duty, Revie as a television commentator, Bremner and Giles for fun – the rest had been captivated by Brazil's dazzling triumph, beamed back to Britain for the first time in sun-drenched colour. Revie might have been tempted to change United's colours again, to bright yellow and blue, but without anything so drastic Leeds joined in the general joie de vivre football found that summer. Leeds had become weighed down by their years of brilliance; Brazil showed playing football at the top level can be a light load, if you know how to carry it.

The rest of football, though, was not willing to let Leeds United become attacking superstars, even if they did outscore every other team in the First Division. 1970's collapse brought a gleeful response from an unsympathetic soccer public, as if Leeds, a club with no heritage in the game, had gatecrashed it for long enough – the tears of Revie and Bremner were deserved for straying so far above their station for so long.

There was more delight when, in the space of a week, Gary Sprake fumbled a shot at Anfield and let John Toshack tap in a winner, then was blamed for all three goals as Leeds fell behind to fourth-division Colchester United in the FA Cup. Hunter and Giles pulled two back but the back pages had their giant-killing, and plenty of readers cheering the story. It was another case of Leeds getting what was coming to them, ironic given the furore earlier that autumn that turned many readers decidedly against Leeds. In a local television interview, while discussing violence in the game, Jack Charlton said he had 'a little book with two names in it, and if I get the chance to do them I will'. He added that he kept bad fouls out of his own game, but 'there are two or three people who have done it to me, and I will make them suffer before I pack this game up'.

Charlton said these things with a light heart, believing grudges between players were common knowledge, not thinking anyone would take the idea of a little black book seriously. But his tone was lost once the newspapers got hold of the quotes and printed them across the country, and 'the Charlton affair' was national news for a month, the FA and Football League convening a joint emergency committee, while everyone from opponents to his own brother condemned him in the press. Eventually the FA, paying attention to the many positive character references for Charlton as a valued international, ordered him to apologise and took no further action. 'I apologise that, through me, the press were given an opportunity to knock football,' he said. But the damage had been done, and not to football. The press, and through them the public, loved football. But they loathed Jack Charlton, and hated Leeds United.

A match against West Bromwich Albion in late April provided more ammunition. English football had not been altogether transformed by Brazil's attacking style, and the teams were frustrating each other with efficient offside traps, strictly policed by referee Ray Tinkler and his linesmen. Until, that is, they weren't. West Brom were a goal ahead but Leeds were pushing for an equaliser, one effort from Jones harshly ruled out for offside, when Hunter's pass hit Tony Brown and ricocheted over the halfway line. Colin Suggett was standing around fifteen yards offside, and when the linesman, Bill Troupe, raised his flag, the game came to a stop. Tinkler, however, refused to stop it, waving play on. Nobody could understand why he wasn't blowing his whistle, but Brown put doing before understanding, running forward with the ball and squaring it across Sprake for Jeff Astle to score.

In the remaining twenty minutes Leeds did everything they could think of to salvage something, but only managed one goal, by Clarke; at the same time, Arsenal beat Newcastle United at Highbury, and for the first time all season Leeds were 2nd in the league. They won their remaining league matches without conceding a goal, including a 1-0 win over Arsenal, but Arsenal had more games left; they won the league title from Leeds by one point.

But the events of the West Brom game brought Leeds not sympathy, but condemnation. The players and staff had surrounded the linesman, appealing with him to tell Tinkler he had made a mistake; he told Tinkler something, but it didn't change the referee's mind. The injustice destroyed the players' tempers, and as they raged at the referee, angry fans joined in from the stands, pursued by police, and for a time it looked like a riot; the linesman on the opposite side was felled by a missile thrown from the Lowfields.

Revie was furious, predicting the decision would cost Leeds the title: 'I have never been so sick at heart. The ref's decision was the worst I have ever seen, and it wrecked nine months' hard work here.' He called for professional referees, as did Leeds' chairman Percy Woodward, and Richard Ulyatt added in the *Yorkshire Post* that he hadn't seen a worse call in 45 years. The anger of everyone in Leeds was justified, but Ulyatt added, with some foreboding: 'The angry spectators who rushed on to the ground will probably get the club into trouble with the FA.'

Elland Road was already acquiring a reputation as one of the grounds worst afflicted by football's growing

problem with hooliganism. Leeds still struggled to fill
the stadium, but had a fiercely loyal core of supporters, as it had since the Supporters' Club was formed
on the same day as the Football Club in 1919, several
hundred of them devoted to following the team across
Europe. But the excitement of the swinging 1960s was
giving way to a depressing swell of social and economic
problems, particularly in northern England, where the
industries that had sustained the region since Victorian
times were declining; the side effects were showing at
football matches, where boring games could be enlivened
by thrilling vandalism or fighting. The pitch invaders
at the West Brom match had not been the long-haired,
T-shirted louts the authorities feared, but respectable
middle-class types in good suits, driven to a furious
reaction by an incompetent referee; but any nuanced
understanding of the situation was impossible in the
aftermath. The public assessment was simple: the Leeds
players had behaved for years like a group of thugs and
this day was no different. The crowd was simply following their lead, and who knew where that would lead?
Revie and Woodward's view that the referee caused the
disorder didn't help when the FA took action; the disciplinary commission fined Leeds £500, and closed Elland
Road for the first four home matches of the following
season.

Leeds didn't help their public image when, desperate
not to end another season without silver, they played

the Fairs Cup semi-final with Liverpool like the Leeds
of old and, thanks to two defensive performances and
a diving header from Billy Bremner in the first leg at
Anfield, knocked out the more popular team. After
watching Arsenal add the FA Cup to their league title,
Leeds travelled to Italy for the first leg of the final against
Juventus, where again the fates seemed to be conspiring
against Leeds. It rained in Turin from the moment United
arrived, and a thunderstorm was drenching the already
unplayable pitch at kick-off, the organisers intent on
appeasing 50,000 soaking spectators by giving them a
game. A few minutes into the second half the referee
called it off; Bremner was furious, as he felt Leeds were
close to securing a 0-0 draw and didn't want to start the
match over again.

Leeds waited two days for the replay, and went for
more than a point; they attacked Juventus but twice
had to come from behind, Madeley equalising first, then
substitute Mick Bates equalising second with his second
touch, scoring only his second ever goal. Despite two
goals against them it was one of United's best European
performances, and the away goals rule put them in a
strong position. There was another good omen for the
second leg; the owl emblem Revie believed brought bad
luck was gone from United's new short-sleeved shirts,
replaced by the letters LUFC. By the end of the night
these shirts had been replaced too; a sharp finish from
Clarke was the best possible start, although an equaliser

forced Leeds to revert to their old cautious selves; the game finished 1-1, and wearing their beaten opponents' plain blue jerseys, Leeds lifted the Fairs Cup in their own ground in front of 42,483. 'When I got that trophy in my hands, everything suddenly became worthwhile again,' said Bremner. 'Gone was the feeling of frustration and despair we at Elland Road have felt so often. In its place was a sense of pride.'

Some of the Fairs Cup's lustre was dimmed because Leeds had won it before. They were playing some of their best football yet in the first seasons of the 1970s but not getting the plaudits, while Arsenal had suddenly progressed from 12th in the league to win a prestige league and FA Cup double. There was intense pressure on Leeds to emulate that success, not least from themselves, although the view outside Elland Road was that time was running out on some of Revie's lads; Jack Charlton was now 36 years old, Johnny Giles was almost 31, Billy Bremner was 28.

The more immediate problem was the punishment for the West Brom debacle; the enforced closure of Elland Road cost Leeds £50,000 in gate receipts, and meant their first eight league fixtures were all played away, four of them technically 'home' matches in not-so-neutral stadiums around Yorkshire. Leeds had only lost five league games the previous season, but with injuries to Clarke, Jones and Gray, by mid-October in 1971/72 they had already lost four, as well as a showpiece play-off against

Barcelona to decide who kept the Inter-Cities Fairs Cup, and a two-legged tie against Lierse SK in the first round of the Fairs Cup's replacement, the UEFA Cup; West Ham United had knocked them out of the League Cup.

But one of the wins, a 5-1 'home' victory over Newcastle United at Hillsborough, was a hint of what was ahead. From mid-November United's best players returned to fitness, form and consistency. Between them, Bremner, Charlton, Hunter and Lorimer only missed two league games; Giles only missed four; Paul Madeley started every match, playing left-wing, left-back, right-back, centre-half and centre-forward. At Christmas they went to Derby County and won 3-0, moving above Derby to 3rd, and began 1972 by beating Liverpool 2-0 at Anfield.

Two games in February proved what Revie's best eleven were capable of when they played without pressure. The public were used to Leeds grinding out results in crucial finals and semi-finals, but in the space of a fortnight *Match of the Day*'s cameras twice caught them carefree. Manchester United led the league at the start of the year but were dropping down the table; when they came to Elland Road, Leeds buried them. Madeley was playing in place of Reaney, but otherwise Revie picked the eleven everybody knew and feared: Sprake, Madeley, Cooper, Bremner, Charlton, Hunter, Lorimer, Jones, Clarke, Giles, Gray. They took the lead two minutes into the second half; calm attacking by Giles and Clarke down the left gave Gray time to aim inside Alex

Stepney's near post; Stepney touched the shot onto that post, but Jones buried the rebound. Then from the left again Lorimer crossed, Jones shot at goal, and Clarke flicked the bouncing ball past Stepney.

Manchester scrambled a goal back, but that was all they got from Leeds. Bremner centred from the right for Jones to head in from close range; Gray nicked the ball from Bobby Charlton, passed to Lorimer, and his shot was diverted in by Jones for his hat-trick and a celebratory smack on the backside from Jack Charlton. Then, with six players inside Manchester's penalty area, a seventh, Bremner, raced to the touchline to keep a stray ball in play and keep the attack going; Jones crossed and Lorimer swept onto the bouncing ball, bringing it under control as he skidded across the penalty area and crashing a shot past Stepney for five. It had taken half an hour, and now Leeds were satisfied to keep the ball and enjoy the rest of their afternoon.

The fun continued at Elland Road two weeks later. Southampton were fighting relegation, but at this point Leeds didn't care who they were playing. Reaney returned and Madeley moved to replace Cooper, but otherwise it was the same team, in the same mood. The first goal came just before half-time; Gray exchanged passes with Jones, danced around a tackle then passed wide to Clarke on the left; cutting in, he shot low and left-footed and scored. There was time for another before the break: Reaney's pass gave Gray time to turn and play a through ball first time to Lorimer, who also shot low and scored.

The second half was savage. At times half United's team was standing in a line across the edge of Southampton's penalty area, passing the ball from side to side, trying to make an opening. A simple through ball from Giles let Clarke beat a player inside the box and make it 3-0; Lorimer collected a loose ball on the right, span past a defender and fired low and hard for 4-0, then repeated the trick with a stray Southampton pass for his hat-trick; from a short corner on the right six passes took the ball to Hunter on the left, whose cross was headed high into the net by Charlton at the back post, 6-0; beginning with Bremner playing keepie-uppies in midfield, another move down the left ended with a dribble and cross from Gray, headed across goal by Lorimer and buried by Jones: 7-0.

Television highlights programmes like *Match of the Day* usually concentrated on goals, incidents and contro-versies, compressing matches into moments and talking points. But the director that day was as bewitched as Southampton and let the cameras absorb Leeds United's brilliance with the ball, as they forgot about scoring more, forgot about league titles and cup finals, referee-ing decisions and fixture lists, and played. They played with Southampton; 'It's almost cruel,' declared commen-tator Barry Davies, echoing what Eric Todd had written in the *Guardian* about the Manchester United match:

'sheer cruelty'. But the backheels, flicks, skills and tricks weren't intended to torture. The roars and cheers from the Elland Road crowd – that used to boo and jeer when United shut matches down to win them – encouraged the high-wire performance, drawing ever more audacious tricks from Giles and Bremner. It didn't matter what Southampton felt or what anybody thought. Leeds were having fun, and Southampton just happened to have a close-up view. 'Leeds have just about reached perfection,' said their midfielder Jimmy Gabriel. 'They are the nearest thing to footballing utopia.'

Champions Arsenal were beaten 3-0 and Nottingham Forest 6-1, but a punishing schedule affected Leeds yet again; those two games were played in three days, followed by three days' rest before a 2-2 draw away to West Ham on Friday 31 March and a 2-0 defeat at Derby the next day. That win put Derby top of the league by a point from Manchester City, who were a point ahead of Leeds. The Football League's secretary Alan Hardaker was again having a significant influence on United's chances; after forcing them to play four more 'away' matches than any other team, Hardaker would not hear of any fixture changes. Their good form had extended to the FA Cup; Bristol Rovers, Liverpool, Cardiff City and Tottenham were beaten on the way to a semi-final against second-division Birmingham City; for once, Leeds had a quiet time in a big match, winning 3-0 for a place in the centenary FA Cup final at Wembley.

Leeds went to Wembley with one league match left; Derby had played all theirs, beating 3rd placed Liverpool 1-0 on the same night Leeds won 2-0 at home to Chelsea. Derby were top by one point, but United's remaining game meant they were superbly placed to overtake them; if they drew with Wolverhampton Wanderers at Molineux they would be champions, and Liverpool would have to beat Arsenal by more than 11-0 to win the league.

If it was prestige Revie wanted, here it was. The FA Cup was held in the highest regard of any club trophy in the world, but had never been kind to Leeds, and was the one domestic honour Revie's team hadn't won. The 1972 centenary final was a grand occasion to celebrate the history of Association Football, attended by the Queen, and the opponents were cup holders Arsenal. A win at Wembley and a draw at Wolves would mean a distinguished and long-dreamed-of double.

Against Arsenal, United were composed, efficient and victorious. Terry Cooper had broken his leg in a game at Stoke City and was replaced by Paul Madeley; Gary Sprake had recovered from an injury but not taken his place back from David Harvey, and an hour before kick-off Revie announced the younger keeper would play. Harvey made a good early save from Frank McLintock but otherwise was hardly tested; the defence were superb, Charlton providing expert cover while Hunter barged forward to stop attacks at source, together subduing flamboyant striker Charlie George to the point of irrelevance, not letting his partner John Radford near the ball. The one time Harvey looked beaten, as a low drive by John Armstrong headed for the bottom corner, Reaney's reflexes blocked the ball on the line.

Leeds nearly took the lead in the first half, when Lorimer's powerful volley across goal was headed against the bar by Clarke; they were patient, and after scoring nine minutes into the second half, confident. Charlton stopped Charlie George's run by moving a foot and taking the ball out of his stride, giving it to Madeley. He ran forward and passed to Lorimer on halfway, who moved the ball on to Mick Jones wide on the right. He strolled towards Bob McNab then burst past him, evading a sliding tackle, and from just inside the right edge of the penalty area he crossed back and away from goal. Pat Rice seemed about to turn and hook the ball clear, but Allan Clarke, and only Allan Clarke, had seen a chance to score. His first thought was to volley, his second thought was to dive, and his third thought was glory as he watched his header flying past the goalkeeper into the bottom corner of the goal.

Leeds attacked with even more purpose after that, although George hit their crossbar with a snapshot to remind them the game still had to be won. Leeds had let strong positions escape them in the finals against Liverpool and Chelsea, but never lost their grip of this one. The FA Cup was won 1-0, and Don Revie lifted

17. Billy Bremner holds the FA Cup aloft, chaired on the shoulders of his teammates after beating Arsenal 1-0 at Wembley, 6 May 1972. Left to right: Paul Reaney, Johnny Giles, Allan Clarke, Jack Charlton, Billy Bremner, Peter Lorimer, Norman Hunter and David Harvey.

Colorsport/Shutterstock

18. The first team in the dressing room with the First Division Trophy following Billy Bremner's testimonial vs Sunderland, 6 May 1974. Back row (left to right): Paul Madeley, Billy Bremner, Peter Lorimer, Gordon McQueen and Paul Reaney. Front row: Frank Gray and Joe Jordan.

Colorsport/Shutterstock

19. Eddie Gray vs Liverpool in the 1974 Charity Shield
at Wembley, 10 August 1974.
Colorsport/Shutterstock

20. Brian Clough (right) glances over at Bill Shankly (middle)
as their sides do battle at Wembley, 10 August 1974.
Colorsport/Shutterstock

21. Allan Clarke takes on Franz Beckenbauer of Bayern Munich during the 1975 European Cup final in Paris, 28 May 1975.

Colorsport/Shutterstock

22. Tony Currie, Chelsea vs Leeds United, September 1978.

Colorsport/Shutterstock

23. John Sheridan, Coventry City vs Leeds United, April 1987.
Colorsport/Shutterstock

24. Mel Sterland, Vinnie Jones and Chris Fairclough
celebrate Leeds United's promotion from Division Two after
a 1-0 victory over Bournemouth, 5 May 1990.
Colorsport/Shutterstock

25. Howard Wilkinson during the 1989/90 season.
Colorsport/Shutterstock

26. Leeds United's title-winning team celebrate with the First Division Trophy at Elland Road, 2 May 1992.
Colorsport/Shutterstock

27. Gary Speed, Tony Yeboah, Brian Deane and Gary McAllister form a defensive wall against West Ham United at Upton Park, 19 August 1995.

Colorsport/Shutterstock

28. David O'Leary and Lee Bowyer talk tactics before Leeds take on Manchester United, 14 August 1999.

Colorsport/Shutterstock

29. Alan Smith and Mark Viduka on the break vs Real Madrid during a Champions League group game at Elland Road, 22 November 2000.

Andrew Cowie/Shutterstock

30. Jermaine Beckford and Matt Heath celebrate an 89th minute winner against Nottingham Forest, 25 August 2007.

Ed Sykes/Shutterstock

31. Marcelo Bielsa, Leeds United's head coach, at the friendly match against Guiseley, 26 July 2018.
Lee Brown for The Square Ball

32. Tyler Roberts, Kemar Roofe, Jack Harrison, Luke Ayling and Pablo Hernández celebrate scoring against Sheffield Wednesday, 2019.
Lee Brown for The Square Ball

Billy Bremner off his feet in a bear hug at the bottom of the Wembley steps. Bremner climbed them with his team, completing Leeds United's sweep of English football's honours by accepting the FA Cup from the Queen.

But Revie had to watch from a distance. In the final moments of the match Mick Jones again drove to the byline and tried to cross, crashing to the floor and not getting up. In the confusion of the final whistle, at first only the TV cameras saw what had happened, and Les Cocker, running past all the celebrations to his player. As cameras zoomed in on United's trainer cradling Jones on the grass, ITV's commentator Brian Moore speculated that Cocker was telling him: 'Son, we've won the cup.' What the microphones broadcast Cocker shouting at the photographers crowding round was: 'Go get the fucking doctor!'

The Leeds players gradually saw that Jones was missing from their celebrations and went to him; Revie was one of the last to realise, making his way over when Bremner was told he couldn't keep the Queen waiting any longer, and would have to collect the cup without Jones. He had dislocated his elbow, and the doctor's advice was to go straight to hospital, but Jones, in agony, wouldn't hear of it. With his arm strapped to his side, he limped to the bottom of the steps, where Mick Bates told him he'd collected his medal for him. That wouldn't do. He nearly went alone until Norman Hunter caught up to support him; in front of the 100,000-strong crowd and millions watching at home, with every step firing intolerable pain through his body, gripping his winner's medal in his hand at the end of his broken arm, Jones climbed to the top to meet the Queen. David Coleman commentated on the moment for the BBC: 'What a tragedy,' he exclaimed, at the moment of Leeds United's proudest triumph, 'and what a moment of emotion.' A group of female Leeds fans next to the steps had stopped Jones on his way up, holding him and kissing him with tears in their eyes.

Apart from the obvious pain of seeing one of the Leeds family so badly hurt, Revie had a practical reason to cry bitter tears, had he wanted. Hardaker's intransigence meant the vital league match at Wolves, on which the league and cup double depended, was being played on Monday night. It was now Saturday evening. Revie could get the players ready by restricting their champagne intake and going straight to a hotel for dinner and an early night, but there was nothing he could do to make Jones fit for Monday. Bremner would have to take his place in attack, and Mick Bates take Bremner's place in midfield. Clarke, Giles and Gray, who had barely been fit to play in the cup final, made it onto the pitch with combinations of painkilling injections and heavily strapped legs.

Revie promised his players would forget about only needing a draw and go on the attack, but what did they have left to attack with? And what did they have to do to get a break? Clarke thought he had a penalty when goalkeeper Phil Parkes brought him down, but the referee, Bill Gow, ruled otherwise. Then Clarke lobbed the ball towards goal but defender Bernard Shaw reached it, apparently using both hands to save the goal; the referee and linesman gave nothing. Wolves took the lead, forcing Leeds to attack in the second half, when there was another handball by Shaw to stop a shot by Lorimer, for which the referee gave nothing; and with Leeds leaving room at the back, Wolves scored again with 23 minutes left. Clarke could no longer run and was replaced by Terry Yorath, so Jack Charlton and Billy Bremner, the two players who had given most to Leeds United's cause under Revie, played as strikers in a desperate attempt to save the double. Madeley drove a pass into Wolves' penalty area and Bremner smashed it into the net with all his frustrated might, but one goal wasn't enough, and a second wouldn't come. Faced with the simple task of not losing a football match, Leeds United yet again found they were taking on more than any mortal team could contend with, and kicked harder against their fate than any other team ever could. But with no reward.

On the same night, Liverpool drew 0-0 with Arsenal, so the rewards went not to Revie's great friend Bill Shankly, but to irksome Derby manager Brian Clough. Like Revie, Clough was Middlesbrough born and raised; he was a prolific striker for Middlesbrough and Sunderland before injury ended his career, after

274 matches and 251 goals, while he was still only 27. As a manager he had, like Revie, built Derby up from the bottom of the Second Division, but otherwise the two could not be more different. Clough spent freely to get Derby to the top, making himself a celebrity. A generation younger than Revie, and four months younger than Jack Charlton, the camera loved him, and Clough loved giving increasingly outspoken opinions on the game and the people who played it – including the ones he didn't entirely approve of at Leeds. To Revie, this brashness was a symptom of football's decreasing decorum, and Clough was its emblem. When he started at Leeds, Revie befriended the tea ladies and regularly gave them money to place bets, sharing a drink with them when Leeds won a trophy. When Clough started at Derby, the story went, he sacked two of the tea ladies for laughing after a defeat.

This time Leeds did attend the civic celebrations; they might have deserved more, but at least had the elusive FA Cup to parade to thousands lining the streets of Leeds, from City Square to Elland Road, where 35,000 cheered a lap of honour. Revie was grateful to the fans, and tried to be magnanimous. Derby, he told the *Yorkshire Evening Post*, were 'one of the most exciting young sides to emerge in the English soccer game in years ... But it would be hypocritical for me to say that Derby won the gripping championship race because they were the best side.' He congratulated them, but: 'Deep down, I cannot accept they deserved to snatch the title from Leeds United's grasp.' Jack Charlton was blunter, but spoke for all at Leeds. 'I'm as sick as a pig,' he said.

Charlton was one of the players Revie had to give most thought to in the summer. He would soon be 38, and had already spoken with Revie about how long he could continue. In contrast to their bitter early relationship, Charlton now trusted Revie so much they agreed that when Revie no longer felt Charlton could do a job for Leeds, he would say so, and Charlton would pack it in without a word. They hadn't got to that point yet, and Revie may have wished it would never come, but he was now forced to think of a future without his favourite sons. Huddersfield Town had just been relegated, and from them Revie bought their 24-year-old captain Trevor Cherry – telling him he would play left-back for as long as Terry Cooper was injured and in the longer term replace Norman Hunter – and their 29-year-old centre-half Roy Ellam, £30,000 worth of competition for Charlton's place. The same fee bought St Mirren's twenty-year-old defender Gordon McQueen, to be prepared as Charlton's replacement.

Ellam started the first match of the new season, with Charlton challenged to win his place back. There was a change in goal, too, as David Harvey, who had waited at Leeds from a schoolboy until he was 25 to become first choice, even trusted with scouting missions to make him feel involved, finally took over from Gary Sprake.

Many thought the change was overdue. Sprake's quality was never in doubt, but he had made too many costly mistakes, and Bremner and Charlton always doubted his relaxed attitude, that bordered on arrogance. They wanted to change as far back as the FA Cup final in 1970; as Houseman's shot squirmed past Sprake for Chelsea's equaliser, Bremner said a prayer: 'Please, not now Gary, not now,' and Charlton said an oath: 'What the hell has the fucking clown done now?' Moments later, in the changing rooms, Sprake acted as if he had done nothing at all. The Leeds players prided themselves on honesty with each other – there would be ludicrous arguments between Hunter and Reaney, each trying to take the blame for conceding a goal – but Sprake seemed oblivious.

Harvey's great asset, as well as agile shot-stopping, was dependability; and after working for so long with Leeds, his game was ready made for the team. His first appearance of the season, though, did not go to plan. Harvey and Jones were both injured early away to Chelsea, and Lorimer had to take over in goal; Leeds laboured on, losing 4-0. Harvey was back for the next game but Ellam was not; Charlton's fight for his place took one match. But Jones' injury was severe and 21-year-old Joe Jordan, signed from Morton in 1970 and trained up as the new Jones, took over in attack.

Leeds shrugged off the defeat, but couldn't find the same stunning fluency that had taken them so close to the double. Only Harvey, Cherry, Bremner and Clarke played more than 35 league games – eight players achieved that number in 1971/72 – with injuries taking their toll on Jones, Gray, Giles and Charlton. There were suspensions too; Leeds struggled with an FA clampdown on behaviour and racked up disciplinary points, FA hearings and accusing headlines, not least from Brian Clough, who said he would punish Leeds by relegating them to Division Two. Another story dominated the autumn's tabloids; allegations that Leeds attempted to bribe Wolves players to help them win the double. There was plenty of sensation but little substance to the stories, but they dragged Leeds' name through the winter, until the FA and the Director of Public Prosecutions announced they saw no evidence to support an inquiry.

Leeds took some revenge. They beat Clough's noisy champions 5-0 at Elland Road and 3-2 at the Baseball Ground, and 1-0 in the FA Cup quarter-finals. They went to Molineux and won 2-0, only wishing they could have done so the previous May; they took on Wolves again in the FA Cup semi-final at Maine Road, Bremner scoring to get Leeds back to Wembley with a 1-0 win. As usual, Leeds were going for as much glory as possible, entering the European Cup-Winners' Cup for the first time and reaching the final, to be played in Greece against Milan.

But their usual form was not coming back. In the league they couldn't rise above 3rd and only won three of the last eleven matches; Revie was relieved that this time Shankly's Liverpool took the title, but three defeats were not an ideal warm-up for Wembley. Their opponents in the FA Cup final were Second Division Sunderland, managed by another of Revie's serial detractors, Bob Stokoe. The underdogs revelled in the build-up, making every television appearance they could, laughing and joking and getting the nation on their side, while quietly reminding everyone that they weren't just up against a First Division team, but 'Dirty Leeds' themselves, with all their skullduggery. 'It's like "Have a go" week,' observed Bremner.

Leeds couldn't lift themselves above their nerves, and they couldn't translate Sunderland's gibes into their old siege mentality. They could barely pass the ball. After half an hour, with the Leeds defence watching Sunderland's Dave Watson, a corner fell instead to Ian Porterfield, who smashed the ball past Harvey. In the second half Leeds were more like their attacking selves, sending Cherry forward from left-back to reach right-back Reaney's deep crosses; he headed one almost into goal, but goalkeeper Jimmy Montgomery dived full length to touch it clear. From five yards Lorimer smashed the rebound past him, or so everybody thought; somehow Montgomery got to his feet and dived again, and the ball cannoned off him onto the crossbar. Cherry, still lying on the ground, tried to flick the ball in with his heel, then tried to punch the pitch into submission, since Sunderland's goal would not give in.

The 1-0 defeat was a triple indignity for Jack Charlton. He had decided to retire and take up the job of managing Middlesbrough, and this was not the way he wished to end his career with Leeds; worse, a hamstring injury meant he missed the game, and he was convinced Leeds would have won if he'd played. Third, as Sunderland did their lap of honour, Stokoe spotted Charlton on the television gantry, and sent him a two-fingered salute.

It was the eighth time Leeds had finished runners-up under Revie. If the other times hurt because Leeds gave so much in defeat, this hurt more, because the tears of the fans confirmed what the players felt; this time they had let everybody down. But there was something more to it. At the post-match banquet Revie stumbled through an emotional speech.

'I feel that our players have done enough in ten years to walk in to your applause even without the FA Cup. We never tried to cheat. We tried to be honest, and we would be less than honest if I did not ask you to salute the most consistent side that ever lived.' Revie's words were tearful, and significantly in the past tense.

Two days later Elland Road said goodbye to Jack Charlton with a testimonial match against Celtic. 'I have not been a footballer to Leeds people,' said Jack, 'I have always felt that I was a friend. I can count on one hand the number of times during the past ten years that I have not been called simply Jack by people who have stopped me in the street.

'I have been fortunate enough to go on longer than most people with one single club and no matter where I go in the future I will always regard Elland Road as my real home. There has got to be change in every walk of life. It is happening to me now and it will happen to others in the team in the future. No player can go on for ever.'

And no manager. Leeds blew off some of the FA Cup final hangover in their last league match, when with nothing at stake but frustration to burn, they took on league runners-up Arsenal at Elland Road with no dossier, and no plan other than to destroy them; they attacked with freedom and won 6-1. But they flew to Greece for the Cup-Winners' Cup final amid a storm of rumours, heightened when Revie only met them at Manchester Airport rather than travelling with them from Leeds; the newspapers claimed he had been in Liverpool that morning, asking directions to the home of Everton's chairman, there to discuss becoming their manager. In public, Revie urged everyone to concentrate on winning the match, for which Leeds were without Charlton, Bremner, Giles, Clarke and Gray. In private, Johnny Giles, Norman Hunter and Mick Bates confronted Revie in his hotel room. They knew Revie wouldn't lie. The deal wasn't done, he said, but the rumours were true: he was leaving. He had planned to tell the players after the game, but called them all together now to break the news.

There were other rumours that week in Greece. Due to his injury Giles was doing television work, and hearing a lot of pre-match talk. 'The word is we can't win this game,' he told the team. Milan were a top-class team in good form, while Leeds would be patched up with inexperienced reserves. But Giles was hearing Milan would also have the Greek referee, Christos Michas, on their side.

The match, played in a howling thunderstorm merging with the howls of outraged local spectators, bore that theory out. In the opening minutes Mick Bates was sent to the floor but Michas gave nothing; seconds later, when with characteristic elegance Paul Madeley took the ball from Alberto Bigon, Michas whistled for an imaginary foul, and Harvey was unsighted as Luciano Chiarugi's free-kick deflected off Madeley and inside his post.

The Leeds players performed well above themselves to stay in the game, but Milan were allowed to get away with all the kicks and punches they liked, and with tripping Mick Jones for what should have been a clear penalty. Leeds could have had two more, but barely bothered claiming for them, knowing they would get nothing. The match continued along a rising trajectory of frustration shared by the Leeds players and the Greek crowd. What was happening was so obvious that at the end of their 1-0 win Milan were booed while Leeds took a lap of honour, the fans chanting: 'You won! You won!'

UEFA and the Greek FA suspended Michas, and UEFA later banned him from refereeing for life for fixing other matches, but they refused to investigate or overturn this result.

The nadir was reached a few minutes from the end. Norman Hunter, his legs already bearing the worst cuts United's doctor had ever seen, felt one more kick on the back of his calf as he chased the ball. He pulled up, limping in pain, raised his eyes to the stormy heavens, and enough was enough. He turned to face Gianni Rivera, chased after him, and landed a punch around his neck. As players and officials ran brawling from everywhere, Hunter took a kick on the thigh from Riccardo Sogliano, and eventually a red card from Christos Michas. In the confusion Hunter thought he might only have been booked, and stayed on the field until Michas furiously ordered him off. Hunter had no choice. It was time to go.

1973–74

THOSE LADS ARE
THE ONES WHO WON

D on Revie accompanied his dejected players back to
Leeds, then returned with his family to Greece, for
a holiday and to think about his future. There were several reasons why he should want to leave Leeds United.

One was the board. Since his friend and mentor
Harry Reynolds had been replaced as chairman by Percy
Woodward and now by Manny Cussins, the boardroom
had become the one part of the club that resisted Revie's
highly prized family atmosphere. He was a friend to the
laundry staff who he thought as vital to the club's success as anyone – somebody had to keep those muddy
shirts gleaming white – but to the businessmen in the
boardroom Revie remained an employee, who had

things his own way too often. Many of them were old
enough to remember when directors ran football clubs,
and managers were merely secretaries; with Revie running the show, the board felt their role was reduced to
writing cheques. Many of their businesses were declining
as the textile trade that built the city's wealth gave in to
overseas competitors, and running the football club was
a way of retaining prestige; but not if Don Revie took
all the credit. The board appreciated Revie's work, and
that of the players. But they were not convinced that
another manager and different players might not have
done better, and given them fewer headaches.

That cold relationship was reflected in Revie's wages.
That was another reason for going to Everton: money.
He wanted to finish working in his mid-fifties and enjoy
retirement, but he'd not earned enough to do that by
working at Leeds. Over the years he had many better
offers, sometimes using them as leverage for a pay rise at
Leeds, but agreeing to stay at Elland Road for less than
was being promised elsewhere. Revie was almost 46, and
stood to earn £122,500 of basic salary from the seven
remaining years on his contract. Everton were offering
to double that and add a £50,000 tax-free signing fee
on top.

The Leeds board couldn't agree how much to offer
Revie to stay this time, but there was a hiccup; Labour
MP Dennis Skinner asked in Parliament if this wasn't a
matter for the Conservative government's Pay Board, a

body that controlled wages and stipulated across industry that new hires should be paid the same as the people they replaced, subject to a maximum £250 annual increase. Everton's proposal could be ruled illegal, but Revie had lucrative offers elsewhere; his presence in Greece alerted the local FA, who wanted him for their national team, as well as top clubs Olympiakos and Panathinaikos. But Revie may have thought twice about managing in a league refereed by the likes of Christos Michas every week.

Another reason was the Leeds team. They had finished as runners-up in league or cup nine times. No club came close to United's record of nine consecutive top-four finishes since 1964/65, but they had still only won the league title once. From six semi-finals, they had won the FA Cup once. And now, seven points behind champions Liverpool in the league, defeated by Second Division Sunderland in the FA Cup final and robbed by Milan, Leeds had finished without a trophy. People had been saying for years that Revie's players were finished. Jack Charlton had gone. If there were to be more seasons like this, Revie might not be able to stand the emotional toll of managing Johnny Giles, Billy Bremner, Norman Hunter and the rest through the decline. He would be taking Les Cocker, Syd Owen and Maurice Lindley to Everton with him; quiet words were had with Hunter and Trevor Cherry about following them. Goodison Park might be a way of taking the machinery from Elland Road, and putting it to work in a less emotional arena.

Emotions, however, bonded Revie and the players together, and to Leeds United. Their explosions of temper and ferocious will to win were expressions of the love the players felt for each other and their club. Billy Bremner had a deep well of statements of his commitment: 'Side before self, every time'; 'Every time Leeds concede a goal, I feel like I've been stabbed in the heart.' Revie had a sign in the dressing room, reading simply: 'Keep fighting.' For the team, for the club, for each other.

It would take a lot for Revie to leave. Whether due to the Pay Board's interest or his obligation to the distressed players he had told he was leaving behind, Revie changed his mind. 'When these offers come along and you have the chance to secure the future of your own family, you just have to give them a bit of thought,' he told the *Yorkshire Evening Post*. 'But I feel my future is resolved and I am completely happy. I never wanted to leave Leeds ... During all the talks I have had recently with Leeds, I have not asked for a penny extra – and I don't want anything. I would like to put it clearly on record that I am not getting anything and I don't want anything.'

What Revie wanted was to win the league. 1972/73 had been a huge disappointment, but helped some of the younger players get used to what the old players had gone through for a decade. Revie's team kept being written off, and the press were stunned that after all the talk of a new job, he didn't buy any new players. But only Bremner and Giles were now over 30, and Paul Reaney, Paul Madeley, Peter Lorimer, Mick Jones and Allan Clarke were all in their prime. David Harvey had taken over from Gary Sprake, who left for Birmingham City; Trevor Cherry had comfortably replaced Terry Cooper, once the best left-back in the world, who now couldn't get back into the team. In 1971 Revie had tried to buy West Bromwich Albion's 21-year-old midfielder Asa Hartford as a long-term replacement in midfield, but a heart defect was uncovered after he was already training with Leeds, and they were advised not to go through with the high-profile £177,000 deal. But since then faithful reserve Mick Bates had filled in regularly and admirably for Bremner or Giles, and youngsters Gordon McQueen, Joe Jordan, Terry Yorath and Eddie Gray's young brother Frank had experienced the Cup-Winners' Cup final and were ready for the first team. Eddie Gray was the only concern, as he couldn't stay clear of injuries.

Half the team were world-class players, half had freshness and potential. Revie had seen something in the 6-1 demolition of Arsenal at the end of the previous season that he later admitted he should have seen sooner; that free of pressure, with less emphasis on dossiers and gameplans, encouraged to attack and left to play, his players could crush even the hardest opponents, and entertain while they did it. Season after season had

started optimistically with the simple aim of winning trophies, but buckled under the pressure Leeds placed upon
themselves; as those trophies became more attainable,
games and expectations piled up, making them harder to
win. Revie now had a simpler plan. They would forget
the cups and win the league, and they would do it the
easy way: by winning all their games.

The target Revie set the players in pre-season was to
go unbeaten, but the tactical plans they worked on left
no doubt that they would be playing to win. Bremner
would forgo defending and drive into the penalty area
from midfield. Goalkeepers would be tested more often
and from new distances and angles; if Leeds shot more,
they would score more. And, importantly, there would be
no dissent, and no fighting. The new-look Leeds would
be as tough as ever, but with a suspended £3,000 fine
imposed by the FA and the papers full of opinion from
Brian Clough and others that 'Dirty Leeds' were a blight
on the game, they would clean themselves up. No more
arguing with referees, no more brawls with opponents.
If they could go unbeaten, they might also go unbooked.

It wasn't the club's first attempt to make over its
image. Since Leeds won promotion in 1965 local pop
singer Ronnie Hilton had recorded a series of tribute
songs that didn't repeat the national success of 'No Other
Love', his number one hit from 1956, but were popular
on the Elland Road terraces: 'Leeds United Calypso',
'The Lads of Leeds', 'The Ballad of Billy Bremner'. The

Anfield Kop was famous for singing songs from the charts; Elland Road had its own songbook. Illustrator and entrepreneur Paul Trevillion helped Leeds United to the top ten in 1972, by convincing songwriter Les Reed, who had written Tom Jones' hits 'It's Not Unusual' and 'Delilah', to write and record a single with the team for the FA Cup final; the A-side was 'Leeds United', but the B-side, 'Leeds! Leeds! Leeds!', was better known by its chorus – 'Marching on Together' – and became the club anthem.

The songs were only one of Trevillion's ideas. He convinced Revie that a touch of razzmatazz could change public perception, and was given free rein. To the astonishment of their opponents, Leeds began running on to the pitch wearing personalised tracksuits with their names on the back, going through warm-up exercises not far removed from dance routines. In days when fans arrived hours before kick-off to secure a view, the crowd at Elland Road loved the entertainment, and the souvenir footballs the players kicked into the crowd for them to keep. During matches they wore tags on their socks, of royal blue cloth with tassels, bearing each player's number, and these would go to young fans as a memento. Then there was the 'Leeds Wave'; after the other team had suffered the boos and jeers of the crowd, the Leeds players would form a line in the centre circle, and wave to each side of the ground in turn, receiving a standing ovation before the match even started.

Trevillion had moved on, but his innovations were kept. For 1973 the tracksuits and shirts had a new look, with a new club badge. The grim landscapes of Britain's industrial decline were brightened by colourful nylon and polyester outfits replacing, for men, the formal suits that were standard for half a century; inadvertently contributing to the general downturn in Leeds, where millions of those suits were made. Leeds United brought that boldness to Elland Road, unveiling a yellow-and-blue badge that placed bubbly L and U letters inside a circle to create a smiley face, placed on the shirts six inches below the scowl of Bremner. Admiral Sportswear took over production of those shirts, one of the first companies to market replica kits, so children across the country could pull on a smiley Leeds shirt in front of the mirror and practise a Bremner scowl of their own.

United had hired Peter Fay, a young public relations expert who co-edited *The Official Football League Yearbook*, and he overhauled the club's match programme into a magazine that gave Leeds a right to reply. The first issue included a lengthy message from Don Revie to the fans, discussing how Leeds would overcome the critics.

'We begin our latest quest for success cast in the roles of music hall villains,' he wrote. 'Not only is it hard for we at the club to take – but it must be even more galling for you fans ... What the critics don't realise is that their attacks have nothing like the effect on us they think.

With every critical word or story we'll work twice as hard to try and prove all these knockers wrong. We hope you will continue to back us with your fantastic support as we try to right one of football's wrongs.'

Just weeks earlier it had felt like those wrongs finally had the better of Leeds, and Revie was departing to put things right elsewhere. Instead, 1973/74 immediately became one of the most successful rebrands and relaunches football had seen. Leeds won all of their first seven games, beating Revie's tempters Everton, then Arsenal, Tottenham Hotspur, Wolverhampton Wanderers, Birmingham City, Wolves again and Southampton, scoring nineteen, conceding four, and receiving not a single booking. For the first match with Wolves, a 4-1 home win, Elland Road's new floodlights were used for the first time in the league; 260 feet tall, they were the tallest in Europe, and didn't only light up the pitch but the sky above the south of the city, like the twinkling steelworks of Leeds soccer's first team of dreamers.

A visit from Manchester United woke things up. Determined to scrap and defend, containing Bremner and Giles with fouls, they left with a 0-0 draw and all the criticism in their ears that used to follow Leeds. Joe Jordan collected Leeds' first booking of the season, but after earlier matches Leeds had already received the personal congratulations of referee Roger Fitzpatrick – it was 'a pleasure to be on the same field' as Leeds

United, 'a model of good behaviour and a credit to the game' – and significantly from Vernon Stokes of the FA disciplinary commission which imposed the suspended £3,000 fine against Leeds in the summer. He visited the Leeds dressing room to tell the players they were 'setting a wonderful example', and Peter Fay made sure his comments had widespread attention.

Leeds were playing their best football since 1972, and possibly exceeding that standard, but inevitably some momentum was lost when Eddie Gray's season was ended by an injury in the Manchester United game, and a month later Giles was ruled out until the end of March. Madeley took over from Gray; and first Bates, then when he was injured Yorath, took over from Giles, and some of the sparkle left Leeds. Teams now approached them with the same wary defensive tactics as Manchester United, and Leeds had to work harder. Two matches were drawn and two won 1-0, and in the changing room Revie reminded his players what was expected now the defensive shackles were off. 'I want to go unbeaten this season and win the league,' he told them, 'but if you lads are not going to do it for me then I'll go out and get someone who will.' The threat of new signings was an old habit and rarely believed, but the team, unbeaten in its first twelve matches, was left in no doubt that standards this season were to be higher than ever.

There was an early exit from the League Cup and, after a gruelling UEFA Cup tie with Hibernian was won on penalties, Revie decided that was enough of that competition and allowed the players to treat the visit to Vitória Setúbal in Portugal as a golfing trip; Leeds went out 3-2 on aggregate. The lessons of nine years of fixture congestion were learned, but even by focusing on the league Leeds were experiencing a different kind of pressure.

As the run continued into 1974, overtaking Liverpool's record nineteen-game unbeaten start to a season, the scoring rate dropped, draws became more frequent, and matches away from Elland Road became more intense. Several commentators, not all of them well-meaning, declared Leeds were as good as champions as early as September, and away matches became like a visit from the fairground's strong man, everybody in every town fancying their chances of knocking him down. Teams with nothing to play for had an attractive target when Leeds visited, of becoming the first team to beat the unbeatables. Leeds were, of course, incredibly difficult to beat; since promotion to Division One they had only lost 69 of 378 league matches, so when teams went for them 'like men possessed,' as Revie put it, as if playing an all-or-nothing cup tie, Hunter, Bremner, Reaney and the rest knew exactly how to steal a win or take a draw. But that wasn't in the spirit of the new, attacking, smiling Leeds United, and even while the run continued, the boss kept reminding the players how good they had to be, until even he realised conspicuous success was becoming counterproductive.

'There isn't a team in the world who could produce their best football under the type of pressure to which Leeds United have been subjected recently,' said Revie. 'When Leeds won the championship in 1968/69, I went on record as saying that our record of only two League defeats throughout the season would never be broken and still hold this view. Certainly, I think it will be a miracle if Leeds reach the end of the current League campaign without losing any games.'

When defeat finally came, away to Stoke City in United's 30th game, it wasn't welcomed, especially as it involved building a commanding 2-0 lead inside twenty minutes, then letting Stoke score twice before half-time and add a winning third in the second half. The critics said that could become a metaphor for Leeds United's season; it came days after second-division Bristol City had used a replay at Elland Road to knock Leeds out of the FA Cup – signs of a trend. From 29 league games Leeds had taken nineteen wins and ten draws, scoring 50 goals and conceding sixteen, creating a nine-point lead over Liverpool at the top of the league. But Liverpool had a game in hand and were building an unbeaten run of their own; and defeat didn't bring the relief Leeds hoped for, just two 1-1 draws and a narrow win over Manchester City before they went, more nervously than necessary, to Anfield on 16 March. Don Revie will have noted that the date marked his thirteenth anniversary as Leeds United manager.

The build-up to the match, and the quality of play by both teams in front of 56,003 fans, suggested a title decider; the result, 1-0 to Liverpool, left Leeds only hoping it wasn't. There were eight games left but worse to follow; a disastrous and bad-tempered 4-1 defeat at home to Jimmy Adamson's exciting Burnley side, and another argumentative match, lost 3-1 at West Ham. Liverpool extended their unbeaten run to twelve, closing the gap to four points with three games in hand; and there was no sign of fixture congestion for Liverpool, the first two games fitting easily into their schedule, the last not due until after the FA Cup final.

The first of Liverpool's games in hand was lost 1-0 to Sheffield United, giving Leeds hope, but 0-0 draws with Coventry City and Sheffield United made it clear Leeds had to concentrate on themselves. The self-discipline they had worked so hard to establish, both in terms of suspensions and consistent results, was threatening to abandon them. The Easter schedule meant a return match at Sheffield United the day after they drew at Elland Road; nervous but in control, Leeds won with two goals from Lorimer in the last half hour. Liverpool brushed Manchester City aside 4-0, but their next opponents were local rivals Everton, who were determined not to help them; they played a 0-0 draw at Anfield while Leeds, getting no help either at home to 3rd placed Ipswich Town, but lifted by Eddie Gray's first match since September, got a crucial result. After 22 minutes

Leeds led 2-0 through Lorimer and Bremner, but there were terrible echoes of the defeat at Stoke when Ipswich equalised with 35 minutes left. Clarke silenced them. Controlling the ball in the penalty area, he shot into the roof of the net, and Leeds knew better than to give Ipswich the ball again after that.

Superior goal average meant a point at QPR from United's final game would be enough. 'It's a bit premature to call us champions yet,' said Revie. 'I'll not really breathe easily until I see the trophy is in Billy Bremner's hands.' He could breathe a little sooner than that. On Wednesday 24 April, while ITV viewers watched a *This Is Your Life* programme about Don Revie, spectators at Anfield watched their side losing 1-0 to Arsenal. The title belonged to Leeds, and the next morning Bill Shankly phoned Don Revie. 'Leeds United are truly great champions,' he said. 'My congratulations to you, your team, and to everyone at Elland Road. I know Leeds care about everyone, from the cleaning ladies right through, and that is how it should be.'

Revie was simply relieved. 'I feel as though someone had come along and lifted six tons of coal off my back,' he said. 'It's a great feeling. I feel as though I am walking on air.' There were celebrations at QPR on the final day, 7,000 Leeds fans travelling to London for the 1-0 win, but Bremner didn't lift the trophy until 6 May, before his testimonial match against Sunderland at Elland Road. He had it again after the game, acclaimed by

37,700 people as he took the trophy on a lone lap of honour.

It was a rare solo tribute to a player who always put the team first, but after fifteen seasons, it was deserved for exactly that reason. Bremner paid tribute to the fans, and Revie paid tribute to the players and staff; 'Those lads are the ones who won the championship, not me,' he said. 'Them and people like Syd Owen, Maurice Lindley and Les Cocker – I am just the figurehead.

'This gives us a second chance to have a crack at winning the European Cup,' Revie went on. 'I've made no secret of the fact that it is my biggest ambition to see Leeds United win the greatest of the European trophies. It is a dream I have had ever since I became a manager, and now the possibilities of that being realised have opened up to us again.'

18

1974–75

I THOUGHT TONIGHT
WOULD BE THE NIGHT

In June 1974 Billy Bremner, David Harvey, Joe Jordan, Peter Lorimer and Gordon McQueen went to West Germany to represent Scotland at the World Cup. Their English international colleagues should have been there; all England needed to qualify was to beat Poland at Wembley in October 1973. Allan Clarke scored a penalty, but a mistake by Norman Hunter had already given Poland a shot at Peter Shilton that the goalkeeper let through, and the 1-1 draw was a national embarrassment. Sir Alf Ramsey, England manager for eleven years and winner of the World Cup, was sacked in May.

There were few outstanding candidates to replace him. Coventry City manager Joe Mercer took temporary charge for the British Home Championship, but didn't want the job. The easy choice, the most successful English manager of the last ten years, was clear in the press that he wanted to win the European Cup with Leeds.

But in private, Don Revie was not at all clear. The European Cup was a huge temptation; seeing Real Madrid claiming that cup inspired much of what followed in his managerial career. But the doubts of the previous summer, when he wanted to leave for Everton, had not diminished in twelve months; winning the league title with such style was a superb achievement, as close to perfection as any team could get, but were those ageing players and naive youngsters capable of finding such strength again in Europe? And if they weren't, how would Revie bring himself to tell players like Billy Bremner, Norman Hunter and Johnny Giles that they weren't up to it anymore – that it was time for them to go?

Elland Road was finally becoming the modern stadium Revie himself had planned – after more than 50 years, the 1920s Scratching Shed was at last demolished, replaced by a South Stand befitting champions of the 1970s – but the uneasy relationship with the board remained. Revie had a nine-year contract to start work at Elland Road as a consultant on the first day of 1980, at £10,000 a year, a sort of pension that required attending four board meetings a year. What he did between now and then was up to Revie, and given Alf Ramsey's tenure, there was not likely to be another chance of the most prestigious job in football.

Revie sent word to the FA secretary, Ted Croker, that he was interested. The messenger was Tom Holley, Leeds United captain of the 1940s, whose career in journalism had taken him to the *Sunday People*. Ignoring the mutterings of Alan Hardaker at the Football League, Croker and the FA chairman Sir Andrew Stephen were delighted, seduced by Revie's Leeds of 1973/74, and a meeting was quickly arranged. On 4 July Revie was announced as the new England manager, and that was that. There was sadness at Leeds, and there were eulogies, but much of what needed to be said had been said the summer before. Leaving for England was different to going to another club; there was pride in seeing the Leeds manager promoted, and his departure was businesslike. On 5 July Don Revie cleared his desk at Elland Road.

The board wanted Revie to stay until his successor was chosen, but he told them what to do: give the job to Johnny Giles. He told Giles too, who hadn't expected it, but accepted Revie's encouragement to speak to the board and get what amounted to a rubber stamp on the job. But before they could meet there was a development. Billy Bremner heard from inside the boardroom about Giles' impending appointment, and let them know he would like to be considered. That changed the situation. By choosing between Revie's choice and Revie's captain, the board feared dividing the loyalties of the squad. And for another thing, they were sick, after so many years, of having employees like Revie, Giles and Bremner dictate how the club was run. There were numerous examples of Revie talking down to the directors, treating them like staff when it should have been vice versa. Vice-chairman Percy Woodward agreed with the press that Revie had 'exceeded his authority' by offering the job to Giles: 'It's not for a manager who is leaving to invite his successor,' he said. 'It's a decision for the board.' As a declaration of independence from Revie, they would advertise the job and choose a manager themselves.

The view inside and outside the club was that Don Revie was right, and Giles was the right choice. Most of the players backed the idea; to them, Bremner was their inspiration, but Giles was their brain, and already proving himself in management as player-coach of the Republic of Ireland. But Giles was ambivalent. If Revie thought he should be the manager and the board offered him the job, he would accept and give it his all, but he wouldn't compete with Bremner for it, and he certainly wouldn't involve himself in an interview process with other candidates. He was 33, happy to be a player for Leeds United, but not happy that the board were disregarding Revie's advice. 'They should have hung on his every word,' he said later. 'But they thought, "He's only a manager. If we advertise this job we'll get a hundred people." But you wouldn't have got a hundred Don Revies, that's for sure.'

In the end nobody was happy with the manager they got, except the man himself. Brian Clough was delighted. He was delighted to be taking audacious charge of a team and players he had criticised for so long, delighted to have the chance to get one over on his rival Revie, delighted at the sensation the announcement caused. He controlled that announcement, although he was not entirely in control of his own situation. At a meeting in a Hove hotel, where with long-time assistant Peter Taylor he was managing Third Division Brighton & Hove Albion, he told Leeds chairman Manny Cussins that he would take the job, but Taylor announced to both Clough and Cussins that he would not be coming.

Observers of their work at Derby County had wondered who should take most of the credit for their success: the high-profile Clough, or the diligent background man Taylor. That Leeds were only getting the accelerator and not the brake was among the first signs that all would not be well. Before Cussins could think too much about that, Clough went straight to the journalists waiting for him in the hotel's lobby, and broke the news: 'Gentlemen, I have just been appointed manager of Leeds United.' Clough might not have been able to control Taylor, but he was now certainly in charge of Leeds. They just had to get around to agreeing with him about that, and they couldn't back out now.

After giving the newspapers a sensational story, Clough flew to Mallorca to resume his family holiday.

Leeds United's players had been in pre-season training for a fortnight, but Clough didn't arrive for several days, bringing his two sons with him as a shield. He arranged extra training sessions then arrived late to most of them, keeping his distance or his sons by his side; the players felt they were being subjected to a strange combination of too much training and not enough rigour, and no communication at all from the new manager. After several awkward days, Bremner suggested to him that, as it was almost two weeks since he had been appointed, Clough might want to say something to the players.

Clough had had plenty to say about them in the past. In 1973, while managing Derby, Clough was invited to speak at Yorkshire Television's Sports Personality of the Year Award dinner at the Queens Hotel in Leeds. Peter Lorimer accepted the award from former Prime Minister Harold Wilson, but as Leeds had an important match the next day, he left before the speeches. There were two or three of these before it was Clough's turn, when he announced to the room that he would not speak until he had been to the toilet. After that delay, Clough began. He had come to pay tribute to sport, he said, but as for Peter Lorimer, he had won this award 'despite the fact that he falls when he hasn't been kicked, and despite the fact that he protests when he has nothing to protest about'. There was more. Billy Bremner was 'a little cheat'; if Eddie Gray, beset by injuries, was a racehorse, he would have been shot; Leeds United should be relegated for 'cheating' and 'cynical football'. Clough had come into the heart of Leeds and insulted its own, and the story kept the newspapers occupied for days; but now he was Leeds manager, the players said they were prepared to let bygones be bygones. 'I took what he said with a pinch of salt,' Lorimer said. 'He was indulging in a bit of games-manship because we were due to play Derby. There is no doubt he is a very good manager.'

The players might have had a policy of appeasement, but Clough did not. Far from apologising, he used that speech as a rehearsal for his first address to the squad, only this time he opened with: 'Right, you fucking lot. The first thing you can do for me is throw your medals in the bin, because you've never won anything fairly; you've done it by cheating.'

Then he took them one by one. Giles was a 'dirty bastard'. No one in football liked Norman Hunter; Hunter told him: 'I couldn't give a fuck.' He rehashed his line about Eddie Gray the racehorse, only this time to his face. Gray pointed out that Clough's own playing career was ended by injury: 'You of all people should know how I feel,' he told him. And Clough should have known what picking on the misfortune of a player who was like a younger brother to the others would do. The only players exempt from criticism were Allan Clarke and Gordon McQueen, the two players the bigger brothers in the room were always knocking the egos out of; the meeting descended into argument, and Clough departed, to reappear that night on TV.

Yorkshire Television cut Clough's speech from their 1973 awards show, but now Austin Mitchell gave him a half-hour special, *Clough Comes to Leeds*, in which Mitchell and three journalists tried to get to the bottom of just what he thought he was doing at Leeds United. Clough referred to speaking with the players, but not to what he said, although he made the same points. 'I think Leeds have always sold themselves short,' he said. 'I think they've been champions, and they've not been good champions in the sense of wearing the crown remarkably well. I think they could have been a little bit more loved ... Leeds were disliked. And are disliked. And it's only been the last twelve months where they've started to earn a little bit of applause from everybody. I want them to be good league champions.'

Clough was proposing that Leeds should do what Revie had made them do the previous season; clean up their act and play more attacking football. But he was bent on dismissing everything Revie had done, while realising that by trying to follow Revie he was trapping himself. 'On certain aspects of me taking over at Leeds, I can't win,' he said. 'Because if I finish 5th, I'm going to get stick, and if I win the European Cup they're going to say it was Revie's side in any case. So on that particular angle I just can't win, and I don't attempt to.' The last part obscured the motive. All Clough could do with the reigning league champions was win the championship again but, in his words, 'a little bit better'. If the league and European Cup were won with Revie's players, it would be done Clough's way. And that seemed to be the whole point.

He quickly bought the very un-Revie Duncan McKenzie, a flamboyant striker forcing his way out of Nottingham Forest, for a club record £250,000. His old players John McGovern and John O'Hare came from Derby's reserves for a combined £130,000, and Clough had already spent more in a few weeks than Revie had in thirteen years. There were suspicions that his old boys were brought in as allies, and Clough did ask McKenzie what was being said in the dressing room. McKenzie knew very well that the players were talking about nothing but Clough, but merely said he hadn't got to know them very well yet.

There was more talk when the season started. The Charity Shield, held at Wembley for the first time and broadcast live on television, showed that imposing Clough's beliefs was going to be difficult; Bremner was sent off, along with Liverpool's Kevin Keegan, for fighting after Giles was booked for punching Keegan. As Bremner and Keegan moped from the field, they threw their shirts to the floor; neither could explain why, but the nation was aghast, and both were banned until the end of September. Leeds lost after goalkeeper Harvey missed in a penalty shoot-out; Clough didn't let

McKenzie take a kick, in case the new signing missed and people blamed the manager.

The league season opened with two more defeats, 3-0 at Stoke City and 1-0 at home to Queens Park Rangers. Before the first match Clough led the players to a nearby motorway and attempted to give his team talk in the central reservation; it began raining, so the team ignored him and went back to their hotel. He was beginning to realise his approach had been wrong; he had also mis-judged who were the true leaders, and what really made the team tick. As well as bringing players in, Clough was rushing to get them out, without oversight from the board. If he clinched a deal for Peter Shilton, Harvey would leave. Giles turned down a move to Tottenham Hotspur that Clough arranged. He was open to offers for Hunter and Terry Cooper.

The players never agreed that there was a revolt against Clough; professional pride wouldn't allow any-thing but trying to win. But it was impossible to perform under the management of a man who had been so scath-ing of their achievements and their character for years, and now to their faces; who was trying to sell many of them against their will; and whose increasingly eccentric and paranoid behaviour was only alienating them more. The players were grilling McGovern and O'Hare, asking if this was how it was at Derby, unable to understand how Clough ever won the league. Preoccupation with the new manager was distracting, and standards were deteriorating. So were results. After six games Leeds had lost three; the previous season they had only lost four. So much for 'better' champions; Leeds were 19th.

Directors Sam Bolton and Percy Woodward wanted him to go but were outvoted until Bob Roberts left for a holiday, when in private meetings they persuaded Manny Cussins. Clough had arranged Cooper's transfer to Nottingham Forest; the board cancelled that, Cussins announcing no players were for sale. The board called a meeting with the squad and Clough, until Giles suggested it would be easier to answer the board's questions about him if he left the room. In the discussion that followed several stayed silent, nobody stuck up for Clough, and there was a sense of unease until Paul Madeley, quiet but astute, spoke for them all: 'What the players are trying to say, Mr Bolton,' he said, 'is that he's no good.' Giles, Hunter and others believed Bolton was trying to goad the players into talking, collecting evidence he could use to sack Clough, with the players taking the blame. There was one more game, a League Cup tie at Third Division Huddersfield Town, that only a last-minute Lorimer goal saved from a 1-0 defeat. At the end, Clough jumped up and punched the air. Then he was told to drive to Manny Cussins' house, where he was told he was sacked.

Where the board were concerned, Clough was still able to exert some control. He met Cussins and Woodward at Elland Road the next day to negotiate his departure, and he and his lawyer sipped tea while the

Leeds directors had gin and tonic. After a long afternoon at the end of Clough's 44 days' work at Leeds United, the lawyer extracted a pay-off of £100,000 after tax. Clough was also allowed to keep his club Mercedes. Then he went back to Austin Mitchell's studio at Yorkshire Television, only this time, unexpectedly, he was seated next to Don Revie.

This programme was called *Goodbye Mr Clough*, and the only journalist present was Mitchell, drawing Clough and Revie into uncomfortable conflict. Clough, his confidence restored by his sober settlement with Leeds and subsequent champagne celebration, relying on the usual slick charm that made him such an engaging presence on television, met his match in Revie, never telegenic but determined, through attention to detail and the force of sense, to put Clough in his place. It was an argument about Revie's legacy and Clough's motivation, started by the Leeds directors, that didn't benefit from being wrung through on television. As Mitchell withdrew from the conversation, Revie pressed Clough on what he had hoped to gain at Elland Road. He got the same answer: Clough wanted to win the league, but better.

'Yes, but there is no way to win it better,' Revie told him.

'Why not? It was the only hope I'd got,' said Clough.

'We only lost four matches.'

'Well, I could only lose three.'

He already had, but Clough insisted. He had wanted to become as involved as Revie had been with the players at Elland Road: 'I wanted to do that and I wanted to do it better than you. You can understand that, can't you?'

'Yes,' replied Revie, 'and I think if you'd said that to our players then you'd have got the message across.'

Revie was probably right. Clarke had liked Clough; Giles had begun to warm to him, and later agreed with his assessment of how restricted Revie's teams had been. Clough was arriving at Elland Road with a message about 'free expression' in football that Revie had already delivered, that the players had welcomed with open arms. It was bewildering that Clough had taken the approach he had – finishing his holiday, bringing his sons when he did turn up, not properly introducing himself to the players or coaches, to 'the laundry ladies and the office staff' as Revie now put it to him. Across several questions for several minutes, Revie kept asking Clough why he had not held a team meeting on his first day.

'Because I didn't think it was necessary,' he said.

'Why?' asked Revie.

'Because I thought I would do it more subtly instead of having everybody, bang, bang, bang. They were all on edge. I was on edge.'

Being on that edge had cost him. The fear of approaching Bremner, Giles and Hunter, unless it was with an insult, getting his retaliation in first against players who, for all their dislike and resentment, were mostly just confused, had cost Clough what he'd come for: to win the European Cup with Revie's players, to ensure that when Revie's team's greatest achievement was written down in history, it would have Brian Clough's name next to it.

It had also cost Leeds United almost £450,000 in settlements and transfer fees, and left them without a manager. The board's attempt to make its own mark on Leeds United's history, to assert itself like Clough in a post-Revie world, had backfired. Until they found a new manager the team was picked by Maurice Lindley, Syd Owen and Billy Bremner, exactly the backroom Revie revolution they wanted to avoid; the first person they offered the job to was the man Revie had told them to hire in the first place, Johnny Giles. Learning the board were only three to two in favour of him, Giles declined, and by the time four directors went to meet Bolton Wanderers manager Jimmy Armfield they were, he said, 'four men in a flap, who needed a manager quick'.

Armfield was not the ideal choice to follow Don Revie; his only achievement in his short managerial career was winning the Third Division with Bolton. But as successor to Clough he was perfect. He played 627 games at right-back for his home town team, Blackpool, most of them in the First Division, and received 43 caps from England, fifteen as captain; if not for injury, it might have been Armfield lifting the

World Cup in 1966 rather than Bobby Moore. Selfless and polite, he earned the nickname 'Gentleman Jim'; once, after seeking a showdown in his office at Elland Road, Norman Hunter emerged exasperated by his pipe-smoking manager's calm enquiries after the Hunter family's health. He was just too nice to argue with.

But he was smart enough to give the job some thought, and to accept Don Revie's advice. Revie met Armfield on the pretext of offering him a job coaching England's under 23 team, but Armfield told him, and suspected Revie already knew, about the offer from Leeds. 'In that case, forget about all this,' said Revie. 'Take the Leeds job.' He told Armfield what he tried to tell Clough on television; that Leeds still had the players to win a trophy, and Clough had tried discarding them too quickly. 'All you have to do with those players is send them out on the field,' he said. 'They'll do the rest. You'll be able to sit in the stand and pick up your bonus. They're the best players in the country.'

They were also 19th in the league. Armfield's first day was a matchday, and he made sure to set a different tone. The team was already picked, so he didn't interfere with Lindley's team talk. Instead he asked questions: 'What the hell are you doing near the bottom of the league?' Few replies were forthcoming from the distrustful, disaffected squad. 'For better or worse, it's you and me now,' said Armfield. 'Nobody is destined to leave the club and nobody is booked to come in. I have a completely clean sheet. I can only believe that we can do better than 19th. Beating Arsenal would be a good way to start.'

From there Armfield went to meet the office staff. Clough had hired a secretary, Maureen Holdsworth, who was waiting nervously, expecting the sack. Instead, Armfield told her he would need all the help he could get, and asked her to consider staying to work for him. How could Maureen refuse this polite gentleman with the kind eyes, placidly asking for her help? Out on the pitch, Leeds won 2-0, and Armfield happily acknowledged it had been nothing to do with him. He made a brief visit to the dressing room. 'Well done, lads,' he said. 'If you can beat Arsenal, you can beat anybody. See you on Monday.' It had been a good first day's work.

Armfield's gentle demeanour didn't go down well with everybody. Despite the smiley badges on their shirts, Leeds had not been a club for nice guys for a long time, and some of the players found Armfield indecisive. But his instinct was correct. There had been enough turmoil for one season, and the players had plenty to give if they were looked after; he retrieved Eddie Gray from coaching the juniors, all but retired since Clough's daggers, and put him back in the first team. Most of the senior players could take a good crack at managing Leeds United themselves, and several of them had wanted to; while Armfield introduced his own ideas, he knew better than to contradict too much where Leeds United were concerned.

His first job was to lift morale, and he took a big risk; asking football's most fearsome team to appear at the City Varieties in a pantomime. With their tentative agreement Armfield wrote his own adaptation of *Cinderella*, starring Duncan McKenzie in the lead role, Billy Bremner as Buttons, Paul Reaney as Prince Charming and the Good Fairy Gordon McQueen. At rehearsals caution became enthusiasm, and one of football's most eccentric team bonding exercises was a success, and a sold-out show.

The second job was ensuring improved morale meant improved results. That took longer, but after Christmas Leeds were more like themselves, only losing three matches and finishing nine points behind champions Derby County; had it not been for the games under Clough, Leeds could have been considerably higher than 9th. Given the league title was unattainable, and after disappointing exits from the League and FA Cups, Armfield's third job was clear: to help the players win the European Cup.

FC Zurich and Újpest Dózsa were beaten without trouble in the first two rounds. Anderlecht promised a test in the quarter-finals, but were beaten 3-0 in a fogbound first leg at Elland Road, and 1-0 by a Bremner goal away. United's semi-final opponents didn't only promise a test; as when they came up against Celtic at the same stage in 1970, Leeds were facing one of the best club sides in the world. If the ageing Leeds overcame

Barcelona, where manager Rinus Michels was continuing the 'Total Football' revolution he started with Ajax, taking with him Johan Cruyff and Johan Neeskens, they would have beaten the best team in the competition.

Few thought they could, even when Leeds ended the first leg at Elland Road with a 2-1 lead. Armfield left out Hunter so that Madeley could mark Cruyff out of the game, and a brilliant half-volley by Bremner, rising into the roof of the net, gave Leeds an early lead. Juan Manuel Asensi scored a free-kick before half-time, after neat theft of the ball by Reaney was harshly judged a foul; but when Reaney's cross was headed across goal by Jordan, Clarke pounced to score a late winner. But Barcelona's away goal was expected to hurt Leeds in the second leg.

Leeds retaliated first, Lorimer chasing a flick by Jordan and lashing the ball in from twenty yards. It then took all United's experience not to retaliate again, as Barcelona belied their skilful reputation. Gallego scythed down any player that came near, then in Bremner's case tried to drag the injured player from the field; after being hit off the ball, Jordan needed four stitches in his cheek, and again Gallego intervened, stealing physio Bob English's sponge and hurling it across the field. In the second half Gallego's free-kick was headed in by Manuel Clares, and with Leeds under pressure, young McQueen cracked; held by Clares, McQueen turned and felled him with a left hook, right in front of the referee. As

McQueen was sent off Hunter rested his head in despair on his teammate's shoulder; the game was already hard enough without raising the ghosts of all United's past semi-final defeats.

It didn't matter if United's determination now blurred with desperation; they won 3-2 on aggregate and were in the European Cup final at last. It wasn't played until a month after the end of the league season, at Parc des Princes in Paris, giving Armfield time to organise friendlies to keep the players fit, and consider his team. There were questions about playing Hunter or Cherry in defence, and accommodating McKenzie, scorer of eleven league goals, in attack. According to Hunter, Syd Owen settled those questions: this was a game for Revie's boys. Eddie Gray had to settle for the bench, as Terry Yorath was used to provide a more defensive shape, and David Harvey had been missing for several weeks after a car accident; Dave Stewart was in goal. But this was a Revie team: Stewart, Madeley, Hunter, Frank Gray, Bremner, Giles, Yorath, Lorimer, Jordan, Clarke. Six of them played their first games for Leeds in the Second Division. Those players deserved to win the biggest game in Leeds United's history.

Their opponents were Bayern Munich, the holders, and they felt they deserved to win it too. They had won the West German championship four times in six seasons, finishing second in the two others, and their last title had been their third in a row; but like Leeds, they were suffering amid managerial changes. Despite players like Franz Beckenbauer, Uli Hoeness, Sepp Maier and Gerd Müller, who all won the World Cup with West Germany in 1974, they dropped to 10th, their worst season since 1957. A trophy was mandatory, and all they could win was the European Cup. They knew how to win it; they had done it before.

As the game wore on, Leeds began to suspect Bayern Munich had done something to make sure they won again. Leeds dominated, while Bayern Munich were disintegrating in front of them; Björn Andersson was injured by a foul by Yorath in the first three minutes, and Hoeness was injured just before half-time. But the substitutions didn't affect Bayern's defensive plan, and even in the first half they played so deep that Hunter and Madeley, United's centre-halves, would be well inside Bayern's half with ten red-shirted players ahead of them.

Getting through that defence was a hard task, and when they did, goalkeeper Maier kept them out, playing one of his best games. Not even the European champions could resist Leeds' attacks; but their captain, the sweeper Franz Beckenbauer, was able to rely on extra help. After twenty minutes Leeds thought they should have a penalty for handball against Beckenbauer, but referee Michel Kitabdjian refused them. After half an hour, everybody thought Leeds should have a penalty when Beckenbauer swept Clarke's legs from under him as he ran into the six-yard box with the ball; Kitabdjian again said no.

After an hour, Giles chipped a quick free-kick to Madeley, who headed across goal, where Peter Lorimer hit the ball on the volley with exceptional power and control, right into the roof of the net. Kitabdjian pointed to the centre circle to indicate a goal, the linesman ran to the halfway line, indicating a goal, but Beckenbauer stayed in the penalty area, as if thinking about something, then raised his hand to indicate that he thought Leeds were offside. As the ball was dropping to Lorimer Bremner had been pushed towards goal by a defender, but he had rushed out past the defender again, just as Lorimer had hit the shot. If he was offside it was by an inch, and only perceptible on replays; both the referee and linesman had given the goal. At Beckenbauer's prompting, however, they discussed it again. The goal was disallowed.

Michel Kitabdjian had been in trouble before, in 1969, when he had to decide a drawn World Cup qualifier on the toss of a coin. The coin chose Tunisia, but Kitabdjian wasn't happy; as in Paris, he changed his mind. He went to his changing room and held another coin toss in private, and now Morocco were the winner. The controversy prompted FIFA to bring in penalty shoot-outs, but Kitabdjian carried on refereeing. He carried on after this match, too; despite needing dozens of stewards to protect him as he left the field and

UEFA's observers giving his performance two marks out of twenty, there was never any formal investigation, although Kitabdjian was never allowed to referee a major game again.

Within ten minutes of the disallowed goal Franz Roth finished a fast counter-attack, hitting Bayern's first shot of the night through Madeley's legs and beyond Stewart's dive; Armfield brought on Eddie Gray for the attack, but resisted adding McKenzie, leaving it up to the Revie lads to sort this. With ten minutes left Jupp Kapellmann sprinted down the right and crossed for Müller, who made it 2-0.

There was trouble off the pitch, too. The Parisian police judged the thousands of Leeds fans in their city by reputation; for English football fans in general and Leeds United fans in particular, that meant hooliganism. They adopted a batons-first approach to policing, so that even before the game kicked off many Leeds fans, the vast majority just there to see the final without trouble, were feeling their cuts, bruises, and a grave sense of injustice. The sporting injustice now taking place fuelled the situation, and fighting broke out with police; when fans saw others being dragged away by groups of officers, fighting became rioting, and seats were broken and hurled towards the police and the pitch. The trouble continued after the match and through the night, and the coverage given to the rioting meant little sympathy for Leeds United when they returned home.

Not that they expected any. Revie's lads were so used to this that most of them left their runners-up medals in the changing rooms; Armfield handed them out later. Billy Bremner had written a book called *You Get Nowt for Being Second*, but you did get summat, and it was the last thing the players wanted: a reminder that this was the end, and that once again fortune had gone against them.

Don Revie was commentating on the match for the BBC, and as Bayern Munich paraded the trophy, he said: 'I think the Leeds lads are stood down there with their heads dropped tonight. And when I think of the boys – Paul Reaney, Billy Bremner, Paul Madeley, Norman Hunter, Peter Lorimer, Johnny Giles, Terry Yorath, all these lads, most of them I brought to the club as boys of fifteen – I've lived with them, I've eaten with them, and I thought tonight would be the night that they would get paid for all the hard work and dedication that they've put into the game. I feel really upset, I feel sorry, I feel very, very sad indeed.'

19

1975–82

WE PAID YOU GOOD MONEY
OVER THE YEARS

Johnny Giles was first to leave. Jimmy Armfield said he wanted Giles to stay, but also said West Bromwich Albion wanted him, and he had arranged a deal. Giles was weary of Armfield being on the fence like this, and as everyone had been saying for a year, he could do a better job himself. West Brom wanted him to be player-manager, and Giles decided to go.

For Armfield it was the start of what Don Revie called 'the hardest job in football', the job he hadn't been able to face: breaking up one of the greatest teams football had ever seen. Brian Clough's intervention had been a dramatic sledgehammer, but Armfield didn't have to be drastic. The team had changed over the years; Eddie

Gray had replaced Albert Johanneson, David Harvey replaced Gary Sprake, Trevor Cherry replaced Terry Cooper, Gordon McQueen replaced Jack Charlton, Joe Jordan replaced Mick Jones – Jones left in 1975, his career ended by a knee injury. Although the three players Revie could least bear to part with – Giles, Billy Bremner and Norman Hunter – were thought to be irreplaceable, when the emotional attachment to Revie was taken out of the equation, their departures could be managed. Giles left in 1975, but Bremner and Hunter played another season before leaving, to Hull City and Bristol City, in 1976. There was still plenty of football in players like Allan Clarke, Peter Lorimer, Paul Madeley, Paul Reaney, Trevor Cherry, David Harvey and the rejuvenated Eddie Gray. There was a lot of faith in Jordan, McQueen, Terry Yorath and Frank Gray for the future.

The attitude in the boardroom made the job more difficult. Despite years of service from the players, the directors refused to budge from the notion that these were anything more than salaried employees. Jack Charlton felt cheated when Leeds kept more than a quarter of the gate receipts from his testimonial as 'deductions'. Even world-class footballers' wages were not high, and players relied on testimonials for security at the end of their careers; several long-serving players suspected the board were delaying them, hoping they would leave and remove the obligation. Giles argued for weeks to get his testimonial guaranteed in writing, then argued again when he discovered the terms of his transfer to West Brom.

Giles expected West Brom to pay him a signing-on fee of around £25,000. He learned instead that the transfer fee Leeds asked was an inflated £50,000, and they would pay Giles out of that – £5,000. Leeds had paid £33,000 for Giles in 1963. They were now selling him for £17,000 more. In between they got 525 appearances, two league titles, two European trophies, the FA Cup, the League Cup and, more than any of that, they got twelve years of blood, sweat and dedication at extreme physical and emotional cost.

'We paid you good money over the years,' said Manny Cussins, the chairman. Giles grabbed him by the throat. 'You miserable little fucker,' he said.

Whether or not Leeds had paid good money was another matter. When Norman Hunter moved to Bristol City, a club near the bottom of the First Division, he discovered his basic wage at Leeds would have made him one of Bristol's lower-paid players. Leeds relied on bonuses to bump up wage packets, usually calculated from and paid out of gate receipts at Elland Road. Hunter had been caught up with playing for Leeds, but now wished he had paid more attention. He also wished, on the day he left, that one of the directors had been good enough to shake his hand and say: 'Thank you.'

The board's cheap disregard for the players' loyalty caused disruption and resentment, and was hard to understand compared to burning through almost £350,000 of settlements and transfer fees in 44 days with Brian Clough. Don Revie had left £2 million in the bank, but the directors seemed to have no idea how he put it there. They resented the way Revie had taken all the credit for Leeds United's success, but his autocratic presence had protected them from the harsh reality of running a football club. Now, without him, they looked lost.

The reaction when UEFA handed down a four-year ban from European football as punishment for the rioting in Paris was typical. The board accepted it, but Armfield wanted to argue. There was no disguising the hooligan element following Leeds, but he heard from supporters about the heavy police tactics used all day against peaceful supporters, and felt the whole event, from start to finish, had been a great injustice. 'I felt exactly as I did when our home was burgled,' he said. The punishment was serious. The club relied on European football to keep it profitable, and replacing Bremner, Hunter and Giles would be more difficult, as the best players wanted to play for clubs in European competitions. Without top-class players to watch, the fickle Leeds public would drift away. That £2 million could soon be gone.

Armfield had to act alone. Armed with supporters' testimonies, he made two trips to the UEFA commission in Geneva, paying for his own flights and hotels. The commission were impressed with Armfield's passionate advocacy, and halved the ban to two years. The directors at Elland Road never bothered to thank him, although they did pay back his travel expenses.

Even without Giles, Leeds improved in Armfield's first full season, rising from 9th to 5th, enlivened by quality football and Duncan McKenzie, who outstayed Clough's other signings and made himself a favourite with sixteen goals, countless tricks, and by hurdling a Mini at Paul Reaney's testimonial. But McKenzie left at the same time as Bremner and Hunter, while Terry Yorath went to Coventry City. Yorath was never a favourite of the fans, who despaired of his errors despite all the good he did; a season trying to fulfil expectations as Giles' heir only highlighted Yorath's deficiencies, and he was glad to get away from the barracking.

It took only a few games for his replacement in the number 10 shirt to hear cheers of delight. Tony Currie was bought from Sheffield United for £240,000, and changed Leeds United's midfield. He had to be looked at, with long blond hair down past his shoulders, and because you never knew what he would do. Giles and Bremner had controlled games between them, creating patterns towards victory as if on a battlefield; with Trevor Cherry and later Brian Flynn alongside him, Currie looked for ways to push games to higher levels of delight, choosing the most audacious pass, trying a mazy dribble, or scoring without warning with a dipping, curving volley.

The disruption caused by players leaving, and injuries to Clarke and new £170,000 striker Ray Hankin, meant Currie's brilliance only took Leeds to 10th in the league; but an FA Cup semi-final offered a return to Wembley, maybe even a vital return to Europe. But at Hillsborough Manchester United scored twice in the first fifteen minutes – the first by Jimmy Greenhoff, one of Revie's first youth players. Clarke scored a penalty with twenty minutes left but Leeds never truly got back in the game. For 1977/78 Arthur Graham was added to the attack, a committed and versatile winger, and Hankin made an impact, scoring twenty goals; Leeds reached another semi-final, losing to Nottingham Forest in the League Cup, but were again only mid-table.

Armfield was efficiently replacing the departing legends with good, popular players, but even before he left Revie bemoaned the declining standard of British players. The schoolboys signing for Leeds weren't a patch on the fifteen year olds of a decade earlier, a problem Revie was now wrestling with on an international level – English players were no longer world-class. But Armfield had chosen well, and after guiding Leeds through the worst of the much-feared rebuilding process, was optimistic about the future.

Armfield's relaxed management style worked well when Giles and Bremner were there to enforce behaviour, with the stern figure of Don Howe working as his assistant. But Giles, Bremner and Howe all moved on, and as well as lacking quality, the new generation of players lacked professionalism, and Armfield's indecisive approach let indiscipline fester. In training and socially, Leeds behaved no worse than any other First Division club, but one of their advantages had been how much more dedicated to winning they were than anybody else. They now looked destined for mid-table every season, so as long as they gave things a good go in the cups, there seemed no need for the old rigour.

Mid-table was not good enough for Joe Jordan and Gordon McQueen. They were in their mid-twenties, reaching their peak, still showing the potential they had when Revie trusted them to replace Mick Jones and Jack Charlton. A physical and ruthless centre-forward and a fast and dominating centre-half, they were Leeds' two best players; but like Jack Charlton at the start of the 1960s, they feared Leeds would be the death of their careers. They didn't hide it. Jordan got the move he wanted in January 1978, for £350,000 to a club that had become an intense rival, Manchester United. The next day, in a heated FA Cup third round match with Manchester City at Elland Road, David Harvey began arguing with McQueen as they prepared to face a corner, shoving him in the chest and receiving a powerful right hook in response. Within a week McQueen was asking for a transfer. A month of speculation followed, with Rangers and Tottenham Hotspur making bids – McQueen was quoted saying Spurs could 'go to hell' but later apologised, saying he was frustrated by the difficulty of leaving Leeds. Eventually he got the move he wanted: for £450,000, a British record, he joined Joe Jordan at Old Trafford. '99 per cent of players want to play for Manchester United,' he said as he left, 'and the other 1 per cent are liars.'

It was a severe blow to Armfield's team building. He paid Blackpool £300,000 for young centre-half Paul Hart to replace McQueen, but Hart started with an own goal on his debut; in the summer, as Paul Reaney and Allan Clarke departed, Armfield took an £80,000 chance on striker John Hawley from Hull City, who had just finished bottom of the Second Division. He never got to see if the experiment would work. In April Tom Holley, the former Leeds captain turned Sunday People journalist, had visited Elland Road as the bearer of bad news; his paper had a story that Armfield was about to be sacked, and he wanted to tell him first. Armfield survived the press speculation; in his guise of lay preacher, he told a congregation of scouts, guides and cubs at York Minster that the letters 'LUFC' also stood for 'Let Us Face Challenges.' But amid the awkwardness of the next board meeting in June, the directors avoided the subject, suggesting a new contract in November once they'd seen how the season was going. That was enough for Armfield. After four years, he didn't think the directors needed three more months to decide if he was up to the job. As the board stared at the floor, Armfield left the room, and left club management for good. He told the papers he had been training as a journalist and had ways of making a living. 'I might even get some of my poetry published now,' he added. Later, he said: 'Leaving Leeds had upset me more than I allowed people to see. It was time to move on.'

That was easier for Armfield than for Leeds. The directors had not been agreed on whether or not Armfield should leave, so he made their minds up for them. Now they had to agree a way to replace him. Leeds advertised the job, but in mid-August, as the new season was beginning, Maurice Lindley was still in charge as caretaker. Cussins made a bold move.

Jock Stein was one of the few managers who could compare to Don Revie. In his twelve seasons as manager of Celtic they won ten league titles, the Scottish Cup eight times and the League Cup six times, and became the first British team to win the European Cup in 1967. In summer 1978 Billy McNeill replaced Stein as manager, and it was assumed Stein would join the board; they offered him a derisory job running the club lottery. At 55, he felt too young to walk away from football; the call from Cussins came at just the right time.

Appointing Jock Stein was almost as sensational as appointing Brian Clough; Leeds were announcing themselves again with a European Cup-winning manager, coming south to prove himself in England by reviving Leeds United. There were doubts about Stein's age, and persistent rumours that, if the job of Scotland national team manager became available, Stein might not stay for his contracted three years. But Cussins was delighted with the man, with the good publicity, and with the instant respect shown to Stein by the players.

Forty-four days later Cussins was looking for a new manager. Whether the rumour that Stein was only filling his time and his bank account until the Scotland job came up was true or not, Ally MacLeod's resignation and the Scottish FA's offer came sooner than anyone expected. The players, led by Hankin and Hart, pleaded with him to stay; so did Cussins, with the added incentive of £35,000 in cash and a new house. Stein would not be persuaded. As soon as MacLeod resigned, Stein was manipulating media contacts in Scotland to ensure the SFA couldn't fail to appoint him.

Leeds were stunned, while the press had great fun with the fact that Stein had lasted exactly as long as Clough, that Lindley was in charge again and that the board were searching desperately for another manager. The fans were not amused. When, after three weeks, the search led to Second Division Sunderland and their manager Jimmy Adamson, the fans were outraged.

Like the Milburns and Jack Charlton, Adamson was born in Ashington, Northumberland; but he became a legend in Burnley. He played his entire seventeen-year career there, won the First Division, was captain when they won the FA Cup, and won Footballer of the Year.

He was offered the job of England manager before Alf Ramsey but felt he was too young, becoming instead a coach at Burnley and then, in 1970, manager. Even though the chairman, Bob Lord, would sell one of them every season, Adamson built one of Burnley's best ever teams by turning 'second-class' young players into First Division footballers. Disputes with Lord meant the sack a few months before relegation in 1976, ending Adamson's dream of Burnley becoming 'the team of the seventies'.

After nearly a year out of work he took over at Sunderland, replacing cup-winning manager Bob Stokoe. The fans at Roker Park wanted Brian Clough, and Adamson couldn't prevent relegation, nor inspire promotion the next season. When Leeds came for him Sunderland were in mid-table, optimism draining away.

From a legend of European football to a legend of Lancashire; Leeds' supporters were not impressed when Adamson arrived with his 'entourage', including his assistant Dave Merrington. Some of the Leeds players weren't happy either; Lorimer had rowed with Merrington after a bad foul on Sunderland's Jack Ashurst, and at their first meeting Merrington told him there were no hard feelings. Lorimer knew what that meant; he never played a game under Adamson, and moved to Toronto Blizzard.

But Brian Flynn was delighted to be reunited with the manager who had been the making of him at

Burnley, and without making any signings – until he spent £357,000 on Kevin Hird in March – Adamson built on Stein's start and took Leeds back to the League Cup semi-final. Leeds took a 2-0 lead in the home leg against Southampton but collapsed in the last twenty minutes, drawing 2-2 and then, despite an urgent attacking performance, losing 1-0 at the Dell; Wembley eluded them for the third consecutive season. But that defeat, and one in the FA Cup to West Brom, were the only losses as Leeds rose from 14th to 5th; a semi-final and qualification for the UEFA Cup were United's best return since Revie's departure.

Things began to go awry as Adamson put his own stamp on the side. There was nothing he could do about Tony Currie; after three brilliant seasons, his wife could no longer bear living away from London. Leeds, ignoring bids from their First Division rivals, made sure Currie went to Second Division Queens Park Rangers. But John Hawley's future was in Adamson's control, and after sixteen goals in 32 league games, few could understand why Adamson sent him to Sunderland and brought in Wayne Entwistle, a less-than-prolific striker he'd managed at Sunderland and Burnley. Frank Gray was quick, dependable, versatile and happy enough at Leeds; he was sold to Nottingham Forest for £500,000.

Adamson's replacements struggled to make an impression. £140,000 was spent on Gary Hamson, but he didn't play until October. Injuries hampered Brian

Greenhoff, 26-year-old brother of Jimmy, an England midfielder who joined from Manchester United for £350,000; and Alan Curtis, a striker from Third Division Swansea City, who became United's record signing at £400,000. The rest of the team was hampered by losing inspiration, goals and energy from Currie, Hawley and Gray, and by Adamson's apparent lack of a strategy.

Leeds received an early shock in the League Cup, a full-strength team losing 7-0 away to Arsenal, and while the return to European football began easily enough, beating Valletta of Malta 7-0 on aggregate, losing 2-0 in each leg of the UEFA Cup second round against Universitatea Craiova of Romania was embarrassing. League form was just as bad; by 1 December, Leeds had lost six, including a 5-1 defeat to Everton. Large sections of the crowd, never enamoured with Adamson, turned against him; as attendances declined, the banners and shouts demanding 'Adamson Out!' became more prominent.

Adamson hatched an audacious plan to pay the £500,000 release clause in the contract of Hamburg's European Footballer of the Year, Kevin Keegan, then play him up front with Newcastle United's experienced striker Peter Withe; he was negotiating with both players, but an estimated £800,000 in transfer fees plus wages on top were too much for the Leeds board, nervously eyeing the impact Adamson's presence was having on gate receipts.

The only bright points were from the youth team; eighteen-year-old goalkeeper John Lukic replaced David Harvey, looking calm beyond his years; Terry Connor, a seventeen-year-old striker from Chapeltown in Leeds, was as exciting as it gets, scoring a winning goal against West Brom in his first substitute appearance, adding another in a 1-1 draw at Old Trafford, one each in wins over Wolverhampton Wanderers and Stoke City, and the only goal in a win at Highbury. The boost from Connor ought to have quieted the complaints, but there was also a 4-1 FA Cup defeat to Nottingham Forest.

As the protests grew louder Adamson was seen less often at training; the players enjoyed working with him, but nicknamed him Howard Hughes, after the reclusive film tycoon. It was a pattern repeating from Sunderland; Adamson's strength was coaching, but when the demands of managing became severe, he would fade away from both. Dave Merrington took the lead. His nickname was simply 'Mad'; powerfully built, prone to violent outbursts, single-minded and a born-again Christian, he brought two American football players to a team meeting to give a lecture on how the Bible helped their careers. The normally sanguine Eddie Gray walked out. 'I have to admit that Merrington was not someone I enjoyed working with,' said Gray later. 'The bloke was a bloody idiot,' said Tony Currie.

The bigger problem was that Merrington's training and Adamson's tactics didn't match up. The team would practise one way of playing all week, only for Adamson to give different instructions when he arrived for the team talk. They might have done better if they had swapped jobs; Merrington was 'in charge, but not in charge,' according to Gray. Adamson felt under severe pressure from the fans. The Yorkshire Ripper serial killer was being hunted in Leeds at the time; the police were playing a recording of a suspect's voice on television and radio, and in pubs across the city, where the north-eastern accent had Leeds fans telling them: 'It's Jimmy bloody Adamson.' He escaped Sunderland with his ears full of Bob Stokoe and Brian Clough, but now he was at Leeds, in the shadow of a serial killer and Don Revie. The fans wanted Giles or Bremner, as they had since 1974; some of the directors did, too. Revie was due to return and take up his nine-year consultancy contract in 1980.

Adamson had withstood worse. He had disowned his father, and taken his mother to live near him in Burnley; as a successful young footballer, he bought her a house of her own. In 1954, when Adamson was 25, she took her own life. With the help of his wife, May, he overcame that, but it was significant that he faltered whenever he left the security of Burnley. One of the reasons he turned down the job of England manager in 1962 was the need to move to London. He never had a permanent home in Sunderland; May stayed in Burnley with their family. When they moved to a house in Roundhay, Leeds, it was the first time Jimmy had lived completely outside Burnley since 1946, and the first time May had moved since she was born.

The anti-Adamson chanting continued for months, as did the dreary football and arguments in the boardroom about his future; Leeds finished 11th, with only 46 goals to their name from 42 matches. In the summer Adamson tried to brighten things by paying Sheffield United £400,000 for Argentinian midfielder Alex Sabella as a belated replacement for Currie, but Sabella had a hard time translating his skills from training to the First Division, where Leeds made another bad start. Police were now required to restrain protesters, but apart from one argument in the car park at Elland Road, Adamson remained stoic and dignified until the end – he was either staunchly determined, or just didn't care any more. When he got home at night to his unfamiliar house, he must have wondered what the point of it all was. The board agreed they would pay up his contract if he resigned, and in early September 1980, Maurice Lindley was once again in charge. Adamson didn't work in football again.

Elland Road had destroyed Adamson's confidence, but his replacement, Allan Clarke, returned to the scene of his greatest days with typical swagger. After inviting Clough, Armfield, Stein and Adamson to create new glories, the board hoped that a link to the past would restore Revie's. Clarke was inexperienced in management, but had won promotion to the Third Division in his first season at Barnsley; he never doubted his own abilities. He was a winner, and said so; before leading the team out at Elland Road for his first game, he promised Leeds would win a trophy within three years.

That first match was against Manchester United, and Clarke gave an indication of his intentions by dropping Alex Sabella and finishing with a 0-0 draw. Anyone who expected 'Sniffer' Clarke to bring his goalscoring knack to Leeds was disappointed, as they scored even fewer than the previous season: 39, the lowest total in the First Division. A 4-1 defeat at Sunderland in Clarke's second match, and a 5-0 home defeat by Arsenal, made improving the defence a priority; with Eddie Gray at left-back and Sabella sidelined, Leeds ended the season by losing only one of their last eight games, 2-0 to Brighton & Hove Albion, and winning or drawing every other game to nil.

A summer search for a powerful striker drew blanks; Tony Woodcock stayed at Cologne, and Joe Jordan moved to Milan. Instead of a finisher Clarke convinced winger Peter Barnes to come from West Brom, where he was holding out for a move back to Manchester City. Clarke also had to convince the board, when the transfer fee was set at £930,000: more than twice Leeds United's record, and £70,000 short of the entire transfer budget. Barnes, furthermore, was being helped to forget about Manchester City by wages of £1,000 per week. The poor football of the previous season hadn't helped gate receipts recover from Adamson, and the board were nervous. But Clarke was a winner, and he won the argument.

He didn't win the opening game. In fact Leeds were trounced, 5-1 away to newly promoted Swansea City. It was a severe shock, but at Elland Road a 1-1 draw with Everton and a 3-0 win over Wolves – all four Leeds goals scored by Arthur Graham – eased the worry. 4-0 defeats away to Coventry City and Manchester City brought the worry well and truly back as Leeds went seven matches without a win, and goals only started coming when Barnes was out of the team; his tendency to aim crosses into the stand behind the goal wasn't much good for young strikers Terry Connor and Aidan Butterworth.

More transfers were required. Frank Gray was brought back from Nottingham Forest to improve the midfield, followed by fearsome centre-half Kenny Burns for £400,000. Burns played in both Forest's European Cup wins, with Brian Clough as manager, in 1979 and 1980; Gray played in the second. But from January to March Leeds lost six games and drew one without scoring a goal; but Clarke, and most of the dressing room, seemed oblivious to the growing risk. The bad run ended with a 1-0 win at Sunderland, the goal scored by 33-year-old striker Frank Worthington, a showman just signed from Birmingham City. His tricks and goals lifted the mood of the fans, and bolstered the self-confidence of the manager and players: as an expensive, experienced team, with a flamboyant and effective striker, they felt sure they were too good to be relegated. But among several of the senior players there was disharmony, and for Eddie Gray there was grave worry; he didn't think they were good enough at all.

Worthington scored nine, but Leeds only won two games he scored in. One of those wins was a stunning 4-1 victory at Aston Villa, with Barnes on top form; another was in the season's penultimate game, against Brighton at Elland Road. Leeds were a goal down with ten minutes left, when Hamson cracked the ball from 30 yards into the top corner; a minute later Gray dribbled down the left, and Hird finished his cross at the back post, to make Leeds believe they were staying up. At the end of the match Allan Clarke saluted the Kop as the fans held scarves aloft, singing *You'll Never Walk Alone*.

Confidence was not what Leeds needed. At West Brom three days later, they were outplayed by their relegation rivals. West Brom's second goal of a 2-0 win, minutes from the end, started a riot in the Leeds end that continued outside the ground, and gave West Brom no incentive to beat Stoke City two days later, the one result that would keep Leeds up. They lost 3-0, and Leeds United lost their First Division status.

THIS IS THE MUSIC THAT I'VE GOT TO FACE AGAIN

The saddest thing about Elland Road in 1982 was how closely it resembled Elland Road in 1962. Back in Division Two with a team of disaffected players, sinking with debt; with low, troublesome crowds and a player-manager hired from within, as Don Revie was, to save the salary of an outsider. Apart from two new stands, both often empty, there were few signs that the years of glory with Revie ever happened.

But the glory years had happened, and relegation to Division Two felt like a punishment for daring to succeed. The memories wouldn't rest, and as Leeds fell, everything they had done was thrown after them.

Don Revie resigned from the job of England manager in 1977. It had not been a happy time. The job was disheartening, and results were poor. Revie missed day-to-day coaching, and without that relationship, the players didn't buy into dossiers and bingo sessions; and without regular games to prepare for, Revie had too much time to brood. Working for the Football Association meant close contact with the game's rulers, many of whom hated what Revie had done at Leeds, and never wanted him to manage England. Revie and Sir Harold Thompson, the FA chairman, loathed each other. In 1977 Revie discovered the FA were working to replace him, so he employed an old Leeds tactic, and got his retaliation in first.

But Revie made several mistakes. He sent his letter of resignation to the FA at the same time as giving the story to the *Daily Mail*, but the FA read it in the newspapers first. Their anger intensified when they read the follow-up story; Revie was taking a coaching job in the United Arab Emirates worth £60,000 a year, plus £100,000 bonuses. In the FA and in the court of public opinion, to resign as England manager to take up a higher-paid job abroad was treachery. To sell the story to a newspaper was greed.

Sir Thompson himself headed the FA inquiry that banned Revie from working in English football for ten years. Revie overturned that in the High Court, so that he could take up his consultancy job at Leeds, but didn't clear his name. The judge agreed the FA's inquiry was a travesty, but agreed with the FA that Revie's resignation was a 'sensational, outrageous example of disloyalty, breach of trust, discourtesy and selfishness'. Revie was free to work, but not from the accusations.

There were now plenty of those. Walking out on England gave the newspapers an excuse to bring out all the gossip the game had to offer about Don Revie. The *Daily Mirror*'s front pages repeated the match-fixing allegations from the Wolverhampton Wanderers match in 1972, but now with testimony: Mike O'Grady, the former Leeds winger who moved to Wolves, was named as the go-between; Gary Sprake, the goalkeeper, as the informant. O'Grady was appalled; he said later he was pressured into talking to the *Mirror*, and disassociated himself from the allegations. Sprake, bitter that Revie hadn't organised a promised testimonial, broke and in poor health, took between £7,500 and £15,000 for his version of events, and was ostracised by his former teammates.

The *Mirror*'s reporters Richard Stott and Frank Palmer claimed to have a large file on Revie, and reported claims by Bob Stokoe and two anonymous players that Revie had tried to fix matches against Bury and Newcastle United to save Leeds from relegation to Division Three in 1962. But what was missing from all the stories about Revie and Leeds was evidence. When the *Sunday People* added Billy Bremner's name to the

Wolves accusations he sued for libel; in 1982 he was awarded £100,000 damages, one of the High Court's most emphatic decisions. Although Revie didn't sue, FA and police investigations found no case for him to answer, and the so-called 'Revie File' was never produced. Against countless witnesses of Revie's good character, and all the examples of United's desperate failures that, had Revie really been corrupt, would surely have been fixed in his favour, were the word of Richard Stott, Bob Stokoe and Gary Sprake. Unfortunately for Revie's reputation, and Leeds United's, for many people that was enough.

United weren't allowed to forget the sins of their glory years, real or imagined. Writing in *The Times*, journalist David Miller identified the pitch invasion after Ray Tinkler allowed West Bromwich Albion's goal in 1971 as 'the definitive moment of moral corruption in English soccer, from which point the domestic game moved steadily downwards. Leeds United under Don Revie stood for everything that was reprehensible in sport'; not only that, but they '[set] the tone of national decline'. This was hyperbole, but it was common, and so were the incidents that allowed it to be repeated. There were the riots in Paris in 1975; the FA Cup tie in 1978 when Gordon McQueen punched David Harvey, and mounted police came onto the pitch to clear invading supporters; horses were on the pitch again in the last moments of Leeds' last match in Division One at West

Brom, although Allan Clarke stuck to his line that he'd been concentrating on the game, and Leeds had the best fans in the country. 'Why should I change my opinion?' he said. 'I didn't see any trouble last night.'

Trouble was harder to ignore in Division Two. It started in the first match, away to Grimsby Town, and was almost a weekly occurrence home and away, becoming more visible as attendances across football dropped in the 1980s. Hooliganism was a national problem but Leeds United supporters, represented much against the club's will by the self-styled 'Service Crew', were regularly in the headlines. Kevin Keegan was hit by a ball bearing thrown at Elland Road; £20,000 worth of damage was caused at Derby County; the new electronic scoreboard unveiled at Stamford Bridge by Chelsea chairman Ken Bates was destroyed; successive weekends away at Barnsley and Huddersfield Town brought local rivalries into the equation. Any incident involving Leeds fans was reported as part of a catalogue going back to 1971; it was the only time anybody seemed to talk about the glory years now.

The FA were reluctant to fine clubs, because few could afford to pay. Ticket-only matches and membership schemes were tried. At Leeds, the terraces were ordered closed for several games; attendances dropped, but as an unintended consequence gate receipts increased, as fans were forced to buy higher-priced seats. But these were treatments for symptoms, not causes. Crumbling stadiums were arenas for young people, left bereft by widespread unemployment and a draconian government, to take out their frustrations, and the escalating violence reached crisis point in May 1985. At St Andrew's Stadium, as Birmingham City and Leeds fans fought police, a wall collapsed, killing Ian Hambridge, a fifteen-year-old Leeds fan attending his first match; at Heysel Stadium in Brussels, 39 Juventus fans were killed when a wall collapsed during fighting with Liverpool fans before the European Cup final. On the same day that Ian Hambridge died, 56 people were killed in a tragic accident at Bradford City's Valley Parade, when the main stand caught fire during a match to celebrate promotion.

In this atmosphere it was difficult to sustain even a First Division football club in the 1980s, and the task of looking after Leeds United in the Second Division was given to Eddie Gray. One of the youngest of Revie's first generation, he was one of its most talented and least fortunate; the injuries behind Brian Clough's heartless taunts held Gray back, and some of his most consistent football came after Revie, and Clough, had gone. He deserved more for his loyalty than relegation. While the job of manager was a sign of trust and esteem, he was also, as chief executive Peter Nash put it, 'a cheap but hopeful option'.

'If I had given it some thought,' Gray said later, 'the chances are that I would have turned the offer down.' Leeds were £2 million in debt, and Gray's job was to dramatically reduce the wage bill while winning promotion; even Revie was not asked to do so much in 1962. But despite the difficulty, Gray and his assistant Jimmy Lumsden, who was a youth player at Leeds with Gray, pieced together one of the most popular teams in Leeds' history. The experienced, high-earning players who came down from the First Division gradually moved on; £930,000 signing Peter Barnes was eventually sold to Coventry City for £50,000. Young goalkeeper John Lukic also left, for £125,000, unable to resist the lure of First Division Arsenal. Gray still had his younger brother Frank, and added vital experience by bringing David Harvey and Peter Lorimer back from Vancouver Whitecaps, allowing Eddie Gray to retire.

What optimism there was came from a crop of young players inspiring memories of Revie's beginnings at the bottom of Division Two. John Sheridan, Tommy Wright, Scott Sellars and Denis Irwin all lived in the same house, and all looked at home in United's first team, Sheridan most of all; he made his debut aged eighteen, and his elegant playmaking and eye for spectacular efforts throughout the 1980s was like having a concert pianist performing on a pub piano. Neil Aspin, Andy Linighan, Terry Phelan and Mark Gavin added more youth, and although Terry Connor was exchanged for Brighton & Hove Albion striker Andy Ritchie – 'One of the saddest things we ever did,' said Lumsden – the club thought it had finally found a home-grown striker, until Aidan Butterworth turned his back on football to go back to college.

Leeds spent most of Gray's first season on the edge of the top six, never able to push through for promotion; his second bore the brunt of the team rebuilding and risked becoming a relegation battle – Lorimer's return after New Year was a vital influence, steadying the team to 10th. 1984/85 started with four wins followed by three defeats, summing up the season; the youngsters were occasionally brilliant and still had a slim chance of promotion on the tragic final day at Birmingham, but the team lacked consistency and strength.

Gray was hampered by the club's finances. In six games on loan from Brighton, Neil McNab looked like the midfield anchor Leeds desperately needed, but the meagre £65,000 fee was beyond their means in 1983. Cheap signings George McCluskey, Andy Watson and John Donnelly didn't make an impact, but goal-keeper Mervyn Day, who won the FA Cup with West Ham United in 1975, was an astute buy at £30,000; and £75,000 for Southampton's Ian Baird gave Leeds a striker with the physicality the division demanded. Desperate to strengthen midfield in the same way, in summer 1985 Gray persuaded vice-chairman Manny Cussins to pay £250,000 from his own pocket for Ian Snodin from Doncaster Rovers, where his manager Billy Bremner had helped him become one of the best mid-fielders outside the First Division.

That rare expense, the good form at the end of the previous season, and the prospect of Sheridan and Snodin controlling midfield with Baird in attack, made Leeds favourites for promotion in 1985/86. Some of the football under Gray was, he acknowledged, dire; some of his signings were poor. But his faith in the young players now reaching maturity was not shaken despite five winless games; in the next six, Leeds were unbeaten. Optimism was high after winning 3-0 at Walsall in the League Cup, so the shock was even greater when, three days later, Eddie Gray was sacked.

Cussins had stepped down as chairman in 1983, replaced by Leslie Silver. Silver's family had moved from London to Leeds when he was fourteen, in time for him to see John Charles' debut; in the early 1980s the company he founded, Silver Paint & Lacquer, was renamed Kalon Group plc as part of its expansion and flotation on the stock exchange. He brought Bill Fotherby onto the board as commercial director, a youth player in Major Buckley's time, who then grew wealthy in the clothing industry. Bolder than the other directors and, in Fotherby's case, alarmingly flamboyant, they were about to do a drastic deal to clear the club's debts and safeguard its future. For £2.5 million, they sold Elland Road to Leeds City Council, agreeing a 125-year lease for Leeds United to keep playing at what was now a municipal stadium.

Silver wanted a new approach on the pitch to match the new start in the boardroom. Neither the players or fans felt the same way. Eddie Gray had signed for Leeds in May 1963, when he was fifteen; ending 22 years of uninterrupted loyalty with the sack brought tears from his young players and anger from the fans. The next day, Leeds played Middlesbrough at Elland Road; there were chants for Eddie and against the board, Silver's car was vandalised, and Lorimer contemplated missing a penalty in protest. He thought again, scored, and Leeds won 1-0; but nothing could raise the heartbroken young players for the Full Members' Cup trip to Manchester City, a 6-1 defeat, and two days later in the same competition only 2,274 turned up at Elland Road to see a 1-1 draw with Sheffield United. Removing Eddie Gray, the Revie protégé who had done so much to lift the gloom since 1975, left Leeds in the dark.

Silver hit upon the perfect strategy for switching the lights on again, and it took a 30-minute interview to decide Doncaster Rovers' manager Billy Bremner should come back to Elland Road. Nobody forgot Eddie, but nobody could resist Billy. Bremnermania gripped the fans, and the board were pleased; Bremner's seven years at Doncaster had been difficult, but with hardly a penny to spend he twice won promotion from the Fourth Division, a skill Silver hoped he could bring to a higher level. He hoped, too, that Bremner would know how to bring Revie's glory back; that he 'had absorbed that touch of magic'.

But as a manager, Bremner was his own man. His

first match was a 3-0 defeat away to Allan Clarke's new team Barnsley, and Bremner decided that was Peter Lorimer's last game for Leeds. He was equally ruthless with the rest of Gray's young team. Bremner didn't share Gray's faith in them, and worried they may not have faith in him: 'They talk about you all the time,' he told Eddie. What Bremner remembered of Revie's use of youngsters in Division Two was that it took Bobby Collins to toughen them up to get anywhere, a view confirmed by his own years managing in Divisions Three and Four. Players like Sellars and Wright looked like they'd never be stronger than schoolboys, and Bremner quickly discarded them, along with Linighan, Phelan and Irwin. The highest fee was £80,000 for Wright, and altogether they went for just £215,000.

Bremner's favourite Ian Snodin survived and replaced Lorimer as captain; Sheridan also stayed. Aspin, Baird, Day and Ritchie kept their places. But Bremner's new players, including two from Doncaster and his own selections from the junior teams, didn't inspire the fans, watching what was meant to be a promotion season becoming a relegation scrap. Leeds finished 14th, and Bremner's summer recruitment looked functional at best. Defenders Jack Ashurst and Bobby McDonald were both 31, joining 25-year-old Brendan Ormsby; Keith Edwards averaged better than a goal every two games for Sheffield United, but was 29. He was expensive, at £125,000, and scored just six league goals for Leeds.

The aim was hard work, strength and honesty, with Sheridan supplying the magic, but it didn't mean consistency. The new-look team rose to second in the table in October, in time for Bremner's first anniversary in the job, but the last match before Christmas was a 7-2 defeat at Stoke City that dropped them to seventh; the season before, under Gray, Leeds had lost at Stoke 6-2. 'It made me want to cry for the fans,' said Bremner, in a 500-word apology in the *Yorkshire Evening Post*. He said that, for the first time, he had talked to the players about his own time at Leeds. 'I spoke about how those players would die for the club, yet we never got the kind of support away from home that the present team are getting ... I have turned things over at this club before and I will do so again. I will bring in new players because I am not having the best support in the world repaid with displays such as that.'

If the players weren't appreciating being at Elland Road, Bremner certainly was; he joined in training on Fullerton Park as keenly as when he played, relished home matches and appreciated, when they behaved, the large groups of away supporters. His enthusiasm was working on the players, raising Sheridan in particular to new standards, but he was putting himself under enormous pressure to succeed, causing explosions of temper if United fell short. 'With support such as that, I would have been prepared to lose an arm and a leg for the club and still keep battling,' he said after one defeat. 'My players have to learn to die for Leeds United.'

The threat of finding new players was not an idle remark, but it meant letting go of one of his stars. The Leeds board could no longer resist offers for Ian Snodin, and with Bremner negotiating at his side, he had his choice between Everton, 2nd in the First Division, or reigning champions Liverpool, in 3rd. Snodin chose Everton, and moved for £840,000 at the start of January; he said later that leaving Leeds 'was the worst moment of my career'.

The money eased the board's constant financial concerns, and gave Bremner cash for more hard-working players – energetic full-back Micky Adams, tall target-man John Pearson, and defensive midfielder Mark Aizlewood – to win the ball and give it to Sheridan. Snodin won the First Division that season with Everton, but the new players helped Leeds challenge for promotion without him.

First there was the FA Cup. The draw was unusually generous, although the third round game away to Telford United had a controversial build-up as the non-league club feared being overrun by Leeds supporters; the game was switched to a Sunday lunchtime at West Brom's ground, and the *Yorkshire Evening Post* declared the change a victory for hooliganism they hoped would be punished on the pitch, beneath the headline, 'Come on Telford!' Leeds won 2-1, then by the same score away to Third Division Swindon Town, setting up a fifth round match at Elland Road against First Division Queens Park Rangers. Good form and big opposition caught the imagination and the stadium, its capacity much reduced since the 1970s, was a 31,324 sell-out; fans clambered onto the rooftops of shops on Elland Road for a view. Leeds took the lead when Baird beat his marker to head into the net; an own goal by David Rennie made it 1-1, but with five minutes left Pearson flicked on Sheridan's corner, while Ormsby hung in the air at the back post until the ball arrived and headed it powerfully into the net, starting wild celebrations on the Kop behind the goal.

Leeds had Third Division opposition again in the sixth round, winning 2-0 away to Wigan Athletic; the cup run took nine weeks, and to reach an FA Cup semi-final so suddenly after so many barren seasons was surreal. Bremner was at the heart of it, feeling the familiar sensations of glory; he had the players compete at carpet bowls, as if to summon the past to the team hotel.

The match, against Coventry City, lived up to United's history. Kick-off was delayed by fifteen minutes as Leeds fans were packed, some thought dangerously, into the Leppings Lane end at Hillsborough; after another fifteen minutes Leeds were ahead, through Rennie's strong near-post header. Leeds were unconcerned by their First Division opponents until the second half when Ormsby, normally decisive, allowed Dave Bennett to keep a ball in play and catch Leeds out; Micky Gynn buried his cross. Ten minutes later the ball broke to Keith Houchen, who calmly took the ball around Day and put Coventry ahead.

With seven minutes left Keith Edwards replaced John Pearson. If transfer fees could be repaid in euphoria, Edwards now became a bargain; within 30 seconds Ritchie fought past two defenders and crossed to Edwards, who gave Ogrizovic no chance with his header. Everything great about Leeds when Bremner was a player had come back; the determination not to be beaten, the quality to make a chance and score. But back, too, was the heartbreak. None felt the impact of Bennett's extra-time winner for Coventry more than Brendan Ormsby, who blamed himself for the first goal and the defeat; the captain was responsible for probably the best moment in five years when he scored against QPR, and now he felt responsible for the worst.

United's dreams had not all deserted them. One league defeat in fourteen games helped Leeds finish the season in 4th, qualifying for a new play-off system and a chance of promotion. In a two-legged semi-final against Oldham Athletic, Edwards scored the only goal in the last minute of the first game; at Boundary Park Oldham cancelled that out, then went ahead on aggregate with seconds remaining, Mike Cecere finishing Denis Irwin's cross. Leeds didn't abandon the fighting spirit Bremner wanted; straight from the restart Aspin launched the ball forward and Edwards again scored a vital goal. Extra time was goalless, sending Leeds through on away goals.

The final was also two-legged, against Charlton Athletic, who were playing to stay in the First Division. Leeds almost came through the away leg with a 0-0 draw, but Jim Melrose scored for Charlton two minutes from the end. At Elland Road, 31,395 came hoping to cheer United's return to Division One; they cheered a goal midway through the second half, when Bob Taylor's shot beat Bob Bolder's dive, and Ormsby, desperate to put the FA Cup behind him, forced the ball over the line. But two 1-0 home wins meant no resolution, and a one-off replay at St Andrews.

United's support was huge; 10,000 travelled to Birmingham. Ormsby's luck again went against him; a serious knee injury in the first half left him watching with everyone else as another tight game went into extra time. In the 99th minute, Sheridan showed the class the First Division could expect if Leeds went up. Twenty-five yards from goal, Sheridan nonchalantly approached a free-kick, shouting at the referee and pointing towards Charlton's wall; suddenly he flicked the ball hard over that wall, his mastery ensuring a dip beyond Bolder's diving hand into the top corner. Now the nonchalance was gone; Sheridan ran to the bench, looking as if he couldn't believe the importance of what he had just done. Ten thousand Leeds fans, and Billy Bremner, could feel the big time belonging to Leeds again.

It wasn't to be. With seven minutes left, the ball bounced around United's penalty area and Charlton defender Peter Shirtliff slotted past Day. Five minutes later Shirtliff scored again, heading in a free-kick, breaking 10,000 hearts.

Leeds United were brought face to face with what success so often brought to Elland Road: pain. They played 55 matches in their best season for ten years, lost in a cup semi-final, were denied promotion in the last seven minutes of a replay, and finished back where they started. Bremner and his teammates made an art of withstanding disappointment and returning stronger, but as manager he couldn't inspire his workmanlike squad to a repeat performance; despite being favourites for promotion in 1987/88, Leeds never rose above mid-table. Sheridan was still sublime; a teenager in midfield, David Batty, was cut from the same cloth as his manager; there were big crowds for matches against Middlesbrough and Bradford City. But the board felt anxious that forward momentum was being lost. After a poor start to 1988/89, Billy Bremner was sacked in October 1988. As when Eddie Gray was sacked, the players were stunned, and told the press so; the fans were furious to see another of their heroes mistreated, again turning on Leslie Silver, and his car.

Bremner's goodbye to Elland Road came a few months after another. The flirtation with glory in 1987 was played against a background of tragedy greater than just losing football matches. Don and Elsie Revie had moved to Perthshire, enjoying retirement near Elsie's home village, and plenty of excellent golf courses. But a round of golf was leaving Don in pain, and when household tasks did the same, he went to his doctor. The diagnosis was devastating. Revie had motor neurone disease, and there was no cure.

That didn't stop Revie's determination to fight it, and with the help of his family he resisted the toll the disease quickly took on his body, seeking experimental treatments in Texas and Moscow. 'I've always been a fella that faced the music,' he said, 'and this is the music that I've got to face again.' But the players who gathered for a match to raise funds for research in Revie's honour, at Elland Road in May 1988, were distressed by the decline of their boss, on whom they had all depended for so much. Now in a wheelchair, he was reunited with them before the game, but overcome by emotion, he left before the match itself. As he was leaving Elland Road for the last time, Revie told the *Yorkshire Evening Post*: 'I am so grateful. I knew the lads would respond. They are always in my thoughts and my heart. I owe them so much and I like to believe I contributed to their success.' Still the boss, he gave £20 to the groundsman, his friend John Reynolds, and told him, 'Make sure all my lads get a drink.'

With his family by his side, Don Revie died in hospital on 26 May 1989; he was just 61 years old. The Revie era, that began when he signed for Leeds United as an inside-forward on 28 November 1958, was over.

1989–92

THEY'VE HAD TO WORK THE HARDEST

Howard Wilkinson's club was Sheffield Wednesday. He played for them, before coaching and teaching became his passion, and managed them, moving from Notts County to take over from Jack Charlton and win promotion to the First Division at the first attempt, as he told the directors he would. He also told the directors he would take Wednesday to the top, and he did that too; they finished 5th in 1985/86, reaching the FA Cup semi-final.

What hurt him, as a manager and a Wednesdayite, was that the directors didn't realise how good they had it. Wilkinson kept telling the board that if they invested again, they could win the First Division; and when

Wilkinson said something would happen, it usually did. But their ambitions were sated, and Wilkinson felt helpless as his best players drifted away. When he decided to leave to take a new job, he broke off from saying goodbye to the staff, sat down in the bootroom, and cried into a blue club towel.

If Howard Wilkinson was going to win the First Division, he needed an ambitious board to back him. If that board was at the bottom of the Second Division, so be it. If it meant moving to a place where he felt no emotional attachment, that might be all the better. Whether he liked it or not, and whether he liked them or not, the most ambitious directors around were Leslie Silver and Bill Fotherby.

Billy Bremner gave them a glimpse of the potential Leeds United still had; Fotherby had been desperate to keep the momentum, launching an audacious bid to sign Argentinian World Cup star Diego Maradona, arguably the best player in the world, to keep Leeds in the headlines. It started as a stunt, but conversations with Maradona's representatives were real enough, and Fotherby was sure he could raise the money. Leeds were still struggling financially, but the recession was easing and there was money in the city, and Fotherby knew where to find it.

Money was coming into football, too. English football had been on its knees; clubs were banned from European competition after the Heysel disaster, so the best English players moved abroad; the Bradford fire failed to awaken the authorities to dangerous conditions in many football grounds, and 96 Liverpool fans were killed by crushing in the Leppings Lane end of Hillsborough at an FA Cup semi-final. Leeds fans who had packed into the same pens two years earlier felt a nervous mixture of anger, sadness and relief; Howard Wilkinson, who worked at Hillsborough for so long, demanded change.

Despite the public image of disasters and violence, and often poor football, satellite television was making the game more valuable. In 1986, ITV paid £6.3 million to show Football League matches for two years; in 1988, with ten First Division clubs threatening to break away into their own 'Super League' and keep broadcast revenue for themselves, ITV paid £44 million for four years. Silver and Fotherby knew that if Leeds weren't in the First Division by the time negotiations started for the next deal, they could be shut out for good.

Leslie Silver's offices were in The Rydings, a mansion house that inspired Charlotte Brontë, now hemmed in by Silver's enormous modern paint factory. He and Wilkinson met there, drank scotch and discussed the Leeds job late into the night. Wilkinson arrived prepared. He had analysed every aspect of the club, the abilities of every player, the role of every director, and outlined to Silver how Leeds could get to the top of the First Division and stay there. The board would have to back Wilkinson's judgement, building a squad to win promotion within two years; after promotion, they would add players to compete at the top, while investing in a ten-year plan to recruit young players to a state-of-the-art academy. It was everything Silver wanted to hear. Wilkinson was taken aback when Silver said money would be no problem; what Fotherby couldn't find, Silver and vice-chairman Peter Gilman would under-write. The important thing was promotion, fast.

Wilkinson was the first outsider to manage Leeds for ten years, and his first task was tackling the problems insularity had created. The club was obsessed with the past, from fading photographs of the glory years in the reception, to decrepit facilities nobody fixed, because it was how things were when Leeds were great. Leeds weren't great anymore, and the memories were fooling everybody. Knowing it would shock the fans, and hoping it would shock the club, Wilkinson removed all remind-ers of the Revie era. 'There can be solace in the past, but you cannot live on memories,' he told the *Yorkshire Evening Post*.

Norman Hunter, employed as a coach by Bremner, was also removed; Mick Bates and Joe Jordan's habit of popping down to training for a kickabout was stopped. The players loved training with Bremner, staying for hours to hear stories about the glory days, but Wilkinson felt that helped the players hide. Why should they work hard to win promotion, when they could just look at

Bremner's medals? Leeds United's history was treated like an inheritance, inflating self-esteem among a group who were, mostly, not good enough to be there.

Wilkinson's first major signing reset the standard. Some Leeds players might think they were big-time but Gordon Strachan, at five foot six, towered over them. At Aberdeen he won the league twice, the Scottish Cup three times, the European Cup-Winners Cup and the European Super Cup; at Manchester United he won the FA Cup; he scored in the World Cup finals for Scotland. He was 32, and like Bobby Collins and Johnny Giles before him, bitterly disappointed to be written off by a First Division manager, Alex Ferguson of Manchester United, with whom Strachan had enjoyed success at Aberdeen. Strachan's years of diligent personal training, and a diet of seaweed pills and bananas, contradicted Ferguson's assessment; Strachan was immediately the fittest player at Leeds, his presence a demonstration to the club's big names that fish, chips and beer were not how things were done at the top level.

Wilkinson gave those players a chance, concentrating on getting the best from them in training. They came close to the play-offs, generating excitement, and publicity courtesy of Fotherby, but Mark Aizlewood's last act of the season demonstrated why players like Strachan had to come; after receiving jeers from the crowd for recent performances, Aizlewood scored against Walsall and ran to the Kop, flicking V signs and shouting. This was Leeds United's captain; before the game restarted Wilkinson substituted him, and he never played for the club again.

John Sheridan left in the summer. The fans loved Shez, their one reminder of quality through the bleak years, but Wilkinson didn't love his indiscipline, and neither player nor manager enjoyed his part in the tough new training regimes. Wilkinson had also seen enough of Sheridan trying to pass the ball on Elland Road's muddy pitch; now also used by Hunslet Rugby League club, it didn't suit passing football. Sheridan went to Nottingham Forest, to impress in the First Division, if he could impress his new manager, Brian Clough.

Sheridan's replacement was, like Strachan, coming down from the First Division. But in every other respect Vinnie Jones was Strachan's opposite, and a shock. Jones epitomised the 'Crazy Gang' spirit at Wimbledon that won the FA Cup, but looked to many like terrace hooliganism on a pitch. He combined trouble with charisma, making him an ideal television chat show guest, and his transfer gave Fotherby the sensation he'd sought from Maradona. 'The most exciting thing to have happened to Leeds United in years,' said Fotherby. 'Don Revie would not have let him through the door,' said Johnny Giles.

Wilkinson thought there was more to Jones than his aggressive public image; that he was, beneath it all, a footballer. He was a perfect counterpoint to the new captain, Strachan; Strachan led by example, and Jones enforced by will. An argument in the players' lounge made the job clear. 'I'm disappointed in you,' Wilkinson told Jones, who arrived in his office expecting to be told to clear out. 'I've just been in there, and there's no blood. Why do you think I brought you to this club? To sort those fucking wankers out.'

Before the start of 1989/90, Wilkinson spent more than £3 million. The policy was quality players Wilkinson either knew, or knew had more to give. Chris Fairclough was a calm centre-back, his confidence low after injuries; Jim Beglin won the double with Liverpool in 1986, another coming back from injury; attacking right-back Mel Sterland and striker Carl Shutt were Wilkinson favourites at Wednesday; John McClelland captained Northern Ireland and Rangers; John Hendrie was an exciting winger yet to prove himself. Leeds signed fourteen players, with a common trait: they were used to better than the Second Division, and would give everything to get it back.

A shock on the opening day, a 5-2 defeat at Newcastle United, didn't stop them. During a fifteen-game unbeaten run they played into form, turning draws into wins; Leeds went top of the league in December. The potential for promotion was being realised, and more players arrived; for £400,000, tall striker Lee Chapman became a vital part of Wilkinson's team, as he was at Wednesday.

When goalkeeper Mervyn Day had the ball, Chapman was his target, and midfield and defence went upfield within 25 yards of him when Day cleared; whether Chapman won the high ball or not, nine players led by Jones and Batty would fight for possession in the opponent's half, then give the ball to Strachan, whose inventiveness on the wing dictated how, not if, a chance to score would come; often a cross from Sterland for Chapman to dive at. Leeds bombarded teams for the first twenty minutes, established a lead, then used their offside trap and strength to keep it; and like Revie's early team in Division Two, their emphasis on winning football didn't make them popular outside the city. London's press had descended on a 1-0 win at West Ham, eviscerating Leeds for their performance. 'Straight out of the Revie textbook at its worst,' wrote Rob Shepherd in *Today*. 'Calculating, clinical, cynical and sly.'

Wilkinson hit back with adjectives of his own. 'Pathetic. Disgraceful. Deep down, very very funny, because it was, in a way, so predictable. A lot of it reads like Barbara Cartland, and a lot of people who have written it are about as over the top as she is.' He resented the comments about Revie's team. 'Ever since I came here that one keeps being thrown up,' he said. 'You only have to commit a foul and on Monday morning it's, "The old, cynical Leeds". If you do something well, nobody ever writes about the old, terrific Leeds.' Wilkinson may have removed all references to Revie, but he was protective of the legacy; he kept one item, a list of his achievements, pinned next to his desk.

The biggest risk to United was, as ever, themselves. Although Leeds stayed top, Sheffield United, Newcastle and Sunderland were close. Wilkinson found more reinforcements; Chapman's arrival upset popular striker Ian Baird, who left for Middlesbrough, replaced by another Wednesday old boy, Imre Varadi; in midfield, David Batty was showing fatigue in his second full season, but another young midfielder, Gary Speed, was in exciting form; boyhood Leeds fan Chris Kamara signed from Stoke City, providing more experience. A vital match against Sheffield United at Elland Road on Easter Monday proved the wisdom of Wilkinson's new investments. Leeds dominated, winning 4-0 with a clincher from Speed, who ran the length of the pitch to score at the Kop end.

The celebratory pitch invasion was premature, as was another at Elland Road two weeks later. The atmosphere when Leicester City arrived for the penultimate game redefined tension, that increased in the second half when Gary McAllister equalised Sterland's early strike. With six minutes left and promotion on the line, Sterland's long throw towards Chapman bounced around Leicester's penalty area until it fell to Speed, whose control put the ball into Gordon Strachan's path, a yard outside the box. First time, as hard as he could, left-footed, Strachan struck the ball, and the ball struck the top corner, and for a moment Elland Road was silent; the goal was scored faster than it could be understood. Then there was pandemonium, in the stands and on the pitch. At full-time, Vinnie Jones announced Newcastle had drawn their match, and Leeds were up; pandemonium became a party.

Jones was wrong. Newcastle won, meaning one more match of agony, at Bournemouth's tiny stadium by the sea. On a blistering day Wilkinson and his assistant, Mick Hennigan, wore the same all-yellow kit as the players, kicking every ball with them. The vital goal came four minutes after half-time: Kamara burst forward and crossed, and Chapman's diving header won the Second Division championship.

As the players partied on the bus home, Gordon Strachan sat up front with the driver, watching the sun set and reflecting on the most satisfying achievement of his career; he had been asked to help Leeds win promotion, and he had. Howard Wilkinson wasn't with them; after Sheffield Wednesday's promotion in 1984 left him looking 'as if I'd just come out of a prison camp', he vowed never to let football cause such stress again, and went to a friend's home in the New Forest. He rose early the next day to listen to the dawn chorus by the pool: 'The garden, with the birds in celebratory song, was the ideal place to be.'

It protected Wilkinson, for a while, from the storm breaking around Leeds. The *Daily Mirror*'s headline summed up the reaction to United's promotion: 'Leeds Scum Are Back.' The match at Bournemouth was played on a Bank Holiday weekend, in a dilapidated stadium with room for just 2,000 Leeds fans. The club pleaded with the Football League to move the fixture, then set up screens in Leeds where 7,500 fans could watch television coverage. But more than 5,000 made the trip anyway, whether they were Leeds fans or not: 'I doubt if any of these people could name half the team,' said Phil Beeton in the *Yorkshire Evening Post*, a fan who hadn't missed a game since March 1967, and didn't recognise a lot of the faces causing trouble that weekend.

The majority revelled in the party atmosphere, but the flash points of violence and vandalism were serious enough to put United's promotion at risk. After a summer-long inquiry, the FA imposed what they called 'a suspended death sentence': one more incident, and the FA would close Elland Road for four matches; any more, and they would close the club down.

It was a bitter blow, as Leeds had worked harder than most clubs to solve the problems their followers caused. Ian Hambridge's death at Birmingham was not the end of the violence, and in the mid-1980s Elland Road was a no-go area for a lot of people in Leeds. As at many clubs, among the hooligans were a small but influential group of far-right agitators, imported to recruit bored kids to join the National Front; outside the ground their members sold the National Front's newspaper, *Bulldog*. After Terry Connor was sold in 1982, Leeds didn't sign any black players until Noel Blake and

Vince Hilaire in 1988; although a majority of decent fans still watched football there, the perception of many people, backed up by bitter experience, was that Elland Road was lost to the racists.

Change began among the supporters. Leeds United Against Racism and Fascism (LUARAF) distributed anti-racist leaflets in 1987, followed by a fanzine, *Marching Altogether*, reminding fans about players like Gerry Francis, Albert Johanneson and Alex Sabella, emphasising that the true voice of Leeds was not the National Front. Getting the club's support was difficult; Leeds initially denied there was a problem, threatening legal action if leaflets used the club badge. The police were reluctant too, fearing confrontation. A different tactic forced the club into action: LUARAF compiled all the coverage of incidents involving Leeds into one report, *Terror on the Terraces*, and sent it to the press, where United could no longer avoid it.

Once Leeds accepted there was a problem, their efforts were sincere. Anti-racist messages from Billy Bremner appeared in the club programme, and in the same month that Howard Wilkinson arrived, former Bradford City player Ces Podd was hired as community officer. He grew up in Leeds, sneaking into Elland Road in the 1960s to watch Johanneson, and now engaged with every part of the city where there were people who might want to watch football, but who were wary of Elland Road. An undercover police operation, 'Wild

Boar', removed several ringleaders, and closed-circuit television and private stewarding added to the atmosphere of security Podd could demonstrate. The team now included black players Chris Fairclough and Chris Kamara, soon joined by Chris Whyte and Rod and Ray Wallace; Fairclough was voted Supporters' Player of the Year in 1989/90. Vinnie Jones, who outsiders feared would appeal to the hooligan element, threw himself into Podd's community work, changing views not only of himself but of the shaven-headed fans who idolised him. Elland Road had a family stand and a creche, and before Bournemouth, the only problems at away games were delayed kick-offs, as grounds struggled to get Leeds' enormous travelling support through the turnstiles.

But perception was stubborn. The punishment for Bournemouth ignored all the good Leeds had done and felt like a penalty imposed against every sin since 1971. Former Liverpool captain Emlyn Hughes spoke for many in 1992 when he said he didn't just want to see Leeds lose, he wanted them 'torn apart'. 'Leeds stood for too much that sickened me when I was a player for just a couple of "goody two shoes" seasons to put right. If Howard Wilkinson sent out eleven vestal virgins and whistled up the Angel Gabriel to captain them, folk would still loathe Leeds United. Me included.'

The important thing was the First Division. In the team bus on the way to Everton for the first match, Howard Wilkinson was filmed riding with a shotgun, gazing through the window, telling ITV he was relieved the football was starting. The shotgun belonged to Vinnie Jones. The players had been told the team, and it reflected the cultural shift Wilkinson was making on the pitch: Jones wasn't in it, and new £1 million playmaker Gary McAllister was. 'Do you want to have another think about the team tomorrow, gaffer?' Jones asked Wilkinson, along the barrel of his gun.

It was in good humour, but Jones was hiding real disappointment; he played the best football of his career at Leeds, bonding with the fans and becoming part of the newly booming city; he had a Leeds United badge tattooed on his leg. To go from being 'more famous than Michael Jackson in Leeds', to watching the team take on Manchester United without him, brought tears of frustration. His old boss Dave Bassett offered to take him to Sheffield United. He left.

McAllister was United's second million-pound player. The first was goalkeeper John Lukic, returning from Arsenal with a league title and a League Cup, and centre-back Chris Whyte came from West Brom for £450,000, as Wilkinson modified his Second Division champions. They made more use of McAllister's sublime passing in midfield, alongside David Batty's tenacious pursuit of possession; Gary Speed, adaptable to anywhere, started as first choice on the left wing. Speed was only twenty, Batty 21, but they stood out among the best players in the division, and Leeds among the best teams;

with endurance to rival a season from the Revie era, Leeds finished 4th in Division One, were knocked out of the FA Cup by Arsenal after three replays, lost a two-legged League Cup semi-final to Manchester United, and the two-legged Northern Area Final of the Zenith Data Systems Cup to Everton. They played 56 matches, their ruthless attacking style surprising television viewers, and Gordon Strachan, aged 34, was voted Football Writers' Footballer of the Year. Crucially, the FA never had to enforce its suspended death sentence. United were back.

Wilkinson was determined to keep the momentum behind Leeds he had lost at Hillsborough; three big signings arrived in the summer. £1.3 million bought left-back Tony Dorigo; at £1.6 million, Rod Wallace was a forward who added pace through the middle or on the wings. For £900,000 Steve Hodge was an experienced international who would prevent the midfield, widely regarded as the best in the league, becoming complacent. Fotherby, typically, was aiming high. The previous season, he said, 'we took things by storm. Our ambition now is quite simply to win the First Division title.'

One defeat in the first 27 league matches was more than even Fotherby expected. Leeds ticked off milestones along the way, beating Liverpool for the first time since 1973 and going top of the First Division for the first time since April 1974. In televised matches they overwhelmed Aston Villa 4-1 and Sheffield Wednesday 6-1, using Sterland and Dorigo to overlap Strachan and

Speed, all supplying crosses Chapman headed in with brave, spectacular dives. Their rivals for the title were Manchester United, who were expected to win their first championship for 25 years, and at New Year they competed in league and cups, playing three matches in two weeks at Elland Road; the league game was drawn 1-1, while Manchester United won the League Cup and FA Cup matches, 3-1 and 1-0. Leeds paid a high price in the last minutes of the last game; diving for a cross at the back post, pressure from defender Gary Pallister sent Chapman off course, and as he landed his wrist fractured beneath the weight of his body.

Chapman was dangerously brave. The previous season, at White Hart Lane, a kick knocked him unconscious in mid-air and he fell face first on a cinder running track beside the pitch. A surgeon compared his injuries to the results of a car crash; with 30 stitches in his face, Chapman played a week later against Manchester United in the League Cup semi-final. He was brave again now, only missing four matches despite doctors' advice that while his wrist was repaired, it would not be fully healed for six months. Chapman put a cast on it and went back in the team. In his absence, Leeds were beaten at Oldham Athletic, only the second defeat of the season.

Wilkinson signed two strikers on loan as cover; Tony Agana, prolific in the lower divisions for Sheffield United, and Eric Cantona, a French international combining flair and intrigue. Cantona's hobbies included painting, poetry and arguing, his temper causing a two-month ban for throwing a ball at a referee and calling each member of a disciplinary panel an 'idiot' to their face. His next move was retiring from football aged 25, until French national manager Michel Platini, backed up by Cantona's psychoanalyst, convinced him to play abroad and return for the European Championships. Leeds were his lifeline.

Wilkinson also lost Mel Sterland to a serious ankle injury, and with Cantona providing an exciting new dimension, he began altering the team to include him alongside Chapman, switching Wallace to the wing and Speed to full-back. Leeds beat Wimbledon 5-1, but lost 4-1 at Queens Park Rangers and 4-0 at Manchester City, a defeat many thought ended their title chances. After the game, Wilkinson told the players to get on the bus and go home. 'We'll talk about all this on Monday,' he said.

Wilkinson and Mick Hennigan spent their Sunday with the detailed performance notes Wilkinson had started paying data analysts to keep at Sheffield Wednesday. Sorting through sheaves of paper-and-pencil records, they discussed what worked at Leeds, which players responded best to their hours of rigorous training drill. It became clear that trying to incorporate Cantona's individualism was giving Wilkinson two problems, when he only had to solve one: replacing Mel Sterland. Jon Newsome could do that, and on Monday

Wilkinson told the players that the team for the final five matches would, Sterland aside, be the team that had taken Leeds to the edge of the title: Lukic, Newsome, Dorigo, Batty, Fairclough, Whyte, Strachan, Wallace, Chapman, McAllister, Speed. There was nothing more to worry about, he said, nothing he could tell them they hadn't heard already. They knew how to win games, and had proved it. He compared their situation to golf; they had done the hard work practising and perfecting their swing, now they had to play the shots. 'Trust your swing,' he told them, again and again.

There was no such calmness at Old Trafford. Alex Ferguson's first team cost almost twice Leeds United's, and he boasted of multi-million-pound players in reserve to deal with fixture congestion. But as congestion increased, he began to crack. On Easter Monday, Nottingham Forest won 2-1 at Old Trafford, before Leeds beat Coventry City 2-0 at Elland Road in a tense, televised game. Manchester United had a game in hand to play midweek at West Ham, who were all but relegated, and an instinctive volley by Kenny Brown settled it 1-0 to West Ham. Leeds and Manchester United both had two games left, and Leeds led by a point.

'They are in the driving seat,' said Ferguson, attempting mind games in the press. 'Though Leeds' players say they have the nerve to take the title, how do they know that? No one in their side has ever won a championship medal.' Wilkinson didn't flinch. He had an appointment, giving a seminar to business people in Bradford, and told the *Yorkshire Evening Post*: 'My message to my players is, keep playing, and leave the comments and the analysing to other people.'

Manchester United's game at Liverpool was scheduled for late afternoon; Leeds played at Sheffield United at noon, aiming to open a four-point lead. Aiming soon became hoping. Playing in bright sunshine, but against a gale, the nerves, tension and conditions were all beyond Leeds United's control. Howard Wilkinson could only watch, and trust his players. They looked nervous and conceded to Alan Cork after half an hour, but equalised just before half-time. Strachan chipped a quick free-kick into the penalty area, where collisions and ricochets ended with the ball in the net, off Wallace's knee.

In the second half McAllister mastered the elements to land a free-kick on Newsome's head, giving Leeds the lead. It lasted two minutes, before a hopeful shot across goal by John Pemberton was deflected in by Lee Chapman: 2-2. Wilkinson embraced the chaos, sending on Cantona almost to see what would happen.

Moments later Speed's clearance bounced over halfway, where David Barnes intervened for the defence but only kicked the ball into the air, looping towards his own goal. Wallace and Cantona chased it, either side of Brian Gayle, who had everything under control as the ball neared the edge of his penalty area, but hit the ball back up into the air with his knee. Cantona and Wallace stopped running and watched as goalkeeper Mel Rees jumped to grab the ball, and Gayle jumped to head it. Gayle won, sending the ball into the empty net.

It was a surreal way to win the Football League. The players couldn't celebrate properly, until Manchester United's 2-0 defeat at Liverpool confirmed the title. Four of them crammed onto the sofa at Lee Chapman's house so ITV could broadcast their reactions. Chapman was a minor celebrity and smoothly answered the hard questions; McAllister mocked Chapman's attempts to translate for Cantona; Batty, reflecting the general confusion, said winning the league was 'a nice bonus'. Spread out across Yorkshire, the players were desperate to get together again at the Flying Pizza restaurant and start the party.

Howard Wilkinson and Gordon Strachan kept to their less stressful path. They both avoided the Manchester United match, Wilkinson eating Sunday lunch with his family, Strachan swimming at a hotel. They underlined the credit due to all the players who had contributed since October 1988, so that the First Division could be won in April 1992; unheralded squad players who worked hard every day. Of all the teams that could have won the title, Wilkinson said, his players 'have had to do the most. They've had to work the hardest, they've had to cope with the most difficulties. So I think it makes the achievement sweeter. They've been magnificent.'

As only the second Leeds manager to win a major trophy, Wilkinson resisted comparisons in the media with Don Revie; the reminders of the past Wilkinson had taken down to take the club forward could now be brought back, to remind the current generation how much more work had to be done.

'At this time, this wasn't a big club,' he said. 'Big clubs win things, and this club hadn't won things. It wasn't a big club, and we weren't a good team. We were fourth from bottom of the Second Division. So we had to start to make our own history, that would go into that new museum that we were building. And all those photographs that were dotted around the place will obviously take pride of place in the new museum, because at this moment in time we have come nowhere near. What we have achieved, in the three-and-a-half years we've been at it, would fill perhaps one corner of that museum. You'd have to find room for us.'

Wilkinson kept coming back to the same word to describe those three-and-a-half years. 'It's been a dream, hasn't it?' he said.

1992–96

IT DOESN'T MATTER
HOW IT MAKES ME FEEL

When the Premier League that top clubs had been seeking since the mid-1980s began, in the 1992/93 season, Leeds United were perfectly placed. They entered as the last champions of the old First Division; managing director Bill Fotherby was part of the committee finding sponsorship for the new multi-million-pound competition.

Other clubs had taken note of Fotherby's work at Leeds, including a £10 million, five-year sponsorship deal with Admiral Sportswear. Howard Wilkinson's promotion plan had been expensive, as he said it would be, and the club had accumulated deficits of more than £8 million; chairman Leslie Silver and vice-chairman Peter

Gilman underwrote a £3 million overdraft. Commercial revenue was increasing, and Fotherby was copying ideas from Old Trafford; the council still owned Elland Road, but a banqueting suite replaced the West Stand's 1950s entrance. The biggest change began days after winning the league; the roof of the Lowfields was pulled down, then the bank of building waste and rubble it was built on, and a new £5.5 million East Stand rose in its place, paid for by a bond scheme; a 17,000 capacity all-seater structure with the biggest family area in the country, and the largest cantilever roof in Europe.

It was in keeping with the 'Whole New Ball Game' adverts promoting BSkyB's satellite television coverage of the new Premier League. But despite being league champions and entering the European Cup, Leeds United was in many ways still a provincial Second Division club, its finances dependent on wealthy local businessmen and its squad eschewing glamour for honest endeavour and hard work. The player with the highest profile was Lee Chapman, footballer husband of film and TV actress Leslie Ash; David Batty and Gary Speed, two marketable young internationals, were close behind, Speed returning for the new season with long, curly hair and a modelling contract. But the team's star player, and its biggest problem, was Eric Cantona.

Within weeks of arriving on loan, Cantona went from enigmatic curio to fan favourite, chants of 'Ooh Ah Cantona' greeting every brilliant piece of control;

his popularity at the end of the title-winning season was far in excess of his contribution. A solo goal against Chelsea was typical, one of the best seen at Elland Road since John Sheridan, Cantona flicking the ball over one confused defender after another before crashing it into the net; it was the third goal in the last minute of a 3-0 win. Trying to accommodate his talents almost derailed United's season, until Wilkinson restricted him to super-sub.

His loan was made permanent for £1 million, and the new season was a chance for Cantona to assert himself properly, as one of the few flair – and foreign – players in a Premier League that couldn't make teams like Oldham Athletic or Ipswich Town chic in one summer. He started in style at Wembley, scoring a hat-trick as Leeds won the Charity Shield against Liverpool, 4-3; another hat-trick followed when Tottenham Hotspur were beaten 5-0 at Elland Road. Believing back trouble may soon end Strachan's career, Howard Wilkinson paid Arsenal £2 million for midfielder David Rocastle, making him United's record signing, but Cantona took Strachan's place as Wilkinson tried three in attack, three in defence, or five in midfield, attempting a new passing style. When Rod Wallace was injured Strachan was back in the side, but Chapman and Cantona up front together were a problem; under pressure the team reverted to playing long to Chapman, leaving Cantona bewildered that they should prefer aiming for his ungainly teammate.

Cantona was not a diplomat, and Wilkinson didn't allow dissent. Cantona's frustration could make his tackling in training matches dangerous, and his efforts on the pitch negligible. In the European Cup, where Cantona was expected to be an asset, his thoughtless attempt to play a cross-field pass with an injured leg, as his manager yelled at him not to try it, cost Leeds an opening goal away to Stuttgart in a game that was already difficult; Leeds lost 3-0.

United's return to the European Cup seemed over as soon as it began, but in the second leg at Elland Road Cantona made an early contribution, leaping like Chapman to head a high ball into Speed's path; Speed volleyed into the net to inspire the crowd and, despite a goal for Stuttgart, a relentless fightback. Gary McAllister scored a penalty and Cantona and Chapman scored one each in a 4-1 win, but Stuttgart won on the away goals rule – until television viewers in Germany spotted they had named four foreign players in their team and broken UEFA rules. A hasty decision reverted the match by default to 3-0 to Leeds, and a quickly arranged play-off was held in front of 7,400 spectators, in Barcelona's 120,000-capacity Nou Camp.

Leeds took the lead after half an hour, Strachan hitting a terrific shot into the top corner, but Stuttgart soon equalised. With fifteen minutes left, Cantona added a misplaced pass to another anonymous performance, and Wilkinson took him off. His replacement was Carl Shutt, whom Wilkinson and his assistant Mick Hennigan took from non-league football when he was 23. Wilkinson was always buying new strikers to take his place, but at Sheffield Wednesday and Leeds, he always turned back to Shutt. Shutt never let him down, and didn't now; within a minute of coming on, he pounced on a loose ball and caught out the Stuttgart defence, running from halfway and shooting past the goalkeeper to win the match. He could hardly believe it; Wilkinson might have known he would do it.

He soon knew what to do about Cantona. He was disappointing again as United's European Cup interest ended in high-profile matches against Rangers, and an argument when Cantona was dropped for a match at Queens Park Rangers ended with the player on his way back to France. Peace talks granted Cantona's wish, Wilkinson dropping Chapman – who had scored six in his last seven games – and playing Cantona up front with Wallace at Manchester City. Leeds lost 4-0 and Cantona contributed nothing. It was time for the experiment to end, if anyone would take Cantona off Leeds United's hands. His agent faxed his transfer request to Elland Road; Leeds tried to find clubs in France, Italy or Spain that would buy him for the million he had cost.

The first to enquire was Manchester United. Bill Fotherby was speaking to their chief executive Martin Edwards about bringing Denis Irwin back to Leeds. Edwards refused, but France's national team manager

Gérard Houllier had tipped Alex Ferguson off about Cantona's unhappiness. A question was asked, and a deal was agreed that day, and Eric Cantona became a Manchester United player.

Leeds thought they were relieving a headache. Buying Cantona had stretched their finances, and getting their money back eased worries at the bank. Wilkinson had tired of him, suspecting he was like a grenade without a pin; when Cantona eventually exploded, he reasoned, it would be better if it happened at Old Trafford. Alex Ferguson had no particular track record for discipline, and had crumbled under the pressure of the previous season's title race. Let him sort Cantona out, if he could.

Leeds' fans were furious. They had quickly fallen for Cantona, and now their favourite was sold to their bitterest rivals. Leeds were out of the European Cup, out of form, and out of the race to defend their title. Cantona's flamboyance, when it worked, looked like the answer, and the future. Wilkinson, they suspected, preferred the tactics of Division Two.

As Cantona revelled in a playmaking role at Old Trafford that ultimately meant it was Manchester United, not Leeds United, who were first Premier League champions, the transfer's aftertaste became increasingly bitter. But selling Cantona was not the only cause of Leeds United's wretched season in 1992/93. A new FIFA rule banning back-passes to the goalkeeper caused havoc across football, as defenders and goalkeepers failed to adapt to having the ball at their feet more often. Although they contributed their share of howlers, Chris Fairclough and Chris Whyte were decent with the ball; Whyte had played indoor league soccer in the USA, where quick control was vital. The problem was Leeds could no longer use their tactic of pressing high up the pitch when John Lukic cleared long to Chapman; they were spread out, and opponents would win the loose ball and attack again, putting the defence under more pressure than it could cope with.

Mel Sterland's absence didn't help; Wilkinson had not bought a new right-back, but Sterland's ankle injury forced his early retirement, and Leeds missed his ferocious overlapping runs and crosses. The team was unbalanced; Jon Newsome, Chris Fairclough, Gary Speed, David Batty, David Rocastle and Scott Sellars, brought back from Blackburn Rovers in the summer, were all tried at right-back; when Leeds tried to buy Denis Irwin to play there, they sold Cantona instead. Attacking at Elland Road, Leeds were still formidable; they only lost once at home, and outscored the new champions. But they didn't win a single game away, where they were forced to defend, and conceded more than all but two teams; Leeds finished 17th, just two points from relegation.

The only optimism came at the end of the season, by beating Manchester United in the FA Youth Cup final; more than 30,000 at Elland Road watched Jamie

Forrester's overhead kick and Matthew Smithard's strike add to Forrester and Noel Whelan's first leg goals, for a 4-1 aggregate victory over a team Manchester United hoped had future stars in Robbie Savage, David Beckham, Paul Scholes and Gary Neville. Leeds were already hopeful about theirs. Forrester and Whelan made promising appearances in the first team, with Rob Bowman, Kevin Sharp and Mark Tinkler; a little older, David Wetherall looked a good first-team replacement for Whyte.

The new East Stand was almost ready, and Leeds were ready to start again the next season, with changes that sentiment had perhaps prevented Wilkinson from making a year earlier. Chris Whyte left; Lee Chapman had scored nineteen goals and seen off Cantona, but now he left too, as did Carl Shutt. Leeds made one major signing, spending a club record £2.75 million on Leeds-born striker Brian Deane from Sheffield United, but in late September there was a major departure that hit the fans even harder than the loss of Cantona.

Wilkinson always struggled with David Batty. Batty was a sixteen-year-old apprentice when Billy Bremner took over as manager, made him captain of the juniors, put him in midfield and let him enjoy himself; for the next three years Batty was never happier than when kicking a ball around with Bremner and fellow apprentices Gary Speed and Simon Grayson. He was Bremner's chosen heir, given the freedom to play and tackle as hard as he wanted. Wilkinson was different. He was fanatical about training, but Batty never saw the point, unless he had a ball at his feet; his pre-match routine was a few keepie-ups and a can of Coke. Batty didn't enjoy playing in Wilkinson's teams; in Division Two, although he loved playing alongside Vinnie Jones, the ball went over his head; in the title-winning season, he felt constrained as a defensive midfielder.

There were transfer requests, and Batty spoke to several interested clubs over the years, but a truce and mutual respect developed with his manager, who trusted Batty would always give his best on the pitch, and knew Batty's best was equal to the best midfielders in the world. But by 1993 Batty felt stale. A £2.75 million offer from Blackburn Rovers made him excited again.

It was a relief to the board. They had spent that on Brian Deane, but bills for the East Stand were coming due. Fotherby always denied it, and chased high-profile transfers across Europe – he pursued Paul Gascoigne, who cost Lazio £5.5 million, to replace Cantona – but cashflow was a perennial problem, and bills were still paid from Leslie Silver's private accounts. Batty wanted to go and the board wanted the money; they withstood the backlash over Cantona, and would have to withstand another now.

The fans loved Batty; he was Leeds born and raised, and had stood among them on the Lowfields as a kid. He reminded the older fans of Bremner, and reminded the younger ones of themselves, if only they could play for Leeds. The midfield that dominated the First Division from August 1990 until it won the league in April 1992 was iconic: for two seasons no team had better than Gordon Strachan, David Batty, Gary McAllister and Gary Speed. It had felt as if, once Rocastle took over from Strachan, success would continue without pause; but Strachan, now 36, endured. It was Batty and soon Rocastle who left. There were banners calling for the board to go too.

Leeds had, at least, won an away match, and the pain of Batty's departure was eased by the team's overall improvement. A solution was found at right-back; young winger Gary Kelly was converted in pre-season and played every match, then went to the World Cup with the Republic of Ireland. Like Cantona, Brian Deane found it difficult to get the team to play to his strengths rather than to their memories of Lee Chapman, but Wallace was a revelation, scoring seventeen goals; one, a solo effort against Spurs that began on the halfway line, was goal of the season.

Leeds were second at Christmas but couldn't sustain a title challenge, falling away to 5th and missing out on UEFA Cup qualification by one point. They finally seemed to be catching up to the Premier League era, although to many fans' regret that meant an all-seater stadium and the removal of terracing from the Kop; the sanitising effect of the Premier League and the reaction to the Hillsborough disaster were making football popular again, but removing some of the exciting edge supporters had grown up with. Wilkinson's buys were a peculiar mix, sourced from both Sheffield clubs – John Pemberton, Paul Beesley, Nigel Worthington, and £2.6 million on midfielder Carlton Palmer – and South Africa, where Leeds found striker Philemon Masinga and defender Lucas Radebe. Fotherby, meanwhile, was travelling Europe, linking Leeds United's name in the press with top forwards in Serie A: Ruben Sosa of Inter, Faustino Asprilla of Parma, Tomáš Skuhravý of Genoa. The constant speculation meant new names were quickly derided as fantasies, until a striker did arrive, from Eintracht Frankfurt in Germany.

To the delight of the fans, Tony Yeboah was not from Sheffield, and even better, he had the explosive talent they had missed since Cantona. A Ghanaian striker with a deceptively big build, it was known that Yeboah had scored 94 goals in 188 matches in Germany, but he was otherwise a mystery. But once he started scoring he was unstoppable, fast and strong, with shooting power like Peter Lorimer; Wilkinson had no problem changing the team to suit him. Strachan finally gave in to back trouble and retired to become assistant manager at Coventry City, leaving a midfield three of Palmer, Speed and McAllister; in attack Wallace and Deane played either side of Yeboah, Deane finding his best form wide on the left where he could attack the ball as he had at

Sheffield United. Despite Yeboah's impact, it was Deane who won Supporters' Player of the Year, and his goal that won qualification for the UEFA Cup; on the final day at Spurs, he ran with the ball from inside his own half and shot to secure the crucial point.

Returning to Europe confirmed that Wilkinson had built another good side at Elland Road, but the optimism at the start of 1995/96 was almost entirely due to Yeboah. He scored twice in a 2-1 win at West Ham United on the opening day; two days later, from 30 yards, he nearly broke the crossbar at Elland Road, scoring an explosive dipping volley against Liverpool. Away to Wimbledon, he scored a tap in, a snapshot from the edge of the area, and a goal to rival the one against Liverpool; rather than volley, he controlled the ball on his chest, then his thigh, then took it inside a defender, gathering pace as he ran towards goal. Twenty yards out, the ball bounced up and Yeboah struck, a knockout shot into the top corner.

Yeboah's shooting power was terrifying for opponents, but delivered with a sort of joy; he never looked more relaxed than when recovering from a high-tension volley into the goal. His finest night was in the UEFA Cup, away to Monaco; Yeboah scored an opportunist overhead kick, a swerving shot into the top corner, and outpaced Basile Boli to pounce for his hat-trick. 'Me and Gary McAllister just looked at each other in amazement,' said Brian Deane later. 'We were saying, he had to be the best centre-forward in the world at that moment.'

Yeboah scored another superb goal in a 3-1 win over Manchester United at Elland Road on Christmas Eve, but Leeds couldn't build any momentum; the previous game had been lost 6-2 at Sheffield Wednesday. PSV Eindhoven put Leeds out of the UEFA Cup 8-3 on aggregate, and in January Yeboah, Masinga and Radebe were absent for the African Cup of Nations. They returned in February, but Leeds had only played one league match, a 3-0 defeat at Aston Villa, due to progress in the cups; Leeds needed a replay to beat Port Vale in the FA Cup, setting up a quarter-final against Liverpool; and in the League Cup they won a two-legged semi-final against First Division Birmingham City, to meet Aston Villa at Wembley, the club's first final there since 1973.

It should have been an occasion for excitement, but it felt like Leeds were only pretending to be an elite European club. Fotherby finally landed his marquee signing from Italy in the autumn, paying £4.5 million for Parma's Tomas Brolin; a star of the European Championships in 1992 and of Sweden's 3rd placed team at the World Cup in 1994, he had lost his place due to injuries and fitness, and after meeting him, Wilkinson was wary; for the first time, he said later, he ignored his instincts, and the deal went ahead. Within a few matches it was clear that Wilkinson should have trusted his judgement.

There had been some dreadful results, including a 5-0 defeat at Anfield. Wilkinson guarded against a repeat in the FA Cup by naming an extremely negative side; only McAllister, Brolin and Yeboah had any attacking intent. He was sarcastic towards critics of the 0-0 result, asking if he should have told his players, 'Go out and put in an own goal, then two of you lie down, let Liverpool go three up and everyone can go home happy, saying they've been entertained.' It all became academic in the replay; Liverpool won 3-0, four days before the League Cup final.

Wilkinson's team selection for the final caused more consternation. Attempting to counteract Aston Villa, he matched their 5-3-2 line-up, with Speed as a left wing-back; Palmer and Mark Ford were two defensive midfielders behind McAllister; Yeboah's partner was winger Andy Gray, Frank Gray's eighteen-year-old son. Fans scoured the team in search of attackers, but two were on the bench, Deane and Brolin; Wallace was in the stands.

It was a disaster. Leeds looked slow and confused, unsure of themselves; after twenty minutes, Villa seized on a misplaced pass, and Savo Milošević hit the top corner from twenty yards; Villa won 3-0. The cheers from their fans were almost drowned out by the jeers from the Leeds fans, most of them directed at Wilkinson, although one journalist suggested the chants were not personal, just expressions of pure disappointment.

'It seemed pretty personal to me,' said Wilkinson, whose first cup final as a manager at Wembley left him distraught. 'They say what a memorable day, they say enjoy it, they say it doesn't last forever, it goes very quickly. None of those things happened today. It went very, very slowly. I didn't enjoy it. But it was memorable.'

He wasn't allowed to forget it quickly, if ever. The new, continental-style Leeds United seemed to have broken beyond repair. Fotherby was angry with Yeboah and Brolin, who said in interviews before the game they might leave if Leeds didn't qualify for the UEFA Cup. Carlton Palmer blamed the players: 'In my opinion, the lack of effort shown by professional players in as big a game as this final was nothing short of disgraceful'; and the fans: 'The criticism dished out to the boss at the end was also a disgrace. I was disappointed with the treatment he received, because he didn't deserve it.' Wilkinson blamed himself: 'It doesn't matter how it makes me feel. I have to take the responsibility whether things have gone well or not so well.' He was thinking carefully about his future.

The collapse had come just too early. In the final weeks of the season more young players followed Andy Gray into the team; Harry Kewell, Ian Harte, Alan Maybury. The FA Youth Cup-winning team of 1993 had not fulfilled its potential at Leeds; Noel Whelan was the brightest hope, scoring seven goals in autumn 1994, but followed Strachan to Coventry after Brolin arrived. But since then the youth system had been working to the ten-year plan Wilkinson outlined in his job interview in 1988. The club opened a new training centre at Thorp Arch, in the countryside near Wetherby, including a purpose-built academy with accommodation for young players. Wilkinson called it 'a football greenhouse', with Paul Hart in charge; Eddie Gray was asked back to coach the youth team, and was repeating the success of his team from the early 1980s, with boys a year or two younger. When Wilkinson bought a cheap, experienced centre-back like Paul Beesley or Richard Jobson, it was with the knowledge that in a year or two a defender might be coming through who could play for fifteen years; when he looked for a new striker, he looked for one who could coach a young player until they were ready to take over. All Wilkinson needed was time.

Decisions in the boardroom meant Wilkinson didn't get it. As the Premier League grew, top clubs were floating on the stock exchange, and United's directors sensed an opportunity to relieve their financial burden, put the club on a sound footing, and make money themselves. Bill Fotherby did not draw a wage, but took a percentage of his commercial deals, making him the highest-paid director in football; Leslie Silver and Peter Gilman were unpaid, and risked £7 million by guaranteeing personal loans to finance Leeds in the Premier League. In August 1995 they restructured the club, forming a

33. Marcelo Bielsa greets Bristol City head coach
Lee Johnson shortly before kickoff, 4 August 2019.

Robbie Stephenson/JMP/Shutterstock

34. Patrick Bamford is mobbed after giving Leeds the
lead over Blackburn Rovers, 9 November 2019.

Lee Brown for The Square Ball

35. The players line up ahead of the centenary game
against Birmingham City, 19 November 2019.
Lee Brown for The Square Ball

36. Kalvin Phillips celebrates scoring the only goal of the game
as Leeds beat Birmingham City 1-0, 19 November 2019.
Lee Brown for The Square Ball

37. Norman Hunter before Leeds United's centenary game, 19 November 2019.
Lee Brown for The Square Ball

38. Luke Ayling leaves the pitch after beating Reading 1-0 at Elland Road, 22 February 2020.
Lee Brown for The Square Ball

39. Jack Harrison scores a late winner away at Reading, 26 November 2019.
Malcolm Bryce/ProSports/Shutterstock

40. Ezgjan Alioski applauds an empty Elland Road
after beating Barnsley 1-0, 16 July 2020.
Greig Cowie/BPI/Shutterstock

41. Pablo Hernández scores a vital goal to beat Swansea 0-1, 12 July 2020.

Kieran McManus/BPI/Shutterstock

42. Liam Cooper celebrates victory over Barnsley at full-time, 16 July 2020.

Greig Cowie/BPI/Shutterstock

43. Fans of all ages gather outside Elland Road to celebrate promotion to the Premier League, 17 July 2020.
Lee Brown for The Square Ball

44. Leeds United players and staff greet the fans stood outside the East Stand at Elland Road, 22 July 2020.
Lee Brown for The Square Ball

45. The Leeds United squad celebrates after winning the Championship, 22 July 2020.

Malcolm Bryce/ProSports/Shutterstock

46. Leeds United player are presented with the Championship trophy, 22 July 2020.

Greig Cowie/BPI/Shutterstock

47. Left to right: Kalvin Phillips, Gaetano Berardi and Gjanni Alioski celebrate winning the Championship, 22 July 2020.

Malcolm Bryce/ProSports/Shutterstock

48. Manager Marcelo Bielsa lifts the Championship trophy, 22 July 2020.

Greig Cowie/BPI/Shutterstock

parent company ready for the stock exchange, Leeds United Holdings plc, granting themselves 98 per cent of the shares.

In March 1996, an armed gang targeting football personalities broke into Leslie Silver's home. He and his wife were overpowered, handcuffed and tied up; the robbers ordered Silver to open his safe, and took cash and jewellery worth £200,000. 'It was a terrifying experience,' said Silver. 'Obviously I was concerned about my wife. There was no indication of any violence, but it was fairly brutal. The worst part was our fears for each other when we were separated. There was no way we could sleep last night.'

Silver was 71; the ordeal exacerbated a heart condition and forced him to reevaluate. In April, he announced he was retiring, handing the chairmanship to Fotherby; Silver's third of the club was for sale, and takeover rumours soon started.

They didn't finish for months. What was billed as the first 'City-backed takeover battle' for a football club appeared to conclude on 3 July; Caspian, a London-based media group, were the successful bidders. On 4 July, Wilkinson entered the transfer market; he had sold Gary Speed to Everton for £3.5 million, but was only able to add veteran striker Ian Rush on a free transfer from Liverpool before the takeover process tied his hands. He now used the fee for Speed to make Charlton Athletic midfielder Lee Bowyer the most expensive teenager in the country at £2.25 million, and was ready to spend some of the £15 million added to his transfer budget by Caspian when business abruptly stopped again.

Peter Gilman claimed a gentleman's agreement meant that if two directors wanted to sell, the other had first refusal on their shares. Another consortium, Conrad, had made a higher offer, but Silver and Fotherby backed Caspian; Gilman objected, taking the matter to the High Court. The frustration got to Gary McAllister first; unsettled all summer, he became sick of the antagonism and accepted a big salary increase from a £3 million transfer to Coventry City. Wilkinson could do nothing to stop him leaving; but the next day, when Gilman's case was thrown out, he invested the McAllister money, making Crystal Palace's Nigel Martyn the most expensive goalkeeper in the country.

Caspian's takeover was finally approved on 4 August. With two weeks to go before the season started, Wilkinson was allowed to spend £4.5 million on Manchester United winger Lee Sharpe, and Fotherby – who stayed as chairman – was almost reported to the FA for his public pursuit of Queens Park Rangers' forward Trevor Sinclair. As injuries accounted for Yeboah, Brolin and Deane, Wilkinson signed striker Mark Hateley on loan, partnering him with Rush to form the oldest strike-force in the league. Wins over Wimbledon and Blackburn Rovers smoothed over a draw and a defeat at the start of the season, but by the fifth game, at home to Manchester United, rumours about Caspian's intentions were filling the papers.

'The team has got to win – it's as simple as that,' Wilkinson told Phil Shaw of the *Independent*, referring to the abuse that had continued from the League Cup final into the new season. 'When the season started, the fans weren't saying: "Well, what a summer of frustration, upset, hold-ups, limbo, injunctions, not being able to sign players, not knowing who's in charge it's been." Whether that's fair or not doesn't come into it.

'A manager's not self-employed. If he's not in the directors' hands, he's in the players' hands. And if he's not in the players' hands, he's in the fans' hands.'

Against Manchester United, he was in Eric Cantona's hands. In stoppage time his volley in front of the Kop made the score 4-0 to Manchester United. All Howard Wilkinson could do to take back control of the situation was pour the champagne, a few days later, at the press conference to announce he was sacked.

'I'm very disappointed, very sad and obviously very shocked,' he said. 'There aren't many clubs in a situation like ours who put up the vacant sign.

'All I know is that I mapped out a ten-year plan when I arrived here, and I know the whole place is much healthier and more vibrant than it was when I came here eight years ago. I know I made mistakes along the way, but nothing catastrophic in the big picture of things.

'The most disappointing thing of all is that I won't have the opportunity to work with the five or six youngsters who are going to be top class acts in a couple of years' time. Apart from Manchester United, I know we have got the best crop of kids in the country.'

1996–2000

WE WILL FORGE
AN EVEN TIGHTER BOND

As a midfielder at Arsenal in the early 1970s, George Graham was nicknamed 'Stroller' for his immaculate elegance on and off the pitch; he passed a football like he combed his hair. When he walked into Elland Road as manager, 24 hours after Howard Wilkinson left, some expected a penitent shuffle; but George Graham's sense of style had not changed.

His suave demeanour was sometimes at odds with his managerial career. At Arsenal he won the First Division in 1989 and 1991, but in subsequent seasons his teams became less exciting, known not for strolling but for being boring. He ruled Highbury with a tight offside trap and strict discipline, yet still allowed alcohol and gambling problems to linger within the team, while his own conduct earned him the sack in 1994. Guilty of accepting an 'unsolicited gift' of £425,000 from Norwegian agent Rune Hauge, Graham was banned from football for a year.

There were no signs of dourness or regret as he stepped back into the limelight at Leeds. After the stress of his exile Graham promised he would be relaxed with the press, confirming his intentions with a wink. 'It's nice to be back,' he said. 'It's a big challenge, a big club. I've seen what Leeds can be like when they're having success, and I thought that, if I can get that back again, Leeds will be very big, up with the giants.'

After six defeats in his first eight league games, Graham was not feeling so easygoing. By the end of the season, neither were Leeds' fans, who saw just 28 goals scored in 38 games as Graham concentrated on making his team hard to beat, and hard to watch. One potential source of excitement, Tomas Brolin, spent the season in dispute with the club and Graham in particular; he eventually left in October 1997. Many fans expected the team to be built around Tony Yeboah, but Graham accused him of being overweight, and the situation disintegrated into another dispute; when Graham substituted him at Tottenham Hotspur in March, Yeboah's last angry act as a Leeds player was to pull off his shirt and throw it at the manager.

Graham's first signing was Gunnar Halle, a veteran defender from Oldham Athletic; then Robert Molenaar, a giant centre-back from Volendam who dominated the defence. Lucas Radebe was blossoming into a calm central defender, and would have plenty of company; Graham packed midfield with defensive-minded players, or actual defenders, often naming just two recognised attackers. He brought in David O'Leary as assistant manager, a centre-half he had managed at Arsenal, who briefly played for Leeds under Wilkinson; in goal was Nigel Martyn, still with plenty of saves to make despite the forest of defenders. He won player of the season. 'Don't give a goal away,' Graham said. 'If you can make the opposition think they are never going to score against you, they will get a negative attitude.' Unfortunately, so did Leeds; nine matches ended 0-0, but Graham was happy to finish 11th.

Such a retrograde season did not match Caspian's ambitions for their takeover. Caspian's main business was owning rights to cartoon characters, but within months of buying Leeds United it sold Paddington Bear, The Wombles, The Shoe People and others for £10.5 million, to finance their young chief executive Chris Akers' vision of a sports and media empire at Elland Road. He started by bidding £5 million to take over Leeds Rugby League and, in a reversal of the plan to move Leeds City in 1915, bring them to play at Elland Road; discussions began about basketball and ice hockey franchises – the latter to be called Leeds Lasers – and when the deal for Leeds Rugby League fell through, attention turned to buying and moving Hull Kingston Rovers.

Caspian bought Elland Road back from the council, unveiling plans to build an indoor arena behind an enlarged West Stand, and hotels and restaurants, creating the 'Madison Square Garden of the North'. It would cost £30 million, but first it cost chief executive Robin Launders and chairman Bill Fotherby their jobs; taking the blame for slow negotiations with the council, they were replaced by Caspian's Jeremy Fenn, and long-term board member Peter Ridsdale became Leeds United chairman. To reflect the emphasis on building a sporting mecca, Caspian's name changed to Leeds Sporting plc.

Media was integral to the strategy. Akers believed the future was in pay-per-view matches on the internet; trials began, streaming live audio and video, and a new website opened with an online shop and advertising space. Talks began about investing in PSV Eindhoven and Sporting Lisbon, to create a European network of clubs at the cutting edge of online broadcasting, retail and advertising; the markets were non-existent in 1997, promising the growth investors desired.

It was essential that Leeds United be worth watching. Akers promised money for transfers, and Graham spent £10 million in the summer. Jimmy-Floyd Hasselbaink, an unknown from Boavista in Portugal, made an impact that symbolised the overhaul. Slim but strong, his bursts into the penalty area ended with emphatic, unstoppable shots, followed up with celebratory cartwheels. He scored 22, and got the best out of Rod Wallace, who scored thirteen; while Alf-Inge Haaland and David Hopkin brought much more energy to midfield.

Graham wasn't allowing total freedom, preferring to use extra full-backs as wide midfielders, and at Chelsea in December Leeds began the second half with nine players and survived an onslaught for a 0-0 draw. Kelly and Haaland were sent off in a brutal first half, recalling the Leeds vs Chelsea FA Cup final of 1970; the game took place days after the shocking early death of Billy Bremner, aged just 54, and while Leeds lacked their greatest captain's quality, they had rediscovered some of his spirit.

Leeds reached the sixth round of the FA Cup and finished 5th in the Premier League, qualifying for the UEFA Cup, but there was a suspicion that George Graham's heart was not really in the job. The youth team won a league and cup double, playing exciting, creative football, encouraged by Eddie Gray's coaching; they scored 112 goals in the Northern Intermediate League, 35 more than any other team, and conceded just 23. But Paul Hart quit as director of youth coaching, complaining that Graham had only watched the team three times. 'The club is now being run differently,' he said. 'I fear the Caspian Group and the manager have no real insight into the ten-year plan laid down by the old board and Howard Wilkinson in 1988. We are just one year off seeing it come to fruition, but the long-term strategy is being ignored.' Gray was promoted to coach the reserve team for the following season, bringing the young players through to the next level and winning the reserve league; but only winger Harry Kewell was given a serious chance in the first team.

In March Leeds followed a 4-0 win over Blackburn Rovers and a 5-0 win at Derby County with an inexplicable 3-0 defeat away to West Ham United. George Graham stayed at his home in London, while David O'Leary and Eddie Gray took the team and staff home on a flight from Stansted Airport. The plane had been in the air for twelve seconds when an engine exploded and the pilot, Captain John Hackett, made an instant decision to bring the plane straight back to the ground, where it slid off the end of the runway, still burning, into grass and mud.

Amid the danger, O'Leary remembered the cabin crew's instructions; he injured his shoulder forcing open the exit, then guided the players out of the plane as emergency services rushed to reach them. There was understandable panic – when Peter Ridsdale paused at the exit, Nigel Martyn said he 'gave him a quick shove – he landed on the wing on his face. I just hope it hasn't ruined my chances of a new contract' – but the plane was cleared within 30 seconds, with O'Leary's shoulder the only injury. On the ground the players took turns borrowing Jimmy Hasselbaink's mobile phone to call their families.

Captain Hackett said later that, had the plane been in the air 30 seconds longer, it would almost certainly have exploded, and the comparisons to the Munich disaster in 1958 were not made lightly; Bill Foulkes, who survived Munich, said: 'I froze when I heard the news. Lord, it was so close.' The players were grateful to O'Leary: 'David saved us,' said young midfielder Stephen McPhail. The whole club was grateful to Captain Hackett and his crew, who were invited to receive the team's thanks before a televised match with Chelsea; as George Graham had missed the ordeal, O'Leary was master of ceremonies. Robert Molenaar praised the way everyone had stuck together on the plane. 'There is a good chance we will forge an even tighter bond,' he said.

Graham's commitment was tested early the next season. Tottenham sacked their manager Christian Gross, and long-whispered rumours that Spurs wanted Graham became pointed questions. 'Why not?' said Graham, at the start of weeks of speculation that reached a bizarre peak when Leeds played Spurs at White Hart Lane. After laughing and winking through questions about his intentions, Graham took a seat in the director's box next to Peter Ridsdale, and listened to the chants of the Spurs fans, who didn't want him as manager: 'The geezer is Arsenal through and through,' said one. At half-time Ridsdale ran down the touchline to appeal to the travelling Leeds fans; if they got behind the manager, he might be convinced to stay. Instead the fans sang 'Fuck off Judas' as Leeds let a 3-1 lead slip to 3-3. By the end of the week Graham had left.

David O'Leary and Eddie Gray took charge for the next match at Elland Road, against Leicester City, who were managed by Ridsdale's choice for the Leeds job, Martin O'Neill, a disciple of Brian Clough when playing for him at Nottingham Forest. As manager he had won promotion with Leicester and took them to the top ten of the Premier League and the UEFA Cup, and won the League Cup. Leicester were determined not to lose him; the fans and local newspaper organised a 'Please Don't Go' protest at their next home match, a 2-1 win over Spurs, with banners and balloons. For two weeks Leicester had denied O'Neill his wish to at least meet Ridsdale, but the fans' affection broke through his frustration: 'The support I have received from Leicester's players and fans alike helped me sort out my mind,' he said, although his new Leicester contract would contain 'about 194 special clauses all written out in block capitals.'

There was unity at Leeds, too. In their second match, O'Leary and Gray gave teenage central defender Jonathan Woodgate his debut, and on the night O'Neill made up his mind, they relied on young players for a difficult UEFA Cup match away to Roma. O'Leary was banned from the touchline and Ribeiro was sent off, but the performances of McPhail, Kewell and Bowyer, with Gray in the dugout, and the brilliance of Martyn in goal, meant a narrow 1-0 defeat and chants for O'Leary from the travelling fans. Ridsdale couldn't ignore public opinion; David O'Leary was appointed manager, Eddie Gray his assistant.

O'Leary had been the main presence on the training pitches for some time; he lived nearby in Harrogate, whereas Graham never committed to moving from London. 'I have had two or three players come to me and say that, for all the right reasons, they wanted David to be offered the opportunity,' said Ridsdale. O'Leary was initially reluctant, but his time as caretaker made him enthusiastic. 'I played at the top for twenty years with Arsenal and now I am starting my management career at the very top,' he said. 'I've played under some great managers – Jack Charlton, Don Howe and George Graham. Now I just want to do better than George at Leeds.'

He won an early coup. Graham had wanted a ball-winning midfielder, and enquired about bringing David Batty back to Leeds from Newcastle United; it came to nothing, but Batty was interested. There were stories of him gazing wistfully from the Newcastle team coach whenever it passed by Elland Road, and eventually he told manager Ruud Gullit that he wanted to go. The return of a prodigal son for £4.4 million, now 30 years old and an established England international, brought fans to Elland Road just to see him photographed, although at first Batty's return threatened failure; he broke a rib on his second debut. Nonetheless, he was seen as symbolic of a new era, combining Leeds roots, a strong bond with the supporters, and a big transfer fee. 'When David Batty left five years ago, the decision to sell was forced on us by our bankers,' said Ridsdale. 'I am determined that Leeds will never again face that kind of selling situation. We are ambitious, David O'Leary is, and we have our sights set on challenging for honours.'

Aside from Batty, O'Leary and Gray were making best use of the young reserves Wilkinson had left and Gray had nurtured. Harry Kewell, just turned twenty, was an automatic choice on the wing, one of the most exciting players in the newly named Premiership. Jonathan Woodgate, a tall, skinny eighteen year old, read the game superbly in central defence. An injury to Nigel Martyn gave Paul Robinson a chance in goal just after his nineteenth birthday, and he became genuine competition; Ian Harte, now 21, didn't let David Robertson back in at left-back. In the heart of midfield Lee Bowyer was nearly 22 and dominating games from box to box; eighteen-year-old Matthew Jones was joining him as substitute. The player Eddie Gray was most excited about was Stephen McPhail, not yet nineteen, but with vision, passing and a left foot Gray thought could be among the world's best. The player the fans were most excited about was Alan Smith, an eighteen-year-old striker who scored an equaliser after coming on as substitute at Anfield, inspiring Leeds to a 3-1 win. Smith kept scoring from the bench, forcing himself into the starting lineup, and into the faces of much older, bigger centre-backs; short, with a tousled mop of blond hair, aggressive with a scoring instinct, he looked like the Leeds-born striker the club had been seeking since 1919.

The players had all been Graham's to use, but O'Leary began referring to them as 'my babies', and they bore the unmistakable stamp of Gray; Charlton Athletic were beaten 4-1, West Ham United 4-0 and 5-1, Newcastle United 3-0, Portsmouth 5-1 and Derby County 4-1; when United's kids caught the mood, they were ruthless. They won five in a row during a nine-match unbeaten run near the end of the season; not enough to challenge for the title, but they did qualify for the UEFA Cup, and had a big say in where the Premiership title went. A televised match against Arsenal put Leeds under pressure, because winning would hand the championship to Manchester United; Leeds' young-sters ignored the rivalry and won the game, Hasselbaink heading in Kewell's cross in the 86th minute. The message on the pitch and in the stands was clear: Leeds didn't care about anybody else.

Hasselbaink, it turned out, didn't care about Leeds; after a summer spent arguing about his wages, he left for Atletico Madrid, for £12 million. O'Leary now spent big on new players, with a policy of buying the best English talent to add to the young players already redefining the club: Michael Bridges, Darren Huckerby, Danny Mills and Michael Duberry together cost more than £18 million, Duberry the eldest at 23, all potential internationals; Eirik Bakke, a 21-year-old midfielder signed from Norway for £1.75 million, already had two caps. The team had new away kits, modelled on Lazio in Serie A, and a new club badge, initially sketched out by Howard Wilkinson to resemble continental teams.

Peter Ridsdale was now in overall charge. After being made chairman of Leeds United, he was initially only a non-executive board member of Leeds Sporting, who questioned his lack of plc experience. But as Chris Akers' dreams of a multi-media, multi-continent group operating a Madison Square Garden of the North became embroiled in negotiations and red tape, and Leeds Sporting's share price dropped, he was ousted shortly before George Graham left; his friend Richard Thompson left a few months later, followed by finance director Jeremy Fenn at the end of the season, who left behind a £1.87 million profit, but argued with O'Leary about transfer funds. Asda supermarket's chief executive Allan Leighton joined the board, and Peter Ridsdale took over the chairmanship, combining it with the role of chief executive, giving him day-to-day control.

It was a dream scenario for Ridsdale. He grew up in Leeds, obsessed with United, queuing overnight, as he never tired of telling people, for a ticket to the

1965 FA Cup final when he was just thirteen. He followed Leeds home and away on his own, and his loner status was underlined on the football pitch where, overweight, he was put in goal. In the mid-1980s Bill Fotherby approached Ridsdale in the Goal Line restaurant at Elland Road, intrigued that he was attending the game with his baby son, and that gave Ridsdale his 'in' at Leeds. He was now working in human resources for the Burton Group, whose menswear factory once employed thousands in Leeds; they owned the Top Man and Top Shop retail brands, and Fotherby soon rustled Ridsdale for a sponsorship, giving him a seat on the board. Ridsdale was ecstatic – 'I was a fan transported from the West Stand paddock to the boardroom' – and never lost his wide-eyed enthusiasm. As chairman, he would go into the dressing rooms to congratulate or commiserate with the players; on away trips, he would join in their singing on the coach. He was still in awe of the Leeds players, even though they were now his employees, and described himself 'standing in the aisle between seats, soaking up every bit of an unforgettable camaraderie'; when Leeds went top of the league and the fans sang his name, Ridsdale had the acceptance he'd been seeking since he was a kid.

The route to the top of the league in 1999/00 was ten consecutive wins in the Premiership, League Cup and UEFA Cup, Bridges combining creativity outside the box with finishing inside, McPhail the playmaker next to Bowyer and Bakke's energy, Woodgate assured at the back and Kewell unpredictable and deadly from the wing. Leeds travelled to Manchester City in the FA Cup at the start of the new millennium; City were top of the First Division, but Leeds were top of the Premiership and unstoppable. City had eight attempts at goal, but Leeds United had 30, seventeen on target, winners by 5-2. Fans, commentators and pundits were left breathless; the players on the pitch were grinning and laughing.

'Leeds were simply terrific,' said City manager Joe Royle. 'Don't let David kid you, they can win the Premiership.'

David O'Leary claimed he wasn't thinking that far ahead. Manchester United's decision to play in the World Club Championship in Brazil postponed their fixture with Leeds, who now had two weeks off. 'I'm going to take this now like a winter break,' said O'Leary. 'Clear up the knocks, get them freshened up again for a tough game at Sunderland in two weeks' time.'

24

2000–02

HE FELT THAT WAS
THE RIGHT THING TO DO

Leeds United's young players did not use their winter break wisely. Two nights after the Manchester City game, several groups of players and friends went for a night out in Leeds, meeting up in the Majestyk nightclub in City Square. In the days that followed, police started knocking on their doors, calling at the training ground, arresting players.

The details weren't clear, but an altercation outside Majestyk after Jonathan Woodgate's friends were thrown out escalated, and some students were chased into nearby streets; one, Sarfraz Najeib, fell and was beaten as he lay on the floor. His leg was broken and his face fractured in six places, showing bite marks and boot marks. Two of Woodgate's friends, Neale Caveney and Paul Clifford, were charged with affray, causing grievous bodily harm with intent, and attempting to pervert the course of justice; but the attention was all on the Leeds United players involved. Woodgate, Lee Bowyer and reserve Tony Hackworth all faced the same charges. Michael Duberry was charged with attempting to pervert the course of justice. The players denied doing anything wrong, but a private investigator hired by United determined they were in a lot of trouble; the case was sent for trial in spring 2001.

Police interviews, meetings with solicitors and intense press speculation had an inevitable impact on the exciting, carefree football that took Leeds to the top of the Premiership at the start of 2000. Aston Villa knocked them out of the FA Cup; defeats to Liverpool and Manchester United knocked them off the top of the league. Resuming the UEFA Cup, in March, helped Leeds rediscover their form. There was a rematch with Roma, for whom Francesco Totti was brilliant in the first leg in Rome; Leeds hardly had the ball, but at the back they had Alf-Inge Haaland, enjoying a renaissance as an emergency sweeper, and Nigel Martyn, developing into United's best ever goalkeeper. The credit for the 0-0 all went to Leeds' defending, and credit for the 1-0 win at Elland Road went to Harry Kewell's brilliant 25-yard strike, although Alan Smith took some of the glory; Roma weren't used to a striker tackling defenders, and two were sent off for reacting to Smith's aggression.

Slavia Prague were beaten 3-0 at Elland Road in the quarter-final, and despite a 2-1 defeat away Leeds qualified to face Galatasaray in the semi-final. Galatasaray prided themselves on the intimidating atmosphere of their Ali Sami Yen Stadium in Istanbul, where 35,000 fans, with banners, drums and red and yellow smoke, would create what the fans called 'Hell'; a sort of macho posturing, believed to give a psychological advantage over European teams. When Leeds visited in April 2000, the hell was tragically real. The night before the match, amid scuffles between supporters outside bars in Istanbul, two Leeds fans were suddenly and senselessly stabbed. One died instantly, and amid chaotic scenes at the hospital as Peter Ridsdale tried to obtain blood supplies, the other died a few hours later. Christopher Loftus was 37, Kevin Speight was 40.

A statue of Billy Bremner, recently unveiled at Elland Road, became the focus for grieving fans who could not understand why two of their own would not be coming back from a football match. In the Ali Sami Yen Stadium, the fans stranded there could not understand why they were now watching one. UEFA refused to cancel the game, and Galatasaray refused requests for a minute's silence. A statement of regret was read over the public address system and jeered by the home crowd; Leeds United's fans turned their backs on the game, a symbolic repudiation of everything happening around them. United's young players were protected by riot shields as they came onto the pitch; they lost 2-0, then drew the second leg 2-2. Nobody at Leeds cared about the result, concentrating on remembering the two lost fans, and an agonising battle to bring their murderers to justice.

The early season optimism collapsed under the weight of the tragedy, but football still went on. The team was tired and playing automatically, but two wins revived hopes of qualifying for the Champions League ahead of Liverpool on the final day. Leeds' own efforts only earned a draw at West Ham United, but at Valley Parade Bradford City had to beat Liverpool to avoid relegation. Bradford's team contained Gunnar Halle and Lee Sharpe, let go by Leeds, and was captained by David Wetherall, who headed in Halle's free-kick and was central to the defending that won the match 1-0, saving Bradford and ensuring Leeds finished 3rd. The Leeds players recognised their hero; they phoned Wetherall from the team coach, chanting his name as they returned north.

David O'Leary and Peter Ridsdale pressed ahead with new signings. Mark Viduka, a burly Australian international striker, arrived for £6 million; Olivier Dacourt, a combative midfielder to take over while David Batty struggled with injuries, became the club's record signing, wearing the £7.2 million fee on his shirt like a squad number as he posed with Ridsdale. A season-long problem with injuries, suspensions and absences was soon apparent, so utility defender Dominic Matteo was bought from Liverpool for £4.25 million.

A calm finish by Alan Smith against 1860 Munich ensured Leeds qualified for the Champions League group stages, but the draw suggested Leeds were stretching too far. Their group brought an unwelcome return to Istanbul to play Beşiktaş, but the two other teams combined prestige and difficulty: Barcelona and Milan. In the Nou Camp Barcelona took Leeds apart, 4-0, and O'Leary's mantra that Leeds were a young team with a young manager, learning about life at the top, sounded well judged.

Leeds learned quickly. A week later United matched Milan in torrential rain at Elland Road, putting in a performance that meant they could be proud of a 0-0 draw. Then, with two minutes left, Bowyer tried a long-range shot, straight into the hands of goalkeeper Dida. The ball seemed to disappear for a moment, and when it reappeared, it was in the back of the net; Elland Road exploded to celebrate a sudden, deserved victory.

Beating Milan restored their confidence, and Leeds beat Beşiktaş 6-0 at Elland Road and drew with them 0-0 away. Bowyer's early free-kick gave Leeds the lead at home against Barcelona; a win would send Leeds through to the next group stage. Young goalkeeper Paul Robinson was brilliant, but Barcelona matched class with persistence, and Rivaldo equalised in stoppage time, the ground falling silent but for the echo of the ball hitting the net.

Leeds needed a point in the San Siro to qualify, and were relieved when Andriy Shevchenko hit an early penalty for handball against the post. It was another night of spirited defending, encouraged by captain Lucas Radebe, and by a goal just before half-time, when Matteo guided his header in front of Dida's dive. Leeds withstood everything except Serginho's individual goal, and the 1-1 draw was a whole world from the 4-0 defeat at the Nou Camp eight weeks earlier.

As the thousands of Leeds fans in the San Siro joined in celebratory singing with the players, it almost felt like this couldn't be Leeds United. Since 1975 the defiant song had been 'We Are The Champions, Champions of Europe' – Bayern Munich's name in the records was a UEFA technicality – and reaching the second group stage felt like an extension of that fierce unreality. For a while in 1999, the exciting form of their young players had elevated Leeds to unusual popularity, but the Champions League felt different. The impending court case took the shine off the club nationally and encouraged a siege mentality; playing against Europe's best teams, written off as hopeless and beset by injuries, they were getting results through hard work, commitment and verve. Leeds were returning to Europe's elite, but with the outsider status that was always theirs. They were now in another difficult group: Anderlecht, Lazio and, at last, Real Madrid.

Although they encouraged it with talk of 'adventures' and a team of 'babies', Ridsdale and O'Leary weren't content with outsider status. Leeds Sporting plc, certainly, stood to gain from a permanent place among the elite. Lucas Radebe was now one of the best defenders in Europe; praised by Nelson Mandela as a hero, his story of recovering from being shot in the back and thigh while a young player with Kaizer Chiefs, then becoming captain of Leeds United and South Africa, symbolised his country's post-apartheid hopes, but injuries were affecting him, and Woodgate had a court case looming. A new centre-back was needed, and United's policy of buying the best young domestic players led them to Rio Ferdinand of West Ham United. To get him, they had to pay a British record fee, and a world record for a defender: £18 million.

Leeds' strengthening wasn't finished; they signed twenty-year-old Robbie Keane from Inter Milan on loan, to be made permanent later at £11 million. 'We felt it imprudent to spend another £11 million immediately,' said Ridsdale, 'but by structuring a loan formula we have the player we want now without impacting on our financial position. As a plc, we have a duty to our shareholders to ensure that we manage our resources with maximum efficiency.'

Keane was not eligible to play in the Champions

League, Ferdinand could not take part until after Christmas, and Leeds were struggling with injuries when Real Madrid made the visit to Elland Road that Don Revie had dreamed of in 1962. They were every bit as good as he might have expected. Raúl, Luís Figo and Guti easily overcame Matteo and Jacob Burns in midfield, although there was no disgrace in Leeds' 2-0 defeat. They quickly reasserted themselves; at Lazio, they matched Juan Sebastián Verón, Pavel Nedvěd and Diego Simeone, scoring ten minutes from the end; Smith tapped Kewell's pass to Viduka, who backheeled the ball into Smith's path as he ran into the penalty area, finishing first time to win the game.

Leeds were back to strength for a double-header with Anderlecht; Martyn in goal, Ferdinand eligible to partner Radebe, Batty forming a dictatorial partnership with Dacourt. They didn't sparkle in the first match at Elland Road but won 2-1, and had a tough task in Belgium, where Anderlecht had won their last twenty home matches. But after hearing coach Aimé Antheunis' criticism of the first leg – 'I did not see Leeds as a strong side,' he said – Leeds produced one of their best ever European performances. Viduka's patient play from the left set up Smith for the first, and he scored the second himself, a looping header. Four minutes later Smith laid the ball off for Batty in midfield, who gave it to Dacourt, who passed forward to Viduka. Viduka backheeled into the path of Batty, and without pausing Batty played a first-time pass that split Anderlecht's defence, Smith following the ball through the breach. When he caught up to it, he chipped gently over the diving keeper, and Leeds United's critics had nothing left to say.

The match finished 4-1, and Leeds qualified for the quarter-finals with games against Real Madrid and Lazio still to play. With the pressure off in the Bernabéu, Smith gave Leeds a sixth-minute lead, but Real Madrid went ahead through a goal scored by Raúl's hand, and another deflected past Martyn by a divot. Viduka equalised, but Raúl headed a winner. The game against Lazio at Elland Road was pure entertainment, finishing 3-3.

The players were powered by self-belief as they entered the knockout stages. Deportivo de La Coruña were Spanish champions, and confident: 'We were very pleased when we found out that Leeds were our next opponents,' said midfielder Victor. 'If you compare Leeds with the other teams in the competition, they are the weakest side left.'

Leeds enjoyed hearing that. Harte opened the scoring at Elland Road with a spectacular free-kick, Smith headed a second in the second half, then Ferdinand headed in from a corner; '3-0 to the Weakest Team,' as the crowd sang loud and clear.

Deportivo didn't learn their lesson, Emerson claiming that scoring four in the second leg would be 'easy'. This time they almost backed it up, scoring an early penalty, hitting the woodwork three times and scoring again with seventeen minutes left. Deportivo played like champions, but couldn't score a third.

Valencia had no choice but to treat Leeds with respect in the semi-final. 'The most important thing about Leeds is their team spirit,' said their manager, Héctor Cúper. 'They play as a block and, with their strong mentality, they can overcome teams who are technically superior.' Their defender Roberto Ayala added that Leeds were 'typical of the English style, with great desire, speed and the willingness to fight for every ball'.

That was also a fair description of Valencia, and the first leg at Elland Road was a tough, even 0-0 draw. Leeds were left happier by not conceding; a score draw in the Mestalla Stadium would win a place in the Champions League final.

In the hours before the match the old shadow of failure at the last crept across United's prospects. To symbolise their solidarity and team ethic, the young players shaved their heads in preparation for the game; except Harte, who was soon to marry, and Bowyer and Woodgate, to protect their image in court. The night before the match, the togetherness was damaged by the loss of one of its pillars; UEFA announced that Bowyer was suspended, guilty of stamping on Juan Sánchez in the first leg. Bowyer had already apologised and Sánchez said it was no big deal, but the ban was immediate. Bowyer had scored six goals in the Champions League, and his all-action performances had symbolised United's journey, but 90 minutes from the final, Leeds had to line up without him.

Fifteen minutes into the match, the target looked much further away. Sánchez dived to meet Gaizka Mendieta's low cross ahead of Martyn, and did, putting the ball in with his arm. Covering for their own suspensions, Valencia exchanged battle for class, and Leeds couldn't cope with Mendieta, Pablo Aimar or Kily González. Alan Smith couldn't cope with defeat; in stoppage time, 3-0 down, he was sent off for putting all his frustrations into a foul on Vicente. Bowyer could only sit and watch the end of another of Leeds' European dreams.

The media, for most of the season, had been watching Bowyer. The trial for the attack on Sarfraz Najeib coincided with the second stage of the Champions League, and with Bowyer's best form. Tony Hackworth was quickly cleared of all involvement, and Woodgate and Duberry were cleared of perverting the course of justice; but Duberry's evidence contradicted his earlier statements to police, and implicated Woodgate and his friends. While Woodgate wilted under the pressure, Bowyer used playing for Leeds to release the tension of hearing the unsparing details, conflicting statements and legal arguments determining his fate. Leeds devised methods of getting him from Hull Crown Court to evening matches, including a helicopter for a game at Everton; some said he shouldn't have been playing, but Bowyer was propulsive on the pitch.

The jury were sent to consider their verdicts in early April, but the *Sunday Mirror* intervened. The paper had interviewed Sarfraz Najeib's father for an article they told him would be published after the trial. In court, both the prosecution and defence dismissed any racial motivations, but Muhammad Najeib told the *Mirror* he had been beaten by a gang of skinheads in Sheffield 30 years earlier, and believed the attack on his son was racially motivated. Inexplicably, the piece was printed the day before the verdicts were expected. The jury read it; the trial collapsed. The *Sunday Mirror*'s editor, Colin Myler, resigned; Mirror Group Newspapers were later fined £130,000 for contempt of court. A retrial was set for October, meaning Sarfraz Najeib was no nearer to justice, and Leeds United would have the case hanging over them for a third season.

Alongside the Champions League run, the Premiership kept optimism high. European adrenalin fuelled a twelve-match unbeaten run, but a bad-tempered defeat at Arsenal between the two Valencia matches set Leeds back so they had to beat Leicester, and hope Liverpool didn't win, to qualify again for the Champions League. Leeds won 3-1, but there was no David Wetherall to deny Liverpool this year. With Gary McAllister key for them in midfield, Liverpool took 3rd place by beating Charlton Athletic 4-0; Leeds would make do with the UEFA Cup.

Nothing had been won, but Leeds fans knew of old that that was not the only measure of success, and the world, as before, had been against them; the injury list, the trial, Bowyer's ban in Valencia, handballs in Europe, a linesman's flag that denied a crucial late winner against Manchester United. The Champions League raised United's international profile, bringing in millions of pounds in revenue, although shareholders were doubtful about the estimated £50 million debt. Ridsdale had no such doubts; it had to be considered against a squad worth £180 million, he said, and a bond issue restructured the deficit. Ridsdale's own high profile generated trust; as well as running Leeds, he was now chairman of the local education department.

But there were hints of dissent when Ridsdale proposed leaving Elland Road for a new, purpose-built stadium at Skelton Grange. For the first time United's matches were consistently sold out, and the new 50,000-capacity ground would effectively be built for 'free', funded by selling Elland Road and sponsorship rights. The idea needed the fans' support, but Ridsdale's letter asking season ticket holders to vote left no doubt about how he felt. The options were presented as an expensive, disruptive and possibly doomed attempt to improve Elland Road, or a simple no-cost move to a new 'state of the art' stadium. There still didn't seem much tangible support for moving, until the result was revealed; Ridsdale claimed an incredible 87.6 per cent in favour, and filmed his media work around the announcement for a new DVD called *Peter Ridsdale: My Leeds United*.

Fans were sceptical about Ridsdale's profile – he was now known as 'Publicity Pete' – the veracity of the vote, and the club's true intentions. The Champions League run was achieved with the core group of young players Howard Wilkinson, Paul Hart and Eddie Gray had raised; Rio Ferdinand was the £18 million icing on the cake, but the fans idolised the home-grown players. Some questioned why more signings were necessary in 2001/02. Robbie Fowler was bought from Liverpool for £11 million; an international striker with undoubted talent, but Leeds already had Smith, Viduka, Keane, Kewell and Bridges. Seth Johnson, a young left-sided international from Derby County, was bought for £9 million and paraded on the pitch by Ridsdale; Johnson seemed expensive competition for Harte, Kewell and McPhail.

Ridsdale still saw himself as a fan in the boardroom, but seemed oblivious to the unease. 'We have moved on from the Wetheralls and Molenaars of this world, and Seth's arrival reflects the progress we have made,' he said, angering the players themselves – 'We were both players who gave 100 per cent on and off the field; obviously it wasn't good enough for this chairman, though', said Robert Molenaar – and fans who appreciated their efforts. Ridsdale was forced to apologise.

Johnson and Fowler joined in autumn, when the team were top of the league; O'Leary assured Ridsdale that if Leeds didn't win the title, they would at least qualify for the lucrative Champions League. But the team was playing unsatisfying football. Smith was told to curb his aggression, but instead his temper was spreading throughout the squad; grudges got out of hand against Arsenal at Highbury, where Bowyer and Mills were sent off, and long suspensions mounted for a succession of incidents. Kewell was off form, and Leeds were no longer the carefree attacking side that had thrilled Elland Road. The fans put the change down to another misjudged step away from the club's soul.

O'Leary's profile vied with Ridsdale's in the media. Although he stuck firmly to his script about being a young manager with young players, that was now ignored; he was obviously flattered by attention. Alex Ferguson's long, successful reign at Old Trafford was believed to be ending, and O'Leary was often suggested as a potential heir. Ahead of Manchester United's visit to Elland Road in 2001, O'Leary publicised a change to his backroom staff, while denying it was pre-match psychology. Ferguson had fallen out with his former assistant, Brian Kidd, who was now working in Leeds' academy; on the eve of the match O'Leary promoted Kidd to head coach, claiming it was a coincidence that Ferguson's old right hand would be beside him in the home dugout.

Leeds fans were more concerned that Eddie Gray was not; he stayed in post as assistant manager, but Kidd was promoted above Gray. Although O'Leary took the credit, his 'babies' were raised by Gray in the juniors and the reserves. Supporters recognised the attacking characteristics of Gray's team of the early 1980s, and Kewell in particular as a player in the Gray mould, a debt Kewell acknowledged. O'Leary, frequently away working on transfers, in the media, or more often now as a VIP guest at Grand Prix or golf tournaments, left a lot of day-to-day coaching to Gray, and the players responded to him; it was an open question whether Gray or O'Leary was most influential. The change when Kidd took charge gave many fans their answer.

'David was the manager of the club, and he felt that was the right thing to do,' said Gray later. 'I disagreed with it. I don't think there's any secret about that. I just felt we changed our approach to the game, and how we approached games.' Four of the first fourteen Premiership games in 2001/02 were drawn 0-0, not what the fans had been used to; the UEFA Cup felt like a grind. Bowyer and Woodgate were called back to Hull Crown Court, but rather than pull the team together, the retrial tore the club apart.

Two weeks before Christmas, Woodgate's friend Paul Clifford was found guilty of grievous bodily harm with intent, and affray, and sentenced to six years in jail. Another friend, Neale Caveney, was found guilty of affray, as was Woodgate; they were each sentenced to 100 hours' community service. Bowyer was cleared of all charges, but ordered to pay legal costs of more than £1 million for lying in police interviews. The Najeib family felt let down; they didn't feel justice was done. Press coverage reflected that view, and went after Bowyer and Woodgate; 'Thug And Liar Walk Free' was *The Times*' front-page headline, and the *Mirror* listed Bowyer's previous arrests and convictions, dating from his time at Charlton, challenging him to sue.

Newspapers focused on the implications of racism in a group of rich white footballers involved in assaulting a young Asian student in the streets of a northern city centre. The entire incident was taken as a symptom of football's irresponsible young millionaires detaching from decent society; Leeds had gathered the best young British and Irish players of their generation and paid them fortunes, and while they reaped rewards on the pitch, loutish behaviour off it brought condemnation.

Leeds moved quickly to impose discipline. Bowyer and Woodgate had broken club rules and brought Leeds United into disrepute; Woodgate, visibly affected by his experience, accepted his fine of eight weeks' wages and community work. Bowyer, never wavering in his stubborn belief that he had done nothing wrong, was also ordered to do community work, and fined four weeks' wages. He was furious. 'I was hoping to put this matter behind me and focus on doing my best for Leeds United and the supporters,' he said. 'Now the club appears to be victimising me and forcing me out, having attempted to impose an unfair penalty by agreement.' He spent three days on the transfer list before relenting, asking like Woodgate that his fine go to community work and a children's hospice, but he didn't let go of his resentment towards Ridsdale.

Ridsdale had his say, in a lengthy interview in *The Sunday Times*. But a large part of the interview was pre-occupied with what O'Leary was saying, and how he was saying it. O'Leary had written a diary of the year, but its serialisation in the *News of The World* within days of the trial's conclusion was unexpected, and the title caught Ridsdale out. At a press conference after the verdicts, he was keen to convey that 'Leeds United were not on trial, two of our employees were.' A reporter told Ridsdale he found that a little odd, given the title of O'Leary's book: *Leeds United on Trial*.

'The book is not about the trial,' insisted O'Leary; but the extracts in the *News of The World* certainly were, and severely critical of the players involved. In chapters about the football, he was scathing about individual performances, and the players believed the book was a breach of dressing room secrets, by a manager who was barely there any more.

Amid the fallout, there was still football. Bowyer scored in a ferocious 3-4 defeat to Newcastle United at Elland Road. Leeds then won three; a Fowler hat-trick beating Bolton away, Bowyer getting the only goal at Southampton, and Fowler scoring again on New Year's Day, a superb finish as Leeds beat West Ham 3-0 at Elland Road and went top of the Premiership.

A visit to Cardiff City in the third round of the

FA Cup ought to have been simple, but in the hostile atmosphere of Ninian Park they found something they couldn't overcome, from which they couldn't recover. Viduka gave Leeds the lead, but Graham Kavanagh equalised with a free-kick, and just before half-time Alan Smith was sent off for tussling with Andy Legg. It was a harsh decision, but was his second red card in six weeks, the sixth of his career; he had a reputation.

In the second half the players were pelted with coins and bottles. Referee Andy D'Urso's head was cut; but rather than calm the situation, Cardiff chairman Sam Hammam left the director's box to stand behind the goal Leeds were defending, stoking the aggression of Cardiff's fans. With six minutes to go Cardiff scored a winner, and after the game Ridsdale had to pull O'Leary and Hammam apart. O'Leary, speaking at his book launch a few days later, admitted he had 'lost it'.

Whatever Leeds United and David O'Leary had now seemed lost too. Leeds didn't win their next nine matches, going tamely out of the UEFA Cup to PSV Eindhoven. In a 0-0 draw at Everton, where Matteo was sent off, Leeds fans targeted Brian Kidd, chanting for Eddie Gray; Ridsdale appealed to the fans to stop. Captain Rio Ferdinand, Nigel Martyn and Alan Smith called their own press conference at Thorp Arch to, as they put it, 'put things straight about Brian Kidd'; 'Brian Kidd is as committed to this club as I am,' said local boy Smith. O'Leary echoed the support, but added a proviso: 'Brian is a great coach,' he said, 'but I think we have reached the point now where the players need to be seeing me fully involved with them again on the training pitch.'

Whether that would be welcome was another matter. Leeds finished 5th and qualified for the UEFA Cup, but O'Leary's behaviour still caused problems. Discussing press attention since the trial, he said Leeds might have had an easier time if Bowyer and Woodgate had been jailed after all. In his column in the *Sunday People* he kept up regular commentary on his own players, saying that if Danny Mills' discipline didn't improve, he would put him on the transfer list.

Mills' response aimed a deliberate touch at O'Leary's nerve, naming the two managers he was used to being compared to. 'The examples of Arsène Wenger and Alex Ferguson, arguably the two best managers in the country, should be noted,' said Mills. 'It's very rare that they come out and comment on what their players do.' He finished: 'Over the years, enough lessons have been learned that whatever you want to say should be kept in the dressing room.'

O'Leary flew to the World Cup to work as a television pundit, fielding questions about United's finances and the future of Rio Ferdinand that were uncomfortable viewing in the Leeds boardroom. The relationship with Ridsdale had broken down after O'Leary's book; he'd had enough. The rest of the plc were concerned by another season without Champions League football. When O'Leary returned, ready for a holiday before the new season, he was called to Elland Road. Within three minutes of entering Ridsdale's office, O'Leary was sacked. The club put out a statement saying he left 'by mutual consent'. O'Leary's adviser told them to put out another statement with the truth. Even in parting, even after so long in the public eye together, Peter Ridsdale and David O'Leary couldn't get their stories straight.

2002–04

I FIRMLY BELIEVE THAT
WE HAVE GOT THE BEST

There was disagreement, once it was done, about who persuaded whom to hire Terry Venables to replace David O'Leary. Initial reports said Peter Ridsdale convinced the rest of the Leeds United board. Ridsdale said later that the board convinced him.

Somehow, though, Ridsdale and Venables persuaded each other. When O'Leary was sacked Ridsdale went back to his original choice three years earlier: Martin O'Neill, now at Celtic. O'Neill was interested, but would not break a contract, and still had a year to work. Next on the list was Steve McClaren, Brian Kidd's successor as assistant manager at Manchester United; he helped them win the Premiership, FA Cup and Champions League treble. The press had him all but installed at Leeds, but he was managing Middlesbrough, and the Leeds board were reluctant to pursue another manager in work.

That problem didn't apply to Terry Venables. Ridsdale met him at his villa in Alicante, where he warmed to Venables' relaxed charm and infectious ambition. That was what Leeds fans feared most. Venables was a well-regarded coach, but 59 years old and lacking silverware; his most recent success was taking England to the semi-finals of the European Championships. Before that he won the Spanish title and cup with Barcelona and the FA Cup with Tottenham Hotspur. The Spurs job was typical of Venables' style; after a failed bid to buy the club, he was employed by Alan Sugar as the club's chief executive, blurring the lines between business and football. His business interests were controversial, almost denying him the England job; in 1998 he was disqualified from acting as a company director for seven years.

Venables had been out of football management for a year, and Leeds fans didn't trust this arch-Londoner's intentions in Leeds; he left his last job, at Middlesbrough, because he was too far from his media work in London. The same day Venables took the job at Leeds, ITV announced another series of his detective drama, *Hazell*; he missed part of the pre-season tour as he was filming a travel programme for Channel 5. Ridsdale was convinced: 'I firmly believe that we have got the best.

The very best,' he said; although he included a one-year break clause in Venables' two-year contract, to give him another shot at Martin O'Neill.

Venables was also wary. United's financial problems were well known from their reports to the stock exchange; in March they announced half-year losses of £13.8 million as a result of missing out on the Champions League. Debts were £77 million, but Ridsdale again pointed to the value of the squad: O'Leary contributed to the debt by spending £97 million on players, but the squad was valued at £200 million. There was an immediate need to recoup around £30 million to make up for another season without Champions League revenue and reassure the shareholders, but Ridsdale had deals lined up. Lee Bowyer was refusing to sign a new contract, so Leeds agreed a £9 million fee with Liverpool. Robbie Keane could go to either Sunderland or Middlesbrough for £10 million. Gary Kelly was going to Sunderland for £2.5 million, and Olivier Dacourt to Lazio or Juventus for £14 million. The player Venables was most concerned about was Rio Ferdinand, who was excellent at the 2002 World Cup, and strongly linked with Manchester United; Venables wanted to play Ferdinand, Jonathan Woodgate and Dominic Matteo as a back three. Ferdinand would only leave, said Ridsdale, if a club paid £30 million for him; and in that unlikely scenario, Leeds would bank more than £65 million from the summer sales, freeing up funds for replacements.

Venables' first inkling that the job would not, as he put it later, match the brochure, came in his first meeting with Ferdinand and his agent, to outline the role for United's captain in Venables' team. After an hour, it dawned on Venables that he was the only person who didn't think Ferdinand was going to Manchester United, whatever happened. A week later Ferdinand followed Joe Jordan, Gordon McQueen and Eric Cantona; the asking price of £30 million had been met, although costs squeezed Leeds' profit to around £6 million.

Ferdinand's departure was a problem for Venables, but the collapse of the other outgoing transfers was just as significant for the club. Kelly's transfer fell through. Liverpool detected Bowyer's desire to move to London and backed out. Dacourt refused Lazio, and Juventus didn't follow up. Keane had no interest in leaving unless it was to Spurs, where he eventually went for £7 million. ITV Digital, holding broadcast rights for the Football League, had collapsed, leaving a number of clubs in financial trouble and frightening others; TV deals across Europe were said to have been oversold, and there were fears over reducing income. Selling players was becoming difficult, and after making clear to several that they could leave, Leeds were forced to keep them on high wages. Dacourt, in particular, was not happy.

Unhappiness was spreading throughout the squad. Nigel Martyn became an expensive substitute after asking to be excused from the same pre-season tour of Australia that Venables missed part of; Martyn had been to the Far East for the World Cup, and now he was 36 years old he felt a rest would be more beneficial. His place went to Paul Robinson. Thinking Dacourt was leaving, Venables signed Australian international Paul Okon, and with Dacourt upset at not moving, Venables offered to 'drive him to Italy myself.' Venables doubted David Batty's fitness, and Ridsdale spoke carelessly at the club's annual meeting in December, saying that in Venables' opinion Batty would never play in the Premiership again. Batty's agent sought legal advice, saying the club themselves had not done Batty 'the courtesy of advising him of this enforced retirement'.

United's form was disastrous. Early wins over Manchester City, Newcastle United and Manchester United inspired optimism, but Venables couldn't get the best out of an unbalanced squad and was soon struggling with injuries and arguments. In eleven Premiership games Leeds won once, a shambolic 4-3 win away to West Ham United; within two months of taking over, there were chants for Venables to go. On an awful night at home to Malaga in the UEFA Cup Michael Bridges ruptured his Achilles tendon, two games into a comeback from two years of injuries; Gary Kelly and Jason Wilcox argued on the pitch; Lee Bowyer stamped on a player and, although he escaped the referee, was removed from future teams by Venables; and Malaga won 2-1, ending Leeds' European campaign. Leeds were

16th in the Premiership, with little prospect of qualifying for Europe again.

The financial implications were serious. The going rate for televising Leeds' European matches had already dropped from £1 million per game to £100,000; now it was zero, and with the team playing so poorly, revenue from the Premiership was also dropping. The introduction of transfer windows, restricting when players could be traded, made January 2003 crucial; the wage bill had to be reduced, and cash brought in, if it could be found.

Bowyer, who Leeds once thought was worth £15 million, went to West Ham United for £100,000. Olivier Dacourt moved on loan to Roma, Leeds hoping to get £4 million in the summer for a player they had also valued at £15 million. Seth Johnson, restricted by injuries since costing £9 million and rumoured to be receiving enormous wages, failed a medical at Middlesbrough, cancelling a £4 million sale. That increased pressure on Leeds to consider bids for Woodgate, but that was a line Venables would not let them cross; he was already using sixteen-year-old James Milner in midfield, and losing a second star defender would bring teenagers Matthew Kilgallon and Shane Cansdell-Sherriff into a weakening squad long before they were ready.

Ridsdale assured Venables that if Robbie Fowler went to Manchester City, Woodgate would stay. But the Fowler deal was difficult; Leeds rejected £7.5 million, and City were reluctant to match Fowler's wage, but with two days of the transfer window left Leeds accepted £6 million, even agreeing to continue paying a fifth of Fowler's wages. They looked desperate, and Newcastle United made a bid for Woodgate; at £9 million, Leeds agreed to sell.

Venables was furious. At an extraordinary press conference he sat next to Ridsdale as they fielded questions for almost an hour, broadcast live at lunchtime on Sky Sports News. Ridsdale made the enraging claim that Leeds had not needed to sell Woodgate, but that in a failing transfer market, the money was too good to refuse. One hundred per cent of Leeds United's shares could be bought for £15 million; amid continuing uncertainty about broadcasting income, the plc could not ignore the money. In an opening statement, Ridsdale sought to justify the previous spending and the current selling.

'As a supporter, I did not want to take the offer,' he said. 'The manager did not want Jonathan to go. As chairman of Leeds United I have a primary responsibility to the shareholders to take the right financial decisions … It was the only decision that could have been taken to give us all peace of mind for the future.

'Should we have spent so heavily in the past? Probably not. But we lived the dream. We enjoyed the dream. Only by making the right decisions today can we rekindle the dream once again in the future, and that is what we intend to do. I am currently the chairman, with all the responsibility that brings. I have not shirked from the responsibility. Whatever the future holds, I will always be a fan. The future is brighter, for all Leeds United fans today, because we took the tough decisions.'

Next to Ridsdale, Venables' face portrayed all the darkness Leeds fans were feeling in that moment, although they felt additional gloom for having Venables there as manager. For the next hour the two spoke at odds; Ridsdale insisting the team was still good enough, Venables adamant no squad could withstand losing so many quality players, any trust between them obviously now dust. The final question was whether Venables would demand that Ridsdale leave in order to stay. 'Would I demand that?' said Venables. 'No.' But his body language said he would welcome it.

Six weeks later it was Venables who left. Three defeats left Leeds eight points from relegation, with eight matches left; he was sacked. Ridsdale arranged for former Sunderland manager Peter Reid to take over, on the basis he would be paid per point, keep Leeds up, and leave in the summer. Ridsdale still hoped O'Neill would be coming; but then, he also hoped he would still be chairman. The anger sent his way by Leeds fans, and mocking chants of 'One Peter Ridsdale' from the Anfield Kop as Reid lost his first game, convinced him that dream was over, too. Ridsdale resigned.

He stuck defiantly to his belief that Leeds were a victim of circumstances, not mismanagement; that despite the results, the strategy and decisions were correct.

Had the transfer market not collapsed, he argued, Leeds could have sold their way out of trouble; but this missed the point that there was no insurance against the transfer market collapsing, and that the huge salaries Leeds were paying their players made them difficult to sell. Ridsdale blamed the unforeseeable economic impact of the terrorist attacks on the World Trade Center in New York in September 2001 for ending the chance of a blue-chip sponsor for the new stadium; anticipated income from the stadium had been used to attract a £60 million loan that was now dragging the club down. Throughout his justifications, Ridsdale seemed caught by the twin role he always struggled with. On one hand, he presented himself as the stubborn financial realist answerable to shareholders of a plc. On the other hand, he was a starry-eyed fan, believing any price worth paying for the glory of the Champions League. He seemed immune to the idea that glory could have been achieved any other way.

Just how much it cost, and how serious the problems were, became apparent after Ridsdale left. Leeds had used a company called Registered European Football Finance Ltd to finance eight player purchases. REFF paid the transfer fee up front; Leeds paid fees to insure the risk, then repaid half the transfer fee in stages to REFF, plus high rates of interest, the rest in a lump sum at the end or when the player was sold. The collapse of the transfer market meant Leeds were stuck. Fees offered for

Viduka, for example, were lower than his initial transfer, and selling him would force a payment to REFF that Leeds could not afford. But Leeds also couldn't afford Viduka's wages. Wages were at least a slower way of losing money than a lump sum, so the players stayed.

The failure to cut other costs now looked unconscionable. Professor John McKenzie, a mysterious shareholder who was Ridsdale's replacement as chair, revealed that 'indulgent spending' continued even while players were up for sale. Bills for company cars and private air travel approached £700,000 per year; £20 per month for goldfish in Ridsdale's office was small but symbolic. Ridsdale protested about being made a scapegoat, saying that every decision was approved by the plc board, including deputy chairman Allan Leighton, who many observers felt held more power behind the scenes than was realised; more than even Ridsdale had realised. It was Leighton who introduced McKenzie, an economics lecturer with links to the Far East and a background in rescuing distressed companies, to the board and supported him as chair.

The priority was Peter Reid's rescue on the pitch. Reid had taken Sunderland to the edge of Champions League qualification, but left them in October after fortunes plunged; they were now bottom of the Premiership, fifteen points below Leeds. The fans were not enthused, but after defeat at Liverpool, a 6-1 win away to 7th placed Charlton Athletic suggested Reid was providing the motivation the players needed. He was getting the best out of Mark Viduka, who scored in all but one of Reid's eight matches, but Leeds couldn't pull clear of trouble. Before their penultimate match, away to Arsenal, they were only above the relegation places on goal difference.

Arsenal were chasing the title, only losing once at home, but Reid reminded Leeds' players about their talents and renewed their determination. Leeds led twice, but their efforts were only gaining a draw that would make the final day's fixtures unbearable. Then, two minutes from time, emergency midfielder Matteo played a long ball forward to the right, where Viduka controlled, ran forward, cut inside, and curled a shot past David Seaman into the top corner. As in 1999, a late winner against Arsenal gave Manchester United the league title; but more importantly it saved Leeds from relegation, and the moment proved that glory existed at the bottom of the Premiership as well as in the Champions League.

United's survival decided McKenzie against chasing Martin O'Neill for the manager's job, or Paul Hart, Gordon Strachan or Micky Adams. Reid was given an incentivised contract and kept on: 'In some ways it was an easy decision and in others it was the hardest decision of my life,' said McKenzie.

There were more hard decisions. It was vital to cut costs, and Reid let a host of physios and coaches go, including Brian Kidd and Eddie Gray; Neil Warnock's assistant at Sheffield United, Kevin Blackwell, replaced them. Mills and McPhail were loaned out to reduce the wage bill, Okon was released, and Dacourt's transfer to Roma was confirmed, for a reduced £3.5 million. Paul Robinson almost joined Aston Villa for £3.25 million but could not agree personal terms; instead Reid let Nigel Martyn join Everton for a nominal fee.

Most attention was paid to Harry Kewell's situation. Despite bids of £7 million from Manchester United and Chelsea, Kewell and his agent Bernie Mandic made clear he would only join Liverpool. Liverpool offered £5 million, and Leeds were forced to accept; McKenzie's naivety cost more when Mandic's Max Sport agency took £2 million of the fee. Kewell received £25,000 for revealing his chosen club in an exclusive interview on Australian television, becoming a zero in the eyes of fans who had worshipped him.

Resolving Kewell's transfer took two months, while Reid's transfer targets went elsewhere. He ended up with Jody Morris on a free transfer from Chelsea; Morris left after a few months, and various kinds of trouble with the police. Jermaine Pennant, on loan from Arsenal, was a more useful player on the wing; but Reid's other signings were a clutch of loan players from France, and Roque Júnior, a Brazilian defender loaned from Milan, for whom he had played against Leeds in the Champions League.

Roque Júnior's time at Leeds summed up Peter Reid's. A World Cup winner with genuine pedigree, he looked completely out of his depth on his debut, was sent off in his next match, and despite scoring twice against Manchester United in the League Cup – a game Leeds lost 3-2 – his Leeds career was halted after seven appearances, and 24 goals conceded.

The League Cup had provided another early-season highlight, goalkeeper Paul Robinson heading a late equaliser in the first round, then helping Leeds through the tie on penalties; but this drama took place against second-division Swindon Town. Leeds only won two of their first thirteen league matches, and Reid's time ended in early November. It almost ended a month earlier, but after a breakfast meeting, Allan Leighton and Professor McKenzie couldn't decide whether to sack him; McKenzie spent the day asking supporters for their thoughts, and finding no strong opinion against Reid, met with him for talks. Then McKenzie slept on it, before releasing a statement from the board about the considerations. 'Our conclusion is that Peter Reid should remain as the team manager to lead the team's recovery performance,' it said. But a 4-1 home defeat to Arsenal, after Mark Viduka was alleged to have told the squad, 'If you want to go down, stick with this fella', and a 6-1 defeat at Portsmouth with Roque Júnior in midfield, changed McKenzie's mind again. 'That second half was the worst 45 minutes of my managerial career,' said Reid, 'and the players don't deserve to pick up their wage packets after that performance.' He went on: 'I'm not sure if the players understand how serious the situation is.'

Leeds were bottom of the Premiership, and Professor McKenzie looked a long way out of his depth; he was as relieved as anyone when Trevor Birch came in as chief executive. Birch was a sign of hope, and of what Leeds were up against. With creditors fearing their money would be lost upon relegation, there was a risk Leeds could be forced into administration; Birch, who briefly played for Liverpool in his youth, had a track record as an insolvency expert. At Chelsea, burdened by £80 million of debts accrued by chairman Ken Bates' determination to build a leisure village at the stadium, Birch was crucial in their takeover by Russian billionaire Roman Abramovich. He was brought to Leeds to repeat the trick.

Birch negotiated a standstill agreement with creditors that would stop payments flowing out of Elland Road; his status in the City secured six weeks, and weekly extensions, a window to sell the club. The players were harder to convince. When asked to temporarily defer 20 per cent of their wages, David Batty pointed out that several players were negotiating transfers, assuming Leeds would be relegated; selling them now would raise more money than deferring wages, leaving Leeds with a squad that wanted to stay. This was interpreted in the press as a refusal to help, and after a backlash from the fans the players agreed to defer, Batty left upset at being made out to be the bad guy.

Birch was finding money where he could, pleading for time, and trying to get one of the bidders for the club to produce funds. There was no shortage of these: Allan Leighton formed a consortium, as did Professor McKenzie, rumoured to be talking to Xu Ming, one of the richest men in China; Michael Ezra, a Ugandan property tycoon, toured Thorp Arch; former Huddersfield Town chairman Terry Fisher and former Leeds player Trevor Cherry expressed an interest; most optimism focused on Sheikh Abdulrahman bin Mubarak al-Khalifa, a Leeds fan since he watched the 1970 FA Cup final, who had a consortium from the Middle East.

A takeover was agreed on 19 March, with the only group to convince Birch they had the money. A consortium of Yorkshire businessmen calling themselves Adulant Force, led by another insolvency expert, Gerald Krasner, completed a deal said to involve 100 lawyers and 60 accountants from fourteen different firms. Leeds United plc was wound up, and the £104 million debts of Leeds United AFC were drastically reduced to £20 million, creditors trusting Birch's judgement and taking something rather than risking getting nothing. He didn't produce a billionaire, but saving £80 million was an audacious rescue by Birch.

The rescue on the pitch was left, as it was in 1982, to Eddie Gray. Gray said being made caretaker manager was 'a fantastic opportunity', and Leeds were hoping his enthusiasm would bring the players together. For a while, it worked. Gray gave Reid's team a chance in a 2-0 defeat to Bolton Wanderers, then made changes. The loan signings were moved aside. Gray wanted players who understood the club, with a deeper feeling; the first 1-0 win, away to Charlton, was clinched by seventeen-year-old Leeds fan James Milner. Leeds went five games unbeaten, but the improvement couldn't withstand the takeover speculation. Controversy over the wage deferral seemed to derail the good form; Gray told Batty he wasn't going to play him again, citing football reasons, but perhaps trying to end the disruption that had brought six consecutive defeats.

With Viduka back from Australia, where his father was ill, Leeds beat Wolverhampton Wanderers 4-1 and were fighting again; Viduka scored six in eight games, and Matteo and Smith were defiant in defence and midfield, Leeds giving themselves a chance with four wins. A 1-1 draw with Everton followed, Leeds foiled by Nigel Martyn's brilliance in goal, but at Highbury Thierry Henry scored four goals in 40 minutes as Leeds were beaten 5-0.

Viduka was crucial to Leeds' effort, but lost his discipline at a crucial time. A second yellow card for time-wasting against Blackburn meant he was suspended against relegation rivals Portsmouth at Elland Road; Leeds lost 2-1, and although there were three matches left, had to win at Bolton to have a chance of staying up. Viduka was back, scoring a penalty just before the half-hour; but in the next six minutes he received two yellow cards for pointless, reckless challenges, and was gone again.

All Eddie Gray could do was stand on the touchline and watch, as stoic as Viduka was stupid. Bolton scored four in the second half, their third a cruel own goal by Ian Harte. Harte was one of the kids in Gray's team when they won the reserve league in 1998; so were Paul Robinson, Stephen McPhail and Alan Smith, all suffering on the pitch now. Gray had seen some tears from those boys when they were growing up, and he was watching them cry again now, listening to the fans singing about being champions of Europe. The only emotion Gray allowed himself was caught by Sky TV's cameras as he walked down the tunnel alone at the end of the game; his right hand made a fist, and he struck the wall with a gentle, resigned punch.

2004–07

TODAY IS THE FIRST DAY
OF A NEW LEEDS UNITED

Even before the relegation season was over, Eddie Gray was gone. He took charge of one more game, at home to Charlton Athletic, but was told before the last day's visit to Chelsea he would not be kept on. The job of getting Leeds back up went to his assistant, Kevin Blackwell.

'I have said before that the club do not owe me anything, and they don't,' said Gray. 'I have had a great life with the football club and it's just sad that it has come to this, but that's life.'

Gray's departure after 40 years was almost lost amid the rush to the doors. The Charlton match ended 3-3, and with a rush to the pitch as fans made for Alan

Smith, the local boy who had done his best; they raised him aloft for twenty minutes, knowing he was leaving. 'There's never been a bigger hero here,' said Gray.

Smith's fall from grace felt as rapid as the club's. He once said he would stay with Leeds even if they were relegated: 'It takes a better type of person to stay.' Finances took that decision out of his hands, but Smith was also famous for saying there was one club he would never play for: Manchester United. Before the game at Chelsea, his tune had changed.

'People say that Leeds and Manchester United are big rivals, but we're not even going to be in the same division, so it's not even a rivalry,' he said. 'I'm not saying I want to walk out of here and go to Manchester United, but they're a massive club. I can't rule anything out. At this stage of my career, if I want to win trophies and do well, then I've got to move on.'

Smith no longer looked like a hero in the Chelsea match. He was barely involved, except when he replied to chants suggesting he wouldn't be welcome back with a single-finger salute. Leeds hoped an auction for Smith would bring much-needed funds, but the deal was quickly done: Smith's agent insisted he would only go to a club in the Champions League; Manchester United offered £6 million cash, plus midfielder Danny Pugh. Smith, in a conciliatory gesture, let his £700,000 cut go to Leeds.

Leeds needed all the money they could wring out of what was left of the squad. Even before the Chelsea

game Paul Robinson went to Tottenham Hotspur for
£2 million. Mark Viduka went to Middlesbrough for
£4.5 million, and youngster James Milner to Newcastle
United for £5.25 million. For the rest, it was a case of
cutting costs, Leeds continuing to pay portions of wages
for high earners leaving on free transfers. Seth Johnson
and Eirik Bakke were injured and had to stay. Lucas
Radebe, sharply critical of some of his teammates during
relegation, underlined his commitment by signing a new
one-year contract. There was no question of Gary Kelly
leaving; he was approaching 500 appearances for Leeds.

The clear-out had Kevin Blackwell claiming there
was 'only me and Gary Kelly' in pre-season, a line
he kept coming back to as he built up a squad, but it
was never entirely true; the Thorp Arch academy kept
producing, and after Milner came Scott Carson, Frazer
Richardson, Simon Johnson, Matthew Kilgallon and
Aaron Lennon. But Blackwell needed players quickly,
signing, trying and discarding anyone he could get. Any
hope of promotion diminished as Leeds used 37 different
players, and there were fears of another relegation when
Leeds dropped to 19th in November. But the response
was one of the most memorable performances at Elland
Road for years; Brian Deane was back to add experience
and effort, and scored four goals in a 6-1 win.

The problems on the pitch were a symptom of
Adulant Force's failure to solve problems in the boardroom. The consortium split almost as soon as they took

over; within six weeks chairman Gerald Krasner and director David Richmond were recommending a take-over bid by local businessman Steve Parkin. Melvyn Helme, Melvyn Levi and Simon Morris were against it, and arguments began. The Adulant Force board was completed by former player Peter Lorimer, and David Richmond's father Geoffrey, an 'unpaid adviser' whose presence caused concern. He had recently been chairman of Bradford City and left them in administration after what he called 'six weeks of madness' in the transfer market; he brought in his former managing director at Bradford, Shaun Harvey, as chief executive at Leeds. Soon Richmond was gone; he stood down for 'personal and health reasons' and a week later was bankrupt, owing £3.3 million to the Inland Revenue.

Adulant Force had taken on Leeds United's £20 million debt, calculating it could be repaid if Leeds stayed in the Premiership. That miracle was beyond Eddie Gray, and Kevin Blackwell was not going to work another. A scheme to sell thousands of twenty-year season tickets sold around 100. They added more debt; former players and staff were owed £8 million, tax bills totalled £9 million, directors put in £4.75 million, and to get the initial purchase done, property investor Jack Petchey loaned £15 million, secured against Elland Road, with penalties of £2 million if repayments were late. Part of the land at Thorp Arch was sold; eight mortgages were taken out against Leeds United's property, and the rest of Thorp

Arch was sold to property investor Jacob Adler, so Leeds could pay off those mortgages. Leeds took a 25-year lease on Thorp Arch with a buyback option, then sold land behind the Elland Road Kop to a casino operator. As Adulant Force struggled to make repayments to Petchey, selling Elland Road itself looked increasingly likely.

There were two takeover offers to bail them out, but they only caused more arguments, some directors favouring Sebastian Sainsbury's Anglo-American consortium, some preferring Norman Stubbs' local group. Sainsbury and Melvyn Helme had a spectacular argument by telephone, broadcast live after a match commentary on Radio Aire; and before a tight deadline for the next payment to Petchey, Sainsbury dropped his bid. Elland Road was sold, also to Jacob Adler on a 25-year leaseback, clearing the debt to Petchey, but not solving United's problems; in December Leeds defaulted on a £2 million payment to the Inland Revenue. Young goalkeeper Scott Carson was hurriedly sold to Liverpool for £1 million to pay wages, but Leeds were desperate, and Trevor Birch's calm negotiating skills were gone.

January put Adulant Force in a whirlwind of negotiations with Birch's old boss. Reports in the *Yorkshire Evening Post* linked former Chelsea chairman Ken Bates to a briefly revived bid from Sebastian Sainsbury; Sainsbury confirmed they met, but Bates said the idea he was investing in Leeds was 'absolute rubbish'. Norman

Stubbs' group, now including Allan Leighton, was believed to be the only viable bid left, with additional funds from one of the independent groups that began arguing the case of the fans during the club's decline, the Leeds United Supporters' Trust; recalling the faith of Alf Masser 85 years earlier, Trust chairman John Boocock believed 5,000 fans could invest £1,000 each. The plan was soon shelved. Ten days after denying any interest, at 2.30 in the morning, Ken Bates completed a £10 million takeover. Simon Jose of the Leeds United Independent Supporters' Association said: 'It's like the four horsemen of the Apocalypse selling to Lucifer.'

Ken Bates' arrival meant Leeds avoided administration, but also meant attention would stay focused on the boardroom, where it had been since 'Publicity Pete' Ridsdale had become the most prominent chairman in football. Bates once had his own claim to that title. He became chairman of Third Division Oldham Athletic in 1965, turning them into his idea of a football club. He spent £45,000 on new seats, fresh paint and executive boxes at Boundary Park, raising ticket prices to match. He replaced the Oldham Supporters' Club with his own Latics Tangerine Club. The matchday programme was replaced by a newspaper, the *Boundary Bulletin*, and a radio station, Radio Latics, so Bates could have his say on all the issues of the day, and he boasted of his plans for a £180,000 stand including an 'exclusive 300 Club', a French restaurant, a bowling alley and a discotheque.

In 1967 Bates took Oldham on a tour of Rhodesia, defying the United Nations' resolution calling on the world 'to refrain from any action which would assist and encourage' the African state's 'illegal racist minority regime'. The *Boundary Bulletin* published a photo, courtesy of the 'Rhodesia Ministry of Information', of Bates and the players posing with the illegal state's prime minister, Ian Smith, who held a rolled-up copy of the *Boundary Bulletin* in his hand.

By 1968 Bates' concrete businesses were struggling, and Oldham fans were tired of being called 'the lambs of Sheepfoot Lane' in his newspaper. Bates sold up, and was next seen in the British Virgin Islands, where he negotiated an incredible 199-year lease on large parts of two islands, Anegada and Tortola, enabling him to redevelop them as leisure destinations and tax havens with no tax on his profits. Bates could make $50 million, and was said to be writing his memoirs, sipping champagne by a beach. The local people feared being confined to a reservation with their island seized, and began to protest; led by Noel Lloyd, the Positive Action Movement marched through Road Town in Tortola. 'Regardless, we got to take back our country from Kenneth Bates,' said one protester, Louella Harrigan, 'and whatever we're going to do we're going to march this morning, and we are going to take our country back! This lease must be revoked, and Kenneth Bates must go!' Weeks of unrest followed, until the British government intervened and bought Bates out, leaving him a personal profit of around $1.5 million. In Road Town the locals put up a statue to Noel Lloyd, in the Positive Action Movement Park.

From there Bates opened a bank in Dublin, the Irish Trust Bank, that failed, leaving the government to reimburse the ordinary people who had lost their money; Bates went to Australia. When he returned to London, he was regarded as a small-time outsider, but forced his way to notoriety by paying £1 to buy Chelsea Football Club and its considerable debts, that Bates failed to clear until a complicated transfer of assets to offshore trusts bewildered the FA and left him head of a new company. In the heart of London, Chelsea gave Bates a voice, and through the 1980s he argued his way into relevance; and it gave him Stamford Bridge, where in the 1990s he built the 'Chelsea Village': hotels, apartments, bars, restaurants, a Chelsea superstore, a club museum, a radio station. The investment was not matched on the pitch until Premier League broadcasting revenue gave Bates the funds, but the Village didn't make the money he hoped, and debts grew over £80 million. Roman Abramovich, a Russian billionaire, solved the problem by buying the club, leaving Bates with £17 million profit to enjoy during retirement in Monaco.

'It's full of people waiting to die,' Bates said after a few months. He had planned to stay on at Chelsea; the deal with Abramovich gave him the right to stay as chairman until 2005 and use the chairman's office and perks for the rest of his life; but the withdrawal of his column from the programme infuriated him and he resigned, suing for breach of contract and contributing a column to Bolton Wanderers' programme instead, for their game against Chelsea. He was 73, but after months of relative anonymity among the glitterati ignoring him in Monte Carlo, Bates was desperate for football's limelight. There was a rancorous attempt to buy Sheffield Wednesday, immediately followed by his successful bid for Leeds.

Using Forward Sports Fund, an investment vehicle in Geneva, Bates took 50 per cent of Leeds United in return for £10 million; Adulant Force's deal with bondholders meant he could not buy the rest until March 2007. A payment to bondholders and a loan from David Richmond were paid off; other directors' £4.1 million loans would stay in the club for four years, and structured repayment of £4.2 million was agreed with the Inland Revenue. Debt was down to £17 million, Bates claiming only £9 million of it counted for anything. Peter Lorimer stayed on the board, joined by Bates' long-term associates: lawyer Mark Taylor, and Yvonne Todd, who became finance director.

'Today is the first day of a new Leeds United,' announced Bates. 'I recognise that Leeds United is a great club that has fallen on hard times. We have a lot of hard work ahead of us to get the club back to where it belongs in the Premiership, and with the help of the fans, who have stuck by the club through thick and thin, we are going to do everything in our power to ensure that happens. Our first task will be to put plans in place to secure the financial future of the club and these will include buying back, in due course, Elland Road and Thorp Arch.' Revelling in the attention at a fans' forum, he said: 'We're gonna have a lorra lorra laughs.'

Bates' presence at least allowed a period of normality. Blackwell's signings became more structured; popular on-loan midfielder Shaun Derry was signed permanently, and strikers David Healy and Rob Hulse were quality additions. Leeds finished 14th in the Championship, and with a second 'parachute payment' from the Premiership, made Hulse's loan move permanent in summer 2005, adding forward Robbie Blake, £1.15 million striker Richard Creswell, winger Eddie Lewis, midfielder Jonathan Douglas and centre-back Rui Marques; although Blackwell still preferred a cumbersome pairing of Paul Butler and Sean Gregan. Seth Johnson's contract was terminated to avoid further payments to Derby County, and Aaron Lennon was sold to Tottenham Hotspur for £1 million; he was the best young player at the club, but Bates said his Ridsdale-era contract could not be carried forward.

United's players were a rough bunch compared to the Champions League team, and Blackwell's sensitivity to criticism was unappealing, but they got results; Leeds were 5th in November when, after falling 3-0 behind at Southampton, on-loan midfielder Liam Miller finished a sensational twenty-minute comeback, scoring with four minutes left to win the game 4-3. That set Leeds up for a successful winter, closing in on Sheffield United's 2nd place. Sheffield were managed by Blackwell's old boss Neil Warnock and the two bickered all season, Warnock angry first at Blackwell's original move to Leeds, then his perceived poaching of Richard Cresswell.

It never became more than a war of words. Leeds lost momentum, and their final ten games brought just one win; six draws secured a play-off place. There was another draw at home in the semi-final, 1-1 with Preston North End, but brawls, a late free-kick by Eddie Lewis and Preston manager Billy Davies' post-match comments – 'It is tremendous to come here in front of their biggest crowd of the season and get what is a fantastic result. It is a case of job done' – helped Leeds find their aggressive side for the away leg. 'Billy has his way of celebrating a draw,' said Cresswell, but he was not so calm at Deepdale. He was sent off, as was Stephen Crainey, six other Leeds players were booked, Preston's Brett Ormerod's leg was broken, and Carlo Nash's cheekbone fractured; a 30-minute delay when the floodlights failed added to the mayhem. Leeds scored twice, through Rob Hulse and Frazer Richardson, trashed the dressing room, scrawled 'Job Done' on a whiteboard, and left for the play-off final at the Millennium Stadium in Cardiff.

Somehow that spirit was lost in the two weeks before the final. Against Watford Leeds were static, listless and beaten 3-0. Hopes of returning to the Premiership were broken amid unwanted memories of losing to Aston Villa in the League Cup final in 1996. Howard Wilkinson had found it impossible to recover from that defeat, and by mid-September, Blackwell was gone too. There were no more parachute payments, and millions were still being paid to players who had left. The previous summer's rebuilding was undone; Rob Hulse was sold for £2.2 million and teenage midfielder Simon Walton for £500,000, eleven others left, and the work to replace them was chaotic; in July Leeds signed midfielders David Livermore and Kevin Nicholls, then sold Livermore to Hull after eleven days, claiming he was 'unlikely to play' ahead of Nicholls, who promptly damaged knee ligaments in a training ground tackle by Paul Butler.

The signs were not good, and Blackwell and his coaching staff told Bates so; he was not impressed by talk of a relegation battle. Bates appointed Gwyn Williams as technical director, a coach and scout with the 'biggest contacts book in Britain' and 27 years behind him at Chelsea, and the rest seemed like a matter of time. The season started with a win, but after five defeats to nil, Blackwell was sacked. 'Life is not fair, is it?' he said.

Bates had been relatively quiet, given his reputation, but was now making his presence felt. Attendances at Elland Road fell below 20,000, a rejection of increased ticket prices. Bates' final meeting with Blackwell took place in the newly opened Billy's Bar, part of an expensive refurbishment of the South Stand, when investment in players seemed more urgent. Blackwell's sacking was not amicable; he sued for compensation, and Bates banned the *Yorkshire Evening Post* from the press box for their coverage. He used his programme notes and a new radio station, Yorkshire Radio, to air grievances with former director Melvyn Levi, and with Chelsea over two young players they took from United's academy.

Most worrying was the revelation that Elland Road had been sold again, to an unknown company in the British Virgin Islands called Teak Trading. Shaun Harvey said it made no difference, as Leeds still had a buyback option that they hoped to exercise soon with a loan from Leeds City Council; 'If the club owned the stadium there would be no longer any mystery as to who owns it,' he said. But the council were sceptical about paying £13 million to persons unknown. The annual rent of £1.5 million, meanwhile, was also going to persons unknown, but Bates was dismissive: 'The straight answer is that neither I nor anybody else at Leeds United knows who it is.'

The new manager at Leeds United was Dennis Wise, whose arrival was rumoured from Bates' first day; Wise was his captain at Chelsea, Bates was godfather to Wise's children. As player-manager he had taken Millwall to an FA Cup final; Swindon Town was his first full-time managerial job, with former teammate Gus Poyet as his assistant, but they were only fifteen games into a good start when they took the job at Leeds. Wise said his aim was the Premiership, but seemed unconcerned when the team showed few signs of rising from the relegation places. The league table, he said, 'wasn't great when I came here, so that isn't going to bother me.' Leeds were stuck on twenty points, but with 24 games left, Wise was confident Leeds would get ten more wins and stay up. 'There's a fair few points to be had and you need between 48 and 50 points,' he said. 'I am confident.'

There wasn't much confidence in the team. Young defender Matthew Kilgallon was sold for £1.75 million, and he left a subdued side, further damaged by Wise's bizarre accusation that a 'mole' had leaked his team to Crystal Palace before a match at Elland Road: 'That player's not going to play again for this football club,' he said, but it transpired to be a fuss about nothing, blown up by Wise's paranoia. A month later his captain walked out. Appointing Kevin Nicholls was one of Wise's first decisions: 'The players know that now I have made a couple of decisions early doors with regards to the captaincy,' he said. Now Nicholls went back to Luton, United's relegation rivals; he said coming to Leeds was a mistake.

Leeds only took eleven points from fourteen matches after Wise set his target, and he could no longer ignore what was happening. Nicholls' desertion inspired five unbeaten games, but when leading at Colchester United with ten minutes to go, Leeds collapsed, losing 2-1 and dropping back into the relegation places. Matt Heath headed in a corner to give Leeds a vital 1-0 win over Burnley at Elland Road, but another late goal conceded at Southampton meant a 1-0 defeat.

To survive, Leeds would have to fight their way to a win over Ipswich Town at Elland Road. Dennis Wise had said he wanted his team to be 'a bit like the Leeds of old; horrible, I want a bit of nastiness and togetherness'. But even after Cresswell's early goal, few among the 31,269 believed. Leeds United had never, in 88 years, played below the second tier. When Alan Lee equalised with two minutes to go, that's where Leeds were heading.

A pitch invasion from supporters trying to get the match abandoned delayed the ending by twenty minutes; play resumed with goalkeeper Casper Ankergren attacking a corner, and a plea from the public address system: 'We cannot emphasise enough how big the last minute of this game is.' If only someone had emphasised to Dennis Wise and Ken Bates how big the previous 46 games had been, before it was too late.

2007–10

THEY DON'T LIKE BATESY
AND THEY DON'T LIKE ME

League One was fun at first. It was a place Leeds
United should never have been, but the new opponents, tiny stadiums, open terraces and determination
to get back to the top gave it the feel of a tour; Leeds
were slumming it, but that was okay. Winning the first
seven league matches was even better, matching Don
Revie's champions of 1973/74, scoring sixteen goals and
conceding just three. Dennis Wise had cracked the camaraderie, and the players were up for the adventure. There
was a common enemy, a familiar one; after a summer
spent in administration, the Football League imposed a
fifteen-point penalty on Leeds that felt like yet another
instance of institutional bias against Leeds United. But

even as seven wins turned minus fifteen points into plus six, dismissing the League's punishment in style, fans were wondering if United's real problems weren't closer to home.

The financial situation had become dire weeks before relegation, and after Leeds missed two monthly payments of £200,000, a winding-up petition arrived from Her Majesty's Revenue & Customs. HMRC now wanted the full amount of £5 million by the end of June. Ken Bates placed Leeds United into administration days after the draw with Ipswich Town that condemned them to League One; it meant a ten-point penalty from the league, but that didn't matter now.

Within days, accountants KPMG announced that the football club, business and assets had been sold to a new company, Leeds United Football Club Limited, pending approval from creditors. The directors of the new company were Ken Bates, Shaun Harvey and Mark Taylor, and the controversy began. 1,350 creditors were listed by KPMG, from HMRC to the St John Ambulance, owed a total of £38,100,038. Bates was offering non-football creditors one penny per pound of debt; HMRC, owed £6.9 million, would get £69,000.

Six alternative bids went before a meeting of 200 people in the banqueting suite at Elland Road, but there was not much to consider. A bid required approval from 75 per cent of creditors, on a one vote per pound basis. A company in the British Virgin Islands, Astor Investment

Holdings, were owed more than 25 per cent of the total and could block any bid; it was made clear that they would only support Bates. Krato Trust, another company in the BVI, also held a large debt and backed Bates; Forward Sports Fund, the company Bates used to buy into Leeds in 2005, administered in Geneva but also based in the BVI, was owed almost as much as Krato. It would also, obviously, go for Bates.

The question in the room was: why were these anonymous offshore companies ignoring better offers, some as high as 18p per pound, to support Ken Bates, when it would cost them millions? He wasn't there to answer, but KPMG had made 'fairly extensive inquiries', finding nothing to link the companies to him, or any clues about the ultimate owners of Astor and Krato. Administrator Richard Fleming said: 'Maybe they had football in their hearts and wanted the club to survive.' Bates and his lawyer, Mark Taylor, signed declarations denying links to Astor; Astor signed one denying links to Bates. But Gerald Krasner found a link in Leeds United's 2006 accounts; Astor had 'an interest in Forward Sports Fund' as of 30 June 2006. 'There was an association on June 30,' admitted Mark Taylor, 'there isn't now.'

The vote went in favour of Bates at 75.02 per cent; close enough for legal challenges, so there were recounts over the weekend, putting the final total at 75.2 per cent. HMRC challenged anyway, determined not to let Leeds be the latest football club to use the administration process to cut a debt worth millions of public money to a few thousand; it emerged that an undeclared debt, £480,000 owed to Yorkshire Radio, was added before the meeting, accounting for around 1.3 per cent of the votes. Bates and Taylor were both directors of Yorkshire Radio.

The football season was due to start, and that meant paying bills. Bates was not prepared to fund the club if he might ultimately lose control on appeal, so KPMG scrapped the Company Voluntary Agreement approved by the vote and announced, on Friday 6 July, that Leeds United was for sale again. Bids had to be received by the end of Monday, the deadline of Bates' original offer. The previous bidders had a chance, but didn't feel it was a fair one: 'It is an absolute travesty,' said Simon Franks of Redbus, one of the leading consortia. 'KPMG have asked us to submit bids by 5pm on Monday, but they are not giving us access to the management accounts. We have no idea what we are bidding for.'

Four bids were submitted; on 11 July KPMG announced Bates was again successful, and Astor were again crucial. As part of the deal with Bates, Astor waived claims totalling £17.6 million; no other bidder had that advantage. Ownership of the club went to Leeds United 2007 Ltd, and 100 per cent of the shares were now owned by Forward Sports Fund.

The sale made both the Company Voluntary Agreement and HMRC's appeal against it redundant, but it did not satisfy the Football League. Its rules said a club must exit administration through the CVA process, and at the end of July there were urgent negotiations to convince the Football League to allow Leeds to take their place in League One. KPMG argued a new CVA was impossible due to the inevitable appeal from HMRC, and the Football League accepted their case; there was an 'exceptional circumstances' clause in the League's insolvency policy, and it was now used for the first time. But, the League added, there had to be a sanction. The price of playing in League One would be starting on minus fifteen points.

Leeds appealed to a meeting of the League's member clubs; unsurprisingly, 64 voted that Leeds should be punished, 54 that a fifteen-point deduction was fair. Bates was furious, and Football League chairman Lord Mawhinney was his target, along with HMRC. Leeds United's press statement after the meeting was headed 'Leeds United 0 Taxman 1', and claimed the decision was 'perverse'; Bates said it was 'prejudiced' and 'a total disgrace'. Bates eventually tried a legal challenge, which failed when the Football League proved Leeds had agreed to the penalty in writing when it was imposed, and agreed not to mount the legal challenge they were now attempting. Bates called for Lord Mawhinney to resign anyway.

Leeds were at least cleared to start the season, but the summer set the tone for Bates' continuing chairmanship of Leeds. His track record and strong association with Chelsea made him unwelcome in 2005, but he was accepted as unavoidable; declaring the club's problems solved, then relegating Leeds to the lowest point in their history was, for many, unforgivable. Administration felt like an opportunity to break with Bates, and fans were bemused that he had survived apparently better offers and somehow still owned the club; there had been interest from Don Revie's son, Duncan, who was much more appealing than Bates. There were protests against Bates all summer, including a spontaneous placing of flowers at Billy Bremner's statue, that the club's official website tried to claim was a show of support; the slogan 'Love Leeds, Hate Bates' made a mockery of that. As at Oldham Athletic and Chelsea, Bates tried to control the debate, taking match commentary rights away from the local BBC station and giving them to Yorkshire Radio, and there was intense distrust of his motives. Bates soon announced plans to redevelop Elland Road, but few could see the benefit of a hotel, shops, offices and nightclubs to a club fighting to stay in League One.

'The supporters don't like Batesy, and they don't particularly like me,' said Dennis Wise, the only one allowed to call the chairman 'Batesy'. 'But they've got us. We're part of this football club.'

Wise, at the end of the chaotic summer's transfer embargo, and a round of pre-season friendlies played in old kits with the sponsors' logos taped over, held a press conference to vent before the season got under way, and didn't hold back. After brandishing his paper's coverage at *Yorkshire Evening Post* reporter Phil Hay, Wise took aim at the Football League. 'It's laughable,' he said. 'They've not only taken my arms and legs off, they've cut my balls off as well. There's a massive point to prove – for everyone. A lot of people want to see us fall flat on our faces and they haven't helped the situation. We've got to fight against it.'

United's aim was promotion; a fifteen-point penalty threatened another relegation. But it also created a mood of defiance at the first match, away to Tranmere Rovers. Wise had kept and added to a core of players who were committed to the club; he feared experienced midfielder Andrew Hughes would stay in the Championship with Norwich City, but Hughes signed the day after the penalty was confirmed. It would be 'no problem', he said; he just wanted to play for Leeds. After a difficult first half at Tranmere, and a half-time 'argument', as Wise called it, Leeds attacked the second half as a team. Trésor Kandol scored a last-minute winner, and players, staff and fans celebrated together; the first win was a significant milestone, getting Leeds ready for the next six.

The spell of solidarity with Wise in charge did not last long. His assistant, Gus Poyet, went to work with Martin Jol in the Premier League at Tottenham Hotspur, and United's subsequent performances made it seem he had taken all the good football with him. Leeds were slipping from the play-off places; performances were deteriorating, and Hereford United knocked them out of the FA Cup in the first round. At the end of January, away at Luton Town, a team at the bottom of the division and in administration, Leeds drew 1-1. Wise, orchestrator of the siege mentality but now short of ideas, resigned to take a lucrative job as director of football at Newcastle United.

It was a shock, but Bates used the opportunity to hire a manager the fans would take to. Gary McAllister's renaissance as a Liverpool player had been tough for Leeds fans to watch; he won the FA Cup, UEFA Cup and League Cup with them in 2001. But he was welcomed back as a treasured member of United's title-winning midfield in 1992, and as a manager who had built an attractive team at Coventry City.

'The job brief is promotion,' said McAllister. Wise left two newly signed midfielders, Neil Kilkenny and Bradley Johnson, and a brilliant local boy from the youth team, Jonny Howson; up front Jermaine Beckford, signed from non-league football in 2006, was having the best season of any Leeds striker since Mark Viduka in 2003. But McAllister's new passing style didn't gel until he signed Crystal Palace's Dougie Freedman on loan; a creative and experienced striker, his intelligence supported Leeds through seven wins in nine matches that secured a place in the play-offs.

If not for the fifteen-point penalty, the team would have finished second with 92 points, one point behind champions Swansea City. Whether it was Bates or the Football League to blame, 36,297 turned out for the play-off semi-final against Carlisle United at Elland Road, ready to see a wrong put right. Carlisle's two goals damaged the mood, but Freedman proved his worth, scoring in the sixth minute of stoppage time to make it 2-1. In the away leg he set Jonny Howson up to equalise the aggregate score; then with a minute of stoppage left Freedman again flicked the ball to Howson, breaking from midfield to the edge of the box, who shot low and hard into the back of the net. A week short of his twentieth birthday, the local boy sent Leeds to Wembley.

Wembley was a chance for McAllister to overcome the memories of 1996, when he captained Leeds in the disastrous League Cup final; for Leeds to overcome the horror of 2007, relegated to its lowest point and rendered insolvent; and for the players to overcome the destabilising effect of Poyet and Wise's departures. But the demand for tickets was more than the club could cope with. A crowd of fans spent a night on Fullerton Park, now a car park, waiting for United's ticket office to open, and by dawn there were 7,000 in a tired, hungry and angry scrum; thousands went home without tickets. Others headed to Doncaster, to try buying tickets from United's opponents.

Doncaster Rovers were more than the team could cope with. Leeds couldn't get to grips with the game, the occasion, the importance; Rovers scored two minutes after half-time. Leeds United had won 27 league games since insolvency, but they couldn't win this one. 'Maybe in a few days we'll realise the achievement,' said goal-keeper Casper Ankergren, echoing the lament of many Leeds players before him. 'But right now we're standing here with nothing.'

The risk was that Leeds would not be able to repeat the achievement. The team had not truly played well between the departure of Poyet and the arrival of Freedman; he now went back to Crystal Palace, and McAllister had to find new inspiration. He had a summer free of distractions, but not much money to spend; the team he put together reflected the cultured football McAllister wanted to play. Robert Snodgrass, a winger signed from Livingstone, had interested Barcelona when he was sixteen; Luciano Becchio, an Argentinian striker signed from the Spanish third tier, had been on Barcelona's books, playing ten times for their B team. Kilkenny was a controlling midfield player to dictate tempo, and Howson was one of Leeds' best young players in years; eighteen-year-old Fabian Delph looked even better, and with Ben Parker and Aidan White proved the value of Thorp Arch's academy, despite its sale.

McAllister's problem was too much choice; he couldn't settle on his best line-up, and away defeats interrupted any momentum. Defending was nervous and fragile, affecting the team's overall form. Beckford and Becchio hadn't clicked, and the team looked doomed to pass the ball around until the opposition scored. A defeat at non-league Histon in a televised FA Cup match broadcast Leeds' troubles to the nation. McAllister's team wasn't bad, but it couldn't get the measure of more physical sides, and there were plenty of those in League One. Before Histon, Leeds lost to Northampton Town; after Histon, they lost to Tranmere, Colchester United and MK Dons. After setting out to dominate the league, Leeds were eleven points from 2nd place, and five points outside the play-offs. 'I feel that I am letting the fans down,' said McAllister. 'There is an expectation, a great expectation, that we should thrive upon.' Four days before Christmas Day – McAllister's birthday – he was sacked.

His replacement was another member of Howard Wilkinson's 1992 squad, although a lot of fans didn't remember him. Simon Grayson signed for Leeds on the same day as Gary Speed, and they were close friends, but Grayson only made four appearances before leaving in 1992. A defender or midfielder, he captained Leicester City to promotion to the Premier League and won the League Cup, and as manager he took Blackpool from League One to the Championship and kept them there.

Grayson was also a Leeds fan. 'It's a club that's obviously close to my heart, being here as a player and supporting the club,' he said. 'I certainly would not have dropped down a division to go to any other club but Leeds United.' He brought as his assistant Glynn Snodin, another from the Billy Bremner and Wilkinson era, and another Leeds fan, credited with popularising the 'Leeds Salute' gesture of a clenched fist over the heart; and he signed Richard Naylor, a centre-back with more than 300 appearances for Ipswich Town, another boyhood Leeds fan who hadn't let go. Naylor became captain of a team including Howson, Parker and White, all young Leeds United fans; and Delph, from Bradford, but a Leeds player since he was twelve.

The influence of Leeds United-minded people was more than sentimental. It added a vital ingredient. Grayson learned from Wilkinson that it was better to play football in the opponent's final third, and Naylor led a new no-nonsense policy at the back, helped by loan signing Sam Sodje. But the problems were psychological as much as stylistic. Leeds were still only 8th when a close defeat at Huddersfield was followed by a 2-0 loss at Hereford United, where Leeds let themselves down and the travelling fans made their feelings clear, chanting: 'We're shit and we're sick of it.' Crammed into the tiny away dressing room, Grayson could communicate that sentiment with the feeling of a supporter and the sense of a boss. 'When you hear your own fans singing things like that at the end of the game, then the players should be hurting,' he told the press. 'We've got to use this result as an example or an inspiration between now and the end of the season.'

The improvement was vivid. Leeds were only beaten once in a run that included eleven consecutive home wins, six goals from Becchio and eleven from Beckford; they went into the play-off semi-finals again in buoyant form. Millwall's New Den, however, was a venue made to burst dreams. Sam Sodje demonstrated the spirit Leeds now had; Millwall were fighting for a first-leg lead but he repelled them, then pushed his own dislocated shoulder back into place before repelling some more. But one half-chance was enough for Richard Harris; he shot past Ankergren, who was punched by Millwall supporters running on the pitch to celebrate.

Leeds had an intimidating stadium of their own for the second leg. 37,036 was almost three times the crowd at the New Den, underlining the absurdity of United's league status. But changing that depended on beating Millwall, and there were few chances to get the goal Leeds needed. Three minutes after half-time, Beckford missed one; he had scored 34 goals, but a poor penalty was easily saved. Leeds didn't give up. Four minutes later Ben Parker ran forward with the ball from left-back, passing wide to Andy Robinson via Beckford. Parker kept running, and Robinson passed into his run, behind two defenders and ahead of another. Becchio was well placed in the middle, and Parker's first touch was a low cross; now Becchio's position was unbelievable, and he bundled the ball in from close range; a counter-attacking goal, and a celebratory crescendo, as good as any in the Champions League.

Millwall were ineffective all night, but as Leeds pushed for a winner, naivety left them vulnerable; after twenty minutes of delirium, Jimmy Abdou scored from Millwall's only real chance. Leeds couldn't do any more.

'It's a bitter pill to swallow,' said Grayson. 'The players were outstanding tonight, we gave it a right go. It was a great atmosphere and the fans deserve to go up, but the players can be proud of what they've achieved. Since the day I walked through the door in December the fans have been with us every step of the way. I think the fans appreciate what we've done as a group, and that's how we will do it next year, by all sticking together as a group.'

He lost one significant player from the group. Fabian Delph was voted fans' Young Player of the Year and Players' Player of the Year for his 51 games in the heart of midfield; he won goal of the season for running from his own half at Brighton and hammering the ball into the top corner. Leeds fans hoped to see the team built around him; £6 million from Aston Villa took him to the Premier League.

'He didn't ask us for a transfer but he did make it clear that he would like a move to the Premier League. We didn't feel it was fair to stop him, so long as we got the right fee,' said Bates, who promised the fee would go into Grayson's 'fighting fund' for new players. 'Bradford City agreed a sell-on clause when they let Delph join us seven or eight years ago,' he added, 'so a big chunk of the money goes to them, and the full fee is obviously related to appearances and so on, which is standard practice these days. We'll use the money carefully.'

Delph's replacement was Michael Doyle, a 28-year-old on loan from Coventry; fans soon realised he wasn't going to hit many shots into the top corner, but Grayson was adept at finding and using players who could offer commitment above their ability. Patrick Kisnorbo dropped from the Championship to lead the promotion challenge alongside Naylor at the back. 'Having spoken to him, his desire and hunger is clear and he is just the type of character I want at the club,' said Grayson.

He was clear about his objective. 'We don't want another season in League One, and I'm well aware of that,' he said. 'I don't need to tell the players either. I followed the club through thick and thin for years, but I'm here now to be a successful manager, one who can take them back into the Championship. That has to be the target.'

Leeds started like a team that understood exactly what was required of them. Leeds won the first six league games, and two more in the League Cup, rivalling the start Revie's team made in 1973. A 2-1 defeat at Millwall was the only loss in the first 24 games; at the start of January Leeds were six points clear of Norwich City at the top of the table. Promotion looked a certainty, and Leeds added an FA Cup run that reminded the fans of what they were heading back up the leagues for, drawn away to Manchester United, the previous season's Premier League champions and Champions League runners-up. At Old Trafford on 3 January, a long pass by Howson found Jermaine Beckford; he miscontrolled as he took the ball down and past Wes Brown, but adjusted superbly to roll his finish into the far corner of the net. For the remaining 70 minutes Leeds defended with all the Leeds United-mindedness they could find, and Snodgrass hit the crossbar; Kisnorbo's bloody face, Naylor's tackling of striker Wayne Rooney and countless replays of Howson's pass, Beckford's goal and Grayson's wild celebration were symbols of a Leeds United renaissance.

There was more to come. Away to Tottenham in the fourth round, Leeds were 2-1 down in stoppage time when Dawson fouled Beckford in the penalty area; Beckford placed his shot into the top corner. In the replay Becchio kept hopes alive with an equaliser just before half-time, but Spurs scored twice in the second half to settle the match. But the 37,704 crowd, and the thousands who went to Old Trafford, had seen Leeds United truly competing with the best teams in the country for the first time in more than six years. It was a sign of how good Grayson's team could be, and of what was at stake.

It was also one of an increasing number of distractions. Leeds did well in another cup, the Johnstone's Paint Trophy, reaching the Northern Area final; winning would take them to Wembley, but it meant two intense matches against Carlisle, eventually lost on penalties. As in the old days, cup games were a disruptive strain.

Another problem was Jermaine Beckford. He was working fitting windscreens when Kevin Blackwell signed him from Wealdstone; the Championship was initially too much, but he became one of Leeds' most important players in League One. A twenty-goal season was followed by a 34-goal season and, in the summer, a transfer request; Beckford's late start as a professional meant he couldn't ignore interest from the Premier League that would make him financially secure for life. Nobody met United's asking price, but after his goal at Manchester United came a revelation; an angry reaction to being substituted had been the prelude to another transfer request, days before the match at Old Trafford. His performance in that game revealed the contradiction of Beckford's situation; he wanted to do his best for Leeds, but he also wanted the riches the Premier League offered.

Beckford soon withdrew the request. 'It was never a comfortable decision to ask for a transfer in the first place,' he said, but there was speculation he had signed an agreement to move to Everton in the summer, at the end of his contract. The situation was affecting both Beckford, who became a target for barracking from the fans, and the team, already distracted by the cups. After Old Trafford, Leeds drew 1-1 with Wycombe, followed by a 2-0 defeat at Exeter City; after the dramatic draw at Spurs, Leeds went to Swindon and lost 3-0. Norwich overtook them at the top of the league, and Charlton were closing in from third. Leeds lost four without scoring a goal, trying four different combinations of attackers, losing Kisnorbo to an Achilles injury. Before playing at Old Trafford, Leeds conceded thirteen goals in 23 games; in sixteen games afterwards they conceded 23, dropping away to 4th.

Leeds had to calm down and start scoring goals. Naylor led by example, scoring two from set-pieces in a 2-1 win at Yeovil Town; Max Gradel, an attacker signed from Leicester in the winter, was hardly a calming influence, but he helped Leeds, and Becchio, start scoring. It wasn't a complete solution; Leeds won three in a row, but lost 3-2 at Gillingham; MK Dons were beaten 4-1, but it took Beckford's two goals from the bench to make the game safe. Leeds got back up to 2nd, unable to catch champions Norwich, and still fighting Millwall, Swindon and Charlton for automatic promotion.

Leeds could have settled things away to Charlton; Millwall went two goals behind at Tranmere, and Grayson involved as many attackers as he could in the last half-hour at The Valley: Becchio, Gradel, Beckford, Sanchez Watt and Mike Grella were all on the pitch when, with three minutes left, Richard Naylor scored an own goal to give Charlton the points.

From being a winning goal away from promotion, Leeds went into the final match at home to Bristol Rovers knowing Millwall, Swindon or Charlton could overtake them. But a win would take Leeds up. Grayson had been ruthless with his team selections during the run in, and he was brave again now. Howson, the local midfielder rated as one of the best outside the Premier League, stayed on the bench. Snodgrass, whose talent could win any game, was dropped to substitute after 40 starts. Beckford hadn't started any of the previous four. He started now, and was made captain. His leadership skills were soon tested.

Gradel's success in attack was due to his unpredictability, but nobody expected his reaction to a foul by Bristol's Daniel Jones. The two began arguing, and Gradel leaned towards him, stamping on his foot; Jones fell to the floor miming a headbutt. Becchio scrapped with Jones, Beckford retrieved Gradel from a crowd of Bristol players, and after the mêlée the referee, Graham Salisbury, sent Gradel off. As Gradel realised what was happening the implications seemed to occur to him one after another, and he fought back, shoving Beckford, trying to get at the referee. Beckford pushed him away, Doyle dragged him away, Johnson took hold; after the intervention of security staff and a long lecture from Andrew Hughes, Gradel finally left the field, leaving the team to find some way of getting through the next hour without him.

A minute after half-time Jones' cross beyond the back post caught Leeds out, and Darryl Duffy scored. Grayson had to act, and took off full-back Shane Lowry, bringing on Howson. If he was looking for heroes, he found them. Within five minutes Becchio controlled Johnson's cross on the edge of the box, and laid the ball off; Howson cracked it first time into the top corner in front of the Kop. Leeds were back in the game; the 38,234 inside Elland Road knew it, every decibel proving it. Four minutes later, Johnson sharply intercepted a throw from Bristol's goalkeeper Mikkel Andersen; Becchio and Beckford were forward, and Johnson fired a cross low and hard across the six-yard box. A defender stretched his leg out to stop it reaching Becchio at the back post, but only sent the ball spinning into the air in front of Beckford; with Johnson already bouncing, ready to celebrate, Beckford buried the ball in the net, and for a few delirious minutes everything was forgiven: Beckford's moods, Gradel's tantrum, the play-off defeats, the relegations. None of it mattered, because United were going back, even if only back to the bare minimum of their history. Elland Road had known greater glories, but few moments like this.

There was still half an hour left, but if over the years Leeds felt like victims of higher forces they couldn't control, now Bristol Rovers were facing something they would never overcome. After Gradel's red card Simon Grayson told Daniel Jones, 'If we don't win, good luck getting off this pitch'; Leeds were going to win, and Jones was wise not to stick around anyway. The final whistle brought chaos and catharsis, and thousands of fans streaming onto the pitch; the public address system boomed warnings, but Leeds fans had long since stopped paying attention to the people in charge at Elland Road. They wanted Grayson, they wanted Snodin, they wanted Beckford and Howson; they found Andrew Hughes, the player who signed up for starting on minus fifteen, and held him aloft in front of the Kop. He was one of the team who got Leeds back, to start again.

2010–14

WHAT WE DO NOT HAVE
IS ENOUGH OF EVERYTHING

Simon Grayson joined Arthur Fairclough, Dick Ray, Raich Carter, Don Revie and Howard Wilkinson on the list of managers who won promotion at Leeds United, and there were good reasons to expect he could emulate them by adding a promotion to the top tier. Leeds had a core group of players coming into their best years – Jonny Howson, Bradley Johnson, Neil Kilkenny, Robert Snodgrass, Max Gradel – and they had momentum, with fans on their side.

Grayson's Leeds United-mind, developed as a fan, player and now manager, contributed to a togetherness that meant when players left, they left reluctantly; Jermaine Beckford went to Everton as expected, but spoke of his tears in the dressing room after promotion was achieved. 'I've enjoyed every single moment,' he said. 'The fans have been amazing, and they have opened up my eyes to what football should be about.' Andrew Hughes also left, realising he wouldn't be part of the team in the Championship: 'Andy Hughes isn't going to make Leeds United better,' he said. 'My wife's upset because she knows how much it has meant to me, to come and say that I played for Leeds United. Alright, it was a promotion from League One, but to say I did something for Leeds United that I set out to do from the start, and to do it in front of these fans, home and away, is the biggest honour. It's up there with the birth of my daughter.'

There were concerns about whether Luciano Becchio could make the step up in attack; transformed from the wispy mystery with long hair down his back who arrived in 2008, he became a physical fighter with a short back and sides, and bridged the gap; he scored twenty goals. Supporting him was Davide Somma, coming off the bench to score spectacular late volleys; but Ross McCormack, signed from Cardiff City for £350,000, didn't make much impact; and Billy Paynter, signed for free from Swindon Town to replace Beckford's goals, didn't score: he managed one.

The ageing defence was another worry, and Grayson added two full-backs, Paul Connolly and Fede Bessone, on free transfers, and two centre-backs, Neill Collins for

£500,000 and Alex Bruce for £300,000. Behind them was a new goalkeeper, signed for free from Notts County, but with pedigree and promise; Kasper Schmeichel was the son of former Manchester United goalkeeper Peter.

Despite the bonhomie, Grayson made clear he wasn't going to settle for less than an attempt at promotion; expectation was part of Leeds United. 'No one who started the game did himself any justice whatsoever,' he said after a 5-2 defeat at Barnsley. 'How our fans can cheer our players off amazes me after that. We brought 7,000, which is huge, and they were still singing and cheering.'

That scoreline was, however, typical; Leeds held a 4-1 lead over Preston North End in the 39th minute at Elland Road; by half-time it was 4-2, and by the end of the night, 4-6. 'I was lost for words,' said Grayson. 'Ashamed.' A 4-0 defeat at Cardiff City was just as shameful, and even when Leeds won or drew, the problems were obvious; 3-2, 2-2 and 3-3 were common, and Michael Doyle, the largely unloved midfielder on loan during the previous season, was badly missed.

Despite the fragility, Leeds progressed. They were unbeaten through November and December, and when league leaders Queens Park Rangers came to Elland Road on a cold afternoon just before Christmas, the 29,426 crowd warmed themselves by twirling scarves, chanting: 'We are the Champions, Champions of Europe' as Gradel scored twice in a superb 2-0 win. QPR manager Neil Warnock didn't appreciate the atmosphere, or the players' response: 'Their celebrations in the tunnel were a bit over the top,' he said. 'They've not won promotion yet. With those celebrations, you'd think they were already there.' Grayson simply observed that Leeds could still get relegated, adding: 'We have a high expectancy level at this club: our fans want and expect the best.'

The fans wanted and expected new signings in January; only around a million had been spent during the summer, and the £6 million received for Fabian Delph was still, as far as anybody knew, in what Ken Bates called 'Simon's fighting fund'. Second in the league at Christmas was surely the time to fight. Andy O'Brien, an experienced centre-back, made his loan move permanent, but the only other arrivals were loans, while Bates became involved in arguments about contracts for two leading players; Johnson and Kilkenny insisted they were asking for reasonable pay rises, given interest from other clubs. 'I really want to stay here and feel honoured to play for the club,' said Kilkenny. 'I want to let that be known. I've made nearly 150 appearances and that's really a very good record over three seasons. Hopefully, the club can sort something out.'

Grayson said later that he had defenders ready to come, but the club didn't complete the deals; what happened next was predictable. Leeds stayed in the top six until four games from the end, but finished 7th, three points behind Nottingham Forest. Their last match was away to QPR, where Leeds won 2-1, but Neil Warnock was celebrating after winning the league.

'You don't like to come to a football ground and see another team celebrate,' said Grayson. 'You want to be celebrating on your ground, and hopefully this time next year we might be the team doing that. You have to have people who can handle pressure situations, who when things are maybe not going right, can stick together. We are a young group and it wasn't for the want of trying that we weren't able to find that person – someone like a Gordon Strachan, or a Billy Bremner-type – to come in and really dig in and take the responsibility on their shoulders and drive other players on.'

Instead, there were more departures. Kilkenny left for Bristol City, and Johnson went to the Premier League with Norwich City; Schmeichel made an unexpected move to Leicester City, for £1 million. Even he was surprised: 'I have never asked to leave, nor did I reject an offer for a new contract, since one was never put to me,' he said.

Their replacements were Michael Brown, a 34-year-old midfielder on a free transfer, and two new goalkeepers, Paul Rachubka for free and Andy Lonergan for £200,000. Bates had told fans since before relegation to League One that if they wanted Premier League football, they would have to 'pay premier prices'; United's season tickets were well above the average Premier

League price, but there was little sign of the money being invested in players. Fans still pointed to the money received for Delph, and windfalls from FA Cup matches against Premier League teams.

When building work began over the summer, adding executive boxes and new offices to the East Stand, fans' anger with Bates boiled over; there were protests at the first match of the season. 'I'm unimpressed by the demonstrations of a few morons,' said Bates. 'The rebuilding of Leeds United is a bit like sex. In an age of instant gratification, Leeds United is having a long, drawn out affair with plenty of foreplay and slow arousal.' Such outbursts were now typical; fans who questioned Bates' ownership were also 'sickpots' and 'dissidents'; he was found to have used the match programme to libel and harass former director Melvyn Levi, printing his home address. Chief executive Shaun Harvey admitted in court that the club were 'spending a fortune on legal fees' as a result of Bates' programme notes.

Another case brought sharp attention onto Bates. His solicitors said in court that Bates and his adviser, Patrick Murrin, were joint owners of Forward Sports Fund, owner of Leeds United, a company incorporated in the Cayman Islands. Five months later Bates swore in an affidavit that the previous information was 'an error on my part'; a letter from Château Fiduciaire, Geneva-based administrators of FSF, said there were 10,000 shares in FSF, none owned by Bates or any Leeds United director.

When the *Guardian* asked who the shareholders were, Château Fiduciaire told them: 'It is not necessary for you to have that information.'

That was the line Bates and Harvey stuck to through the newspaper and parliamentary investigations that followed. Football governance was a political topic and United's high-profile administration and obscure offshore ownership put the club at the centre of attention. In summer 2010 the club published an 'ownership statement' to comply with Football League rules, stating that none of the offshore trusts' owners had rights to more than 10 per cent of shares, and so did not have to pass the League's 'fit and proper' test for club owners. Documents at Companies House revealed more of the story; a complex structure of holding companies stretching back to Road Town in Tortola, where Noel Lloyd's statue commemorated that island ridding itself of Ken Bates.

At a parliamentary inquiry in March 2011, Harvey gave evidence as a late replacement for Bates, and said he did not know the identities of the ultimate beneficiary owners of Leeds United. Harvey and Bates didn't know who they were working for, and Harvey didn't view that as unusual, or something that should interest the fans. 'We're 5th in the league, and everyone seems to be happy with how the club is progressing,' he said.

That was not strictly true. In 2008 the club failed to buy back Thorp Arch at £5.8 million before the deadline for that agreement; Fabian Delph had just been sold, but the club was depending on a loan from Leeds City Council, and Bates complained bitterly when the deal collapsed. The main problem, from the council's point of view, was loaning such a large amount of public money if they didn't know who they were loaning it to. When United looked close to promotion in spring 2011, the Premier League made clear it would want more assurances about ownership than the Football League, and Bates relented; he announced he had bought FSF's shareholding and now owned the club, but not who he bought it from, or how much he paid.

Similar problems slowed the grant of planning permission for Bates' scheme to replicate Stamford Bridge's 'Chelsea Village' at Elland Road. Nobody knew who owned the stadium; only that it was an offshore company, also registered in Tortola. The works in summer 2011 were a small part of the overall scheme, but United's accounts showed £5 million of future season ticket income mortgaged and put towards building, while little was spent on the team. The accounts also showed that, since 2007, the only money invested by FSF was £500,000 to buy Leeds United out of administration; gate receipts paid by supporters since came to £42,410,000, and they wanted their money spent on players.

The war of words intensified as the 2011/12 season began. Bates' attempts to control media coverage, banning critical newspapers and refusing to engage beyond scripted interviews on Yorkshire Radio, or frequently offensive programme notes, fuelled the counter-arguments across social media, blogs and in fanzines like *The Square Ball*. The Leeds United Supporters' Trust was a focal point for a growing campaign against Bates' ownership, and after the protest by about 500 fans at the first game of the season, Bates didn't hold back. 'Bring back both corporal and capital punishment, slash benefits, and put single mothers into hostels instead of giving them council flats,' he wrote, just part of a bizarre rant. 'This is a rather long way of saying that I am unimpressed by the demonstrations of a few morons last Saturday and ain't going anywhere soon.'

At the end of August, Max Gradel was sold to Saint-Étienne for £2.3 million; his replacement was Danny Pugh, the utility defender who was once part of Alan Smith's transfer to Manchester United. Grayson no longer hid his frustration, although he stopped short of criticising his employer; despite the good form of Ross McCormack and Robert Snodgrass, he couldn't lift Leeds into the play-off positions. The players were struggling; Paul Rachubka had to be substituted at half-time in a 5-0 defeat to Blackpool at Elland Road. Grayson wanted to replace the whole lot after a 4-1 defeat at Barnsley: 'Embarrassing, shambolic,' he said. 'When you play for Leeds United you have to earn the right to wear the shirt. Too many of them didn't do that.'

However, there was a hint of what the team was capable of, and the bond that still existed between players and fans, in a 4-0 win at Nottingham Forest. Promotion and title-winning midfielder Gary Speed had died days earlier, aged just 42, and Snodgrass opened the scoring at Forest at the end of eleven emotional minutes of the fans singing Gary Speed's name, a rare and welcome moment of poetry.

Bitterness soon returned. The sale of club captain Jonny Howson, following Bradley Johnson to Norwich for £2 million, was the sale of a local boy, a valued Thorp Arch academy graduate, an improving player and a key part of the team. From being one or two additions short of promotion to the Premier League, Grayson's team was being dismantled from above, and there were fears Snodgrass, McCormack and midfielder Adam Clayton would leave in the summer. There wouldn't be much left. Delph returned seeking fitness on a short-term loan, but he was a reminder of what Leeds were letting go; Bates justified the lack of signings by claiming Leeds hadn't received as much money from transfers as fans thought, blaming the exchange rate for reducing the value of Gradel's transfer to France.

Grayson initially backed Howson's transfer, but said later that he had only agreed to it if he was given the transfer fee to spend. A week after Howson left, Grayson was told that Robbie Rogers, an American international signing for free, was all he was getting;

arguments followed, as did the closure of the transfer window on 31 January. Leeds lost 4-1 that night at home to Birmingham City, and a statement was placed on the club website the next day, announcing Leeds had 'dispensed with the services of Simon Grayson and his coaching staff'.

Protests against Bates restarted in earnest. Leeds United Supporters' Trust began a 'Campaign for Change', explaining how, with reference to the club's history and resources, Leeds United ought to be run and implying that if Bates couldn't do it, he should find someone who could. Before a game against Brighton & Hove Albion, more than 1,000 fans marched from City Square, through Holbeck to Elland Road, and the East Stand's new corporate facilities; only 23,171 watched the game, and given the fans' reputation for acquiescence since the raucous early meetings at Salem Hall in 1919, the march was a significant statement. Bates responded by attacking LUST's chairman, Gary Cooper, in the programme, and banning the group's board from buying tickets; Shaun Harvey made his attitude to criticism clear, telling the Football Supporters' Federation that 'players play, managers manage, and supporters support'.

Into all this came Neil Warnock: former manager of, among others, Huddersfield Town, Sheffield United and QPR, star of several behind-the-scenes documentaries about old-school football management, gifted at delivering controversy and quotes, but not necessarily at producing attractive football. He had been sacked from QPR after rediscovering his taste for the limelight in the Premier League, and Bates persuaded Warnock, now 63, he could get back into the Premier League by taking Leeds there; the play-offs were not yet out of reach. 'We believe the appointment is arguably the most important we have made,' said Bates, but despite talk about long-term ambition, Warnock's contract at Leeds was for just fifteen months, with a break clause after three.

He may have wished he'd used it. Warnock's basic style of launching the ball into the penalty area brought just three wins, and Leeds finished 14th, far from the play-offs; a 7-3 defeat at home to Nottingham Forest helped Warnock realise what the previous lack of invest-ment had left him with. After a 2-0 defeat to Derby County he told their manager, Nigel Clough: 'Enjoy this Nigel, because you'll never ever see another Leeds United team or a Neil Warnock team like this'; but a 2-0 defeat at Watford was arguably even worse. 'What we are miss-ing are quality players,' said Warnock. 'What we do not have is enough of everything. We have not got enough guts, quality and desire. You name it and we do not have it.'

Robert Snodgrass, captain since Howson was sold and wanted by Premier League clubs, was sceptical. 'As a footballer everything here is first class. I love where I live, the only thing missing is the Premier League,' he said. But, he said: 'We're missing Howson. It's weird that we never replaced him. How can you say you're aiming for promotion and then sell your captain?'

He repeated his concerns in the summer. 'The chairman is trying to put a bit of pressure on me,' he told the *Scotsman*. 'He's telling me what plans he has got for the club. But they told me the same type of plans the season before and it didn't work out. So it's hard to buy into these things again.' Warnock wanted to keep him, but Snodgrass was wary. 'He's already said he won't be sticking around as manager for much longer. Who knows whether he's got one or two more years left at Leeds? My future doesn't lie in the hands of Neil Warnock, it's in the hands of Robert Snodgrass.'

The future of Leeds United lay in the hands of Ken Bates, but with a twist; on 29 May, the club confirmed it was in talks with an investor. Information from the club was minimal, but pointed to a takeover. Consortia from Canada were linked; a group of Americans were seen touring Thorp Arch; the Information Affairs Authority of Bahrain claimed Sheikh Abdulrahman bin Mubarak al-Khalifa, the fan who had tried to bid in 2004, was 'involved in a takeover bid for the club with financial investors'. As summer wore on, the Middle East became the most likely source.

The process drove supporters to distraction, and almost drove Warnock out of the club. It was the end for Snodgrass; during the pre-season tour of Warnock's

favourite haunts in Devon and Cornwall, his patience
ran out and he left, a third player joining Norwich, for
£3 million. Warnock was frustrated but pressed on. 'I've
always been trying to sign Luke Varney for that role,'
he said, and he got him, for £300,000 from financially
stricken Portsmouth. The takeover meant transfers
were difficult, and Warnock was relying on experienced
players; 36-year-old Michael Brown, a favourite from
Sheffield United, signed a new contract, and eleven new
signings were 29 or older, including Frank Gray's son
Andy returning, controversial former Bolton Wanderers
striker El-Hadji Diouf, and 34-year-old goalkeeper
Paddy Kenny, for £400,000, whom Warnock was signing
for the fourth time. There were two academy graduates
to lower the average age; Tom Lees was a stern central defender in his second season, and right-back Sam
Byram started with an outstanding pre-season and ended
with the Player, Young Player and Players' Player of the
Year awards.

How Warnock's team would work on the pitch was
secondary while the takeover dragged on. Three days
before the season started, Shaun Harvey was in Monaco
with Ken Bates, trying to complete the deal before the
end of the exclusivity period; he failed, and rumours said
Bates' intransigence was causing the delay. The *Yorkshire
Evening Post* was told the deal 'isn't definitely on but
isn't definitely off either', and fans posted pens to Ken
Bates, encouraging him to sign the contracts and go.

It took until late November. The new owners, revealed over several weeks by long-lens photographs of the Elland Road director's box, messages on social media and statements to the Bahrain stock exchange, were Gulf Finance House Capital, a subsidiary of private equity investment firm Gulf Finance House. The group, and their main representatives Hisham Alrayes, Salem Patel and David Haigh, had no track record in football, but at 10.30pm on 20 November 2012 the deal was done; GFH-C announced they were buying Leeds United from Ken Bates – and keeping him as chairman. At the end of the season Bates would become club president; Shaun Harvey was staying as chief executive. 'Nothing has changed,' said Bates.

There were hopes that investment might follow in January to at least change the dire football, but instead of £8 million of new signings as rumoured, Warnock did yet another deal with Norwich City that almost seemed motivated by spite; hard work and sharp finishing made Luciano Becchio the first player since the Revie era to be added to the club's top ten league goalscorers, but he wasn't committed enough for Warnock's liking. There was interest from other clubs, that interested Becchio, but he had scored nineteen goals in the first half of the season, and a new contract seemed a more sensible idea than exchanging him for Norwich's Steve Morison and £200,000, which is what Warnock did. 'He'll be a legend here in a few years,' Warnock said of Morison. 'The fans will love him to bits and say, "Bloody hell, that was one of Warnock's signings."' Morison scored three goals, and Warnock later said: 'The final straw was losing Becchio. After Becchio went we scored eleven goals in thirteen games.'

Belligerence came easily to Warnock at Leeds. An FA Cup match with Birmingham brought just 11,447 to Elland Road. 'One or two people have been going on about the style of football over the past few weeks,' said Warnock, 'but that's rubbish.' As a game at Middlesbrough dragged towards a 0-0 draw, the away fans chanted for substitutions; Warnock applauded sarcastically, and Middlesbrough promptly scored, sending him scrambling for changes, too late. In his final match, at Elland Road against Derby County, Warnock's tired refrains about Paddy Kenny, Michael Brown and Luke Varney were sung back at him from the Kop: 'Can't fault their effort, they're a great bunch of lads.' Ross McCormack, a frustrated substitute, showed his feelings when he came off the bench and scored; he yelled at Warnock to 'fuck off'. Leeds lost 2-1. Warnock was sacked.

Brian McDermott, a quietly spoken former scout who had managed Reading to promotion from the Championship, was appointed before the summer as a contrast to Warnock, and GFH-C began dismantling Bates' work; with every announcement, the mood of the fans lifted. Shaun Harvey left; Gwyn Williams, the

sporting director Grayson blamed for stopping transfers, was dismissed; weeks after assuming the role, Ken
Bates 'ceased to be President of Leeds United Football
Club', a dispute over a private jet giving GFH-C a reason to break the deal. Leeds signed Luke Murphy, the
first £1 million transfer since August 2005, and in bright
sunshine on the opening day of the season, as Elland
Road celebrated Bates' demise, Murphy scored a last-
minute winner.

The joy did not last. As part of a charm offensive,
GFH-C were meeting and talking to fans, but these were
strange conversations. One supporter had to explain the
FA's new rules about youth academies; others received
text messages with lists of potential signings, asking
for advice. The front man, David Haigh, used a separate public relations company and had his own website,
listing his favourite Leeds matches; most of the games
dated from before he was born. Where he was born was
another question; he told the *Daily Mail* it was 'Beeston,
a stone's throw from Elland Road', but fans uncovered
birth records that said Salford; his personal website,
meanwhile, said he was from Cornwall, and had 'never
lived anywhere that wasn't walking distance from the
beach'. The inconsistencies accumulated, from gaps in
his employment record to his bizarre claim about managing a branch of McDonald's when he was sixteen.

Haigh and Patel were promoting their ownership as
a rejection of Leeds' recent past under Bates, asking fans

to trust them with the club's future, but Gulf Finance House's story wasn't adding up either. A 2010 report by three academics at Reading University analysed GFH's work before the 2008 credit crisis, describing their business model as 'highly questionable' as it was based on taking profits in fees at the start of projects, rather than waiting for investments to pay off. GFH's financial statements described Leeds as a 'bargain purchase', saying: 'The group has an active plan to sell its stake in LUFC Holdings,' and has 'commenced negotiations relating to the sale of its stake.'

Haigh and Patel insisted this meant investment, not another takeover; soon 10 per cent of the club went to International Investment Bank, and 3.33 per cent to IIB's former employee Salah Nooruddin, who was named chairman, did a video interview, and disappeared. In his place came more takeover speculation, as new company names were added to an already confusing situation, and at the end of November there was a typical contribution from Salem Patel: he posted a smiley face on Twitter, prelude to a statement from GFH-C that confirmed David Haigh was attempting to buy the club.

Haigh's consortium, Sport Capital, said they intended to appoint Lucas Radebe as 'international ambassador'; an early sign of confusion, as Radebe was already fronting another consortium with former Sunderland marketing director Mike Farnan. As managing director with the inside track, and backing from club sponsor

Enterprise Insurance, Haigh confidently promised a quick deal and funds for the January transfer window. But after two months nothing was concluded, and at the end of January 2014 Haigh announced his backers had pulled out, although he hoped for new ones.

The next night, a Friday, as fans were settling down to watch coverage of the last hours of the transfer window on television, checking Twitter for updates on the rapidly developing takeover and hoping Ross McCormack would not be sold before Saturday's home match against Huddersfield Town, news broke from Elland Road: Massimo Cellino, owner of Serie A club Cagliari, was in the building, and he'd sacked Brian McDermott.

2014–17

I THOUGHT I KNEW EVERYTHING ABOUT FOOTBALL

Massimo Cellino had owned Cagliari for 22 years, and at first his interest in Leeds United looked like the latest part of a long-running battle with local authorities over Cagliari's stadium; he had moved home games to Trieste, 500 miles away, while the fans hung banners around Sardinia reading '*Cellino Vattene*' – 'Cellino Get Out' – and 'We have no stadium, you have no dignity.' After Cagliari lost a match in January, he stormed away to his second home in Miami, local newspaper *L'Unione Sarda* reporting that he was ready to buy Leeds.

He had been interested in English clubs before; an attempt to buy West Ham United was blocked by the FA, and he met Sheffield Wednesday's owners before becoming part of David Haigh's consortium to buy Leeds. He toured Thorp Arch in October, then split from Haigh to make his own bid. The ten days between *L'Unione Sarda*'s report and the end of January were frantic, as Haigh and Mike Farnan's consortia reacted to news that Cellino had jumped the queue, and former Cagliari coach Gianluca Festa was shadowing Brian McDermott at the training ground. Festa was refused permission to go in the dugout for a match against Ipswich Town, but on Friday afternoon a text message from Salah Nooruddin let Cellino believe he could do what he liked: 'Congratulation [sic]. You are now the new owner of Leeds.' Within hours he was at the stadium, and McDermott received a phone call from Cellino's lawyers, telling him he was sacked.

Amid the hourly speculation about the takeover, the football had been forgettable. After a bright start McDermott struggled to get a better style from what were mostly Warnock's players; one positive was Ross McCormack, who scored 28 goals, winning points for the team almost on his own. McDermott was desperate for attackers, but was refused permission to sign Ashley Barnes from Brighton after Gulf Finance House checked his profile on the *Football Manager* video game, and concluded he was no better than Luke Varney. McDermott did acquire two wingers, Jimmy Kébé and Cameron Stewart, and a centre-back, Marius Žaliūkas, but the results were two embarrassments: a 2-0 defeat in the FA Cup away to Third Division Rochdale, and a 6-0 loss to Sheffield Wednesday at Hillsborough; at that game, GFH-C talked about sacking McDermott during the half-time break.

Cellino hadn't sacked him for football reasons, though; he didn't like what McDermott said in the press about managing through the takeover. 'I don't know Brian but he was talking with the papers, with everyone, which was not fair,' said Cellino. 'In the end we didn't have any choice – he did everything to get fired. He started arguments with everyone and made it impossible.' Complaints about the presence of Festa were believed to be the catalyst.

Not many people saw McDermott that way. His grace under pressure kept a lot of fans, despairing at the football, on his side. Friday night descended into chaos. Acting chief executive Paul Hunt was also sacked, David Haigh resigned as managing director, sponsors Enterprise Insurance – who were part of Haigh's bid – and Flamingo Land withdrew support. Ross McCormack telephoned Sky Sports News to state his support for McDermott, adding what many interpreted as a transfer request; midfielder Andrea Tabanelli arrived days after signing for Cagliari, Danilo Avelar's move from Cagliari fell through, and angry fans descended on Elland Road, blocking exits and chasing Cellino in his taxi as it lapped the stadium, trying to find a way out.

Cagliari's fans raised a collective, sympathetic

eyebrow. In Italy Cellino was nicknamed the 'Manager Eater' after changing managers 35 times in 22 years; at the start of his ownership Cagliari had reached the UEFA Cup semi-finals, but there were few highlights after that, as the team bounced between Serie A and Serie B, and the fans argued about Cellino's behaviour. He inherited his wealth from the family grain business, but was isolated from the company after being accused of defrauding the European Union of several million euros; he was convicted of false accounting relating to Cagliari's transfer of Daniel Fonseca, and spent several days in jail over the disputes about the stadium. An arrest warrant in 2013 described him as a man 'of marked criminal tendencies – capable of using every kind of deception to achieve his ends'. And yet, for all the trouble, he was popular with some who saw him as an anti-establishment rebel; tying a bandana into his thick hair, he played guitar with his band, Maurilios, performing covers of AC/DC and Jimi Hendrix, but not Deep Purple; purple, and the number seventeen, were unlucky according to Cellino's strong superstitions.

The weeks after 'Mad Friday' were not much calmer; McDermott was reinstated, but stayed away from the next day's 5-1 win over Huddersfield Town, McCormack scoring a defiant hat-trick. GFH-C confirmed they were selling 75 per cent of the club to Cellino's company Eleonora Sport Ltd, but the sale remained subject to the Football League confirming Cellino passed their 'owners and directors test'. His previous convictions were considered 'spent' according to the rules, and he was expected to pass; but in mid-March there was a new conviction, for evading Italian import tax on a yacht brought from Miami. He had been ready to sell Cagliari, but changed his mind: 'When I realised that the team needed me,' he said, 'I came back.' But he was saying different things in different countries; in England: 'There is only one place in my heart for one club and that is Leeds. When I get the right offer I will sell Cagliari.' In Italy: 'If you were to ask me who I would choose between Cagliari and Leeds, I answer Cagliari all my life.' His mind was made up when an independent review overturned the Football League's block; on 8 April 2014, Cellino left Cagliari for Leeds.

He made plenty of promises. 'I don't want to make promises I can't keep,' he said, 'and I admit it will be difficult to get promotion next season. But in 2015/16 we will earn our way back to the Premier League, which is where Leeds belong.' In the days after Mad Friday he had been ready to move fast: 'On Thursday I am going to the bank and I will buy our stadium. I have the funds to buy Leeds and to run Leeds. A club like Leeds has big potential. I want to see Leeds United versus Manchester United like it used to be. I want to make the fans happy. I know what it means to be a fan.'

Cellino celebrated his takeover, taking the stage at the end-of-season dinner with local band The Pigeon

Detectives and partying through the weekend with nightclub owner Terry George. His three children, Edoardo, Ercole and Eleonora, soon joined in the fun, the two sons taking up senior but obscure roles at the club; Ercole's contribution to the takeover was writing 'Cringe – ugly. You make puke!' beneath photos of Mike Farnan's daughter on Instagram. When Ken Bates took over in 2005, he promised 'a lorra lorra laughs'. It felt like Cellino might finally deliver them.

'I'm dying,' he told ITV two weeks later, in a bout of dramatic self-pity that revealed his true tone. Owning Leeds United was hard, and the years that followed were spent trying to find the party, when all he had was the hangover. The club, he said, was like an over-loaded aeroplane, a 747 or 'even bigger', that he was trying to push along the runway; 'I'm down there,' he said. 'You just try to imagine myself down on the floor on the ground, pushing this plane full of people and luggage. And I'm dying.' He didn't know where Brian McDermott was. 'Brian. Where's Brian? I sent a letter to Brian – help us.'

McDermott was, as the club was aware, with his mother, who was ill; he eventually left Leeds at the end of May, after Cellino returned from his own trip to Miami, apparently more contrite now. 'I did not fully understand the mess [Brian] had to work in, and the broken promises he had to deal with, until I have got involved trying to turn Leeds around,' he said.

McDermott had never been Cellino's biggest problem. The problem was that Cellino rushed into his deal with GFH-C without doing due diligence, and now he had seen 'the mess', he didn't know how to get out of it. In their brief time in charge a £15 million debt was added to the balance sheet, payable to GFH-C; in the months before the takeover, they had stopped funding the club, leaving it threatened by winding-up orders for unpaid bills, some of the largest from David Haigh. Haigh was soon involved in his own predicament; after being interviewed by police in Leeds amid rumours of spy cameras in the Elland Road boardroom, he flew to Dubai, expecting to discuss a new role with GFH-C. He was arrested in their offices and jailed, accused of defrauding millions from GFH-C but held without charge, in atrocious conditions, for more than a year. He was convicted of 'breach of trust' but denied any wrongdoing.

Without personal wealth to pay the debts off, Cellino's recourse was to cut costs, attempt to renegotiate with GFH-C, and hope his experience of Italian football would translate to the Championship and Leeds would be promoted; the Premier League offered broadcasting revenue and prize money that would wipe out United's debts at a stroke. At a press conference to present McDermott's replacement, Cellino boasted of his own credentials. 'I know Maradona personally, I know van Basten, Gullit, I know all these people, that is my life,' he said. But the new head coach sitting next to him was Dave Hockaday, who in his only managerial job had taken Forest Green Rovers to the bottom of the Conference Premier. Nobody knew who he was or where Cellino found him, but he seemed confident. 'My journey has not just involved Forest Green,' Hockaday said. 'I've been at other clubs and I'm sure you'll do your homework.' To everyone's surprise, he said getting the Leeds job was not a surprise to him, and after his first day of training he announced: 'I've got myself back in the groove, and I'm raring to go. The king is dead, long live the king.'

The king lasted 70 days, six matches, one league win; Cellino sacked him, and published an apology in the matchday programme. The new coach was Darko Milanič, manager of Austrian club Sturm Graz. 'I don't know why I've chosen him,' said Cellino. 'Coaches are like watermelons. You only find out about them when you open them up. His particular qualities? He's good looking, what can I tell you?' Milanic was the handsome but silent type; after six games but no wins in 32 days, with barely a word to anybody, he was sacked. 'I made a mistake with this guy,' said Cellino.

The mistakes on the football side were a serious problem. After a public spat with Ross McCormack, that Cellino admitted was for 'my satisfaction', the striker went to Fulham for £11 million, that was spent on eighteen new players, most from Serie B, that Cellino later regretted; the money 'went all on the garbage', he said. He assumed Serie B was equivalent to the Championship, but the players were out of their depth. Cellino's third manager was the long-serving head of academy Neil Redfearn, who focused on a group of young players he brought through the junior teams: Sam Byram, Lewis Cook, Alex Mowatt and Charlie Taylor. There were signs of improvement; Leeds won eight of twelve games at the start of 2015.

But Cellino's cost-cutting hit Thorp Arch hard. The swimming pool was empty, the cleaning and kitchen staff were dismissed, players were bringing packed lunches and Redfearn had a first team staff of one, his assistant Steve Thompson, only granted after several weeks working alone. Thompson was soon sacked over an obscure disagreement with Cellino's sporting director, Nicola Salerno, and the team lost the next five matches; before the last, at Charlton, six of Cellino's signings claimed to be injured and withdrew from the squad, causing bitter arguments with supporters who accused them of disrespecting Leeds United.

Cellino had, by this time, been banned by the Football League from owning Leeds again. Another ruling on his yacht tax case came from Italy, calling it a 'Machiavellian simulation'; an initial three-month ban was extended to the end of the season, and Cellino said he wouldn't come back. In May, he came back, with Adam Pearson as his new chief executive, a former commercial director of Leeds who had wisely left before the recklessness of the Champions League season took hold. It was hoped he would be a steadying influence, but at a summer press conference, Cellino went even further out of control.

For an hour Pearson sat with a face like thunder, as Cellino thundered forth; even a cigarette break didn't calm him down. He was angry, apparently jealous of the relationship between the fans and Neil Redfearn, who grew up as a Leeds fan in the 1970s and now seemed to be inspiring a positive future from the academy, as Eddie Gray had. 'Who put Neil Redfearn in that position?' demanded Cellino. 'Me. I did it. Who wants Neil to succeed more than anyone else? It was me. It's me. Because it was my choice. I take the risk.'

After a year of fighting GFH-C and the Football League, Cellino wanted more of the credit, and more of the love. He brought film star Verne Troyer to a match, but the fans weren't impressed; he cooked a pre-match meal for the players, but all Terry George's video captured was a group of frowning, confused footballers. While he was banned, he said: 'I never heard [from] anyone, no one called me. When I got back my employees made a little champagne glass to welcome me back, I was touched. But Neil was not there.' He was angry with Redfearn, and angry with the fans who exchanged the 'Leeds Salute' with their favourite. 'Less touching the crest!' yelled Cellino. 'And start putting the money! ...

Tell them to start to buy season tickets! Then we talk about the club!' He carried on in the *Daily Mirror*. 'Redfearn tried to play the fans against me to keep his place,' he said. 'Do you think that Neil Redfearn loves Leeds more than me?'

Redfearn was sacked, as was his wife Lucy Ward; a former Leeds United Ladies player, Ward was with the club for seventeen years, and as head of education at the academy helped the personal development of James Milner, Fabian Delph, Jonny Howson, Sam Byram and more, whether they'd made it in football or not. She held the academy together as Cellino's cuts took hold; in his paranoia, Cellino decided Ward's relationship with Redfearn meant he had to sack them both, a decision that cost Leeds £290,000 in a sex discrimination case.

Expensive court cases were costing the club dear, as all Cellino's attempts to 'fix the club' only caused more problems, as if he didn't already have enough. Autumn came, and another conviction for another tax offence, this time over a Range Rover, meaning Cellino was disqualified from owning Leeds for a third time; he appealed, so he could carry on, but how much further would Leeds have to carry him?

A new manager, Uwe Rösler, had been and gone after twelve games. His replacement was Steve Evans, a lower league manager with convictions of his own; he won promotion at Boston United after signing players on higher wages than their competitors could pay, funded by not paying the tax and national insurance required. He was given a suspended jail sentence after his defence counsel told the judge: 'He is terrified of spending one day in prison.' The first thing he wanted to do at Leeds, he said, was make other teams terrified of playing there: 'Let's get Elland Road into a place where everyone fears going. It's seven months since the supporters saw their team win there.' He would change that, he said, but Blackburn Rovers didn't get the message before Evans' first home match. They took the lead after seventeen seconds, scored again in the sixth minute, and had no problem keeping their 2-0 lead to the end.

The fans sang 'Massimo, time to go,' and two days later he offered to sell the entire club to Leeds Fans United, a supporters' group trying to buy a stake; when they took him at his word and started producing funds, he changed his mind. Instead, Cellino put a £5 charge on tickets for the South Stand, where singing against him was loudest; you got a voucher for a pie, but you didn't get a choice, and in a filmed interview over a bottle of wine in Sardinia, he admitted it was a punishment. Sam Byram, the home-grown full-back central to the fans' affections, was sold to West Ham United for £3.7 million in January, Cellino claiming to be 'hurt inside' by the player: 'He maybe thinks he deserves to be in a bigger team and a bigger club, and maybe he's right'; Lewis Cook went in the summer, to Bournemouth for £7 million. In between, protests against Cellino started in earnest: 'Time to go, Massimo' became the rallying cry of a group that projected the case against him in a huge light display on the side of the East Stand.

Something had to give, and it seemed to be Cellino's spirit. The promises and boasts were gone. 'I do not want Premier League football; I wish for it,' he said. 'I am very superstitious. If you want something in football you never get it. If you wish for something then you get it.' That was his best plan now; wishing for success, and finding someone in the summer to replace Steve Evans, not even waiting to sack him first. Evans clung on, hoping to stay, while Cellino flew to Italy in search of a new manager. 'I have a good feeling,' he said. 'I can not make a mistake this time. My players need someone special.' He was clear about what he didn't want: 'I cannot work with English managers,' he said. 'I never want to learn. I give up.'

Naturally he hired an English manager, but there was something different about Garry Monk. If not something special, he at least had pedigree; as a centre-back for Swansea City, he rose from League Two to the Premier League, becoming captain as managers Roberto Martinez and Brendan Rodgers associated Swansea with fluent, attacking football. Monk took over as manager, taking them to 8th in the Premier League. A difficult start to the next season had cost his job, but many looked at Monk and thought him too good for Cellino's inevitable mistreatment.

Cellino, however, had other things on his mind. A short statement in September was significant: 'The club is delighted to confirm that Leeds United Football Club is now 100 per cent owned by Eleonora Sport Limited, it having purchased all of the shares previously held by GFH Capital.' It had taken 30 months, but Cellino finally 'fixed' GFH-C; they were still owed £17 million, but they no longer had a say. That left Cellino clear to seek new investment, which added to the constant state of takeover speculation that had burdened United for more than a decade, but proceeded without any repeat of 'Mad Friday' or flirtation with administration; the only interruptions were the conclusions of yet more court cases, and yet another ban; eighteen months, for making illegal payments to an agent. 'I feel that I am guilty of one thing,' said Cellino. 'Protecting Leeds United since I took charge of the club.'

It was left to another Italian businessman, Andrea Radrizzani, to talk about the future. Radrizzani had recently sold most of his stake in sports media agency MP & Silva, where he became wealthy buying and selling sports media rights, and announced he was buying 50 per cent of Leeds in January, with an option for the rest in June. 'Leeds are exciting,' he said. 'They are a sleeping giant as everyone knows. Probably the only big brand left in English football that could grow in terms of value.'

Supporters didn't appreciate hearing Leeds United called a 'brand', but it reflected Radrizzani's background, and the way football had changed, with broadcasting revenue much more valuable than gate receipts. It also reflected the club Radrizzani was buying into. Cellino's day-to-day running of Leeds United was horrendous, a nightmare clash of his fragile ego, explosive temper, a history of litigation he could not shed, and a failure to look properly into what Ken Bates and Gulf Finance House had done to the club he was buying; a two-and-a-half-year expression of buyer's remorse. He cut everything there was to cut, argued with everybody there was to argue with, and at times made a once proud club a laughing stock; it was unforgivable. The club was still losing more money than Cellino could cope with, but he hadn't destroyed it. He had to keep the club alive to save himself, and had found a way to make GFH-C's claims manageable, so someone else could do what he could not: run Leeds United properly. Elland Road was empty, cold and dark for much of Cellino's time in charge, fans choosing to stay away rather than watch Steve Evans' version of football. But you could still imagine it full.

Early in Garry Monk's tenure, it was full. He had a bad start; the team barely looked competent, and after losing to Huddersfield Town at Elland Road, there was a tetchy argument with BBC Leeds reporter Adam Pope about the team's 'identity', its playing style. It was an awkward moment, but it was arguably the nearest thing to a sensible conversation about football a Leeds manager had been involved in for years.

The match was Pontus Jansson's debut, a central defender from Sweden, and after tackling a Huddersfield player in the first half he turned to the Kop, pumping his fists and roaring as if he'd scored a goal. That was arguably the most passion a player had demonstrated for years. Leeds were waking up, winning seven of the next ten as Jansson's partner Kyle Bartley, playmaker Pablo Hernández and striker Chris Wood came into form; youngsters Kalvin Phillips and Ronaldo Vieira impressed in midfield. At the end of the run 36,002 came to Elland Road to watch Leeds play Newcastle United, the first time a league match was sold out since the Bristol Rovers game that won promotion from League One; Leeds lost 2-0, but they weren't bad, and 32,648 came back for a 2-0 win over Aston Villa. 'I thought I knew everything about football, but here I have had to start from zero again,' Cellino said in the summer. 'Until now I've only spent about five per cent of my time looking at the playing side.' Now the playing side had good players playing good football, and winning games, and it was working.

It stopped working so well in spring; Monk suffered from the shared ownership, as it created a vacuum when he needed decisions. The chance to strengthen in January was missed; Leeds won just one of their last eight games, finishing 7th. But after five seasons of finishing between 13th and 15th, this sort of failure felt like success, and the start of more.

At the end of May, Andrea Radrizzani completed his 100 per cent buyout of Massimo Cellino. 'I have been proud to work at Leeds United, with nice people who have worked at the club with me,' said Cellino. 'If you can survive working with me, you can survive anything.'

2017–19

THEY'RE ASKING FOR A PICTURE WITH THE HEAD COACH OF LEEDS

When Andrea Radrizzani bought Leeds United, 98 years after the club was founded, he didn't just buy a football club. He bought into an immediate future bound to be among the most emotionally significant in the club's history. Leeds United had never been outside the top tier of English football for so long, and the impending centenary meant unavoidable comparisons between where Leeds United had been, in its greatest days, and where it was now. Leeds United needed something to celebrate, something to show for the past 100 years.

Garry Monk's management of the team had given United's fans a desperately needed reminder of glory, but nobody had brought that touch, attention or success to the boardroom for fifteen years. The club's offices still echoed with the arguments of its fall from the Premier League in 2004, and problems had multiplied, while the patience of the weary supporters grew shorter. Massimo Cellino had declared himself the 'Sheriff of Elland Road' and attempted to run the club, with his children and lawyers, as a one-man show; Radrizzani began by bringing experience and expertise to the executive levels of the club. Ivan Bravo joined the board, former Director of Strategy at Real Madrid and now Director General of the Aspire Academy, integral to Qatar's plans for hosting the World Cup in 2022; in summer 2018 the investment arm of American football team San Francisco 49ers bought a minority stake that gave their Executive Vice President of Football Operations, Paraag Marathe, a seat on the board. Angus Kinnear, former Marketing Director of Arsenal and Managing Director of West Ham United, joined as Chief Executive.

The practical efforts to rebuild the club's infrastructure were combined with the symbolic. Negotiating the repurchase of Elland Road from its offshore owner was a practical and powerful act, saving £1.7 million a year in rent, closing a painful gap between the club, the fans, their home and their history. Radrizzani went further, allowing the Leeds United Supporters' Trust to register

Elland Road as an 'Asset of Community Value', giving fans and the local community a meaningful stake in the stadium's future.

'When I met with management and supporters during my first few months at the club, the purchase of Elland Road was very high on their list of priorities,' said Radrizzani. 'I'm delighted to be able to announce that we have completed that process today.'

The fans were delighted too. Ken Bates and Massimo Cellino, when they bought Leeds United, each said buying Elland Road back was their priority; all they did was preside over emptiness, of crowds and of spirit. The days of queues for the bus from the city centre, of pubs busy with fans, had been lost; it was possible to be in central Leeds and not know United were playing just down the road. Garry Monk's team brought some of the excitement back, and now Radrizzani was working on the pride; enormous images of Don Revie, Howard Wilkinson and current and former players were hung from the stadium walls, and asbestos was removed from the neglected West Stand's roof. Billy Bremner's famous statement, 'Side Before Self, Every Time', was emblazoned above the main entrance.

The option to buy Thorp Arch back had lapsed during Ken Bates' ownership, and while Leeds announced plans to build a new training centre and academy on land around Elland Road, the existing facilities were given the investment they needed to recover from the shoestring budgets imposed by Cellino. The project was overseen by a new Director of Football, Victor Orta, a former journalist who had been successful at Sevilla and arrived from Middlesbrough. Thorp Arch's rooms were renovated, reopened, and filled with new players; Orta brought in 30, restocking the Under-23 and first teams.

Such an overhaul of players was a surprise. Leeds had only missed the play-offs by one place in 2016/17, and after eight managerial changes during Cellino's ownership, fans had been hoping that stable ownership would mean stability in the dugout, and that Garry Monk would be building on his good first season. But discussions about how to extend his one-year rolling contract, and for how long, quickly broke down, and two days after Radrizzani took 100% control, Monk resigned.

His replacement was Thomas Christiansen, who had just left a job coaching APOEL in Cyprus. He took APOEL to the group stages of the Europa League, but was a relative unknown in English football. Born in Denmark, his mother was Spanish, and he made his breakthrough as a striker with Barcelona, learning under Johan Cruyff, training with Michael Laudrup, Pep Guardiola, Romario. He'd made his debut in the European Super Cup, and scored an audacious backheel in his second international match for Spain, but he struggled to establish himself and goals only came after a move to Germany, where he was top scorer in the Bundesliga in 2002/03.

Christiansen lacked coaching experience, but came

to Leeds as someone who had learned from and trained with the best; he understood high standards. Thoughtful, intense and polite, he was determined to play attractive football and committed to his work. Early in the new season top scorer Chris Wood, around whom the fans had hoped the team would be built, moved to Burnley in the Premier League for around £15 million, but Christiansen would only speak about the squad about he had. 'These are my players,' he said. 'And for them I would die.'

In the first weeks of the season Christiansen and his players made Elland Road come alive. Of the new signings Samuel Saiz was the star, a tiny playmaker who played like nobody Elland Road had seen for years, an individual and an artist. Ezgjan Alioski provided pace on one wing, while Pablo Hernández provided thought on the other; Ronaldo Vieira was becoming one of the best young midfielders outside the Premier League; Luke Ayling was an attacking full-back, and Gaetano Berardi was a full-back who liked to attack opponents. He was a survivor from Cellino's first summer, and with Pontus Jansson he patrolled the pitch, looking for trouble.

On 12 September 2017, Leeds United beat Birmingham City 2-0 at Elland Road, and went top of the Championship for the first time since May 1990, when it was called the Second Division, and Leeds United had won it. It was the first time they'd been top of any division since January 2010, in a season that ended with promotion from League One; the attendance,

31,507 on a Tuesday night, was the largest midweek crowd at Elland Road since 2004. The positive feeling of a fresh start, symbolised by bringing Elland Road back into the club's ownership for the first time since 2004, was enhanced by winning seven and drawing two of the first nine league and cup matches, including a 5-0 demolition of Burton Albion in the Championship at Elland Road. All the goals in that game were scored in the first hour; for the rest of the match Leeds stroked the ball around like the great team of the early 1970s. At the end of September, with Leeds still top of the league, a headline on the BBC Sport website asked, 'Are Leeds United finally set for Premier League return?'

By that time, though, Leeds had lost their first game of the season, 1-0 away to Millwall. The game was billed as the first big test of Christiansen's attacking style, and he said he had 'lots of information' about the hostile, hard tackling tactics of Millwall, who gave Leeds no space to attack and countered quickly themselves through a team built for flair. Afterwards, he said, 'I believe there was nothing new in what I expected from Millwall – they did exactly what I expected them to do.' But he hadn't been able to stop them winning, and although a 3-2 win over Ipswich Town took Leeds top of the table again, that was followed by a 3-1 defeat to another of the division's roughhouse teams, Cardiff City, on their way to promotion with manager Neil Warnock and his assistant Kevin Blackwell.

Seven defeats in nine games, including a 4-1 defeat away to eventual champions Wolverhampton Wanderers, doused United's expectations. Liam Cooper, the captain, said later that the Millwall game had been a turning point. 'Teams, I think, after that game set up a lot differently against us,' he said. 'They did try and bully us and maybe we weren't used to that. The lads who'd come in, it was maybe an eye-opener for them.'

The joy had gone from the performances, and soon discipline went too. In an FA Cup match away to Newport County, Christiansen named an inexperienced team that struggled against their physical opponents; Saiz was brought on as substitute in search of a winner, but was sent off for spitting in a fracas after Newport scored their own winner in the last minute. He was banned for six matches, and in the four games that followed, Liam Cooper, Eunan O'Kane and Gaetano Berardi were shown red cards as Leeds lost three and drew once. After Cardiff came to Elland Road and won 4-1, Thomas Christiansen was sacked. Leeds were 10th.

There was still a chance of overcoming a seven-point gap and making the play-offs, but where Christiansen had been unable to prepare the players for the physical demands of the Championship, his replacement, Paul Heckingbottom, was unable to inspire a push up the table. Heckingbottom had a good reputation for improving young players, several Premier League clubs opting to loan their youngsters for him to work with at

Barnsley, where he'd won promotion from League One and secured a 9th place finish in the Championship. He spoke about restoring discipline, aiming for the play-offs, and planning for the following season, but produced little to suggest he was the right man for the job. For one thing, while at Barnsley, his home town club, he'd spoken about growing up there and hating Leeds United, which didn't endear him to Leeds' fans; for another, Leeds only won another four games, finishing 13th, and while the recklessness leading to red cards had gone, so too had the fight. The players didn't look interested; Saiz admitted later that, as the play-off chances disappeared, he lost motivation, and he was obviously not alone.

Two consecutive seasons that promised a return to the Premier League but failed to deliver it were met with dismay by United's supporters. Each new owner for fifteen years, and each new manager, had asked them to be patient, and that patience was now all worn out. Leeds United needed to change quickly to meet the fans' demands for success, but in their first full season the new owners had tried to change too much too soon. Too many players had been brought in at once, too few of them prepared for the Championship; goalkeeper Felix Wiedwald had seemed terrified of the strikers he was facing and was eventually replaced by Bailey Peacock-Farrell, a resolute but inexperienced 21-year-old. The repurchase of Elland Road was followed by a new club badge as a precursor to the club's centenary;

intended to symbolise what the next 100 years would mean to the fans, the graphic rendering of the 'Leeds Salute', a fist-to-heart gesture of obscure origins that the fans exchanged among themselves, had to be withdrawn within seven hours amid a reaction so hostile it became international news.

Impatience for promotion was one thing Radrizzani and the fans had in common. He estimated that buying the club, the stadium, and taking immediate steps to reverse the decline of both had cost an initial £100 million, and was clear that he would only lose more money if Leeds stayed in the Championship. Despite being regarded as one of the most competitive and popular leagues in European football, the broadcasting deals negotiated by the Football League, now run by former Leeds chief executive Shaun Harvey, didn't meet the costs of running the clubs; a system of 'parachute payments' that guaranteed higher income for clubs relegated from the Premier League forced other clubs into excessive spending to try to compete, while 'Profit and Sustainability' tests punished clubs that took those risks and failed. 'There is no income for the clubs, so everyone loses money,' said Radrizzani. 'I don't think anyone in the world wants to own a business that at the end of the year is making losses. Therefore, there is a timeline in my mind – three years, maximum five – to make it to the Premier League. If we're there, everything changes.'

To get there, everything would have to change, again.

Reviewing 2017/18, the new executives running Leeds didn't deny their mistakes. The failed badge design became a rueful running joke in Angus Kinnear's programme notes. The players who had not proven up to the task of playing in the Championship were moved on, and Victor Orta refocused his recruitment strategy on finding players with English football experience. The most significant decision was about the head coach. Paul Heckingbottom was sacked, and United decided to aim as high as they could for his replacement.

An inquiry was made to Antonio Conte, who had just left Chelsea, and an interview held with Claudio Ranieri, who had overcome odds of 5000-1 to win the Premier League with Leicester City in 2015/16. Contact was made with Roberto Martinez, but he was engaged taking Belgium to third place in the World Cup. Later, Orta recounted a conversation with Radrizzani, who asked him to name his ideal coach. Orta's first thought was Marcelo Bielsa, but his second thought was that hiring him would be impossible. Radrizzani told him to try. Orta picked up his phone.

The gospel of Marcelo Bielsa had arrived slowly to England, first through the testimony of Pep Guardiola, the coach who had redefined the sport by developing 'tiki-taka' football at Barcelona, Bayern Munich and now Manchester City, who described Bielsa as 'the best coach in the world' for the way he 'has influenced football and his football players.' One of those players,

Mauricio Pochettino, manager of Tottenham Hotspur, called him 'a genius.'

Bielsa and Pochettino's relationship began when, in search of players for the youth team at Newell's Old Boys, Bielsa drove 200 miles across Argentina and arrived at Pochettino's home at two in the morning to look at the sleeping thirteen year old's legs. 'These legs look like those of a very good player,' declared Bielsa, and by the time he as coach and Pochettino as centre-half won two league titles with Newell's Old Boys at the start of the 1990s, the story had become a key part of the growing Bielsa legend. Newell's were Bielsa's chosen team in his home city of Rosario, Argentina, the club where he'd almost made it as a player, returning for a ten-year apprenticeship as a coach before taking charge of the first team. The players soon realised he was unlike any coach they'd had before. To win the derby match against Rosario Central, Bielsa told young player Fernando Gamboa, he would cut off a finger. 'But if we're lucky enough to win five clasicos, you lose your hand,' replied Gamboa. Bielsa became angry, telling him, 'Gamboa, you do not understand anything.' By the time Bielsa left Newell's, in 1992, saying he had exhausted himself and the players on the way to narrowly losing the Copa Libertadores final, his nickname was fixed – El Loco Bielsa, 'The Crazy Bielsa' – and his legend in Rosario was assured. Newell's stadium had never had a formal name, but in 2009 it became Estadio Marcelo A. Bielsa.

By that time Bielsa had coached Argentina's national team, winning Olympic gold and qualifying for the 2002 World Cup with a record of just one defeat in eighteen matches, scoring 42 goals and conceding fifteen; at the World Cup itself Argentina crashed out in the group stages despite attempting what Guardiola said was 'the football idea' that appealed to him most at the tournament. He qualified from the World Cup group stages as head coach of Chile in 2010, an outcome that completed a transformation not only of Chile's underachieving football team but of its national psyche, making the country believe in itself. Jimena Castro, a doctor in American Studies at the University of Santiago, said, 'We were thirsty for heroes, we lacked epic language, we lived the boring part of failure ... Bielsa arrived with a particular ethic that I think was what we needed. He was a kind of Messiah who came with a discourse far removed from grandiloquence and taught us a new language.' Claudio Borghi, the coach hired after Bielsa disagreed with the Chilean FA and resigned, struggled with the scale of the nation's mourning. 'Bielsa left more widows in Chile than the Second World War,' he said.

Bielsa inspired similar devotion in Europe during typically intense spells as manager of Athletic Bilbao and Marseille, but the years before Leeds contacted him had been difficult. His time at Marseille was characterised by disagreements with the club's president; on the eve of his first season, Bielsa held a press conference to explain that the president had broken their agreements over transfers, but that he would continue with the players he had anyway. Bielsa didn't just continue; he took Marseille to the top of the table, until the loss of players to the African Cup of Nations exposed the lack of squad strength he had complained about. Marseille finished the season 4th, and summer brought detailed renegotiation of his contract; after one game of the new season Bielsa declared that promises had been broken once more, and resigned. At Lazio Bielsa was head coach for just four days, resigning as soon as he arrived to find agreed plans had not been carried out; at Lille he lasted thirteen games before, again, disagreements with the club's sporting director about recruitment ended with Bielsa suspended, then sacked. The last view of him as a working coach was a photograph taken of him sitting alone at a Formica table in the back of a side street restaurant, intently watching Lille losing to Montpellier on his laptop.

Bielsa's obsessive watching of football was key to his success. His enormous video library was part of his legend, and a practical tool for his deep analysis of the game; it was said that he could watch two matches simultaneously. But European club football had not been kind to his reputation. With Athletic Bilbao he reached the finals of the Europa League and the Copa Del Rey, but lost both, and Bielsa's last club trophy was an Argentinian title with Vélez Sarsfield in 1998. Many felt his style of football, based on players aggressively pressing their opponents in a 3-3-1-3 formation designed for exhilarating attack, had been refined and overtaken by the younger generation of coaches, including his admirers Guardiola and Pochettino; his own reputation for intensity and for demanding exhausting commitment from his players made him seem too volatile for the luxurious world of modern elite football.

When Bielsa received Orta's call, asking if he'd be interested in coaching Leeds United, he had taken charge of just fourteen games of football in three years. He told Orta he would look into the job, and invited him and Angus Kinnear to meet him in Argentina. What looking into the job meant to Bielsa became clear when they arrived; Bielsa had watched all 51 games Leeds had played the previous season, drawing initial conclusions on each member of the playing squad; asked what he knew of the Championship, he presented his analysis of a match played between Burton and Bolton the previous season, including a discussion of every formation each team had used during the rest of the season; he had obtained architectural blueprints of Thorp Arch and outlined the changes he would need to create a training centre that could be used from morning until night. The question of his compensation was swiftly dealt with; Bielsa was happy with a salary less than at Lille, but still making him the highest paid manager in the Championship; he would fund his own coaching staff and, it turned out, a new training centre he was paying to have built for Newell's Old Boys. Bielsa's more pressing concern, as it had been at Marseille, Lazio and Lille, was whether Leeds United could agree a realistic plan of work and stick to it. After lengthy negotiations Bielsa flew to Leeds in mid-June and gave English football its first experience of a Marcelo Bielsa press conference, speaking through an interpreter for almost ninety minutes, then went to commence pre-season training. The players were brought back earlier than scheduled for a programme of twelve-hour sessions to inculcate Bielsa's philosophy and prepare them for its physical demands.

'There is a desire to change mentality in the club,' said Radrizzani, 'and to do it in a strong way with a man who can bring innovation to improve the football and the players, but also in the way we run the entire football department and the academy. We believe that Bielsa's philosophy and his vision reflect our desire to become a winning club and affect the mentality of the club.' If Leeds had made mistakes the season before, they now had a coach who would keep them accountable for their actions. To make the players understand their responsibility to the supporters, Bielsa made them pick litter around Thorp Arch for three hours, the average amount of work a supporter would have to put in to afford a ticket to watch them play.

Such stories about Bielsa's methods didn't emerge until the season was underway, as after his initial presentation, United's new coach avoided the press and defied interpretation. In an intense programme of pre-season games Bielsa fielded confusing line-ups, using midfielders Ronaldo Vieira and Mateusz Klich as central defenders, experimenting with youth and reserve players while the fans clamoured for transfers. Leeds only made two major signings, striker Patrick Bamford and left-back Barry Douglas, and added a clutch of loan players; seeing the improvement of Klich, a midfielder Orta had signed but Christiansen had quickly rejected, Bielsa permitted the club to sell Vieira, one of its brightest young players, to Sampdoria. Supporters were bewildered and nervous; when Leeds lined up against Stoke City at Elland Road for their opening match, the team only contained one player who hadn't been part of the previous season's disappointment.

It took 45 minutes for Bielsa to prove that there had been stunning method behind his pre-season madness. Stoke arrived with an expensive team that had just been relegated from the Premier League but was expected to dominate the Championship on its way back up; they were dominated all over the pitch by the same Leeds United players who had looked sluggish and lost just two months earlier. Leeds led 2-0 at half-time and won 3-1, then set about proving that the transformation was permanent: they won 4-1 at Derby County and 3-0 at Norwich City, overwhelming teams that were expected to challenge for promotion.

Two of the main doubts about Bielsa had been

whether his football would suit the Championship, and whether United's players would suit his football. He stuck resolutely to both as a matter of principle. 'Faithfulness to the style' was one of the tenets of his philosophy; and although he maintained a distance from them personally, he maintained, 'I love my players.' Improving the players rather than replacing them was the part of Bielsa's project carrying most risk, but that he seemed to be relishing. Kalvin Phillips was given intensive individual training to make him capable of playing as a '6', a defensive position in midfield key to Bielsa's system, and in two early season matches he was substituted after just thirty minutes when he couldn't assert himself in the game. It could have been humiliating, but to Bielsa it was part of the process; Phillips was given more individual training and put straight back in the team for the next games, soon becoming one of the most impressive midfielders in the league.

With his team answering questions on the pitch, curiosity grew around Bielsa himself, swiftly becoming affection, then adoration. His practice of refusing one-to-one interviews made his pre and post-match press conferences must-watch events, the online broadcasts attracting sponsorship from South America. Through his interpreter Salim Lamrani, an academic with expertise in US-Cuban relations, Bielsa frequently spoke for more than an hour with thoughtfulness that, compared to the clichés and commonplaces of most football coaches, felt revolutionary. Asked to discuss differing playing styles, Bielsa spoke at length about the corrosive pursuit of success at all costs, using climate change as an analogy for the commercialism of football: 'The fact that we are not taking care of the planet, [means] our children will pay the consequence of our acts. And with football it will be the same. Because we are destroying football and in the future we will see the negative effects of this.'

Talking about his habit of never refusing a request for a photograph, Bielsa returned to a regular theme, the importance of using football's privileged position in society to make people happy: 'They're not asking for an autograph or photo of me. They're asking for a picture with the head coach of Leeds ... The most significant thing in football is the love people have for their club and the identification of many around something which allows them to gather together and express themselves. We live in an individualist society but this is something which unites people.' With that permission, fans started sharing photographs of Bielsa wherever they met him, usually in the town of Wetherby, where Bielsa could be found working on his laptop in the local coffee shop or buying groceries in the supermarket, or taking his daily 45 minute walk to the training ground. Despite the language barrier and his genial inscrutability, Bielsa was becoming a part of the Yorkshire landscape, as appreciated and respected as the moors. For many fans, he said, 'It's harder to have access to another kind of happiness than they get from football, and they don't have many opportunities to feel proud of things like they do for their club. It's a big opportunity for us to fill this hope for all of the fans, especially the poor ones.'

Hope and happiness took Leeds fans over in a way most had not experienced for years. Two extraordinary matches in three days over Christmas were unlike anything the club had ever seen. First, a 2-0 half-time deficit at Aston Villa was turned into a 3-2 win by Kemar Roofe's goal in the fifth minute of stoppage time. Then, at Elland Road, Blackburn Rovers took a 2-1 lead in the 90th minute, surely winning the game. But Leeds restarted with a visible conviction that they would score again, and did within a minute through Roofe, who incredibly added another in the 94th minute, heading in Hernández's cross to seal an impossible victory.

Leeds were top of the league by three points, and Bielsa's work was becoming impossible to ignore. Leeds fans had grown to love not only his results but the old-school integrity of his attitudes towards football and life, but it was modern media that brought his work in the Championship to national attention. Derbyshire Police used social media to announce they'd apprehended 'a suspicious male' who had been reported at the perimeter fence of Derby County's training ground. 'All checks above board!' they added, and 'Keeping the team safe to bring home a win against Leeds! Spying is cheating.'

At first it was thought to be some sort of joke, but over the next 24 hours Derby's manager, the former Chelsea midfielder Frank Lampard, made clear that he was taking the matter seriously. In an interview minutes before Leeds and Derby kicked off their match at Elland Road, Marcelo Bielsa shocked television viewers by confirming the rumours. 'It's true,' he said, 'There was someone from Leeds United. I'm responsible for this incident.' He had telephoned Lampard to tell him, and that he'd been watching other teams training since he was coach of Argentina, as there was nothing in the rules to say he couldn't. Lampard complained that Bielsa's actions were against the unwritten rules of fair play; Bielsa accepted that point of view, and that Derby's feelings about the matter were important, but he didn't apologise.

Leeds won the game 2-0 with one of their most emphatic performances, but that was far from the end of the matter. The storm of criticism that followed was like a throwback to the arguments against Don Revie's use of dossiers, his players' use of 'foreign' gamesmanship and tactics; Leeds were once again successful, and once again judged to be contravening English football's unwritten sense of moral superiority. There were demands for the result against Derby to be reversed, for Bielsa to lose his job, even for him to banned from English football.

Attempting to end the debate, Bielsa only confused commentators even more, by calling the press to an unscheduled lecture describing his approach to analysis. For seventy minutes he described how he and his team put more than 200 hours of work into analysing match videos of each team, understanding the effect of their different formations, the roles and abilities of their players in different roles. He explained that he didn't hold all this information in his mind, but that having it documented allowed him to quickly answer any question he might have. 'I don't need to watch a training session to know how they play,' he said. 'Why do I go? Because it's not forbidden, I didn't know it would create such a reaction, and even though going and watching an opponent is not useful, it allows me to keep my anxiety low.'

'I know I am not trying to get an advantage,' he added, addressing the main accusation against him. 'I already have the information. I repeat: Why do I do it? Because I think I'm stupid. I thank you for your patience.'

The press, commentators and several opposition managers and players were even more mystified; concentrating on Bielsa's admission that he had observed the training sessions of every team Leeds had played, eleven Championship clubs wrote to the Football League, forcing them to open an investigation even though, as Bielsa rightly pointed out, he had not broken any rules. Anxious for the affair to be finished, Leeds accepted a fine of £200,000 for 'breaching good faith', that Bielsa later revealed he paid himself. Asked for his reaction at the time, Bielsa only said, 'Yes, I am happy it's over.'

In the minds of the media, and the fate of the season, the episode was not over. The second half of the season became increasingly difficult for Leeds, with wins harder to find. Bielsa insisted that performances were still all they should be, and statistics supported him: Leeds were among the hardest teams to create chances against, and were creating the most and best chances of any teams in the division; measurements of work rate showed that the players' fitness was still high, belying a claim that dogged Bielsa that his teams suffer tiredness. But they couldn't score goals. The strikers, Kemar Roofe and Patrick Bamford, succumbed to injuries and lost form; Samu Saiz left to play in Spain; apart from midfielder Mateusz Klich, every member of United's squad was injured during the season, an extraordinary record that gave chances to impressive youngsters like Jack Clarke and Jamie Shackleton, but disrupted the team.

At Easter, Leeds took a 1-0 lead against relegation-threatened Wigan Athletic at Elland Road, whose Cédric Kipré was sent off in the first fifteen minutes. It was a chance to maintain a three-point lead in 2nd place ahead of Sheffield United, and perhaps score enough to overcome their goal difference. Instead, Leeds froze, conceding twice, losing the game and 2nd place; three days later, away to Brentford, they lost again, and were suddenly three points behind Sheffield United, and nine goals. In his first press conference, Bielsa had said, 'I know everything I, as a foreigner, could possibly know and have absorbed about Leeds United, and what Leeds United means to supporters in this country.' He was now learning first-hand about what happens to Leeds United when glory is there to be grasped. A near certain chance of automatic promotion behind Norwich City had evaporated, leaving Leeds in the play-offs, and a rematch with Frank Lampard's Derby County.

While Bielsa was trying to overcome United's fated characteristic of achieving less than they ought – fourteen times runners up in the Revie era – he was publicly acknowledging an identical failing in himself. His teams had finished runners up in the Copa Libertadores, the Europa League and the Spanish Copa Del Rey; after leading Ligue 1 at Christmas, his Marseille team had finished 4th. 'You're a coach that knows how to win titles,' one reporter told him after a Leeds game. 'I would actually say the opposite,' replied Bielsa, chuckling. 'I thank you for the generosity of your concept, but people would find out the truth very easily.'

'Let's see if here in Leeds I can change this feature of my career,' he added, and five minutes before half-time in the second semi-final match against Derby, Bielsa was as close as he could be to changing his and Leeds United's fortunes. Leeds had beaten Derby 4-1 and 2-0 in the league, and won again at Pride Park in the first leg, 1-0. Now, at Elland Road, Stuart Dallas had scored to give Leeds a 2-0 aggregate lead and the confidence that they would be playing Aston Villa in the final at Wembley.

Everything changed in fifteen minutes of football. A minute before half-time, goalkeeper Kiko Casilla missed a bouncing ball through the middle, leaving Liam Cooper floundering and an empty net for Derby to score. Forty seconds after half-time Derby scored again, a tactical change catching Leeds out, again through the centre of the pitch. Ten minutes later Derby won and scored a penalty and now they had an aggregate lead.

Although Stuart Dallas scored again to equalise, United's studied programme of tactical plans gave way to chaos in the second half. Gaetano Berardi was sent off for a foul after losing the ball in midfield, and Derby scored their fourth with five minutes left, to lead 4-3 on aggregate. Leeds tried everything to equalise but nothing, now, was working. At half-past eight Leeds were going to Wembley, and hopefully the Premier League; at half-past nine their season was over, and Leeds were going nowhere. At full-time Frank Lampard ran onto the pitch, joining his players in goading the Leeds fans with gestures about spying and crying, returning the songs Elland Road had been singing an hour before. Kalvin Phillips was crying now, as other Leeds players either comforted him or slumped to the floor. Marcelo Bielsa gathered his coaching staff and waited, with them in a line inside the technical area where they'd worked all season, for Lampard to come and shake his hand; he didn't. After watching Derby's celebrations for five minutes, Bielsa turned and walked back to the changing rooms.

31

2019–20

PROFE, ¿MAÑANA LIBRE?

Deep in the second half of Leeds United's centenary celebration game at Elland Road, a league match against Birmingham City 100 years and two days after the meeting at Salem Hall that marks the club's beginning, Kalvin Phillips pushed forward into the opponent's half.

A Leeds attack had come to nothing but, for a team coached by Marcelo Bielsa, that was never the end of the story. Phillips chased the ball from Fran Villalba to Jude Bellingham, forcing the Birmingham players into passing backwards to right-back Maxime Colin. Unbalanced, trying to pass to his goalkeeper, Colin lost the ball to Jack Harrison, who surged into the penalty area. Tapping the ball to the right put it into the path of

Phillips, and the Leeds-born player, a symbol of United's renaissance, swept the ball past the 'keeper in front of the Kop, scoring the goal that won the game, 1-0.

Depressed by the play-off defeat and tempted by a shortcut to the top, Phillips had come close to moving to the Premier League with Aston Villa, but this goal was the sort of moment he had stayed at Leeds for. In a week heavy with symbolism and celebration, when the current team had emulated famous photos of the Don Revie era and Revie's players and staff were awarded the Freedom of the City, the highest civic honour Leeds could bestow, Phillips' goal was beautifully placed between the stories of Leeds United's first 100 years, and its next.

'Sometimes, God puts things in the right place,' said Bielsa after the game. 'Phillips has continued playing here in the club, and now he will stay in the history of the club for this goal. It's a fair act from God.'

Fairness had been the theme of controversy a month earlier, as Bielsa struggled to shake off his and the club's more recent history. At FIFA's lavish annual ceremony, Leeds were named winners of the Fair Play Award for allowing Aston Villa to equalise towards the end of the previous season. 'It was a strange decision for them to win that,' said Frank Lampard, now manager of Chelsea despite losing with Derby County in the play-off final. 'I think everyone had the same reaction.' Lampard, and the English media, still had Spygate on the brain, not to mention United's longstanding reputation as 'Dirty

Leeds' that appeared to rule them out of such awards by definition.

That was the sort of perception Bielsa was working against. He tried to defray credit for the gesture away from himself, saying that in the few seconds when he made the decision, he was trying to act as the city and the club's supporters would wish. He wanted to share the award with the people in society who have least, who make difficult ethical decisions every day without being praised for them. Recognising football's influence in society, Bielsa said he tried to let people outside the game be his guide. 'It starts in a city, but comes to all working in here,' he said. 'Everybody, players, people working at Thorp Arch, the gardeners. I thought the decision represented this group of people.' He added, 'Nobody working 30 years in football is doing the right thing all the time. You cannot avoid this. Football makes you worse. If not, football does not accept you.'

The reaction to FIFA's award confirmed that football was as unwilling to accept Leeds United as ever and formed a distracting contrast to the work Bielsa was doing in his second attempt at promoting Leeds to the Premier League. Although he thanked FIFA for it, the award was an unwelcome reminder of the season before while Bielsa was trying to cope with the residue of those bitter memories, of sixteen years accumulating scars outside the top flight, of the expectations of a century. The centenary celebrations were a demonstration of his priorities, when he lined up for a photograph with dozens of former players and managers, all wearing dinner jackets, and he arrived from the training ground in his tracksuit, for which he apologised. The current players were there briefly and Liam Cooper represented them with a speech before a celebration dinner, before they were whisked away for yet another early night before more training. History was important, but not as important as winning the next game.

The squad working with Bielsa had changed in small but significant ways that increased their collective dedication to his methods. Keeping Phillips had been one of the first requests Bielsa made of United's board. Another was selling Pontus Jansson, who left for a surprisingly low fee to Championship rivals Brentford. Jansson had been the only player to resist Bielsa's order to let Aston Villa equalise and had been photographed alone on the pitch at the end of the play-off defeat to Derby while the squad consoled each other elsewhere. He had also, for a second summer, requested a later return to training after international duty, and while the infractions were individually minor, they added to Bielsa's early impression of a player who could not completely submit to working for the collective goal of promotion the way the coach required.

When he arrived at Elland Road in 2016, Jansson had been the noisy, almost cartoonish character Leeds had needed for years, but the changes he helped inspire put his strengths out of fashion. Jansson had noticed it himself, saying Bielsa was now, 'The main man. Maybe when I came here I saw myself as the main man but not anymore,' but after a season trying to fit the former main man into a side without stars, Bielsa was choosing a way forward without him. Replacing Jansson was Ben White, a 21-year-old unknown on loan from Brighton and Hove Albion.

The other addition was Helder Costa, a £15m winger from Wolverhampton Wanderers, and the concern among fans was that outgoing players were not being adequately replaced. Goalkeeper Bailey Peacock-Farrell went to Burnley and striker Kemar Roofe to Anderlecht, both replaced by players on loan. Jack Clarke, the teenager who made a big impact in his breakthrough season, was sold for a big fee to Tottenham Hotspur and loaned back. Jack Harrison joined for another year on loan from Manchester City. Bielsa's planning felt risky to fans who were still suffering from the end of the season before. The same small squad, the same players, the same style of play: Bielsa planned for a better result, but the fans, though relieved to have the same head coach in charge, feared he was building towards the same failure.

The season started with five wins and two draws and all the same attacking impetus as the previous campaign, with the invention of Pablo Hernández to the fore, and White showing class beyond his experience as opponents struggled to get the ball past him and Cooper into United's penalty area. But when defeat came in the season's sixth game, at home to Swansea City, followed by conceding a stoppage time equaliser to Derby in the next home match, it amplified the tangible anxiety refusing to lift from Elland Road.

'It feels like the same as last season, we feel like we lost the game,' Mateusz Klich had said, after the season started at Elland Road by letting a one goal lead slip and drawing with Nottingham Forest. 'It's like last season, we created a lot of chances and we should have scored more goals, but didn't.'

Defeats in London to Charlton Athletic and Millwall and a dour late-October draw with Sheffield Wednesday, only the second goalless game of Bielsa's time at Leeds, frayed the nerves of careworn fans. League leaders West Bromwich Albion had only lost once while Leeds were beaten three times, twice by teams expected to finish near the bottom of the table, and had given points away through defensive errors. They were dominating possession and creating chances to little effect, while Bielsa's press conferences became preoccupied with questions about whether Eddie Nketiah, an exciting loanee from Arsenal, could finish more chances than Patrick Bamford. He might, was Bielsa's consistent reply, but without Bamford's hard work for the team, he couldn't guarantee Leeds would have as many chances to score.

West Brom's single defeat, though, had come at Elland Road, and when Leeds were relaxed, their football was the best they'd played yet under Bielsa. Form improved through victories at Luton Town and Reading character-ised by resilience and counter-attacks that made the most of United's fitness, and a brilliant performance dismissed Middlesbrough 4-0. Seven consecutive wins were becom-ing eight when early goals and a devastating first half gave Leeds a 3-0 lead over Cardiff City as the hour mark was approaching at Elland Road, while anxiety in the stands was replaced by certainty that, after an uncertain start, nobody could stop Leeds this time.

The exception, as Leeds fans can never forget, was Leeds themselves. Only those in the changing rooms could explain what happened to Leeds United between half-time against Cardiff and a 2-0 defeat at Nottingham Forest in February, but even the players seemed first baf-fled and in the end depressed by the way their powers abandoned them. What had statistically been the best defence in Europe let in three goals in thirty minutes as Cardiff stole a point, and the only wins in the next eleven games were a comeback from two goals down against Millwall at Elland Road, and before that a bewil-dering 5-4 win at Birmingham City in the last match of 2019. Compared to the firmness with which Leeds beat Birmingham in their centenary game, they now looked like they had lost all control, allowing Birmingham to equalise three times, losing then retaking the lead twice in the last seven minutes of a match that was exhilarat-ing, but exhausting, and finally worrying.

By the end of the match at Forest, what had been an eleven-point gap to 3rd place was gone, and all United's confidence with it. It was their fourth game of the year without scoring, while goalkeeper Kiko Casilla was littering scorelines with his mistakes, and would soon be banned for eight games for racially abusing Charlton's Jonathan Leko during the match in October. Luke Ayling told the club's media department that, as a senior player, he would take responsibility for speaking to the press, but looking uncharacteristically bleary and lost in the dark of Nottingham, he didn't seem to know what to say, or how Leeds could change their course.

'I don't know. We'll keep working hard, keep trying our best,' he said, grasping for ideas. 'I think that's all we can do, and hopefully things can change around and we can get some kind of form back.' The season so far, the points advantage the team had worked hard to build and lost, was all history now. 'Now it's about scrapping those 31 games and starting again. We're back on equal points with other teams, so we've got a certain amount of games to outscore the other teams. We start again now.'

With fifteen games left Leeds were 2nd, four points behind West Brom, but 5th placed Brentford could overtake them by winning their game with Leeds at Griffin Park three days after the defeat to Forest. Brentford manager Thomas Frank raised eyebrows in Yorkshire by claiming, 'They couldn't pick a worse place to play on

Tuesday night. I am 100 per cent sure that they fear us';
but the words Leeds said among themselves had more
impact. Eschewing his usual post-match video analysis,
Bielsa used the footage from Nottingham in a motivational session with his players, talking through all the
good qualities of their football in that game and the run
of defeats they'd been suffering. His argument was that
their performances were as good as ever and that, by
keeping faith in what they had been working for almost
two years to refine, better fortunes would follow. The
biggest risk was losing confidence in their ideals because
of a few defeats, when the team was still well placed in
the league and doing the right things on the pitch.

The game at Brentford began with a goal given
away by another Casilla mistake, and Frank's pre-match
confidence and the memories of automatic promotion
slipping away at the same ground a year before were
closing in on Leeds. But Liam Cooper prodded in an
equaliser when David Raya proved other goalkeepers were also fallible, and the 1-1 draw, and Fulham's
identical result at Millwall the next night, kept Leeds in
2nd place, and changed the mood.

Ayling had lamented the time passed since Leeds
scored first in a game and now he took charge, opening the scoring in wins over Bristol City, Hull City and
Huddersfield Town, the last a stunning volley after just
three minutes of play. It was a sign that Bielsa's assessment of the character of his squad was well founded.

Ayling had started his career at Arsenal but dropped down the leagues to Yeovil Town, Liam Cooper had fallen from then Premier League Hull to League Two Chesterfield, Stuart Dallas came late to professional football after working as a labourer. Mateusz Klich had left Poland to sign for Wolfsburg but was never given a proper chance in the Bundesliga; now 29, he had started every league match for Bielsa, and scored the winner in an important 1-0 win over Middlesbrough. Bielsa was satisfied with their ability but, knowing that many of his important players were of similar age and background, he had confidence in their commitment to his arduous training methods and strict ideals. They knew time was against their teenaged ambitions of becoming Premier League footballers, and that Bielsa's strenuous and exhausting coaching was their best chance. Now their leadership was vital as Leeds took control of their destiny, winning five games in a row, scoring nine and conceding none.

As each performance improved on the last, excitement and anticipation grew about the manner with which Leeds looked ready to clinch promotion, even if West Brom's form meant they were only a point behind in the title race. But United were not in control of their destiny for long. After a 2-0 win over Huddersfield at Elland Road, the club announced that the Thorp Arch training ground was closing to all but essential first team players and staff, responding to a novel coronavirus,

Covid-19, that chairman Andrea Radrizzani had seen first-hand was causing chaos in northern Italy. Within a week Thorp Arch was closed altogether, United's game in Cardiff was called off, and all football, and much of ordinary life, was put on hold while the pandemic spread across Europe and the United Kingdom.

There was soon no part of the world untouched by the virus, and in the following months more than 45,000 deaths in the United Kingdom alone were attributed to Covid-19. Among them was Norman Hunter, the iconic defender of Don Revie's Leeds, as well as a coach, commentator and ambassador at Elland Road, beloved by every generation of Leeds fans. It was a painful time for the football club, as Hunter's protégé, Trevor Cherry, who played more games as Leeds United captain than anyone but Billy Bremner, died from a heart attack a week later; soon Jack Charlton, Hunter's defensive partner, a World Cup winner and holder of United's record for appearances, died after a long illness.

With the country under lockdown to control the spread of the virus, fans had to delay public respects for the achievements of these three of Leeds United's greatest representatives. And the weight of history increased on the shoulders of the players who were being frustrated from carrying on their season and completing the job Hunter had hoped to live to see done. In October, he had contributed a foreword to James Willoughby's book, *Ups and Downs*, concluding: 'It would be a dream for me to see Leeds United back in the Premier League in my lifetime.'

Teams in the Championship had nine games left to play and even counting suspensions in wartime, the English league season had never been paused at such an awkward stage. The weeks while the country grappled for control of the pandemic became months, time that football filled with debates and then arguments about how to finish the season.

First came the question of when or if it might be safe to play, or if the season must be cancelled. Ideas like letting the tables stand or calculating final positions based on points-per-game so far were proposed. Most mathematical options kept Leeds in the promotion places, but the situation was complicated by clubs in the Premier League objecting to being relegated without being given a chance to play out of trouble. Germany demonstrated a way forward on the pitch, completing the Bundesliga season by playing 'ghost games' without crowds, relying on rigorous testing to keep players and key staff safe from the coronavirus. There were objections to following that example in England, some clubs feeling they would suffer unfairly without gate receipts from big matches, others that playing behind closed doors would distort the home advantages teams had enjoyed earlier in the season. Players, some of whom were being asked to extend contracts to take part in the lengthening season, raised concerns about potential infection or injury.

Leeds United were consistent. They wanted to play their remaining games and win promotion, or lose it, on the pitch. The players were united, and Leeds United-minded, quickly agreeing to defer large parts of their wages to ensure the club could pay its staff throughout the crisis, and adapting to new forms of training required by the new concept of 'social distancing'. The club's medical staff had noted early reports of the developing pandemic in January and were ready, supplying players with exercise equipment and tailored routines to keep them as close as possible to Bielsa's physical requirements.

Training and diet were the cornerstones of Bielsa's work, centred on a midweek session he had used for more than twenty years. 'He just calls it football,' said Kalvin Phillips, but the Leeds players dubbed it 'murderball', an intense eleven-a-side match with no fouls and no stoppages, a constant supply of balls denying the players any respite, Bielsa and his staff roaming the pitch and bellowing instructions to ensure constant motion. The players said it was more exhausting than a league match, and high performance in murderball was a prerequisite for playing in Bielsa's team. The club was aiming to keep the players ready to start the season again at any moment, and after two years, the squad knew what would be demanded of them when they were allowed back to Thorp Arch.

Despite, or perhaps because of the rigours of murderball, the players said they couldn't wait to get back to it.

The final nine games held symbolic importance after the suffering at the end of 2018/19. Their record in the last nine games of that season included four defeats and a draw as the team lurched from 2nd place to 3rd, and disaster in the play-offs. The players were drawn into the critical picture of Bielsa that followed him from job to job, the accusation that his methods burned players out, leaving them physically and mentally vulnerable at the end of long seasons and too fragile to sustain performances through a second campaign. Promotion was the target and Leeds had got themselves back to the top of the Championship despite the perpetual doubts surrounding them, but promotion secured mathematically in a curtailed season would not correct a record that both players and manager felt was unjust.

'It's going to be a formality for us. That's my personal view on it. I think we'll romp it,' midfielder Adam Forshaw told the *Leeds That* podcast once the authorities decided the season would be played to a finish. But he also alluded to the strangeness of the antiseptic training methods imposed on the players as the pandemic continued around their closeted training ground; Forshaw was injured meaning he couldn't mingle too closely with his teammates, so was basing his confidence on watching them from a distance and on conversations held over WhatsApp messages.

United's fitness didn't look in doubt when they began playing league football again, starting with a game away to Cardiff City. But concentration was at fault for an uncharacteristic mistake by Kalvin Phillips, who gave the ball to Junior Hoilett to score Cardiff's first goal; then Liam Cooper did the same, letting Robert Glatzel make it 2-0, ending United's run of five wins without conceding a goal. They played better at Elland Road, where 15,000 cardboard cutout 'crowdies' bearing images of fans replaced flesh and blood supporters in the stadium, and a second half show by Pablo Hernández unlocked promotion rivals Fulham in a 3-0 win. But when Luton Town visited, desperate for points to avoid relegation, they defended in deep numbers to frustrate Leeds into a 1-1 draw. Brentford had restarted in strong form, and bravado about wrapping up promotion quickly was beginning to look misplaced.

This time it didn't take Marcelo Bielsa to inspire a reset. Frustrations spilled over into arguments on the pitch against Luton, and the next morning the players came together to clear the air and review their aims. As after the Nottingham Forest match in February, Leeds United's future was still in the players' control, and determination and self-belief were again their key assets. With the right focus they could trust that the football would take care of itself, and it only took seven minutes for Patrick Bamford to put Leeds ahead in a 3-1 win over Blackburn Rovers at Ewood Park. That was followed by their biggest post-lockdown statement yet, a 5-0 win over Stoke City at Elland Road, inspired again by a goal, an assist and ceaseless creativity from Pablo Hernández.

The revised fixture list meant Leeds were playing their match in each round after their promotion rivals. On 11 July Brentford beat Derby, their sixth consecutive win since the restart, including one over West Brom that compressed the top three. West Brom won their three games after that, keeping them a point behind Leeds at the top, but their 1-1 draw at Blackburn on the 11th made Leeds' trip to Swansea an opportunity too important to miss.

It also meant more tension than many Leeds supporters thought they could bear, restricted to a strange new role watching live internet streams of games in empty stadiums. The match at Liberty Stadium was grinding towards a 0-0 draw that would at least keep Leeds a point in front of West Brom, but their training was to keep playing for a winner. In the 89th minute Ayling collected the ball from his own six-yard area, and started a counter attack encapsulating the players' fitness and desire. Klich then Costa then Ayling again set up Hernández, for a precise finish off the post that summed up his outstanding contribution since the restart, a goal equivalent to Gordon Strachan's pivotal winner against Leicester in 1990.

The celebrations mixed relief, triumph, and a recognition that although the pressure was now on United's rivals, their own nervous tension was building as the points needed for promotion were being gained. One more win would put Leeds beyond all but the most bizarre outcomes, and it came from their worst performance in two years under Bielsa. Brentford had won again and West Brom had drawn again before Leeds played Barnsley at Elland Road, and the players couldn't pretend the suspense was not affecting them. Barnsley unsettled Leeds by throwing players forward and pressing enthusiastically, but gave away the lead through a Michael Sollbauer own goal in the first half. Leeds clung to that, bringing Hernández on then taking him off again, replacing attackers with defenders, shifting from one defensive formation to another as the players pleaded with Bielsa for clarity, reaching for any habit they could summon from exhausted muscle memory to get them through to full-time. It was desperate, but it was done.

It was no longer Leeds United's mental strength being tested now. They had beaten Swansea and Barnsley under immense pressure, and over the next two days the attention was on their rivals, both expected to win against struggling sides and prolong United's wait for promotion. Instead Emile Smith Rowe scored an 86th minute winner for Huddersfield Town against West Brom that confirmed Leeds were going up, and Brentford's run was ended by Lee Gregory's winner for Stoke, making Leeds United champions with two games left to play.

Romantics spotted that when Smith Rowe's shot hit the net for Huddersfield, the club that had nearly moved into Elland Road 100 years earlier, digital clocks showed the time was 19:19, the year of Leeds United's foundation. As fans crowded onto Lowfields Road that night, trying to forget the coronavirus amid a surreal socially-distanced celebration with players looking down from the East Stand windows and dancing from a distance on the stadium steps, Marcelo Bielsa was snuck into the stadium through a side entrance, his demeanour of strict discipline giving way to the night's euphoria.

Leeds had a game two days away at Derby, who in a reversal of the previous season's play-offs now owed Leeds a guard of honour. But as Bielsa embraced his players with more smiles and emotions than they'd seen from him in two years, the preparations his staff had been diligently working through just hours earlier were all forgotten. 'Profe, ¿mañana libre?' Barry Douglas asked him as the beer flowed – 'Day off tomorrow?' '¡Mañana!' shouted Bielsa, replying in Spanish the cheering players all understood in spirit if not in word. 'Tomorrow, Sunday, Monday, Tuesday!' Against Derby, said Bielsa, the fanatically ordered genius admired and derided for his intensive pre-game planning, 'Let anyone play who wants to!'

Epilogue

LOOKS LIKE WE'RE
GETTING THERE, BOYS

Mañana was not libre. The players were given two hours off, allowed to start training late, sweating out their hangovers and, when he arrived, embracing and singing Marcelo Bielsa's name. There cannot have been many such popular taskmasters.

Near the end of the season, a reporter had asked Bielsa if he would settle for promotion without winning the title. Bielsa laughed, and said that question could only have one answer. The game at Derby County was important until the title belonged to Leeds, so the players had to be ready for it; a couple of hours after Leeds started training, though, Brentford lost their lunchtime match, and that settled things. Now it wasn't about who wanted to play, but who would be fit enough after a second night of celebrations. After starting 92 consecutive matches for Bielsa, Mateusz Klich succumbed to two days of partying and only made the bench.

Leeds won 3-1 anyway, pride guaranteeing victory after Derby took the lead. Charlton Athletic were taken more seriously in the season's final game, at Elland Road. They were fighting against relegation and, after having his integrity questioned during the 'spygate' episode, Bielsa was determined to name his strongest side out of respect for the competition. Charlton's manager, former Leeds player Lee Bowyer, offered his own respects, a bottle of Malbec for Bielsa and one for Eddie Gray, but his team were swept aside 4-0. Since the pivotal match at Nottingham Forest in February, Leeds had won twelve, drawn two and lost one, coping with the unprecedented 106-day gap in the middle, silencing all talk of burnout.

'Everything that happened here was very, very beautiful,' said Bielsa. 'I will never forget this. This is a moment everybody was waiting for, wishing for, and deserving as well. That links the players with the supporters who are in love with the club. For this reason, the ideal is to try to keep this moment as long as we can. Later, naturally, this moment will go. But we should not put another feeling on this moment that is very special. I am so happy in this moment, I don't want to make this moment pass quickly.'

The Covid-19 pandemic meant the trophy wasn't given to captain Liam Cooper after the Charlton game; due to social distancing it was placed on a table so he could help himself to it and carry it across to his team. Behind the fireworks and streamers, the stands were dark and empty except for the surreal presence of the cardboard cut-out 'crowdies' bought by supporters. Among them were images of relatives and friends who had passed during the 100 years and more of history that brought Leeds to this point, a poignant way of including absent fans on the terraces.

The life of the party was outside. Knowing that pleas for fans to observe coronavirus protocols and stay away would only work to a point, the club arranged for an open top bus outside the East Stand, from which the players could send the inevitable crowds home happy with a sight of their heroes and their trophy. It was a bizarre pastiche of the traditional bus tour that the club promised would take place one day when it was safe; the bus couldn't move from its place on Lowfields Road, but then, Leeds United were not in the mood for moving. They were back in the Premier League where they felt they belonged, determined to stay there.

It was a night of glory mixed with regrets, of fans happy that Leeds were going up, but disappointed they couldn't join the celebrations. The players were wrapped up in the emotional confusion. Gaetano Berardi, the longest-serving among them, extended his contract to help Leeds through to the end of his most mature and effective season with the club, to secure the promotion he had signed up to deliver six years earlier; in the game at Derby, he damaged his knee so badly he would be unable to play again for six months. Like Mick Jones carrying his dislocated elbow up the Wembley steps to give his muddy hand to the Queen in 1972, Berardi and his crutches went to the top of the bus, where he was given a microphone and asked to explain how he felt. 'I feel fucking great!' he roared, a winner's medal round his neck, his knee broken, Billy Bremner's 'Side Before Self' motto written across the stadium behind him.

It always felt too uncanny that Leeds might finally win their longed-for promotion in their centenary season, but every other circumstance prevented anyone from thinking Leeds were living out a fairytale. If this had been a Hollywood moment, Jack Charlton, Norman Hunter and Trevor Cherry would have been there, linking 1950, when Jack moved from Ashington to join the groundstaff at Leeds, to March 2020, when Norman strolled off Elland Road's press gantry after the 2-0 win over Huddersfield Town, declaring aloud, 'Looks like we're getting there, boys.'

Those three players, who died before the end of the 2019/20 season, encompassed much of Leeds United's story. Jack Charlton joined a club pining for its lost pre-war promise and watched Elland Road being graced by John Charles, the world's greatest footballer, who had the temerity to be wearing the number five shirt Charlton wanted. Then he played as that greatness gave way to the need for a new main stand, standing as a singular concession to modernity at a club sinking into the comforting oblivion of mediocrity. Then he took part in building a club the world would recognise.

Trevor Cherry's reputation suffered from coming to Leeds at the end of the glory years, and because a preoccupation with failure has always haunted Leeds: defeat in the European Cup in Paris has persisted in the memory longer than the success that took them there. Cherry captained Leeds through the decline and fall back into Division Two, but he also played 37 games in the 1973/74 First Division title-winning season, arguably United's finest achievement. His pride was quiet, but he was appreciated across West Yorkshire: in Huddersfield, where he was born, for helping Town to the First Division before joining Leeds; and in Bradford, where he was manager at City on the day of the terrible fire in 1985 that claimed 56 lives at Valley Parade, and led them with effective dignity through the aftermath. Taken altogether Cherry was highly regarded everywhere as a decent person who, when people paused to think of it, was also a superb football player.

Norman Hunter was the icon of 'Dirty Leeds', right down to his shy insistence that he wasn't that way at all. That was the point of the 'dirty' tag to people at Elland Road; Don Revie's team would fight with everything they had to win every honour they felt was being denied to them; and they would smile bashfully, wiping the blood from their boots, wishing it didn't have to be this way. Leeds, and Hunter, only ever wanted to play fair. But they were playing in a world that wasn't bloody fair.

Like many at Leeds, Hunter had to work hard for his accolades. He was part of the World Cup-winning squad in 1966, but not given a medal until 2007. He was lumbered with a hard reputation that diminished his skill as a footballer, but when his peers held their first ever vote, he was immediately named the Professional Footballers' Association Footballer of the Year. In the late 1980s he was part of the old guard Howard Wilkinson felt were keeping the club living in its past; a perfectly good coach, he was cleared out with the old photos, then watched in his new role as a BBC Radio Leeds commentator as Wilkinson worked to build a team he hoped Norman Hunter would be proud to see wearing Leeds United's shirt.

It was in that role that many younger fans knew Hunter, the kind, knowledgeable voice from a past that, before the internet, felt dim and old-fashioned. People always knew his 'Bites Yer Legs' nickname, though, and Hunter's presence as a commentator and later as a club ambassador meant everybody who saw him at Elland Road could recognise the determined character from the black and white photos. There were as many smiles as grimaces in the photos of Hunter's playing career, as he alone of the supposed hard-act generation of footballers always seemed on the verge of breaking character into giggles when he remembered they were all just playing a game. They had to take it seriously, but Hunter didn't think they should forget how lucky they were. He always said the best moment of his career was the day Don Revie signed him as a schoolboy for Leeds, because that was the moment from which every joy of his life followed.

The South Stand will carry Norman Hunter's name into the Premier League, meaning he will still be spoken about at Elland Road as often and as fondly as he has been for nearly sixty years, by the ordinary supporters Norman would always want speaking well of him.

Such hero status is more difficult for modern players to achieve, because associations don't last with clubs the way they once did. Except, perhaps, at Leeds. Reviewing the ten year anniversary of his goal that took Leeds up from League One in 2010, Jermaine Beckford remembered feeling like a fan not only of the club he was playing for but of the team he was playing in; he knew how the fans felt about him, because he felt the same way about his teammates. Leeds United is the club ex-players keep looking back to with fondness, dreaming they could have signed sooner, wishing they had never had to leave, finding something at Elland Road that no other modern club could give them.

The title winners of 2019/20 will feel that. Mateusz Klich scoured eBay for an old Premier League Leeds shirt, wearing it around Harrogate to celebrate promotion, bemoaning the difficulty of finding a Champions League version. After Klich's goal beat Middlesbrough in February, former Leeds captain Jonny Howson approached him on the pitch to tell him to 'Get it done', and win the promotion he had wanted to be his ten years earlier.

The sixteen years outside the Premier League have been decorated here and there by players who felt and responded to the desperation among the fans for a return, but it took until 2020 for enough of them to come together, feeling it, and capable of delivering it. How much they needed Marcelo Bielsa to help them achieve it, only they will know. And what part emotion played in the way Bielsa led them to it, only he will know.

Bielsa insists that his victories with Newell's Old Boys, his childhood club, where he was raised as a player, a coach and, he says, a person, will always mean more to him than any other success. But he is close to managing more games for Leeds than for any other club, and some at Leeds felt that had promotion not been achieved in his second season, he may have committed to a third to get the job done.

Something more than professional pride seemed to be at stake for Bielsa, despite the opportunity to show a trophy to his detractors in Argentina. At home he was accused of 'selling smoke,' he said, of preaching success without anything to show. But if his two seasons at Leeds had ended in smoke he could have been forgiven for walking away with his head high, admitting that Elland Road's heavy history of complexes and anxieties was more than he could fix. We'll never know, because at the end of his second season he was walking towards the Football League Championship trophy, albeit almost dragged there by Kalvin Phillips and Patrick Bamford, and being urged by his players to take it in his hands and hold it aloft as they sang his name.

Bielsa soon slipped away from the front of the celebrations. He had changed from the young manager who celebrated a title at Newell's on the shoulders of the supporters. He had learned to leave the limelight to others, developing a way of thinking that Don Revie would have approved, speaking at the end of the season about the contribution of everybody behind the scenes at Leeds. 'The ladies in the kitchen are wonderful people,' he said. 'In this [pandemic] isolation period, my wife couldn't be here with me, I am living alone now. And this lady, Vera, once a week used to leave a container outside my door with very tasty soup. Those things are not linked with the food itself, but it's linked with the emotion, and it's a big contribution.'

In 1919, rousing the supporters inside Salem Hall to back the building of a new football club from the ashes of Leeds City, Alf Masser told them, 'Unless I have you behind me, I finish.' One hundred years later, with Leeds behind him, Marcelo Bielsa made a new Leeds United, ready to start their second century.

BIBLIOGRAPHY

Right Back To The Beginning, Jimmy Armfield with Andrew
  Collomosse (Headline, 2004)
'*Not Playing The Game*'?: *Leeds City in the Great War*,
  A. J. Arnold (The International Journal of the History of
  Sport, 1990)
'*Shall it be Bradford or Leeds?*': *The Origins of Professional
  Football in the West Riding Textile District*, A. J. Arnold
  (Thoresby Society, 1988)
The Unforgiven, Rob Bagchi & Paul Rogerson (Aurum
  Press, 2014)
Bremner!, Bernard Bale (André Deutsch, 1998)
The Life and Times of Herbert Chapman, Patrick Barclay
  (Weidenfeld & Nicolson), 2015
David Batty: The Autobiography, David Batty with Bill
  Thornton (Headline, 2001)
*Meet The New Boss; Same As The Old Boss: A Social
  History of The Football Manager, 1880–c.1966*, Neil
  Carter (University of Warwick, 2002)
Herbert Chapman on Football, Herbert Chapman, ed. Greg
  Adams (GCR Books, 2011)
King John, John Charles with John Harris (Headline
  Publishing, 2004)
Jack Charlton: The Autobiography, Jack Charlton with
  Peter Byrne (Partridge Press, 1996)
Goals Are My Business, Allan Clarke (Pelham Books, 1970)
The Square Ball Magazine, Ian Dobson et al (The Square
  Ball, 1989–2018)

Raich Carter: The Biography, Frank Garrick (SportsBooks, 2003)

Forward With Leeds, Johnny Giles with Jason Tomas (Stanley Paul, 1970)

John Giles: A Football Man, John Giles with Declan Lynch (Hodder & Stoughton, 2010)

Marching On Together: My Life With Leeds United, Eddie Gray with Jason Tomas (Hodder & Stoughton, 2001)

Keep Fighting: The Billy Bremner Story, Paul Harrison (Black & White Publishing, 2017)

Leeds United: From Darkness Into White, Phil Hay (Mainstream Publishing, 2008)

Ozwhitelufc.net.au, Tony Hill et al

The Only Place For Us: An A–Z History of Elland Road, Jon Howe (Pitch Publishing, 2015)

Biting Talk: My Autobiography, Norman Hunter with Don Warters (Hodder & Stoughton, 2004)

The Matador: The Life and Career of Tony Currie, E.J. Huntley (Pitch Publishing, 2015)

Leeds United: A Complete Record 1919–1986, Martin Jarred and Malcolm MacDonald (Breedon Books, 1986)

Peter Lorimer: Leeds and Scotland Hero, Peter Lorimer with Phil Rostron (Mainstream Publishing, 2002)

Jock Stein: The Definitive Biography, Archie Macpherson (Racing Post Books, 2014)

Jack and Bobby, Leo McKinstry (CollinsWillow, 2003)

Don Revie: Portrait of a Footballing Enigma, Andrew Mourant (Mainstream Publishing, 1990)

The Essential History of Leeds United, Andrew Mourant (Headline, 2000)

Leeds United: Player by Player, Andrew Mourant (Guinness, 1992)

Leeds United On Trial, David O'Leary (Little, Brown, 2002)

The Major: The Life and Times of Frank Buckley, Patrick A. Quirke (Tempus Publishing, 2006)

Soccer's Happy Wanderer, Don Revie (Museum Press, 1955)

Cantona: The Red and The Black, Ian Ridley (Vista, 1996)

United We Fall, Peter Ridsdale (Pan Books, 2008)

John Charles: Gentle Giant, Mario Risoli (Mainstream Publishing, 2003)

Leeds United: Trials and Tribulations, Phil Rostron (Mainstream Publishing, 2004)

We Are The Damned United, Phil Rostron (Mainstream Publishing, 2011)

Careless Hands, Stuart Sprake and Tim Johnson (Tempus Publishing, 2006)

Bremner: The Real King Billy, Richard Sutcliffe (Great Northern Books, 2011)

Revie: Revered and Reviled, Richard Sutcliffe (Great Northern Books, 2010)

Jimmy Adamson: The Man Who Said No To England, Dave Thomas (Pitch Publishing, 2018)

MightyLeeds.co.uk, Dave Tomlinson et al

Managing To Succeed: My Life in Football Management, Howard Wilkinson with David Walker (Mainstream Publishing, 1992)

Brian Clough: Nobody Ever Says Thank You, Jonathan Wilson (Orion Books, 2011)

ABOUT THE AUTHOR

Daniel Chapman was born and raised in Leeds, but found his nerdish fervour for Leeds United during an enforced exile, returning to the city and a season ticket as soon as he could. He has co-edited Leeds United fanzine *The Square Ball* since 2011, taking it through its 25th anniversary, and seven nominations for the Football Supporters' Federation Fanzine of the Year award, winning twice. He has written a film and book about Howard Wilkinson's title-winning team at Leeds, both called *Do You Want To Win?*, and can be found reporting weekly on Leeds United through Twitter, as MoscowhiteTSB.

ACKNOWLEDGEMENTS

This book is the product of archival work to piece together 100 years of football history – and more – making intensive use of the British Library's Newspaper Archive to find dates, quotes and reports from local, regional and national publications from too many journalists to mention; although Tom Holley's transformation from Leeds United captain to sports journalist kept him in the story for more than 40 years.

Other excellent resources were Tony Hill's Ozwhitelufc website, a peerless record of stats and biographies, Dave Tomlinson's Mighty Leeds website's excellent accounts of Leeds City and United's early years, and Andrew Mourant's *Player by Player*, a book I pored over for hours and hours when I was younger, and that remains a priceless piece of work.

This book is for my mum, my dad and my sister; with thanks to Michael, Duncan, Philip, Andrew, Victoria, Lucy, Lydia and everyone at Icon Books; and Dan, Eamonn, Michael, Oddy, Wayne and everyone at *The Square Ball*.